Deleuze and Derrida

In loving memory of my mother, who taught me to dream

'Je vous aime et vous souris d'où que je sois.'
'I love you and am smiling at you from wherever I am.'
Jacques Derrida

Deleuze and Derrida

Difference and the Power of the Negative

VERNON W. CISNEY

EDINBURGH
University Press

Edinburgh University Press is one of the leading university presses in the UK. We publish academic books and journals in our selected subject areas across the humanities and social sciences, combining cutting-edge scholarship with high editorial and production values to produce academic works of lasting importance. For more information visit our website: edinburghuniversitypress.com

© Vernon W. Cisney, 2018

Edinburgh University Press Ltd
The Tun – Holyrood Road
12(2f) Jackson's Entry
Edinburgh EH8 8PJ

Typeset in 11/13 Adobe Garamond by
Servis Filmsetting Ltd, Stockport, Cheshire,
and printed and bound in Great Britain.

A CIP record for this book is available from the British Library

ISBN 978 0 7486 9622 2 (hardback)
ISBN 978 0 7486 9623 9 (webready PDF)
ISBN 978 1 4744 0470 9 (epub)

Contents

Acknowledgements

This book is a revised version of my doctoral dissertation. When I submitted my completed dissertation to the faculty at Purdue University in 2012, the dedication page read as follows: 'For Jody, Jacob, and Hayley, who have sacrificed so much, so that I could chase a dream.' Though the journey of our life together post-graduation has offered entirely different challenges than did the journey through dissertation, defence, and graduation, this sentiment is now stronger than ever. To Jody, it is undeniably the case that I would not be the person I am today without you. From high school through grad school to today, you have been my partner and my love. Thank you for your willingness to embark upon this journey with me; to sell our home, give up our steady factory jobs, uproot our children and move them halfway across the country; and most importantly, thank you for your steadfast love and friendship. You have provided me with moral encouragement when your own faith was weak, you have never let me give up on myself, and you have often provided the much-needed gentle (and not so gentle) prodding to keep me on track. It is, and always has been, you and me against the world, baby. For all this and so much more, thank you.

To Jacob and Hayley, you are the centres of my world, and the lights in my moments of darkness. Your mother and I began the academic journey when you were both too young to really understand *why*, much less to offer your own input or words of protest. From Illinois to Tennessee, to Indiana, to Pennsylvania, your lives have been repeatedly disrupted and restructured by my dreams; but, showing little concern for yourselves, you have been my most inspired and fiercely loyal supporters. I thank you. You are now pretty much grown, complete with your own scars, goals, ambitions, and perspectives on the world. I am daily amazed at your strength of character, as well as the depth and richness of your mental, emotional, philosophical, and moral landscapes. You are my two favourite people in the world. I am so grateful for the way you fill my life, and so excited to see where your own lives will take you in the years to come.

This book would not have been possible without the wonderful folks at Edinburgh University Press. I am incredibly lucky to have landed with you, as I could not have asked for a more supportive and encouraging professional relationship. This is now our third book together, we are in talks for a fourth, and I look forward to what I hope will be a long and productive partnership. To Carol Macdonald, thank you for taking a chance on me when I was but a graduate student, thank you for taking a chance on this book in particular when I know that there were forces working against it, but most importantly, thank you for your faith in me. To Carol, to Ersev Ersoy, and to Kirsty Woods, thank you so much for your seemingly infinite patience as I continued, in true Derridean fashion, to infinitely defer my submission of the manuscript. To Rebecca Mackenzie and the design staff, thank you for creating such a kick-ass cover for my book. Thank you to the two anonymous reviewers whose insights and suggestions have helped me immeasurably. To countless other unknown persons – typesetters, designers, press operators, laminator operators, bindery workers, truck drivers, sales and marketing staff, conference workers, and others I am certainly forgetting – thank you.

I want to thank Gary Aylesworth, for first exposing me to the thought of Derrida in an undergraduate course on continental philosophy at Eastern Illinois University. I would also like to thank Mary-Beth Mader, for giving me my first classroom exposure to Deleuze, in a graduate seminar at the University of Memphis titled 'Continental Philosophies of Science'. Those pages on Aristotle from *Difference and Repetition* were what first hooked me. Thank you to Valentine Moulard-Leonard and Erinn Gilson for very early conversations and presentations on Deleuze at the University of Memphis in 2005 that fanned the flames. Thank you to Peter Gratton for conversations on the negative at IPS in Italy, July 2014. Thank you as well to Henry Somers-Hall for an extremely important conversation on the question of contradiction at the 2014 SPEP in New Orleans. This discussion in particular greatly impacted the final version of this book. In addition, thank you to Justin Litaker for countless illuminating conversations on Deleuze. I want to thank Jonathan Beever and Nicolae Morar – who feel more to me like brothers than friends – for providing emotional support and philosophical input through the initial writing of this book. To Jonathan in particular, who provided indispensable comments on the final version of this book, I thank you.

I would also like to thank the students in the philosophy programme at Gettysburg College. In particular, thank you to the students in my spring 2015 Spinoza seminar, who grappled extensively with me over the question of the 'yes' and the 'no', affirmation and negation. In addition, thank you to Spencer Bradley and Ian Garbolski, who have conducted independent studies with me on Deleuze, Guattari, and Badiou. Thank you to Matthew Bajkowski, who conducted an independent study with me on the Medievals. Thank you as well to Jonathan Lucido and Frank Scavelli, with whom I worked closely in an independent study on Goethe, Nietzsche, and Heidegger.

There are a few friends whose support has been positively indispensable to me through the past few years. To Kerry Walters, Steve Gimbel, and Loretta Gruodis, thank you. Steve and Kerry, not only are you both outstanding and accomplished scholars, but you are, more importantly, both genuinely good and decent human beings, willing to go to the mattresses for a friend, no matter the personal cost to you. I owe you all more than I could ever possibly repay. Thank you.

Some sections of this book have been published elsewhere, and I am grateful for the permission to reuse these passages in this book. Some content from my 'Differential Ontology' entry on the *Internet Encyclopedia of Philosophy* appears in Chapter 2, and is reprinted with kind permission from James Fieser, the founder and general editor of the IEP. Then, material in Chapter 9 is reprinted with permission from Springer Science and Business Media, and was originally published as 'Jacques Derrida and the Future' in a collection titled *Husserl's 'Ideen'*, edited by Lester Embree and Thomas Nenon (Dordrecht, 2012).

Finally, I would like to thank the members of the dissertation committee who oversaw this project in its earlier incarnation: Arkady Plotnitsky, Chris Yeomans, Leonard Lawlor, and Daniel W. Smith. You are all of you tremendously accomplished scholars, whom I respect both personally and professionally. Your criticisms were invaluable as I reconsidered this project over the past few years. To Chris, Dan, and Len, thank you for your continued friendship and professional support. Thank you to Dan for countless Sgt. Preston burgers and glasses of Lagavulin during the writing of this book. Thank you to Len and to Dan for stoking the fires of passion for the thought of Derrida and Deleuze. Thank you to all of you for the professional and scholarly examples you have set for me. Thank you.

To anyone I may have forgotten, thank you.

Abbreviations

Unless otherwise noted, in-text citations refer to English translations listed here.

Works by Gilles Deleuze

B	*Bergsonism*
CC	*Essays Critical and Clinical*
DI	*Desert Islands and Other Texts*
DR	*Difference and Repetition*
EPS	*Expressionism in Philosophy: Spinoza*
LS	*The Logic of Sense*
N	*Negotiations 1972–1990*
NP	*Nietzsche and Philosophy*
SPP	*Spinoza: Practical Philosophy*
TRM	*Two Regimes of Madness*

Works by Gilles Deleuze and Félix Guattari

AO	*Anti-Oedipus*
ATP	*A Thousand Plateaus*
WP	*What is Philosophy?*

Work by Gilles Deleuze and Claire Parnet

Dialogues   *Dialogues II*

Works by Jacques Derrida

AL	*Acts of Literature*
C	*Cinders*
D	*Dissemination*
FK	'Faith and Knowledge: The Two Sources of "Religion" at the Limits of Reason Alone'
FL	'Force of Law: The "Mystical Foundation of Authority"'
G	*Glas*
LI	*Limited Inc.*
MP	*Margins of Philosophy*
OG	*Of Grammatology*
P	*Positions*
PIA	*Psyche: Inventions of the Other, Volume II*
Points	*Points . . . Interviews, 1974–1994*
SNS	*Spurs: Nietzsche's Styles*
VP	*Voice and Phenomenon*
WD	*Writing and Difference*
WM	*The Work of Mourning*

Works by Georg Wilhelm Friedrich Hegel

EL	*Logic*
GL	*Science of Logic*
PH	*Phenomenology of Spirit*

Works by Friedrich Nietzsche

BGE	*Beyond Good and Evil*
BT	*The Birth of Tragedy out of the Spirit of Music*
EH	*Ecce Homo*
FW	*The Gay Science*
GM	*On the Genealogy of Morality*
TI	*Twilight of the Idols or, How One Philosophizes With a Hammer*

WTP	*The Will to Power*
Z	*Thus Spoke Zarathustra: A Book for All and None*

Works by Edmund Husserl

CES	*The Crisis of European Sciences and Transcendental Phenomenology*
CM	*Cartesian Meditations*
IPP	*Ideas Pertaining to a Pure Phenomenology and to a Phenomenological Philosophy, First Book*
LU	*Logical Investigations, Volume I: Prolegomena to Pure*
PCT	*On the Phenomenology of the Consciousness of Internal Time (1893–1917)*

Other Works Cited

GS	Jean Hyppolite, *Genesis and Structure of Hegel's* Phenomenology of Spirit
ID	Martin Heidegger, *Identity and Difference*
LE	Jean Hyppolite, *Logic and Existence*
OBT	Martin Heidegger, *Off the Beaten Track*

'So my life is a point-counterpoint, a kind of fugue, and a falling away – and everything winds up being lost to me, and everything falls into oblivion, or into the hands of the other man.

I am not sure which of us it is that's writing this page.'

Jorge Luis Borges

Part I
Introduction

Chapter 1

The Question

If one were to crystallise twentieth-century continental philosophy into a single problem, it would be the 'problem of difference'. The demand to think a concept of difference and differences that is not subordinate to a primary conception of identity, but would be constitutive of those given identities, is evident in Heidegger's 'ontico-ontological difference' and in his later '*dif-ferenz*', Merleau-Ponty's chiasmatic notion of 'flesh', Levinas's 'face of the other', Foucault's 'thought of the outside', Irigaray's 'sexual difference', Butler's 'gender performativity', and Lyotard's 'differend'. These point to the ubiquitous sense in twentieth-century continental thought that, across all domains – ontological, ethical, social, political, and so on – our efforts to think the nature of things will always be short-circuited by the same self-enclosed, representational categories by which we attempt to think them in the first place. When confined to only what things have in common, thought cannot get at the heart of what makes them singular, what John Duns Scotus called 'haecceity', or the 'thisness' of a thing. To truly think the nature of the thing, thought must reach to the constitutive conditions of those identities, and to the differences and relations between those identities.

The 'problem of difference' is that difference and relation necessarily elude the stasis of representational thought, which traditionally seeks to fix borders around conceptual content, thereby halting the passages between various concepts. In order to truly think difference, then, it must be conceptualised on its own terms, constrained neither by the logic of identity, nor, consequently, by the requirements of a standard philosophical concept. It must not be thought as a merely empirical relation between given things, nor should it be conceived in the Hegelian manner as a diametrically opposed contradiction which, by virtue of its bipolar and reciprocal nature, would ultimately unite dialectically into a higher, homeostatic identity. The 'philosophy of difference' is the designation for the philosophical response to this problem.

Standing out in this tradition are Gilles Deleuze and Jacques Derrida, who address the problem of difference directly, formulating their own explicit conceptions, respectively 'difference in itself' and '*différance*'. While other philosophers are frequently occupied with questions of difference in specific contexts (ethical, epistemic, subjective, sexual, etc.), Deleuze and Derrida grapple with difference 'itself'. Hence, we can say, in a sense that I shall have to define and defend in what follows, that their conceptions of difference operate at the level of the ontological. Theirs are rigorous engagements with questions of being and time, identity, force, and meaning, across the history of Western metaphysics – spanning from Heraclitus and Parmenides to Hegel, Nietzsche, and Heidegger – and culminating in original and highly unique conceptions of difference constructed to engender the thinking of the impossible: the conditions of identity and thought themselves. It is to Derrida and Deleuze that Vincent Descombes refers when he speaks of the 'remarkable point of modern metaphysics which all preceding discourse had indicated like a flickering compass', calling the philosophy of difference the 'crux' of contemporary French philosophy.[1] The aim of the present book is to articulate the fundamental distinction between the philosophical conceptions of difference as formulated in the works of Derrida and Deleuze.

Given their shared desire to formulate non-dialectical, non-Hegelian conceptions of difference, we might, with some justification, suspect that Deleuze and Derrida have the same or very similar conceptions of difference. In what little textual dialogue occurs between Derrida and Deleuze, it seems as though they themselves would agree with this assessment. While I cannot agree entirely with Jeffrey Nealon's conviction that 'Deleuze and Derrida so scrupulously avoided writing about each other's work',[2] it is certainly the case that they address each other only rarely; and almost always in laudatory ways. On the event of Deleuze's death, Derrida famously cited the 'experience of a closeness or of a nearly total affinity' with Deleuze with respect to the thesis 'concerning an irreducible difference in opposition to dialectical opposition', later adding that, 'one day, I would like to try to provide an account of such an agreement in regard to philosophic "content. . ."'.[3] On occasions when they point to differences between them at all, the differences are typically brushed aside as merely stylistic or methodological. Derrida cites disparities in 'what I would call – lacking any better term – the "gesture," the "strategy," the "manner" of writing, of speaking, of reading perhaps'.[4] Deleuze also cites Derrida in an affirming way on a number of occasions, and appears to emphasise their differences as strictly methodological: 'As for the method of textual deconstruction, I know what it is, and I admire it, but it has nothing to do with my own method.'[5] Given these expressed affinities, and given their obvious similarities in formulating productive, constitutive concepts of difference, one might suspect that I am attempting to forge distinctions where there are none.

On the contrary, I shall demonstrate that these methodological differences are rooted in deeper conceptual tensions between the two thinkers, and precisely at the point on which they may seem most completely to converge – their conceptions of difference. While this claim will have to be defended in what follows, there is sufficient evidence, even at the surface level of their comments, to warrant the investigation. Just moments after fondly recalling the 'nearly total affinity' he shared with Deleuze, Derrida qualifies this affinity with a hesitation: 'even if I happened to grumble a bit . . . about the idea that philosophy consists in "creating" concepts',[6] noting elsewhere that 'deconstruction does not consist in passing from one concept to another, but in overturning and displacing a conceptual order'.[7] While Derrida treats this grumbling as a trifle, we must note that Deleuze's understanding of philosophy as concept-creation is not a minor or peripheral element of his thinking but one of the defining principles that pervades the entirety of his thought.[8] Likewise, just after professing his admiration for deconstruction, Deleuze relegates it to one among many practices of 'textual commentary', a characterisation that Derrida would almost certainly reject.[9] Moreover, Deleuze (with Guattari) famously claimed that 'the death of metaphysics or the overcoming of philosophy has never been a problem for us: it is just tiresome, idle chatter',[10] no doubt with deconstruction in mind. Thus, there are philosophical tensions between the two, sufficient to warrant this inquiry.

The landscape of work dedicated to comparing and contrasting these two figures has been somewhat sparse, especially considering their shared philosophical heritages, milieus, and concerns. In 2001, John Protevi writes, 'Although Jacques Derrida and Gilles Deleuze are the leading philosophers of French post-structuralism, very little has been done to compare their work on common issues.'[11] Since that time, the situation has changed somewhat. Besides Protevi's book, there has been the groundbreaking edited collection by Protevi and Paul Patton,[12] Jeffrey Bell's *Philosophy at the Edge of Chaos*, an edited collection by Gabriele Schwab,[13] and in French, Sergeant's *Deleuze, Derrida: Du danger de penser*. Besides these, there have been a handful of works dedicated to themes or other figures, or to contemporary French philosophy in a broad sense, in which discussions of Derrida and Deleuze are prominent.[14]

From this body of work, there have been two major strategies for differentiating the philosophies of Derrida and Deleuze. The first is the systems-oriented approach, which distinguishes them on the basis of their respective conceptions of systems and systematicity. The major proponents of this approach are Jeffrey A. Bell and John Protevi. In *Philosophy at the Edge of Chaos*, Bell distinguishes Derrida and Deleuze by arguing that, for Derrida, 'the very identity of a system presupposes . . . a fundamental difference that prevents the system from ever attaining any sense of completion or closure'. This fundamental difference is the condition of the system, and the system is its 'effects', but in its constitutive play this difference also continually destabilises the system. For Deleuze, by contrast, 'what is implicitly developed is the notion of a fundamental both/and or difference that is inseparable from dynamic systems that are at the "edge of chaos"'.[15] For Derrida, systems are always both constituted and subverted by a rupture or difference which prevents their completion, while for Deleuze, systems, while ever in flux and always open to the force of the outside, are nevertheless, in their own way, whole. This open completeness entails that the system itself, as a nexus of relations, informs and modifies the relations by which it is constituted, and affords Deleuze's thinking with a dynamism that is denied of Derrida's, according to Bell, in so far as Derrida understands the system as a mere 'effect' of its *différance*.

Similarly, in his *Political Physics*, John Protevi argues that 'deconstruction is top-down: starting with claims of bodies politic to natural and simple identity it shows *différance* or its cousins worrying and shaking those pretensions and thus opening those inhabiting that body to the critical claims of the call of the other in the democracy to come'.[16] Beginning from the self-contained 'presence' of phenomenological consciousness, Derrida's analyses consistently demonstrate the contamination of the 'I' by the 'not-I', exposing the play of forces out of which both are constituted. Nevertheless, this 'force' itself remains, for Derrida, unthinkable and in his terms 'mystical'. So, Protevi argues, while Derrida's thought is effective in destabilising the presumed finality and completion of given political systems, its capacities are almost exclusively critical. Contrary to this 'top-down' approach, Deleuze's thinking is 'bottom-up', demonstrating the material, historical forces by which bodies politic are produced. Hence, Deleuze's thinking is also critical, in that it illustrates the ways in which present systems have come to emerge, but it is better equipped than deconstruction to point to positive alternatives and 'avenues for nuanced pragmatic intervention and experimental production of immanent and democratic bodies politic'.[17] What Protevi and Bell hold in common is that they distinguish the philosophies of Derrida and Deleuze on the basis of their understandings of systems.

The other major strategy by which the two figures are most often distinguished is through their respective views on immanence and its relation to transcendence. While Deleuze remains committed through the entirety of his professional career to the principle that philosophy must be rooted in immanence and must abolish all transcendent modes of measure and evaluation, Derrida is much more comfortable overall with the language of transcendence, even if it is a transcendence always constituted within the immanence of the phenomenological subject. This is evident through a number of different emphases between the two philosophers. First, while Derrida cuts his philosophical teeth on Husserl and Heidegger, culminating in 1967's *Voice and Phenomenon* where he formulates the strategies that will occupy him for the remainder of his life, Deleuze maintains a comfortable distance from the phenomenological tradition and its emphasis on subjectivity, critiquing (with Guattari) the tradition for turning immanence into an immanence 'to' a consciousness, thereby reinstating a transcendence in the breach between the plane of immanence and the subjectivity by whom it is cognised.[18] Second, while Deleuze retains the Kantian language of the 'transcendental', seeking a 'transcendental empiricism' to think 'not the conditions of all possible experience . . . but the conditions of real experience',[19] Derrida famously characterises his concepts as 'ultra-transcendental',[20] where 'the condition of possibility of those effects is simultaneously . . . the condition of their impossibility'.[21] Third, while Deleuze seeks to think being *as* difference, a concept wherein 'being is said of becoming, identity of that which is different, the one of the multiple, etc.',[22] Derrida's 'difference is older than Being itself' and 'still more unthought than the difference between Being and beings'.[23] Finally, in their respective engagements with theological language and thinkers, Deleuze is aligned most closely with the tradition of univocity, and hence, immanence and affirmation – stemming from the Stoics, Lucretius, Duns Scotus, Spinoza, and Nietzsche – in which being 'is said in turn *in a single and same sense*'[24] of all of which it is said. For Derrida, on the other hand, given that '*différance* is not',[25] his operations and strategies 'resemble those of negative theology'[26] or apophatic mysticism, which attempts to secure the absolute transcendence of the divine by way of the negation of any positive characteristics one would ascribe thereto. In each of these cases, Deleuze's allegiances fall more on the side of uncompromising immanence, while Derrida is more immersed in a certain experience of transcendence. One of the early and major proponents of this transcendence/immanence distinction is Giorgio Agamben, who traces two distinct lines in contemporary continental thought: a line of transcendence extending from Kant, through Husserl and Heidegger to Levinas and Derrida, and a line of immanence extending from Spinoza, through Nietzsche and Heidegger to Deleuze and Foucault.[27] Daniel W.

Smith has also argued quite effectively for this reading,[28] while Leonard Lawlor rejects the transcendence/immanence distinction, arguing instead that 'both are philosophers of immanence', and that 'there is only a formal difference between Deleuze's thought and [Derrida's]', stemming from the single point of their respective concepts of 'simulacra'.[29]

My reading is deeply indebted to these major strategies, and to the excellent analyses by those who have both articulated and critiqued them. Nevertheless, what these two strategies share is that they operate primarily at the macrocosmic, aggregate level, focusing on large-scale questions of commitment with respect to the concept of the whole or the system. In a certain sense, the transcendence/immanence distinction is a variation of the system-oriented distinction: is it possible to think the inside of systems without also looking outside, toward the beyond of the system? My aim, on the other hand, is microcosmic. Given that Derrida and Deleuze are both thinkers of the minute, elemental, constitutive force – that is, difference – by which systems are constituted, given that this is their shared, express task, especially salient in their 1960s texts, my question is: is there a difference between them at the microcosmic level? Are their conceptions of difference *different*?

The response I shall defend in what follows is that there is indeed a distinction in their conceptions of difference, that this distinction is deep and undeniable, and that it factors into everything else that separates the two thinkers. To state my thesis clearly – for Deleuze, difference is understood as pure affirmation and relationality, while for Derrida, difference is always formulated in terms of a fundamental negative, rupture, or breach. *Différance*, for Derrida, is always a 'not', a conflictuality that he calls in 'Violence and Metaphysics' a 'transcendental violence',[30] while for Deleuze, the 'not' is a secondary 'epiphenomenon'[31] that indeed makes itself felt in the 'bloody and cruel'[32] movement of human history and experience, but is not a fundamentally constitutive or definitive aspect of being itself. This difference marks the two thinkers from Deleuze's emphasis on immanence to Derrida's experience of transcendence, from Deleuze's 'bottom-up' 'constructivism'[33] to Derrida's 'top-down' 'deconstruction', from Deleuze's notion of being as 'full positivity and pure affirmation'[34] to Derrida's 'cinder [or ash, *cendre*] as the house of being',[35] and in countless other minute ways.

My strategy will be to differentiate Derrida and Deleuze on the basis of specific decisions they make in their interpretations of key moments in the history of philosophy. It is true that Derrida and Deleuze are both uniquely preoccupied with differing primary groups of thinkers. Derrida focuses much of his philosophical effort, especially early on, with unorthodox readings of 'the three H's'[36] of French philosophical orthodoxy

– Hegel, Husserl, and Heidegger. Deleuze, on the contrary, refers to phenomenology as 'our modern scholasticism',[37] and 'wrote his first book on Hume . . . as if he wanted to add a fourth "H" of his own to the list',[38] and in his other published writings turned to a multitude of other heterodox figures, such as Bergson, Lucretius, and Spinoza, in whom he found a 'secret link . . . constituted by their critique of negativity, their cultivation of joy, the hatred of interiority, the externality of forces and relations, the denunciation of power . . . and so on'.[39] Nevertheless, despite these differing influences and objects of philosophical engagement, when it comes to the question of difference, the distinction between Derrida and Deleuze is most evident in the shared triumvirate of Hegel, Nietzsche, and Heidegger. Deleuze and Derrida will each reject the Hegelian understanding of difference. Likewise, each will reject a crucial aspect of Heidegger's important and influential reading of Nietzsche, thereby valorising Nietzsche as contributing to a post-Hegelian conception of difference. But at each of these three points, their reasons for these commitments differ, and it is in these differing commitments that their respective conceptions of difference emerge.

In this book

The next chapter, Chapter 2, constitutes the second part of the introduction, in which I ground the question of difference in the history of philosophy. I do this by characterising the history of philosophy as the thought of the centre, where the 'centre' functions as a kernel or kernels of identity and stasis that have traditionally anchored some aspect of Western thought. I then show that the question of difference has operated throughout the history of philosophy, in so far as that history has frequently vacillated toward and away from that emphasis on the centre. This movement culminates in the nineteenth century, bookended as it is with Hegel's efforts at the most comprehensive and systematic centring in the history of philosophy, and Nietzsche's radically Dionysian and Heraclitean decentring. I then conclude with Heidegger's reading of Nietzsche as the last metaphysician, predicated upon three specific critical points: (1) that the will to power is to be understood in a substantialist way; (2) its essence is understood as the ever-expanding desire for more power, which relies upon the securing of the power it has gained; (3) that this amounts to a reversal of the binary terms of the metaphysical tradition, but that in so far as it reverses, it remains enchained to what it reverses.

Part 2 of the book, consisting of Chapters 3, 4 and 5, looks at the ways in which Derrida and Deleuze engage with and critique the philosophy of Hegel. In Chapter 3, 'The Two Pillars of Deconstruction', I isolate what I understand to be the two guiding impulses of Derrida's project: (1) the closure of Western metaphysics as embodied in the philosophy of Hegel, making impossible any would-be radical anti-Hegelianism, according to Derrida; (2) Heidegger's critique of ontotheology – that Heidegger demonstrated throughout the history of Western metaphysics the commitment to privilege *presence* in both its temporal and spatial senses – this too reaches its apogee in Hegel's system, with his notion of the *Aufhebung*. But in critiquing Hegel, Heidegger also points toward a constitutive absence or difference that the *Aufhebung* ignores, while also falling prey to the ontotheological impulse himself. Hegel, and Heidegger after him, posit difference only in order to ultimately cancel it out in the name of presence or primordiality. The question for Derrida will be, then, how to think beyond the system when the system has already thought all that can be thought?

In Chapter 4, 'Deleuze and Hegelian Difference', I look at three specific criticisms of the negative, Hegelian notion of difference as offered by Deleuze. The first is that the concept of negation is in fact *less than*, which is to say, *less profound than*, the concept of difference that Deleuze is looking for – things must *differ* before they can be *opposed*. The second is that the impulse to conceive of difference in terms of the negative derives from a nihilistic spirit of *ressentiment*, that sees negativity at the heart of being itself, and is incapable of thinking being *except* in terms of its negative relations with others. Finally, Deleuze critiques the *Aufhebung* on the grounds that its *difference* is ultimately overcome, and that, in each case, *this* difference is only constituted *as* this difference, precisely because it *will be* overcome.

In Chapter 5, 'The Tremendous Power of the Negative', I examine the different understandings of the concept of 'force' as found in the writings of Hegel, Derrida, and Deleuze, as it is here that the distinction between Derrida and Deleuze becomes salient. For all three figures, force acts as the constitutive and genetic conditions that make thinking possible. Both Derrida and Deleuze critique Hegel on the basis that his conception entails the harmonious balance of two opposed but equipoised forces, subsisting in a homeostatic relationship. The very concept of force is bound up with the notion of difference in quantity. But the difference between Derrida and Deleuze is that, where Derrida understands this imbalance as essentially oppositional, Deleuze does not. This distinction has further implications. Where Derrida, like Hegel, understands forces as operating in specific, interdependent relationships, for Deleuze forces can potentially interact with any other forces (even if they do not do so in fact). For Derrida, forces are conflictual, and hence conflictuality resides at the heart of being; while for Deleuze, conflictuality or cooperation are predicated upon the fundamental fact of difference itself. For Derrida, Hegel's concept of difference is *almost* right – it is right in the sense that it is oppositional, but it is *wrong* in assuming a counterbalance of specific relations. This is why, as we will see in Chapter 3, deconstruction seeks merely the *displacement* of, not the escape from, the Hegelian system. It seeks to unleash the power of a *negativity so negative* that it can no longer be assimilated beneath the traditional definition of the negative. For Deleuze, Hegel's negative concept of difference is the enemy, the antithesis of life and of philosophy.

While Part II was primarily critical, Part III aims to articulate the positive conceptions of difference for Derrida and Deleuze. Where Hegel is the touchstone for Part II, Nietzsche, read through the lenses of Heidegger, serves as the touchstone for Part III, which consists of Chapters 6, 7 and 8. Both Derrida and Deleuze understand a certain Nietzscheanism as the key to thinking difference beyond Hegelian trappings, and both reject Heidegger's famous reading of Nietzsche, but they do so for different reasons.

Chapter 6 is titled 'Traces and Ashes', and weaves a thread through Husserlian time-consciousness and Freud's understanding of the trace, to Nietzsche's emphasis on truth as a mobile army of metaphor and metonymy. Husserl's phenomenology provides the contemporary and most impassioned defence of the interiority of consciousness as the guarantor of presence. Through his deconstruction of Husserl's 'living present', Derrida exposes the thought of the 'trace', as the imprint of the other in the ipseity of the same, the structural possibility of repetition itself. This thought is prefigured in the works of Freud and Nietzsche, who first undertook the radical deconstruction of consciousness. But of these two thinkers, Freud remains committed to a notion of the trace as, in some senses, unerasable, and hence, he remains bound up in the metaphysics of presence. Nietzsche, on the other hand, liberates the signifier from any pretence to truth or being. Thus, Derrida rejects the first of Heidegger's criticisms, denying the substantiality of will to power, and thus denying that Nietzsche is in any way carrying out an ontology. The trace, constituted by the oppositional play of *différance*, is the mark of its other. It is only ever understood as the trace of other, absent traces, and is, hence, akin to ashes and ghosts.

In Chapter 7, 'Deleuze, Plato's Reversal, and Eternal Return', I show that for Deleuze, the reversal of Platonism does not affect from the outside a simple binary structure, but rather liberates a suppressed third term in the Platonic paradigm, that of the *simulacrum*. Where the copy (the icon) is for Plato predicated upon its internal *resemblance* to the model (the eidos), the simulacrum is understood only in terms of its internal *differ-ence*. This internal difference is the difference at the heart of being that allows one to think the *thisness* of the thing. Against Aristotle's analogical understanding of being, Deleuze posits, with John Duns Scotus, Spinoza, and Nietzsche, the univocity of being. This thought finds its fullest expression in Nietzsche's notion of eternal return, according to Deleuze. I highlight three specific aspects of eternal return, according to Deleuze: (1) the affirmation of chance with no fresh, 'transcendent' injections thereof; (2) the disjunctive synthesis – understood as the affirmation of incompossibility; (3) the selective heartbeat of time that casts out the self-identical and the negative in the constitution of the 'same' as a play of the different. Eternal return makes it possible to think being as a multiplicity, a purely differential and purely relational field of pre-individual singularities and intensities.

In Chapter 8, 'Derrida, Deleuze, and Difference', I look more closely at the ways in which Deleuze and Derrida reject aspects of Heidegger's Nietzsche reading. Point by point, I show that Deleuze rejects each of Heidegger's criticisms. He *accepts* that Nietzsche is in fact an ontological thinker, but denies that this entails a substantiality to the will to power. Deleuze formulates his understanding of being as purely relational. Deleuze rejects that there is an isolable *as such* to the will to power, because the will to power, according to Deleuze, is *essentially* multiple. Finally, he rejects that the reversal merely inverts a binary relation, because for Deleuze, to cast the Platonic tradition as binary is to overlook the suppressed term of the simulacrum. Derrida, on the other hand, *accepts* that *if* Nietzsche is carrying out an ontology, the rest of Heidegger's criticisms would prevail against Nietzsche. Instead, Derrida rejects the claim that Nietzsche is doing an ontology at all. Nietzsche, instead, is attentive to the *production* of sense, and this production takes place by way of the interval-creation that occurs as a result of the oppositional play of forces, pressing outwardly against each other. For Deleuze, the constitutions of difference are positive and relational, while for Derrida they are negative and oppositional, understood only in terms of *what they are not*.

Part IV focuses on the implications of the book's discoveries. Given that the question of the nature of philosophy is raised throughout Chapter 8, this becomes the explicit object of Chapter 9, titled 'Deconstruction vs. Constructivism'. While Deleuze embraces the characterisation of philosophy as ontology, Derrida explicitly rejects the language of ontology, and consistently gives very good reasons for doing so. To address the *nature* of philosophy for these two thinkers, my analysis focuses on two specific *origins*, both of which are arguably formative for Derrida and Deleuze: Plato and Husserl. From Plato, I take the motivation from the *Republic* that the philosopher is the one who actively disrupts the *doxa* – the prevailing 'common sense' opinions of her day – in pursuit of the 'fundamental'. Understanding this fundamental in the broadest sense possible, I characterise it with the term 'being', and therefore, the pursuit of this fundamental I define as 'ontology'. From Husserl, I take the emphasis on the *epoché* as the reduction of being to the sphere of sense, which opens up the structure of temporalisation, in light of which I perform a phenomenological analysis of the consciousness of time. From this analysis, I derive a differential structure at the very heart of the present itself, on the basis of which I posit that philosophy for Derrida and Deleuze is differential ontology. Using terminology from Eugen Fink, I then characterise Derrida's project as a negative differential ontology, while Deleuze's is understood as a positive differential ontology.

Finally, in Chapter 10, 'Conclusion(s)', I further clarify and defend my thesis by: (1) distinguishing Derrida and Deleuze on the specific question of affirmation; (2) discussing in depth the role of the negative in Derrida's concept of 'undecidability'; (3) revisiting the criticisms of Hegel offered up by both Derrida and Deleuze, redirecting them this time against each other, in order to assess the projects of each. On the question of affirmation, I show that while both Derrida and Deleuze employ a notion of 'double affirmation', Derrida's sense of 'archi-originary affirmation' is always already torn open by the threat of oblivion and of radical evil. Deleuze's sense of affirmation, on the contrary, is the Dionysian, expressive power of becoming. With respect to undecidability, I show that while the negative differential aspects of Derrida's thinking still apply with respect to the question of the 'decision', nevertheless this does not divest one of the responsibility of *deciding*. My reading of deconstruction as a negative differential ontology does not, therefore, amount to the assertion of a quietism or political ineffectuality embedded therein. With respect to the Derridean and Deleuzian criticisms of Hegel, I argue that Deleuze would indeed find in Derrida a spirit of *ressentiment*, and that Derrida would likely locate in Deleuze a spirit of naivety, but that I myself understand that particular question (of affirmation or negation) to be a matter of taste. However, on Deleuze's criticism that a negative conception of difference amounts to a concept that is *less than* difference, I agree with Deleuze, on the grounds that *différance* maintains a lingering affinity with binarism, with *two*-ness, and hence, with the *this-not-that* of identity. I then offer one last bit of argumentative support, concluding the book with brief reflections on political and ethical engagement, through the lenses of the early feminist engagements with Derrida and Deleuze. I argue that while deconstruction is potentially more useful for addressing the immediate needs of excluded and marginalised *others*, when it comes to imagining a world beyond the binarity of *I* and *other*, of *us* and *them*, Deleuze's thought is more useful.

Notes

1. Descombes, *Modern French Philosophy*, 136.
2. Nealon, 'Beyond Hermeneutics: Deleuze, Derrida and Contemporary Theory', in Patton and Protevi (eds), *Between Deleuze and Derrida*, 158.
3. *WM*, 192–3.
4. *WM*, 192–3.
5. *DI*, 260.
6. *WM*, 193.
7. *LI*, 21; *MP*, 329.
8. See *DI*, 22; *DR*, xx; and *WP*, 2.
9. *DI*, 260.
10. *WP*, 9. We should note, however, that while the 'overcoming of metaphysics' is a motif that Derrida adopts from Heidegger, the matter is not so simple for Derrida. He is ever suspicious of philosophical themes of 'death', whether of the subject, of God, or of philosophy: 'I try to keep myself at the *limit* of philosophical discourse. I say limit and not death, for I do not at all believe in what today is so easily called the death of philosophy (nor, moreover, in the simple death of whatever – the book, man, or god, especially since, as we all know, what is dead wields a very specific power)' (*P*, 6). As Derrida frequently notes, at the heart of deconstruction lies the suspicion that it is not 'possible *simply* to escape metaphysics . . .' (*P*, 17). Moreover, it is possible, perhaps likely, that Deleuze and Guattari have in mind Heidegger as much as Derrida in this proclamation. Immediately prior to the remark about the overcoming of philosophy, Deleuze and Guattari write, 'To say that the greatness of philosophy lies precisely in its not having any use is a frivolous answer that not even young people find amusing anymore' (*WP*, 9). This is almost certainly directed at Heidegger, who in his 1937–8 Freiburg lectures claims that 'philosophy is the immediately useless, though sovereign, knowledge of the essence of things'. Heidegger, *Basic Questions of Philosophy*, 5. Nonetheless, to invoke the theme of 'overcoming metaphysics' is to put one's critique in the vicinity of deconstruction.
11. Protevi, *Political Physics*, 1.
12. Patton and Protevi (eds), *Between Deleuze and Derrida*.
13. Schwab (ed.), *Derrida, Deleuze, Psychoanalysis*.
14. Roudinesco, *Philosophy in Turbulent Times*; Cusset, *French Theory: How Foucault, Derrida, Deleuze, & Co. Transformed the Intellectual Life of the United States*; Gendron, *Repetition, Difference, and Knowledge in the Work of Samuel Beckett, Jacques Derrida, and Gilles Deleuze*; Davis, *Critical Excess: Overreading in Derrida, Deleuze, Levinas, Žižek, and Cavell*; Choat, *Marx Through Post-Structuralism: Lyotard, Derrida, Foucault, Deleuze*; Goddard, *Violence et subjectivité. Derrida, Deleuze, Maldiney*; Sato, *Pouvoir et Resistance: Foucault, Deleuze, Derrida, Althusser*; Halpern (ed.), *Foucault, Derrida, Deleuze: Pensées rebelles*.
15. Bell, *Philosophy at the Edge of Chaos*, 3–4.
16. Protevi, *Political Physics*, 5.
17. Ibid.
18. *WP*, 46.
19. *DI*, 36.
20. *VP*, 13.
21. *LI*, 20; *MP*, 328. See also *VP*, 87.

22. *DR*, 40.
23. *MP*, 67.
24. *DR*, 35.
25. *MP*, 21.
26. *MP*, 6.
27. Agamben, 'Absolute Immanence', in *Potentialities*, 238–9.
28. Smith, 'Deleuze and Derrida, Immanence and Transcendence: Two Directions in Recent French Thought', in Patton and Protevi (eds), *Between Deleuze and Derrida*, 46–66. This essay also appears as Essay 16 in Smith's *Essays on Deleuze*.
29. Lawlor, 'The Beginnings of Thought: The Fundamental Experience in Derrida and Deleuze', in Patton and Protevi (eds), *Between Deleuze and Derrida*, 67. This essay also appears as Chapter 8 in Lawlor's *Thinking Through French Philosophy*.
30. *WD*, 128.
31. *DR*, 54.
32. *DR*, 268.
33. *WP*, 35–6.
34. *DR*, 269.
35. *C*, 23.
36. Smith, 'Deleuze, Hegel, and the Post-Kantian Tradition', in *Essays on Deleuze*, 62.
37. *NP*, 195.
38. Smith, 'Deleuze, Hegel, and the Post-Kantian Tradition', in *Essays on Deleuze*, 62.
39. *N*, 6.

Chapter 2

Grounding the Question

One might reasonably wonder, 'why difference?' Why does difference matter so much? Or *does* it matter so much? If this question is of such vital philosophical importance, why does it appear primarily within the continental tradition of the late twentieth century, without so much as a whisper elsewhere in Western philosophy's two-and-a-half-millennia-long history? In his work, *Reconsidering Difference*, Todd May speaks of the problem of difference as a 'pattern . . . in the French philosophy of this generation, of the generation running roughly from the mid to late sixties up to the present',[1] claiming that 'For philosophers outside the French tradition, there may be some puzzlement as to why one should be so concerned about difference.'[2] Indeed, in the previous chapter, I myself referred to it as the defining problem of twentieth-century continental philosophy. So, why should anyone besides a continental philosopher care?

Moreover, we might reasonably wonder: is a philosophy of difference, *as* a philosophy, even possible? Given that philosophy has traditionally attempted to think the universal, and given that, as we noted in Chapter 1, difference necessarily eludes the stasis of representational thinking, which attempts to freeze borders around conceptual content, will attempting to formulate a *concept* of difference not simply result in obscurity, paradox, contradiction, in a word, *non-philosophy*?

By way of introduction, we can say that the question of difference matters in so far as the question of *identity* matters. Prima facie, to characterise the identity of a thing means to be able to say things *about* that thing, to characterise that thing in ways that augment our understanding of it. This requires predicating of the thing qualities, characteristics, or attributes that are not *essential* to that thing, but are *different* from it in some senses. To say that A is A – *the sky is the sky*, or *blue is blue*, for instance – requires no thought at all. Each proposition is a simple expression of the principle of identity, and as such, each is tautologically, but trivially, true. But to say that A is B – *the sky is blue* – compels thought to ask how it is that a thing can *be* what it *is not*.

In a second way as well, to comprehend the identity of a thing requires that we understand what it is, beyond all those attributes that we mentioned, that makes it *this* thing in particular, as opposed to *that* thing. Of any given thing we encounter, we can indeed characterise it with a litany of generalities, but however many of these generalities are compounded in our account, there will always be something that makes this entity irreducibly singular and different from every other entity that shares these generalities with it. For example, we might characterise a given ball as rubber, red, spherical, inflated to a particular degree of air pressure, of a certain size, texture, and so on. Nevertheless, however accurate it may be to say that the ball *is* all these things, it is also the case that it is *other* than these characteristics as well. For we can imagine any number of balls that each shares this list of qualities, but nevertheless, only *one* is *this* specific ball. Difference therefore lies at the heart of our understanding of identity, not as a superficial or accidental add-on, but as fundamental to the very nature of identity itself.

Thus, from a certain perspective, difference can be thought of as *the* central question of the philosophical tradition. For this reason it is little surprise that we see it explicitly manifested at various points throughout the history of philosophy. In this chapter, I ground the question of difference by conceptualising philosophy as the 'thought of the centre', demonstrating that throughout its history, philosophy has moved closer to and further from its emphasis on 'the centre', and that operating ever against the emphasis on the centre is the problem of difference. This oscillation culminates in the Hegelian and Nietzschean moments, which correspond, respectively, to philosophy's most comprehensive efforts at centring and its most radical and fundamental decentring. It is then Martin Heidegger who attempts to think through the relation between these moments, and in so doing, lays out the terms and questions that will occupy Derrida and Deleuze. In their own formulations, the philosophy of difference is the thought of the decentred centre. As such, it remains within but at the limits of the philosophical tradition.

Philosophy as the thought of the centre

The history of Western philosophy is a history of centrings, decentrings, and recentrings, of oscillating movements toward and away from central-ity or 'the centre', with an emphasis on an absolute kernel or kernels of stasis and identity. Derrida himself refers, repeatedly and insistently, to the importance of the 'centre' in Western thought:

> structure – or rather the structurality of structure – although it has always been at work, has always been neutralized or reduced, and this by a process of giving it a center or of referring it to a point of presence, a fixed origin. The function of this center was not only to orient, balance, and organize the structure – one cannot in fact conceive of an unorganized structure – but above all to make sure that the organizing principle of the structure would limit what we might call the *play* of the structure.[3]

Clare Gorman writes, 'Prior to deconstruction there was a norm or centre in Western thinking, which held true for institutions, texts, traditions, beliefs, and society. This thinking presupposed a centre or origin at the core of every structure and was seen as the ontological ground of such structures.'[4] This term 'the centre' effectively functions in my historical narrative as a linking term for what Derrida will call 'presence' and Deleuze 'representation'. This historical oscillation between centring and decen-tring corresponds roughly to the movement between the polar emphases on identity and difference, or on being and becoming, and it corresponds, as well, with the perennial debate in the history of philosophy between Parmenides and Heraclitus, the two fountainheads of the Western philo-sophical tradition.

Heraclitus

From its beginnings, what distinguishes ancient Greek philosophy from its mythologically oriented ancestors is philosophy's attempt to offer a rationally unified view of the operations of the universe, rather than think-ing the cosmos subject to the fleeting and conflicting whims of various deities, who differed from humans only in virtue of their power and immortality. The early Milesian philosophers had each sought to locate among the various classical elements a first principle (*archê*) to serve as the underlying principle of reality, in order to thereby better understand the phenomena of that reality. Thales had argued that water was the primary principle of all things, while Anaximenes had argued for air. According to these Milesian thinkers, through various processes and permutations, this first principle assumes the forms of the various other elements with which we are familiar, and of which the cosmos is comprised. All things come from this primary principle, and eventually return to it. In these early philosophers, we should note, we hear the first whispers of a centre, in the effort to reduce the myriad phenomena of the cosmos to the permutations of a singular and irreducible substance, a 'centre' that is the source and destination of all the others. Yet they remain whispers as, in its nascency, philosophy has not yet explicitly declared the self-identical as the ground of thought.

Against the Milesians, Heraclitus of Ephesus (fl. c.500 BCE) argues for fire as the *archê* of the cosmos: 'The cosmos, the same for all, no god or man made, but it always was, is, and will be, an everlasting fire, being kindled in measures and put out in measures.'[5] The most obvious innovation here is that Heraclitus names fire as the basic element, rather than water, air, or, in the case of Anaximander, the 'boundless' (*apeiron*). But moreover, unlike the Milesians, Heraclitus does not hold in favour of any ultimate origin of the cosmos. The universe 'always was' and 'always will be' the self-manifesting, self-quenching, primordial fire, expressed in nature's limitless ways. So while fire, for Heraclitus, may be ontologically basic in some sense, it is not temporally basic: it did not, in the temporal or sequential order of things, come first.

However, like his Milesian predecessors, Heraclitus appears to provide at least a basic account as to how fire as first principle transforms: 'The turnings of fire: first sea, and of sea, half is earth, half lightning flash.'[6] Elsewhere we can see more clearly that fire has ontological priority only in a very limited sense for Heraclitus: 'The death of earth is to become water, and the death of water is to become air, and the death of air is to become fire, and reversely.'[7] Combined with the two passages above, we can see that the basis of the ontological priority of fire is its transformative power. Fire from the sky consumes water, which later falls from the sky nourishing the earth. Likewise, fire underlies water (which in its greatest accumulations rages and howls as violently as any conflagration), out of which comes earth and the meteorological or ethereal activity itself.

Thus we can see the greatest point of divergence between Heraclitus and his Milesian forbears: the first principle for Heraclitus is not an irreducible substance. Fire, though one of the four classical elements, is of its very nature dynamic – a vital element that 'is' nothing more than its own transformation. It creates (volcanoes produce land masses; fire tempers steel and hardens wood; heat cooks food and protects from exposure), but it also destroys in countless obvious ways; it hardens and strengthens, just as it weakens and consumes. Fire, then, does not constitute a substantial unity, but an elemental process. In contemporary scientific terms, we would say that fire is a chemical reaction; its essence for Heraclitus lies in its obvious dynamism. As Deleuze writes, 'Fire is the element which plays, the element of transformations which has no opposite.'[8] When we look at things (tables, trees, homes, people, and so on), they seem to exemplify a permanence which is noticeably missing from our experience of fire.

This brings us to the next point: things, for Heraclitus, only *appear* to have permanence; their apparent permanence is an ephemeral result of the processes that make up the identities of the things in question. Here it is appropriate to cite the famous river example, found in more than one Heraclitean fragment: 'You cannot step twice into the same rivers; for fresh waters are flowing in upon you';[9] and 'We step and do not step into the same rivers; we are and are not.'[10] These passages highlight the seemingly paradoxical identity of the cosmos. On the one hand, it is obvious that there is a meaningful sense in which one may step twice into the same river; one may wade in, wade back out, then back in again; the river is marked between the same banks, the same land markers, and the same flow of water, and so on. But therein lies the paradox: the water that one waded into the first time is now completely gone, having been replaced by an entirely new configuration of particles of water. So there is also a meaningful sense in which one cannot step into the same river twice. But it is this *particular* flowing that makes this river this river, and nothing else. Its identity, therefore (as also my own identity), is an effervescent impermanence, constituted on the basis of the flows that make it up. We gaze into nature and see things – rivers, people, animals, and so on – but these are only temporary constitutions, even deceptions: 'Men are deceived in their knowledge of things that are manifest.'[11] The essence of nature itself, however, continuously eludes us: 'Nature tends to conceal itself.'[12]

The paradoxical nature of things (that their identities are constituted on the basis of processes), helps us to make sense of Heraclitus' proclamation of the unity of opposites (which both Plato and Aristotle held to be unacceptable). Fire is vital and powerful, raging beneath the appearances of nature like a primordial ontological state of warfare: 'War is the father of all and the king of all.'[13] The very same process-driven nature of things that makes a thing what it is, by the same operations tends toward the thing's undoing as well. Given that fire is responsible for the complementary functions of both creativity and destruction, the nature of things is to tend toward their own undoing and eventual passage into their opposites: 'What opposes unites, and the finest attunement stems from things bearing in opposite directions, and all things come about by strife.'[14]

It is in this sense that all things are, for Heraclitus, one. The creative-destructive operations of nature underlie all of its various expressions, binding the whole of the cosmos together in accordance with a rational principle of organisation, recognised only in the universal and timeless truth that everything is constantly subject to the law of flux and impermanence: 'It is wise to hearken, not to me, but to the Word [*logos* – otherwise translatable as 'reason', 'argument', 'rational principle', and so on], and to confess that all things are one.'[15] Thus it is that Heraclitus is known as the great thinker of becoming or flux. The being of the cosmos, the most essential fact of its nature, lies in its becoming; its only permanence is its impermanence. For our purposes, we can say that Heraclitus was the first philosopher of difference. Where his predecessors had sought to identify the one primordial, self-identical substance or element, out of which all others had emerged, Heraclitus had attempted to think the world, nothing more than the world, in a ceaseless 'state' of flux.

Parmenides

Parmenides (b. 510 BCE) was likely a young man at the time when Heraclitus was philosophically active. Born in Elea in Lower Italy, Parmenides' name is the one most commonly associated with Eleatic monism. While there is no one standard interpretation (ironically enough) of Eleatic monism, probably the most common understanding of Parmenides is filtered through our familiarity with the paradoxes formulated by his successor, Zeno, who argued, in defence of Parmenides, that what we humans perceive as motion and change are mere illusions.

Against this backdrop, what we know of Parmenides' views come to us from his didactic poem, titled *On Nature*, which now exists only in fragmentary form. Here, we find Parmenides, almost explicitly objecting to Heraclitus:

> It is necessary to say and to think that *being* is; for it is to be/but it is by no means nothing. These things I bid you ponder./For from this first path of inquiry, I bar you./then yet again from that along which mortals who know nothing/wander two-headed: for haplessness in their/breasts directs wandering understanding. They are borne along/deaf and blind at once, bedazzled, undiscriminating hordes,/who have supposed that being and not-being are the same/and not the same; but the path of all is back-turning.[16]

There are a couple of important things to note here. First, the mention of those who 'suppose that being and not-being are the same and not the same' hearkens almost explicitly to Heraclitus' notion of the unity of opposites. Secondly, Parmenides declares this to be the opinion of the 'undiscriminating hordes', the masses of non-philosophically-minded mortals.

Therefore, Heraclitus, on Parmenides' view, does not provide a philosophical account of being; rather, he simply coats in philosophical language the everyday experience of the mob. Rejecting Heraclitus' critical diagnosis that humans deceptively see only permanent things, Parmenides claims that permanence is precisely what most people miss, preoccupied as we are with the mundane comings and goings of the latest trends, fashions, and political currents. The being of the cosmos lies not in its becoming, as Heraclitus thought. Becoming is nothing more than an illusion, the perceptions of mortal minds. What is, for Parmenides, is and cannot not be, while what is not, is not, and cannot be. Neither is it possible to even think of what is not, for to think of anything entails that it must be an object of thought. Thus to meditate on something that is not an *object* is, for Parmenides, contradictory. Therefore, 'the same thing is for thinking and for being'.[17]

Being is indivisible; for in order to divide being from itself, one would have to separate being from being by way of something else, either being or not-being. But not-being is not and cannot be, so not-being cannot separate being from being; and if being is separated from being by way of being, then in this thought experiment being itself is continuous, that is to say, being is undivided and indivisible: 'for you will not sever being from holding to being'.[18] Being is eternal and unchanging; for if being were to change or become in any way, this would entail that in some sense it had participated or would participate in not-being which is impossible: 'How could being perish? How could it come to be?/For if it came to be, it was not, nor if it is ever about to come to be./In this way becoming has been extinguished and destruction is not heard of.'[19]

Being, for Parmenides, is thus eternal, unchanging, and indivisible spatially or temporally. Heraclitus might have been right to note the way things appear (as a constant state of becoming), but he was wrong, on Parmenides' view, to confuse the way things appear with the way things actually are, or with the 'steadfast heart of persuasive truth'.[20] Likewise, Parmenides has argued, thought can only genuinely attend to being – what is eternal, unchanging, and indivisible. Whatever it is that Heraclitus has found in the world of impermanence, it is not, Parmenides holds, philosophy. While unenlightened mortals may attend to the transience of everyday life, the path of genuine wisdom lies in the eternal and unchanging. Thus, while Heraclitus had been the first philosopher of difference, Parmenides is the first Western thinker of 'the centre', first to assert explicitly that self-identity, not difference, is the basis of philosophical thought.

Plato's forms and the discovery of the different

Plato attempts to address and fuse these two accounts, the Heraclitean and the Parmenidean (with an emphatic privileging of the latter), with his theory of forms. As Plato's problems are rooted in the soil of the Parmenides-Heraclitus debate, they bear the marks of both voices, and the final decision in favour of the centre is not yet made. As Deleuze writes, 'the Heraclitan world still growls in Platonism'.[21] Throughout his *Dialogues*, Plato consistently gives credence to the Heraclitean observation that things in the material world are in a constant state of flux. The Parmenidean inspiration in Plato's philosophy, however, is that, like Parmenides, Plato will explicitly argue that genuine knowledge must concern itself only with what is eternal and unchanging. So, given the transient nature of material things, Plato will hold that knowledge, strictly speaking, does not apply to material things, but rather to the forms (eternal and unchanging) of which those material things are instantiations or copies.

Everything that exists in the world 'participates' both in being and in not-being. For example, every circle both is and is not 'circle'. It is a circle to the extent that we recognise its resemblance, but it is not 'circle' as such because we also recognise that no circle as manifested in the world is a perfect circle. Even the most circular circle in the world will possess minor imperfections, however slight, that will make it not a perfect circle. Further, even supposing we *were* to find some beautiful, apparently perfect circle, every point of which were evidently equidistant from its centre, the fact that the circle is *visible* entails that the arc has *breadth* (which points do not), and the fact that it is determinate (and hence exclusionary of all other such circles), entails that it would not be 'circle' as such. Thus all material things participate both in being and in not-being, and this is the nature of becoming. Since being and not-being each has a specific capacity proper to it, respectively 'knowledge' and 'ignorance',[22] we can say that becoming, lying between being and not-being, must have a capacity that is proper only to it. This capacity, Plato argues, is 'opinion', which, as is fitting, is the epistemic mode between knowledge and ignorance.

Therefore, when one's attention is turned solely to the things of the world, one can possess only opinions regarding them. Knowledge for Plato applies only to the form of the thing, or 'what it means to be x and nothing but x'. If one has knowledge of the form, then one can evaluate each empirical particular in the world, in order to accurately determine whether or not it in fact accords with the principle in question. If not, one may have only opinions about the thing. Possessing knowledge of the form of the beautiful, one may evaluate particulars in the world – paintings, sculptures, bodies, and so on – and know (not opine), whether or not they are in fact beautiful. Without the knowledge of the beautiful, one may hold opinions in such matters, but these opinions are closer to what we might call 'tastes' – ('I like this poem', 'I do not like that painting', and so on). This is why Socrates, especially in earlier dialogues,[23] insists that his interlocutors not give him examples to define or explain their concepts ('a pious action is doing what I am doing now'). Examples, he argues, can never tell us what the form of the thing is (such as piety in the *Euthyphro*). The philosopher, Plato holds, is concerned with being, or the essentiality of the form, as opposed to lovers of opinion, who concern themselves only with the fleeting and impermanent.

From this point, however, things in the Platonic account get more complicated. 'Participation' itself is a vague notion that Plato never satisfactorily explains. What does it mean to say, as Socrates argues in the *Republic*, that the ring finger 'participates' in the form of the large when compared to the pinky, and in the form of the small when compared to the middle finger?[24] It would seem to suggest that a thing's participation in its relevant form derives, not from anything specific about *its* nature, but only in so far as its nature is related to the nature of another material thing in the realm of becoming. This is problematic in so far as the form is purported to define the thing itself, not its relation to other things. But it gets even more complicated in that at multiple points in his later dialogues, Plato argues explicitly for a form of 'the different', which drastically complicates what we typically call 'Platonism', almost beyond recognition.[25]

The most important of these discussions takes place in Plato's late-period *Sophist*, which, combined with the *Parmenides*, marks a careful revaluation of earlier Platonic presuppositions regarding the nature and purpose of the forms. Through the course of their inquiry, the anonymous Eleatic visitor asks Theaetetus to speak as a representative of the 'friends of the forms',[26] or the Platonists, with respect to the question concerning being and becoming. A friend of the forms, they agree, holds that being is distinct from becoming, that being remains eternally the same, whereas becoming varies from one moment to the next. Moreover, the friend of the forms holds that becoming is approached through the body and its perceptions, whereas being is grasped through reasoning by way of the soul; and as we saw above, knowledge pertains only to the domain of being.

This agreement points to a subsequent question, having to do with knowledge as a 'capacity' of the soul. The visitor defines 'capacity' as the ability of a thing 'to do something to something else or to have even the smallest thing done to it by even the most trivial thing, even if it only happens once'.[27] But 'doing to' or 'being done to' imply an entanglement with change, which for the Platonist, as we have defined one, would thus forbid any relation between any 'capacity' and being, for being remains eternally the same. But as knowledge is a capacity of the soul, this would suggest that there can be no relation between knowledge and being.

This complicates the accepted understanding of the Platonic relation between the soul and being, because 'knowledge' is Plato's name for that relation, and knowledge concerns itself only with being, not becoming. In the *Phaedo*, existence is divided into two categories, the visible and the invisible,[28] corresponding with the division in the *Republic* between the visible and the intelligible.[29] The soul belongs to the realm of the intelligible, and in the *Phaedo* famously dwells in the body as a prisoner in a cell. The primary domain of the soul then is that of being, as opposed to becoming. Likewise, the divided line in Book VI of the *Republic* establishes the distinction between the knowable and the opinable. When the soul is fulfilling its task, it is striving for the attainment of knowledge, the jurisdiction of which is being. But, incorporating this definition of 'capacity', if the soul learns, the soul does something, and undergoes change in the attainment of knowledge that it did not previously possess. This contamination by change touches even the notion of 'being' itself. 'Being-known' or 'coming-to-be-known' is itself an affection, because after something is known, one can attribute to it something that was not attributable before, namely, that it is known. Thus, if being itself can be *known*, then being, too, undergoes change.

We see, thus, that the Platonic paradigm has brought us to a tentative conclusion that would be positively unacceptable for Plato. 'Soul' and 'being', as designators for members of a class of things that are not subject to change, can have nothing to do with knowledge, as knowledge is a capacity, which, as Plato has defined it, involves becoming in the form of 'doing to' and 'being done to'. However, neither the visitor nor Theaetetus is willing to concede this point. As the stranger exasperatedly exclaims:

> Visitor: But for heaven's sake, are we going to be convinced that it's true that change, life, soul, and intelligence are not present in *that which wholly is*, and that it neither lives nor thinks, but stays changeless, solemn, and holy, without any understanding?
> Theaetetus: If we did, sir, we'd be admitting something frightening.[30]

One of the primary purposes of the forms, after all, through the entirety of Plato's corpus, is to provide a basis for an account of knowledge. Divesting being of its relation to understanding would undermine the entirety of the Platonic project. Knowledge and understanding, then, are essential accompaniments of Platonic being, a conclusion to which both the visitor and Theaetetus agree. It then seems that being should also involve 'life', given that understanding, which is an activity, pertains to being. It seems unlikely that something that is not living can engage in or involve itself with understanding. Furthermore, if it involves life, it must include becoming, as all living things in some sense undergo change.

The interlocutors are thus forced to concede that change cannot be excluded from the concept of being. With that, Plato begins revolutionising his own earlier ontology from the ground up. Whatever else one might say about being, 'both *that which changes* and also *change* have to be admitted as being'.[31] But change and being cannot be coextensive or coexhaustive. Being must also include rest, for while knowing involves a change in the knower and in the object known, it also implies an acquisition on the part of the knower, in the sense that the knower possesses something that they formerly did not. This possession itself does not readily change. The immutability of genuine knowledge is one aspect of Plato's earlier thought that he does not relinquish.

The reformulated ontology must then at the very least include being, rest, and change. From here, the visitor begins to construct a concept of essential 'blending' between forms. If change *is*, then change must participate in being. Likewise, if rest *is*, then it must participate in being. For either of these forms to be, they must in some way blend with the form of being. At a basic level, Plato thus acknowledges that his ontology cannot get off the ground without some inter-mingling of the forms. The visitor claims, 'the most ridiculous account is the one that's adopted by the people who won't allow anything to be called by a name that it gets by association with something else'.[32] This prompts still another concern, namely, do all forms intermingle or only some and not others? Theaetetus and the visitor conclude that not all forms can blend. This is especially clear in the case of contraries. If rest, for instance, blends with or participates in change, it is not truly rest at all.

Given that there are at this point three fundamental forms, and given that they are distinct from each other – and we know that they are because not all forms blend with all others, and though both rest and change participate in being, being is not coextensive with either – we can begin to draw conclusions about 'the same' and 'the different'. Though change participates in being, it is *different* from being, and we have already established that it is different from rest. Nonetheless it is the *same* as itself. Such can be said for the other two forms as well: each is the same as itself, but different from each other. It follows then that the same and the different are also two distinct forms, distinct from each other, and from the other three.[33] At last, we have found the form of the different.

On the face of it, that Plato articulates a form of 'the different' should not be surprising. If a finger sometimes participates in the form of the large and sometimes in the form of the small,[34] it should stand to reason that any given thing, when looked at side by side with something similar, can be said to participate in the form of the 'same', while by extension, when compared to something that differs in nature, will be said to participate in the form of the 'different' – and participate more greatly in the form of the different, the more different the two things are. A baseball, side by side with a softball, will participate greatly in the form of the same, but when looked at side by side with a cardboard box, will participate more in the form of the different.

But consistently articulating the form of the different is more complicated than it may at first seem. To say that the form of x is 'what it means to be x and nothing but x' is comprehensible enough when one is dealing with an isolable characteristic or set of characteristics of a thing. If we say, for instance, that the form of circle is what it means to be a circle and nothing but a circle, we know that we mean all of the essential characteristics that make a circle a circle (a closed plane curve consisting of points, equidistant from a centre; an arc of 360°; and so on). Each individual form, to the extent that it is completely what it is, participates equally in the form of the same, in that it is absolutely the same as itself; it is self-same or self-identical. But what can it possibly mean to say that the form of the different is what it means to be different and nothing but different? This would suggest that the 'identity' of the form of the different is that it differs, but this requires that it differs even from itself. For if the essence of the different were that it is the *self-same* as the different (in the way that the essence of circle is self-identical to what it means to be 'circle'), then to the same extent that it is different, it would participate equally in the form of the same – like the rest of the forms, it would be self-identical. But the form of the different is defined by its being essentially and absolutely different from the form of the same; it must bear no trace of the form of the same. This entails that the form of the different must be different from the different as well; put otherwise, while for every other conceivable Platonic form, one can say that it is self-identical, the form of the different would be absolutely unique in that its nature would be defined by its self-differentiation.

But there are further complications still. Each form in Plato's ontology must relate to every other form by way of the form of the different, in that each form is different from every other. As the visitor says, 'And we're going to say that it [the different] pervades all of them. . .'.[35] To the extent that change is different from rest, it is so because it participates in the form of the different. So just as the form of the same pervades all the other forms (in that each is identical to itself), the form of the different also pervades all the other forms (in that each form is different from every other). What is even more interesting about Plato's formulation, however, is the implication that difference assumes a co-constitutive role with the same. The passage proceeds: 'And we're going to say that it pervades all of them, since each of them is different from the others', and Plato's wording here is crucial, 'not because of its own nature but because of sharing in the type of the different'.[36] Change, for instance, differs from rest *not* because change has its own self-contained identity, which is different from the self-contained identity that rest possesses, but rather because change participates in the form of the different. The same must be said for rest as well. The implication of this, however, is a step that Plato does not take: it must follow that change would not be self-identical without this differing relation. In order for change to be change, it must differ from rest; and if it differs from rest, not because of their respective identities, but because of their participation in difference, then this difference is primary to the self-identity that it engenders. Given what Plato has said, therefore, the sheer articulation of a form of the different would threaten the dissolution of any centrality of identity.

This complication reaches its apogee, however, when we consider the form of the same specifically. As we said, the form of the different is defined by its being absolutely different from the form of the same. The form of the same differs from all other forms as well. For instance, while the form of the beautiful participates in the form of the same (in that the beautiful is self-identical), nevertheless, the form of the same is different from (is not the same as) the form of the beautiful. The form of the same differs, similarly, from all other forms. However, its difference from the form of the different is a unique relation. If the form of the different is defined by its being absolutely different from the form of the same, we can say reciprocally that the form of the same is defined by its being absolutely different from the form of the different; it relates *to* the different *through* the different. But this means that, to the extent that the form of the same is self-same, it is so because it differs absolutely from the form of the different. This entails that its self-sameness derives from its maximal participation in the form of the different itself. Put otherwise, its self-identity would have to be constituted by its absolute difference from the different. Its self-sameness is an absolute difference. Moreover, it is clear that this threat does not run both ways – the same does not threaten the different in the way that the different threatens the same. Given that all forms differ, according to Plato, on the basis of the different alone, not on the basis of their respective identities, the different is not contaminated by the same (because it differs from the same by way of the different); however, the same is absolutely contaminated by the different, in so far as it too must differ from the different by way of the different.

Plato thus stands tottering on the edge of a great precipice off of which, ultimately, he does not allow himself to fall, but which nevertheless complicates any so-called traditional understanding of Plato's ontology. We can therefore see the danger posed by Plato's form of the different, and consequently, by any attempt to formulate a 'concept' of difference itself. Plato's form of the same is ubiquitous throughout his ontology; it is, in a certain sense, the glue that holds together the rest of the forms, even if it rarely makes an explicit appearance. Simply by understanding what a form means for Plato, we can see the central role that the form of the same plays for this, or for that matter any, essentialist ontology. By merely introducing a form of the different and attempting to rigorously think through its implications, one can see that it threatens to fundamentally undermine the form of the same itself, and hence by implication, difference threatens to devour whole the rest of the ontological edifice of essentialism. Plato, it seems, was playing with Heraclitean fire. Given that the *Sophist* is, according to most Plato scholars, a dialogue that appears very late in Plato's life, one cannot help but wonder what might have become of Plato's system had he lived many years longer. Nevertheless, Plato never makes the decisive turn that would allow him a genuine concept of difference, as he never quite permits himself to think that the form of the different is primary, and his forms remain the unaltered, unquestioned, centres of identity in accordance with which the world is created and operates; moreover, they remain hierarchically organised beneath the form of the good beyond being,[37] from which all others ultimately derive their reality.

Aristotle

Next comes what Deleuze calls the 'propitious moment' in the philosophy of difference.[38] The concept of difference threatens to destroy the very identity that enables all representational thinking. In the *Metaphysics*, Aristotle attempts to correct Plato's missteps. Aristotle inserts into the discussion of difference a presupposition that Plato had not employed, namely, that 'difference' may be said only of things which are, in some broader sense, identical. Where Plato's form of the different may be said to relate everything to everything else, Aristotle argues that there is a conceptual distinction to be made between 'difference' and 'otherness'.

For Aristotle, there are four ways in which a thing may be said to be one: (1) continuity; (2) wholeness or unity; (3) number; (4) kind.[39] By 'continuity', he means the most general sense in which a thing may be said to be a thing. A bundle of sticks, bound together with twine, may be said to be 'one', even if it is human effort that has made it so. Likewise, an individual body part, such as an arm or leg, may be said to be 'one', as it has an isolable functional continuity. Within this grouping, there are greater and lesser degrees to which something may be said to be one. For instance, while a human leg may be said to be one, the tibia or the femur, on their own, are more continuous (in that each is numerically one and independent, and the two of them together comprise the leg).

With respect to 'wholeness or unity', Aristotle clarifies by saying, 'the substratum does not differ in kind; it does not differ in the case of things whose kind is indivisible to the sense'.[40] Each of the parts of a human being (the legs, the arms, the torso, the head), may be said to be, in their own way, 'continuous', but taken together, and in harmonious functioning, they constitute the oneness or the wholeness of the individual human being and their biological and psychological life. In this sense, the person is one, in that all of the parts function naturally together toward common ends. In the same respect, a shoelace, each eyelet, the sole, and the material comprising the shoe itself, may be said to be, each in their own way, continuous, while taken together they constitute the 'wholeness' of the shoe.

Oneness in number is fairly straightforward. A human being is one in the organic sense above, but is also one numerically, in that their living body constitutes one person, as opposed to many persons. Finally, there is generic oneness, the oneness in kind or in intelligibility. There is a sense in which all human beings, taken together, may be said to be one, in that they are all particular tokens of the genus 'human'. Likewise, humans, cats, dogs, lions, horses, pigs, etc., may all be said to be one, in that they are all types of the genus 'animal'.

'Otherness' is the term that Aristotle uses to characterise existent things which are, in any sense of the term, 'not one'. There is, as we said, a sense in which a horse and a woman are one (in that both are types of the genus 'animal'), but obvious senses in which they are other as well. There is a sense in which my neighbour and I are one (in that we are both tokens of the genus 'human'), but in so far as we are materially, emotionally, and psychologically distinct, there is a sense in which I am other than my neighbour as well. There is an obvious sense in which I and my leg are one but there is also a sense in which my leg is other than me as well (for if I were to lose my leg in an accident, provided I received prompt and proper medical attention, *I* would continue to exist). Every existent thing, Aristotle argues, is by its very nature either 'one with' or 'other than' every other existent thing.

But unlike Plato's form of the different, Aristotle's 'otherness' does not satisfy the conditions for what Aristotle understands as difference. Since everything that exists is either one with or other than everything else that exists, there need not be any definite sense in which two things are other.

There might be (as we saw above, my neighbour and I are one in the sense of tokens of the genus 'human', but are other numerically), but such a definite sense is not a necessary condition of 'otherness'. For instance, a human being is so drastically other than a given place, say, a cornfield, that we need not even enumerate the various ways in which the two are 'other', nor would we really know where to begin distinguishing the two.

This, however, is the key for Aristotle: otherness is not the same as difference. While a human being is other than a particular cornfield, she is not, in Aristotle's sense, different than a cornfield. Difference, strictly speaking, applies only when there is a definite sense in which two things differ. This requires a higher category of identity within which a distinction may be drawn: 'For the other and that which it is other than need not be other in some definite respect (for everything that exists is either other or the same), but that which is different from anything is different in some respect, so that there must be something identical whereby they differ. And this identical thing is genus or species.'[41] In other words, two human beings may be different (one may be taller, have a different skin tone, a different sex, and so on), but this is because they are identical in the sense that both are specific members of the genus 'human'. A human being may be different than a cat (one is quadrupedal while the other is bipedal, one is non-rational while the other is rational, and so on), but this is because they are identical in the sense that both are specified members of the genus 'animal'.

But between these two, generic and specific, specific difference or 'contrariety' is, according to Aristotle, the greatest, most perfect, or most complete difference. This assessment too is rooted in Aristotle's emphasis on identity as the ground of differentiation. A difference in genus in Aristotelian terminology means primarily belonging to different 'categories' of being (substance, time, quality, quantity, place, relation, and so on). A cat is other than '5', to be sure, but Aristotle would not say that the cat is different from '5', because the cat is a 'substance' and '5' is a 'quantity', and given that these two are distinct categories of being, for Aristotle they cannot relate in any meaningful sense, and hence, they do not differ in any meaningful sense. Things that differ in 'genus' are so far distant (more akin, really, to otherness) as to be nearly incomparable. However, a cat may be said to be different than a human being, because the characteristics whereby they are distinguished from each other are 'contrarieties', occupying opposing sides of a given either/or: for instance, rational versus non-rational. Special difference or contrariety thus provides us with a binary of affirmation or privation, a 'yes' or a 'no' that constitutes the greatest or most perfect difference, according to Aristotle. Differences in genus are too great, while intra-special differences are too minute and numerous (skin tone, for instance, is manifested in a myriad of ways), but special contrariety is 'complete', embodying an affirmation or negation of a particular given quality whereby 'genera' are differentiated into species.

There are thus two senses in which, for Aristotle, difference is thought only in accordance with a principle of identity. First, there is the identity that two different things share within a common genus. (A rock and a tree are identical in that both are members of the genus 'substance', differentiated by the contrariety of 'living/non-living'.) Second, there is the bipolar self-identity of the characteristics whereby two things are differentiated: material (versus non-material), living (versus non-living), sentient (versus non-sentient), rational (versus non-rational), and so on.

We can see, then, that it is only with Aristotle that difference becomes fully codified within the tradition as the type of 'empirical difference' that we mentioned in the previous chapter: it is understood as a recognisable relation between two things which, prior to and independently of their relating, possess their own self-contained identities. Difference then is a way in which a self-identical thing 'A' is not like a self-identical thing 'B', while both belong to a higher category of identity (in the sense of an Aristotelian genus). While in Plato the apparent co-constitutive nature of the different remained an open question, Aristotle closes the issue, completely subordinating difference to identity. Moreover, despite his relentless attacks on the forms as abstract, ideal universals, he leaves virtually untouched their status as final causes. The forms for Aristotle, especially within the living substance, are *teloi* or *entelécheia* drawing the substance in its living activity and change, and hence his hylomorphism in no way alters Plato's centrality of the forms.

Augustine and the mind of God

The next decisive moment in the thought of the centre takes place with Plotinus, and subsequently, with St Augustine of Hippo who Christianises Plotinus and with him, the Platonic tradition. Where Plato's Demiurge of the *Timaeus* had created in accordance with the forms or ideas, which were at least in some sense distinct from the Demiurge himself, Plotinus conceives the Platonic ideas as inhering in and synonymous with the divine *nous*. The divine itself, for Plotinus, is absolutely transcendent, beyond all comprehension, the 'One'. Of the One it must be said first and foremost that there is no multiplicity. There is no thought, because thought requires a thinker *and* an object; no efficient causality, because *acting* implies a distinction between agent, action, and object, and it moreover implies a dispositional change in the agent itself; there is not even self-consciousness, which would turn the selfhood of the divine into both subject and object, thereby introducing multiplicity. Plotinus formulates the concept of the One by thinking through the implications of Plato's form of the good which, though beyond being, is not non-existent, but rather utterly exceeds and transcends all the categories by which we typically understand existence.

Such a transcendent unity cannot create by a free act of the will, but creates by way of 'emanation' or 'circumradiation'. Like the rays of the sun (Plato's material analogue for the form of the good), goodness emanates from the One, and as it does, it posits and is received by a 'matter' necessary for its realisation. This goodness and its material correlate decrease in intensity, and hence perfection, the further the strata get from the divine. All emanates from the divine, and all strives toward the divine – the source and telos of all being. The first of these strata is *nous*, or the divine mind. Following logically from the unity of the One, we have first the not-one, the first differentiation. At this stratum, the attributes of the One (such as the beautiful, the just, and so on), which inhere in the One in a purely undifferentiated form, are distinguished into what we know as the archetypes that are Plato's forms. *Nous* emanates from and turns its gaze back toward the One, attempting to think the eternality and perfection of the One, but is only capable of doing so in this differentiated way. For Plotinus, then, the absolute centre is the One, which is ineffable, undifferentiated, pure, and unknowable as such. As this absolute centre, it also encompasses in a pure and undifferentiated way all those discrete (for Plato) centres of the forms, which for Plotinus exist independently only in a differentiated, and hence imperfect, domain.

Augustine accepts this position almost entirely, but rather than thinking the ideas as inhering in a derivative, deficient, and impersonal *nous*, he understands the ideas as belonging to the mind of a personal God:

> Hence in Latin we can call the ideas either 'forms' (*formae*), or 'species' (*species*), which are literal translations of the word. But if we call them 'reasons' (*rationes*), we obviously depart from a literal translation of the term, for 'reasons' (*rationes*) in Greek are called *logoi*, not 'ideas' (*ideae*). Yet, nonetheless, if anyone wants to use 'reason' (*ratio*), he will not stray from the thing in question, for in fact the ideas are certain original and principal forms of things, i.e., reasons, fixed and unchangeable, which are not themselves formed and, being thus eternal and existing always in the same state, are contained in the Divine Intelligence. And though they themselves neither come into being nor pass away, nevertheless, everything which can come into being and pass away and everything which does come into being and pass away is said to be formed in accord with these ideas.[42]

With this, Augustine consolidates all knowledge in the divine mind. Like Plotinus, Augustine unambiguously interprets Plato's form of the good theologically, and like Plato's form of the good, Augustine's God is the necessary condition for all genuine knowledge. Any glimmers of knowledge available to humans are available only by way of their looking to that epistemic centre, and by the divine light that, like Plato's sun, permits that seeing: 'This was the condition of my mind when I did not realize that light must come to it from another source than itself, that it must *share* in the truth because it cannot *be* the truth.'[43] Unlike Plotinus, however, Augustine's divinity is not an undifferentiated, non-thinking, pure unity, but a personal and loving God, and it is only because of God's *grace* that humans are drawn to look to the divine in the first place. Human intelligence or determination alone are insufficient. Augustine's doctrine, which would come to be known as the doctrine of divine illumination, deposits all of Plato's centres of meaning into the absolute centre of the divine mind. For nearly a millennium to come – through Boethius and Anselm, through Al-Fārābī and Ibn Sīnā,[44] up through Aquinas – the Western philosophical tradition would rest safely within that figure of the centre, as its most foundational and unassailable assumption. As Copleston writes, 'This doctrine was the common doctrine in the Middle Ages up to and including the thirteenth century.'[45]

The movement of decentring in Duns Scotus and Ockham

In the wake of St Thomas Aquinas, however, a shift is inaugurated, and a decentring begins to rumble beneath the philosophical theology of the Middle Ages. This movement of decentring continues until the emergence of modern rationalism, and occurs in three basic phases: ontological, epistemic, and cosmological. The first of these moments, the ontological, occurs in the late thirteenth century with John Duns Scotus, who rejects Augustine's divine illumination. Scotus reasons that if the human capacity for knowledge is inherently flawed and incapable of certainty, then God's self-illumination would in no way remedy the deficiency. If our assumption is that the human mind is fundamentally incapable of knowledge, then even if God *were* to illuminate truth for us, we would not be capable of recognising it *as* truth, any more than a squirrel could understand special relativity, however clearly a physicist might explain it to her. There must be, according to Scotus, a 'natural knowledge of God'.

This brings us to Scotus' doctrine of the univocity of being.[46] Accompanying this natural knowability of God are the proofs for the existence of God. Nearly all of these proofs rely upon an inference made from some fact about the human mind to the existence of God, and hence, they rely upon a commonality between God and humankind. In whatever ways and to whatever degrees God's existence is unlike human existence, human thought is incapable of knowing God's existence. Thus, in an effort to ground more decisively the persuasive force of the proofs for God's existence, Scotus argues for the univocity of being. Being, he claimed, must be said in a single sense of everything of which it is said. Scotus' doctrine of the univocity of being, posited with the most pious of intentions, nevertheless amounts to a rejection of the Aristotelian and Thomistic doctrine of analogy, whereby being is distributed analogically and hierarchically. An analogical and hierarchical distribution of being entails that there are greater and lesser degrees to which a thing may be said to be, both 'horizontally' (across the things of the world – substances *are* to a greater degree than are their qualities) and 'vertically' (God *is* to a greater degree than is his creation). A substance exists to a greater degree than do its properties, because the properties *require* the substance in order to manifest, but the substance will persist despite changes in its properties. There is no red 'as such'; there are only red things, and if I paint a red thing black, its quiddity remains unchanged.

Likewise, vertically, the early Medieval period had given us the *scala naturae*, often translated as the 'great chain of being'.[47] Similar to Plotinus' notion of emanation, the *scala naturae* imagines all of being as ranging from pure being (pure spirit) at the top, down to bare existence (inert matter) at the bottom, with the human being the only thing in all of existence to straddle the matter/spirit divide. On this model, things further down the scale exist to a lesser degree than those things further up the scale, with God being at the apex of the chain, and, like Plotinus' 'One', external to creation. The doctrine of analogy accords nicely with the Christian demand for an ontological distinction between God and creation, maintaining God's transcendence while still, in some sense, affording us the means to speak of him. To say that being is univocal, as Scotus does, is thus to depose the absolutely transcendent centrality of God, even if only in a subtle way, replacing it instead with the abstract notion of being: being is said in the same sense of everything of which it is said, whether God, human being, or spider.

Despite his rejection of illuminationism and his proclamation of the univocity of being, Scotus nevertheless remained a metaphysical realist when it came to the ideas themselves. In keeping with our historical narrative, we might therefore say that he dispersed them from the centrality of the divine mind while maintaining at the same time their own self-contained and independent centrality. William of Ockham thus launches the epistemic moment of this decentring, by abolishing the Platonic forms. Again, Ockham operates with the 'holiest' of intentions. In his case, it is in order to salvage the absoluteness of the divine freedom that he disposes of the ideas. To assert the discrete 'real existence' of the ideas, Ockham holds, is to imply that God's creative freedom is restrained, in that God would be constrained to create in accordance with the ideas. If there is an eternal, abstract 'idea' of the human being, then when God creates human beings, he must do so in accordance with the idea of human. The same applies to God's moral freedom; to assert the discrete reality of the good, an idea or form distinct from God, is to constrain God to act in accordance with its dictates.

Moreover, to assert the real existence of the ideas is, according to Ockham, incoherent, inasmuch as *anything* that exists, in virtue of its existence, is an individual. However, the very purpose of Plato's idea is to explain the commonality among different things. Hence, it is ascribable to a plurality of differing individuals. Supposing the 'real existence' of the forms, then, according to Ockham, is tantamount to saying that each form both is an individual (in so far as it exists) and is not an individual (in so far as it is univocally ascribable to countless individuals), which results in a logical contradiction. A universal, therefore, is a term that may stand in the place of an individual in a proposition, but to ascribe to a universal its own real existence, other than that of mental abstraction, is for Ockham both illogical and heretical. Thus, the figures of Scotus and Ockham represent the beginning of a shift of decentring in the history of philosophy – Scotus by displacing the absolute centrality of God, and Ockham by jettisoning the centres of Plato's ideas themselves.

Scepticism and the scientific revolutions

This movement of decentring, begun in the thirteenth century by Duns Scotus, would reach its extremity in the sixteenth and seventeenth centuries in a series of earth-shattering discoveries, both scientific and philosophical. One of these, continuing Ockham's epistemic moment of decentring, was the rediscovery of ancient scepticism in the Western world. While theologians beginning with Augustine had presented and objected to sceptical arguments, the texts of the philosophical sceptics themselves were largely lost to the West, and the arguments themselves were often misrepresented – presented in bare, 'straw person' forms – and thus, not given due credence. This changed with the 1562 rediscovery and Latin translation of the texts of Sextus Empiricus. As Jonathan Barnes notes, 'In 1562 Henri Etienne published a Latin translation of the sceptical works of the Greek philosopher Sextus . . . If ancient skepticism was not wholly unknown before the publication of Etienne's Sextus, it was little regarded and little respected: the Sextus put it in the limelight and made it the talk of the day.'[48] In its developed and mature formulations, philosophical scepticism challenges the bases of human knowledge, calling into question the reliability and extent of the sensory faculties and seriously questioning the validity of human reasoning (the two epistemic vehicles, we should note, which are suspended in the first of Descartes' *Meditations*).

Among those seriously influenced by the rediscovery of the Sextus text was Michel de Montaigne, who constructed a Christianised form of scepticism in which the only way beyond the unreliability and limitations of reason and the sensory faculties is faith in God. Given that we can't *know*, our only recourse is to *believe*. Montaigne popularised anew for the European world the arguments of ancient scepticism. However, once we've called into question the human ability to *know* anything at all, it doesn't require much imagination to ask, akin to Duns Scotus, on what basis can one *know* that one needs to have faith in God? It appears but a stone's throw from Montaigne's Christian scepticism to a full-blown scepticism.

Finally, we come to the cosmological decentring, the heliocentric model of the cosmos posited by Nicolaus Copernicus in his 1543 text, *De revolutionibus orbium coelestium*. Prior to Copernicus' text, Western thought, still in the shadow of Aristotle, Ptolemy, and Al-Fārābī, held a geocentric view of the cosmos, which provided a comforting spatial analogue to the prevailing views concerning God, the world, and humankind's place *in* the world. God, it was believed, had created the vast cosmos, and at its centre, he had placed his most special project, Earth. On this nucleus was a myriad of species of life, the apex of which was humankind itself, just a bit beneath the angels and the only being anywhere on the *scala naturae* who straddled the line between the material and the spiritual. Humankind was both literally and figuratively the centre of God's world, on the geocentric view. Thus it is difficult to overstate the tremendous impact that Copernicus' text had, followed shortly by the innovations of Kepler and Galileo, sparking the emergence of the modern scientific revolution. Copernicus had displaced humankind from the centerpiece of God's creation to one form of life among others on one among many planets which, like the rest, flies through the vast blackness of space around the old, rival god of Christianity's nascency, the sun. Ontologically, epistemically, and cosmologically, humankind and its hope for securing a totalising understanding of the whole of being within its web of static kernels of identity had apparently irredeemably lost its footing, and philosophy – the thought of the centre – seemed in grave peril.

Rationalist redemption and empiricist threat

To the rescue came a robust rationalism, reborn in the form of René Descartes, who conducted a massive recentring by revolutionising the Western understanding of the very structure of knowledge. He provides a decisive response to philosophical scepticism by instituting absolute certainty as the condition of knowledge and by pushing scepticism as far as it can possibly go, culminating in the figure of the infamous evil genius. Once he has doubted everything that can possibly be doubted, Descartes discovers that the only thing that is certain is the existence of the thinking subject, along with the self-presence of the ideas by which it thinks. For Augustine and the religious philosophical tradition that followed, ideas had existed only in the mind of God who, transcendent to his creation, had brought everything into being in accordance with those eternal templates. Knowledge, then, consisted in the ability to adequately see those eternal ideas in the mind of God by way of divine illumination. Descartes recentres the conditions of knowledge in the mind of the individual cognising human being, thus establishing what comes to be known as the 'way of ideas'. As humankind has been torn gradually from its access to the centres of knowledge, Descartes brings those centres into the human mind, thereby establishing the human subject as each its own little 'centre' of the cosmos.

Like Augustine's divine ideas, Descartes' way of ideas – that the foundations of knowledge reside in the mind of the knowing subject – would endure for centuries beyond Descartes, despite vastly different views regarding the *sources* and *natures* of those ideas. For Descartes, all ideas, including that of God, are innate; they do not rely upon external or sensory experience for their illumination. Though God will finally serve for Descartes as the guarantor of all other clear and distinct ideas, it is nevertheless only on the basis of the innate idea of God that the cogitator can be sure that God exists. The Cartesian apodicticity of consciousness now plays the role formerly ascribed only to God – the absolute guarantor of truth and knowledge. Rather than God illuminating the mind, the mind now illuminates God. In so doing, Descartes restores philosophy's demand for centrality, making it once again possible to access those absolute cores or kernels of identity and truth. It is also worth noting that, in nearly all its manifestations – particularly its Malebranchian and Leibnizian ones[49] – robust rationalism[50] endeavours to so restore the centre.

But just as continental rationalism reaches its fever pitch in Leibniz, across the channel a resurgent empiricism is beginning to chip away at the carefully constructed rationalist edifice, once again shifting philosophy in the direction of decentring. This begins with the relentless attack on the doctrine of innate ideas, carried out by John Locke in his two-volume *An Essay Concerning Human Understanding*. The implications of this attack, which all subsequent empiricists would take for granted, are staggering. If the ideas by which the mind cognises the world are not *innate*, then they must be constructed somehow, and the empiricists will hold that the only plausible explanation is that this construction takes place by the mind's deriving simple ideas from sensory experience and combining these simple ideas into ideas of greater and greater complexity. Naturally, it stands to reason that if our ideas are constructed by the mind, they are, like all human constructions, subject to error; and while the empiricists take great pains to outline strategies for avoiding epistemic errors, gone forever is the ability to satisfy Descartes' certitude condition of knowledge with respect to the external world. Along with it, many of the cherished Cartesian 'ideas' are either discarded or seriously attenuated. The notion of 'substance', the linchpin of Descartes' dualism and the unassailable foundation of his cogito argument, is for Locke merely a word we use to explain why certain properties often appear together, 'only a supposition of he knows not what support of such qualities, which are capable of producing simple *ideas* in us – which qualities are commonly called accidents'.[51] As we do not *see* the so-called substantiality of a thing but by its various properties, our idea of substance is, at best, obscure and confused. Likewise, the notion of personal identity, no longer resting in the self-identity of the Cartesian substance, is reduced to the active human consciousness, along with whatever memories it has of past modes of consciousness: 'For as far as any intelligent being can repeat the *idea* of any past action with the same consciousness it had of it at first, and with the same consciousness it has of any present action, so far it is the same *personal self*.'[52] The idea of God as well, no longer innate, must be derived from our observations of the natural world; and as a result, it is stripped of its Cartesian omnipotence and omniscience. While we might conclude on the basis of observation that the creation and operation of the cosmos requires vast knowledge and power, but we are not thereby justified in concluding *infinite* knowledge and power. Thus the idea of God, for Locke, is an idea of a being '*most powerful*' and '*most knowing*'.[53]

The empiricist tradition reaches a crescendo in David Hume who, following the Cartesian implication that 'the centre' of the sciences is 'human nature itself',[54] proceeds to demolish nearly all of the cherished centres of the rationalist tradition that had been left tottering precariously by Locke, starting with the centrality of reason as the cornerstone of human nature: 'Reason is, and ought only to be the slave of the passions,' and can never pretend to any other office than to serve and obey them.'[55] As our ideas are compounded from the simple ideas of sensation, they will *always* be more obscure the further removed they are from experience. Moreover, Hume will argue that any obscurity pertaining to our ideas can be cleared up permanently if we abide by the following principle: upon encountering an idea that *cannot* be traced to a particular sensation (of which there are many), we unflinchingly acknowledge this fact and either employ such ideas only in so far as they are *necessary* to explain sensations (but with the constant awareness that we are doing so), or we discard them entirely: 'By bringing ideas into so clear a light, we may reasonably hope to remove all dispute, which may arise, concerning their nature and reality.'[56] The litany of such ideas is vast, and includes the cause-effect relation, our prediction of future events, the connection between mind and body, power, substance, moral facts, the self, the freedom of the will, and the nature of the divine. Even identity, in the hands of Hume, will be reduced to an ascription that human beings apply, not arbitrarily but relative to our own perspective, to what are in fact nothing but diversities.[57] Little wonder, perhaps, that Deleuze's first monograph is written on Hume. David Hume finalises philosophy's next major decentring, in the reactivation of a plausible form of modern scepticism. Immanuel Kant would then attempt to correct this decentring shift with his transcendental idealism, reinstating the centrality of knowledge in accordance with the categories of subjectivity. However, Kant is only able to do so by predicating his entire system upon the distinction between phenomenon (the thing as it appears) and noumenon (the thing in itself), salvaging a genuine possibility of objective knowledge (objective because it is the same for all rational subjects) by paring off the realm of being as irredeemably inaccessible. The Kantian recentring is thus in one way radical, but in another limited.

Hegel and Nietzsche[58]

This recentring would thus be insufficient for most of Kant's successors, who would, each in their own way, attempt to bridge or cancel the distinction between noumenon and phenomenon, thus restoring to reason the jurisdiction over the whole of being. The greatest of these efforts indisputably occurs with Hegel, who attempts to reconcile the divisions not only between noumenon and phenomenon, but to reconcile *all* of the divisions and ruptures within the history of philosophy, and bring them under the scope of Absolute Spirit. Hegel thus returns to the Greek origins[59] of the Western tradition, and conceives Aristotle's self-thinking thought of the *Metaphysics* in accordance with Hegel's notion of the Absolute, understood in the sense of the whole. But where Aristotle's self-thinking thought consists of self-reflection in the mode of pure immediacy, Hegel's history of Spirit consists of this immediacy's gradually and progressively becoming other to itself, and reconciling this otherness within a richer, more complex notion of identity. The self and its other – thesis and antithesis – are *aufgehoben*, simultaneously cancelled in their self-standing opposition while also *elevated* and *sublated* into a higher whole. This elevating cancellation – the negation of the contradiction – is commonly referred to as the *Aufhebung*. The unfolding of Hegel's 'True' is an ongoing dialectical process that culminates in the self-consciousness of Absolute Spirit: 'The True is the whole. But the whole is nothing other than the essence consummating itself through its development. Of the Absolute it must be said that it is essentially a *result*, that only in the *end* is it what it truly is; and that precisely in this consists its nature, viz., to be actual, subject, the spontaneous becoming of itself.'[60] Contrary to Spinoza then, for whom substance alone *is*, while all else consists of mere modes of that substance, for Hegel 'everything turns on grasping and expressing the True, not only as *Substance*, but equally as *Subject*'.[61] Being becomes aware of itself no longer in Aristotle's simple immediacy, but in the mediated complex 'reflection in otherness within itself'.[62] The history of philosophy is thus reconceived under Hegel's system as the vast unfolding of the Absolute, such that all of its apparent disputes and contradictions, all of its centrings, decentrings, and recentrings, are necessary stages in this unfolding, anchoring the entire progression of nature, culture, art, history, and thought within an absolute centre. Incorporating elements of Aristotle's self-thinking thought, Augustine's divine mind, and Spinoza's substance monism, along with the Trinitarian structure of Christian theology, Hegel creates philosophy's most centralising system yet, which Deleuze refers to as a 'monocentring of circles'.[63]

Following Hegel in our story comes Nietzsche, who conducts philosophy's most aggressive movement of decentring. If Plato's thought led out of the cave, Nietzsche's self-described inversion of Plato leads unapologetically back in, to a labyrinthine realm of depths, echoes, shadows, and dissimulations. No longer does the light of the Platonic sun illuminate, but rather Heraclitus' fire; no longer do facts (in the sense of static 'givens') prevail, but perspectives. Nietzsche's early thought is deeply indebted to the work of Arthur Schopenhauer. Though mired in relative obscurity for much of his life, Schopenhauer comes of age at the height of the Idealist phase of German philosophy, boldly (if foolishly) scheduling his own classes at the University of Berlin to conflict with those of Hegel, whom Schopenhauer despised. Against Hegel's thought, Schopenhauer reasserts a drastically revised Kantianism, laced with a dash of Spinozistic parallelism. In place of Kant's noumenon/phenomenon distinction,

Schopenhauer posits the analogous will/representation distinction, where will is the principle of the universe as it *is*, and representation as it *appears*. For Schopenhauer, this is evident upon introspection – turned inward the mind recognises immediately the constant striving of will within, the outer expression of which is its bodily representation. Contrary to Kant, however, Schopenhauer does not conceptualise this will as fundamentally rational, but rather as blind, irrational, and insatiable, like Freud's *id*. Also contrary to Kant, for Schopenhauer there is no justifiable basis by which one can distinguish different *noumena* (or wills) from each other. Anything that could distinguish one noumenon from another for Schopenhauer would have to be restricted to the phenomenal (or representational) sphere, and hence could not be trusted to reflect the reality of things. For this reason, Schopenhauer understands the principle of will as *singular*, though in constant striving. Finally, Schopenhauer disagrees with Kant in that will does not *cause* representation (as Kant's noumenon causes the phenomenon) – rather, like Spinoza's parallel attributes, will and representation are two ways of understanding the same thing. But most significantly, and against the entire tradition of German Idealism, for Schopenhauer will is decidedly *not* teleological – its striving is purposeless and insatiable, and it does not tend toward any just, final, or holistic resolution. Our only respites from the striving of the will are in brief moments of absolute absorption in the sphere of representation – the appreciation of the beautiful in the domain of art.

Nietzsche shatters Schopenhauer's ontologically singular will. As Deleuze writes, 'Nietzsche's break with Schopenhauer rests on one precise point; it is a matter of knowing whether the will is unitary or multiple.'[64] In Nietzsche, the will is dispersed into a play of multitudes of forces at the heart of life, dubbed the 'will to power': 'Where I found the living, there I found the will to power.'[65] For Nietzsche, the 'will to power' is a will not to persist or survive but to expand and grow. This fundamental impulse to expansion and growth produces diversity, without which adaptation (and hence, survival), would be impossible. The will to power thus presupposes, demands, and thrives on multiplicity: 'The will to power can manifest itself only against resistances; therefore it seeks that which resists it.'[66] But for Nietzsche, this multiplicity does not teleologically point toward, nor is it for the sake of, some ultimate unification or assimilation; it is for the sake of difference itself: 'The greater the impulse toward unity, the more firmly may one conclude that weakness is present; the greater the impulse toward variety, differentiation, inner decay, the more force is present.'[67] Nietzsche decries the state apparatus, favours polytheism over monotheism (which he calls 'monotono-theism'[68]), and reduces the ego to a nexus of active and reactive forces. Nietzsche thus reinstates the madness of the

Heraclitean world, conceiving the being of the cosmos in terms of its becoming, dispersing and disrupting identity in all its forms, and launching the torpedo of thought that will dominate continental philosophy in the twentieth century.

Accompanying this philosophy of the will, however, is a more perplexing notion, the concept of eternal return: 'Herewith I again stand on the soil out of which my intention, my *ability* grows – I, the last disciple of the philosopher Dionysus – I, the teacher of the eternal recurrence.'[69] The eternal return is an ancient idea, with precursors in both Eastern and Western religious and philosophical traditions – the idea that the entire history of the cosmos repeats in precise detail, an infinite amount of times throughout eternity. Nietzsche himself interprets (or reinterprets) eternal return as the marriage of Heraclitus and Parmenides: 'To impose upon becoming the character of being – that is the supreme will to power . . . That *everything recurs* is the closest *approximation of a world of becoming to a world of being.*'[70] What Nietzsche *meant* by this marriage, however, is not immediately evident. It *is* clear that Nietzsche had read some texts of contemporary physics, and had speculated in his notes that eternal return might be 'the most *scientific* of all possible hypotheses'.[71] As a result, some prominent Nietzsche scholars interpret eternal return in the strictly straightforward cosmological sense, as the precise repetition of the history of the cosmos.[72] The imposition of the character of being onto becoming then is that, despite the eternal fluctuations of the cosmos, the process of fluctuations always starts over in perfectly identical repetition, playing eternally like a film that begins again each time the credits have faded to black.

However, the cyclical reading is not without problems. As Deleuze notes, Nietzsche's own conception of the eternal return was formulated precisely in opposition to the ancient doctrine of cyclical, cosmological, repetition, and Nietzsche himself saw his concept of eternal return as something completely new: 'Why did Nietzsche, who knew the Greeks, know that the eternal return was *his* own invention, an untimely belief or belief of the future?'[73] Deleuze's response is that eternal return is formulated by Nietzsche as a concept of repetition in a world where Identity, the Same, and the Similar have already been abolished. 'The same' in the eternal return of the same is a repetition of the different itself, according to Deleuze. Whatever we make of the eternal return (and we will deal with it in more detail in what follows), it is clear that in the wake of Hegel's decisive recentring of philosophy, Nietzsche pushes it further in the direction of decentring than it has been since Heraclitus, providing us with the seemingly paradoxical combination of a philosophy of will to power that abolishes all fixed identities, and a conception of repetition that would seem to presuppose the very identities that the will to power destroys. In so doing, he throws down the gauntlet for philosophy in the twentieth century.

Heidegger's engagement with Nietzsche

The most important philosopher to take up that gauntlet early on is Martin Heidegger, who grappled with Nietzsche's work more vigorously, more aggressively, and more enduringly than he did any other single philosopher in the history of the tradition.[74] Alan Schrift notes that 'Heidegger published a greater volume of material on Nietzsche (over 1,200 pages devoted specifically to interpretations of Nietzsche) than any other figure in this history [of metaphysics].'[75] As early as *Being and Time* (1927), Nietzsche, like Kierkegaard, lurks in the margins of Heidegger's overall project:[76]

> Anticipation discloses to existence that its uttermost possibility lies in giving itself up, and thus it shatters all one's tenaciousness to whatever existence one has reached. In anticipation, Dasein guards itself against falling back behind itself, or behind the potentiality-for-Being which it has understood. It guards itself against 'becoming too old for its victories' (Nietzsche).[77]

Stephen Aschheim writes that 'Heidegger's initial solution for the overcoming of nihilism – through a heroic, existential, self-affirmative will – was unexceptionally Nietzschean.'[78] Nevertheless, though Nietzsche's influence is perceptible early on in Heidegger's work, according to Aschheim, Heidegger will only fully embrace Nietzsche around the time that he becomes enamoured with the far-right political thought of the Weimar Republic in 1929.

When Heidegger commences his Nietzsche lectures in 1936, it is in order to discredit the more explicitly National Socialistic readings of Nietzsche, as found in the writings of Alfred Bäumler,[79] who, 'along with Heidegger', writes Richard Steigmann-Gall, 'was the most notable philosopher to back the Nazi regime with his intellectual prestige'.[80] As Heidegger begins to work through Nietzsche, however, he comes to reject Nietzsche for his own reasons. But in so doing, Heidegger undergoes a self-transformation, coming to reject certain aspects of his own thinking, which for Heidegger had been bound up with Nietzsche. The will to power, which had found its way into Heidegger's thought as the 'resoluteness of Dasein', would come under criticism, and would ultimately be rejected, thus pushing Heidegger's thought toward the *Kehre* that would mark the distinction between the early and late periods of Heidegger's thought. Heidegger would ultimately come to view his own political failures as bound up with his earlier Nietzscheanism, such that he reportedly confided to a family member, 'Nietzsche hat mich kaputt-gemacht', or 'Nietzsche did me in.'[81]

Nevertheless, one could argue that the entirety of Heidegger's thinking from 1929 on is wrapped up in the set of problems and questions that he finds in Nietzsche. Aschheim again writes: 'throughout the 1930s and 1940s, Heidegger's categories and thematic, his *Fragestellung* and metadiscourse, depended upon the Nietzschean frame', and, 'If he later chose to dissolve self-assertion and metaphysics in complete submission to the Voice of Being, his problematic nevertheless remained cast within the radical Nietzschean critique of reason and the end of Western philosophy.'[82] Nietzsche's primary task – the reversal of Platonism, the decentring of philosophy, the break with the metaphysical tradition,[83] the conviction that this tradition had run its course and that a new way of thinking lay on the horizon – this framework, along with Heidegger's own conviction that Nietzsche had not in fact gotten beyond metaphysics, undergirds the entirety of Heidegger's late thinking.

We cannot here offer a comprehensive account of Heidegger's engagement with Nietzsche, and must proceed in a summary fashion, extracting from Heidegger's late criticisms the three principles of that engagement that will play a central role in the readings of Deleuze and Derrida: (1) Heidegger understands Nietzsche's concept of 'will to power' substantially, as having a quiddity or substantiality in line with Leibniz's concept of the 'monad'; (2) this allows Heidegger to isolate an essence of will to power itself, one that can be framed in singular terms, as what 'a' will to power is, ultimately determined as an ever-expanding striving for self-presence; (3) through the course of this explication, Heidegger reveals that, though Nietzsche indeed reverses the tradition of metaphysics, this reversal does not amount to a disentanglement, since Nietzsche remains, despite his efforts, ensnared in the metaphysical tradition:

> Yet, because the hitherto highest values ruled the sensory from the height of the supersensory, and because metaphysics is what structured that rule, to establish the new principle of the revaluation of all values is to bring about the reversal of all metaphysics. Nietzsche takes this reversal as the overcoming of metaphysics. However, every reversal of this kind will only be a self-blinding entanglement in what is the same though become unrecognizable.[84]

The notion that any reversal remains enslaved to what it reverses often goes by the shorthand expression of the 'Heideggerian criticism' of Nietzsche. Let us now look to Heidegger's influential reading, 'Nietzsche's Word: "God is Dead"'.[85]

Nietzsche, metaphysics, and nihilism

By his own admission, Heidegger reads Nietzsche in the context of his own specific project, and it is out of this context that his criticisms arise: 'It is the concern of preparatory thinking to clear a free scope within which being itself would again be able to take man with regard to his essence into an initial relationship. To be preparatory is the essence of such thinking.'[86] Elsewhere, Heidegger writes, 'metaphysics is thought as the truth of beings as such in their entirety, not as the doctrine of a thinker'.[87] Heidegger then is not attempting to engage with Nietzsche's thinking as such on its own terms, even less with a would-be uniquely 'Nietzschean' metaphysics, but rather with Nietzsche's role within 'the' history of metaphysics. Thus, like Hegel (and in his own way, Nietzsche), Heidegger views the history of philosophy historically,[88] as a 'story' that, beginning with the Greeks, already included its destiny within its origins. Heidegger's project then, in light of the completion of this story, is a preparatory thinking that opens anew the possibility of a primordial appropriation of humankind by Being:

> in the history of Western thinking, right from the beginning, beings have been thought in regard to being, but the truth of being has remained unthought. Indeed, not only has the truth of being been denied to thinking as a possible experience, but Western thinking itself (precisely in the form of metaphysics) has specifically, though unknowingly, masked the occurrence of this denial.[89]

This history of the West as Nietzsche and Heidegger understand it is the history of nihilism: 'Nietzsche uses *nihilism* as the name for the historical movement that he was the first to recognise and that already governed the previous century while defining the century to come, the movement whose essential interpretation he concentrates in the terse sentence: "God is dead."'[90] The death of God means, in Nietzsche's words, 'that the belief in the Christian god has become unbelievable'.[91] But for Nietzsche, the collapse of this belief entails far more than the epistemic negation of the 'confession of faith' or the apostolic creed. Tangled in our cultural conception of God is everything that we have hitherto believed about art, love, morality, truth – in short, value itself – but we have yet to accept that this death, liberating though it may be, brings with it terrible repercussions the likes of which the West has never seen. With the death of God, the West has utterly lost its horizon. As Nietzsche writes, 'One interpretation has collapsed; but because it was considered *the* interpretation it now seems as if there were no meaning at all in existence, as if everything were in vain.'[92]

Nietzsche compares it to being adrift on the ocean with no frame of reference – it is at once exhilarating and terrifying. As Heidegger understands it, 'God is dead' expresses the historical self-devaluing and self-exhaustion of humankind's highest values, the depreciation and final collapse of the Western faith in all transcendent, supersensory values: '"Christian God" also stands for the "transcendent" in general in its various meanings – for "ideals" and "norms," "principles" and "rules," "ends" and "values," which are set *above* the being, in order to give being as a whole a purpose, an order, and – as it is succinctly expressed – "meaning."'[93] This interpretation of history is what Nietzsche means when he refers to 'Platonism', 'metaphysics', and in most cases, 'Christianity'.[94] Where Hegel had understood history as the unfolding of Absolute Spirit, or God, Nietzsche understands history as the decline and ultimate collapse of our highest values, and sees himself as the thinker who diagnoses this history and motions toward a way beyond it. Heidegger writes: 'his [Nietzsche's] thinking sees itself under the sign of nihilism'.[95] Nietzsche recognises the impending dark cloud that awaits us when we finally accept the death of God, and longs to deal the final blow, so that creation can begin again. His thinking seeks to affirm the death of God so that new 'gods' – embodiments of values – can be created.

Heidegger will agree with Nietzsche's characterisation of metaphysics as the history of nihilism, saying that 'nihilism, thought in its essence, is on the contrary the fundamental movement of the history of the West'.[96] However, the end of this movement for Heidegger is not merely Nietzschean revaluation. Rather, the history of nihilism is consummated in what Heidegger elsewhere calls the '*Ge-stell*', or the 'Enframing'.[97] The essence of the Enframing is revealed in modern technology as the situatedness of humankind in the throes of power, such that all of the world, nature, even humanity itself, is revealed in terms of the 'Bestand', or the 'standing-reserve',[98] their ability to be ordered and mobilised for the purpose of the expansion or enhancement of power. Thus nihilism, on Heidegger's reading, is 'the world-historical movement of the peoples of the earth who have been drawn into modernity's arena of power'.[99] Heidegger situates Nietzsche not *beyond* the tradition of metaphysics, but rather at its end, the thought that recognises and designates 'will to power' – the explicit basis of Nietzsche's metaphysics – as the defining thought of the modern age, inaugurated by Descartes.[100] To speak in Heidegger's language, Nietzsche's overturning is not an overcoming: 'the oblivion of Being is only completed and the suprasensuous is let loose and furthered by the will to power'.[101]

Nietzsche and value

The question of 'God' is not a question of 'existence' or 'truth' for Nietzsche, but a question of 'value'. The relevant consideration for Nietzsche with respect to God is not, *does God exist or not?*, as though there were an ultimate and discernible fact-of-the-matter regarding that question, but rather, what God *means* and what different conceptions of the divine indicate about the cultures and peoples who hold them. Rather than signifying 'it is true that God does not exist', the death of God signifies on the contrary that God, and more generally, all transcendent concepts and modes of valuation, have ceased to serve as bases of value; they have lost the importance or the efficacy they once held in Western culture. The question of nihilism, and hence, the interpretation of history's movement as one of nihilism, is a question inextricably tangled in the question of value. But, as the source of all preceding historical values has collapsed, the problem becomes that of locating a new source of value.

For centuries, Nietzsche thinks, humanity has responded to this death by leaving intact the space that God occupied, filling in his absence with new doctrines that recast the transcendent within the robes of immanence. The 'kingdom of God' is reinterpreted as an earthly kingdom;[102] other-worldly heavens become this-worldly utopias. The Enlightenment ideals of modernity – socialism, democracy, humanism, utilitarianism, egalitarianism, and so on – have perhaps abolished the designator 'God', but have left its meaning untouched. They are both symptoms and prolongations of the death of God: set in this world with no promise of or reliance upon another, they indicate that the transcendent absolute has lost its explicit grasp; but in attempting to instantiate the transcendent within the worldly, humankind has yet to recognise and affirm the death of God and to grasp the magnitude of its demise. It is primarily of the bearers of these ideals that Nietzsche's madman speaks when he says, 'This deed is still more distant from them than the most distant stars – *and yet they have done it themselves.*'[103] Elsewhere Nietzsche refers to this as 'incomplete nihilism', the 'attempts to escape nihilism without revaluating our values so far: they produce the opposite, make the problem more acute'.[104] If the highest values have become devalued 'by coming to understand that the ideal world is not, and not ever, going to be realized within the real world',[105] then the task that remains is not for us to tarry with the vestiges of the dead, but to seek to posit values anew. As Heidegger says, 'since (in Nietzsche's view), this yes neither negotiates nor compromises with the previous values, an absolute no is part of this yes to the new dispensation of value'.[106]

Radically shifting the evaluative eye is no simple task. Everything that we have ever held dear, everything we have ever believed about how evaluation is conducted, has thus far been wrapped up in the supersensory. Nietzsche himself notes, 'If one disregards the ascetic ideal [the ideal of life turned against itself toward the otherworldly]: man, the *animal* man, has until now had no meaning . . . man would much rather will *nothingness* than *not* will.'[107] The questions then are, how to shift our view, and toward what? In Heidegger's words, 'No longer can the principle be the world of the supersensory, now grown dead. Therefore, nihilism aiming at revaluation (understood in this way) will seek out what is most alive.'[108] Nietzsche therefore says of nihilism that it is 'an ideal of the highest degree of powerfulness of the spirit, the over-richest life – partly destructive, partly ironic'.[109] The question of value becomes a question of life, and, more specifically, of the enhancement of life; and, as Heidegger notes, Nietzsche defines value in precisely these terms: 'The point-of-view of "value" is the point-of-view of *preservation-enhancement-conditions* for complex forms of relative life-duration within the flux of becoming'.[110]

Value is essentially related to a point-of-view. Heidegger interprets this in two ways. First, value is a point-of-view in the sense that it is the point from which the activity of viewing is carried out, the position of the subject. Secondly, it is the point-of-view as that on which the viewing is concentrated, the object. The point-of-view can only value something that it has beforehand represented to itself 'as' a something, worth valuing. A value is never simply present, it is only ever present as a value being valued by an evaluative eye. The evaluative eye, which does the valuing or establishing of the preservation-enhancement-conditions, is the will to power. There are thus two moments, subjective and objective, contained in the term 'value'.

The substance of the will to power

Having moved from the *Nachlass* reference regarding value in terms of a point-of-view, to the establishment of the dynamic and mutually constitutive relation between valuing eye and value itself, Heidegger next posits:

> To see is to represent; since Leibniz, this representation has been grasped more explicitly in its fundamental character of striving (*appetitus*). All beings are representing beings to the extent that *nisus* is part of the being of beings: *nisus*, the urge to make an appearance, the urge that enjoins a thing to arise [*Aufkommen*] (appear) and so determines its occurrence [*Vorkommen*]. The *nisus*-like essence of all beings takes and posits for itself in this way a point of sight. The point of sight provides the perspective which it is essential to follow. The point of sight is value.[111]

Heidegger's invocation of Leibniz at this point instantly hearkens to Leibniz's concept of the *monad*, and with it, the concept of substance:

> I understand matter as either secondary or primary. Secondary matter is, indeed, a complete substance, but it is not merely passive; primary matter is merely passive, but is not a complete substance. And so, we must add a soul or a form analogous to a soul, or a first entelechy, that is, a certain urge [*nisus*] or primitive force of acting, which itself is an inherent law ... But Spirit is to be understood, not as an intelligent being ... but as a soul or as a form analogous to a soul, not as a simple modification, but as something constitutive, substantial, enduring, what I usually call a *monad*, in which there is something like perception and appetite.[112]

One might wonder if Heidegger's connection of Leibniz to Nietzsche is merely incidental, but statements he makes elsewhere suggest that, for Heidegger, this connection is essential. In further discussing Nietzsche's reference to 'complex forms of relative life-duration within the flux of becoming', Heidegger writes:

> Here, and generally in the conceptual language of Nietzsche's metaphysics, the stark indefinite word 'becoming' does not signify just any flux of all things, nor the mere alteration of states, and not just any development or vague evolution. Becoming means the transition *from something to something* [my emphasis], that movement and being moved which Leibniz in the *Monadology* (§11) calls *changements naturels*, which govern the *ens qua ens*, i.e., the *ens percipiens et appetens* [perceptive and appetitive being]. Nietzsche takes this governance as the fundamental trait of all reality, i.e., he takes it in the very broad sense of beings. He understands that which thus determines beings in their *essentia* as the 'will to power'.[113]

Heidegger reads Nietzsche's 'becoming' more precisely as a 'coming to be', and he reads this 'to-be' as a 'being-something', a static presencing, fixed and in some sense permanent. This is developed more thoroughly in the Nietzsche lectures:

> Nietzsche's philosophy is the end of metaphysics, inasmuch as it reverts to the very commencement of Greek thought, taking up such thought in a way that is peculiar to Nietzsche's philosophy alone ... What are the decisive fundamental positions of the commencement? In other words, what sorts of answers are given to the as yet undeveloped guiding question, the question of what being is?
> The *one* answer – roughly speaking, it is the answer of Parmenides – tells us that *being is*. An odd sort of answer, no doubt, yet a very deep one, since that very response determines for the first time and for all thinkers to come, *including Nietzsche* [my emphasis], the meaning of *is* and *Being* – permanence and presence, that is, the eternal present.
> The *other* answer – roughly speaking, that of Heraclitus – tells us that

being becomes. The being is in being by virtue of its permanent becoming, its self-unfolding and eventual dissolution.

To what extent is Nietzsche's thinking the end? That is to say, how does it stretch back to both these fundamental determinations of being in such a way that they come to interlock? Precisely to the extent that Nietzsche argues that being *is* as fixated, as permanent; and that it *is* in perpetual creation and destruction. Yet being is *both* of these, not in an extrinsic way, as one beside another; rather, being is in its very ground perpetual creation (Becoming), while as creation it needs what is fixed. Creation needs what is fixed, first, in order to overcome it, and second, in order to have something that has yet to be fixated, something that enables the creative to advance beyond itself and be transfigured.[114]

As noted, for Heidegger, the will to power is the fundamental characteristic of everything that is. Nietzsche himself refers to will to power as 'the innermost essence of being'.[115] Everything that is, is substantial and must have permanence (or 'presence' in Heidegger's language), in order to become something else. There can thus be no doubt: Heidegger reads Nietzsche's will to power in a substantialist way. It has an essence, a fixedness, a permanence to it: 'Will to power, becoming, life, and being in the broadest sense have the same meaning in Nietzsche's language.'[116] To speak with Heidegger, will to power *is* presence. This is the first characteristic of Heidegger's reading that I wish to emphasise here.

The essence of the will to power as the preservation-expansion of power

Secondly, the fact that Heidegger reads will to power in this way then allows him to isolate this essence and speak of 'the' will to power in a singular sense, to isolate and define what 'a' will to power is, without reference to any other will. Here Heidegger emphasises the hyphenated German expression, 'Erhaltungs-Steigerungs-Bedingungen', or *'preservation-enhancement-conditions'*.[117] The instinctive thirst for enhancement is fundamental to and constitutive of the struggle for survival. Heidegger rightly notes that 'to preserve life is to serve the increase of life. Any life that is restricted to mere preservation is already in decline.'[118] Nietzsche makes this point repeatedly throughout his own writings:

> Indeed the truth was not hit by him who shot at it with the word of the 'will to existence': that will does not exist. For, what does not exist cannot will; but what is in existence, how could that still want existence? Only where there is life is there also will: not will to life but – thus I teach you – will to power.[119]

> *Anti-Darwin.* As for the famous 'struggle for *existence*,' so far it seems to me to be asserted rather than proved. It occurs, but as an exception; the total

appearance of life is not the extremity, not starvation, but rather riches, profusion, even absurd squandering – and where there is struggle, it is a struggle for *power*.[120]

Physiologists should think before putting down the instinct of self-preservation as the cardinal instinct of an organic being. A living thing seeks above all to *discharge* its strength – life itself is *will to power*, self-preservation is only one of the indirect and most frequent *results*.[121]

Indeed life itself is defined as an ever more purposive inner adaptation to external circumstances (Herbert Spencer). In so doing, however, one mistakes the essence of life, its *will to power*, in so doing one overlooks the essential pre-eminence of the spontaneous, attacking, infringing, reinterpreting, reordering, and formative forces, upon whose effect the 'adaptation' first follows; in so doing one denies the lordly role of the highest functionaries in the organism itself, in which the will of life appears active and form-giving.[122]

The wish to preserve oneself is the symptom of a condition of distress, of a limitation of the really fundamental instinct of life which aims at *the expansion of power* and, wishing for that, frequently risks and even sacrifices self-preservation.[123]

Once the concept of will to power is articulated, Nietzsche never shrinks from the position that this instinctive drive for expansion is itself responsible for the secondary drive toward preservation. The fact and mechanism of adaptation – that certain members of a particular species exhibit characteristics making them more suitable for survival given changing ecological and environmental factors, thus enabling their passing those characteristics onto their progeny – would not be possible without the already expansive nature of life itself, which differentiates and complexifies the members of the species in the first place. Life's instinct to grow beyond itself makes possible the diversity that enables adaptation. Without diversity there is no adaptation, and without expansion no diversity. The expansion thus precedes and conditions the adaptation. As Ernst Mayr writes, 'The availability of variation is the indispensable prerequisite of evolution.'[124] The will to self-preservation only manifests in conditions in which the organism is in a state of distress, when its well-being or its existence hangs in the balance. Without survival, its possibilities for expansion will be forever denied, so in conditions of existential threat, its impulse for expansion appears as the impulse to survive. For Nietzsche then, preservation is inherently tied to enhancement, with the drive for enhancement in the role of primary and constitutive importance.

But for Heidegger, though the expansion impulse is constitutive of the preservation instinct, at the same time expansion is not possible without preservation – hence the significance of the hyphen between 'preservation' and 'enhancement'. Without preservation, there is nothing to enhance. Citing *Thus Spoke Zarathustra*, Heidegger notes that, 'to will is to will to be master'.[125] To be master means to command, and to command means to have authority over, for the purpose of deploying and further fortifying, one's resources and capabilities. The will's resource, what it has at its disposal, is the will itself. For the will to command, therefore, it must both gather itself under its own authority and seek to expand its dominion. It therefore preserves by stabilising what it has already attained and mastered: 'In order for will, in the overpowering of itself, to be able to overcome the level it has reached at a given time, this level must already have been attained, secured, and retained. To secure a given level of power is the condition necessary for intensifying power.'[126]

At the same time, in so stabilising its acquisitions, the will seeks its own further enhancement by bringing more power under its dominion. Heidegger claims: 'Will already has what it wills. For will wills its willing. Its will is what it has willed. Will wills itself. It exceeds itself. In this way will as will wills above and beyond itself, and therefore at the same time it must bring itself beneath and behind itself.'[127] Heidegger compares this to an act of creation: 'To create, in the sense of creation out beyond oneself, is most intrinsically this: to stand in the moment of decision, in which what has prevailed hitherto, our endowment, is directed toward a projected task. When it is so directed, the endowment is preserved.'[128] Thus to will at all is to will to be more powerful. The God-like infinitude of the Cartesian will is made explicit in Nietzsche's will to power.

In stabilising itself and projecting itself forward, the will is also constantly in the mode of redirection, turning its focus back onto itself. Heidegger writes: 'it [the will], as the same, is constantly coming back unto itself as the Same'.[129] Thus, Heidegger will tie essentially together Nietzsche's notion of will to power with the concept of the 'eternal return of the same'. Eternal return, as we have said, is an old idea – its roots are visible in strains of ancient Indian philosophy, as well as in various cosmological positions of the Stoics.[130] Nietzsche often formulates it in cosmological terms as well:

> What, if some day or night a demon were to steal after you into your loneliest loneliness and say to you: 'This life as you now live it and have lived it, you will have to live once more and innumerable times more; and there will be nothing new in it, but every pain and every joy and every thought and sigh and everything unutterably small or great in your life will have to return to you, all in the same succession and sequence – even this spider and this moonlight between the trees, and even this moment and I myself. The eternal hourglass of existence is turned upside down again and again, and you with it, speck of dust!'[131]

Nevertheless, Nietzsche's insistence that the eternal return is his own discovery – 'thoughts have arisen such as I have never seen before'[132] – casts significant doubt on interpretations suggesting that Nietzsche understood this ancient concept in a straightforwardly cosmological way. For Heidegger, the eternal return has an explicitly ontological, rather than a cosmological, meaning. The eternal return is the presencing of the being in its becoming:

> 'Recurrence' thinks the permanentizing of what becomes, thinks it to the point where the *becoming* of what becomes is secured in the *duration of its becoming*. The 'eternal' thinks the permanentizing of such constancy in the direction of its circling back into itself and forward toward itself. Yet what becomes is not the unceasing otherness of an endlessly changing manifold. What becomes is the same itself, and that means the one and selfsame (the identical) that in each case is within the difference of the other . . . Nietzsche's thought thinks the constant permanentizing of the becoming of whatever becomes into the only kind of presence there is – the self-recapit-ulation of the identical.[133]

Heidegger thus understands will to power as the essence, and eternal return as the existence, of the being: 'The two fundamental terms of Nietzsche's metaphysics, "will to power" and "eternal return of the same," determine beings in their being in accordance with the perspectives which have guided metaphysics since antiquity, the *ens qua ens* in the sense of *essentia* and *existentia*.'[134] Will to power, the impulse for expansion essential to all of life, is the essence of the being. Eternal return – that the being, in its essential impulse for expansion, stabilises and solidifies its own level of power – is the existence of the being. Elsewhere Heidegger writes, '*Will to power, in its essence and according to its inner possibility, is eternal recurrence of the same.*'[135] Nietzsche's eternal return is the name that Heidegger gives to the actual presencing of the being in its mode of becoming. Its becoming, its existence, is a becoming-permanent.

Nietzsche's thought as the inversion of Cartesian certitude

The final element of Heidegger's Nietzsche reading that pertains to our discussion of Derrida and Deleuze is that Heidegger reads Nietzsche as reversing the tradition of Platonism, but holds that in reversing this tradition, Nietzsche remains imprisoned by it. The history of Platonism is the history of nihilism, the devaluing of our highest values. Nietzsche diagnoses this history, recognises the hollowness of our idols, and seeks to abolish them forever, in order to restore the possibility of creation. To do so, he shifts the philosophical paradigm from one of truth to one of value, and explicitly articulates the essence of Being as will to power. In this way, however, he merely punctuates what Heidegger understands as the essence of modern metaphysics: 'The metaphysics of modernity begins with and has its essence in the fact that modern metaphysics seeks the absolutely undoubtable, what is certain, certainty.'[136] This brings us to Descartes.

In his *Meditations on First Philosophy*, Descartes famously calls into question the foundations of everything he believes, methodologically jettisoning everything that is in any way subject to doubt, in search of a foundation conducive to absolute certainty:

> Anything which admits of the slightest doubt I will set aside just as if I found it to be wholly false; and I will proceed in this way until I recognize something certain, or, if nothing else, until I at least recognize for certain that there is no certainty. Archimedes used to demand just one firm and immovable point in order to shift the entire earth; so I too can hope for great things if I manage to find just one thing, however slight, that is certain and unshakable.[137]

Descartes discovers his 'Archimedean' point in the cogito. His unshakable certainty lies in his awareness that he is a thinking thing, and so long as he is thinking, he cannot possibly doubt that he exists. 'I am, I exist – that is certain. But for how long? For as long as I am thinking.'[138] It follows that the certainty derived from the cogito must be renewed at every single moment (though Descartes will elsewhere deny this implication) because, as we know from Descartes' concurrence argument,[139] there is no necessary continuation from one moment of time to the next, and if there is no necessary causal connection between t_1 and t_2, then I can in no way conclude from my memory of self-certainty at t_1 that I still exist at t_2. At every single moment, therefore, my certainty and hence my existence is called back into question; *unless* I affirm myself again at each moment, or, in Heidegger's words, unless the subject is 'enduringly [*beständige*] present'.[140]

For Heidegger, what is most significant is the status that Descartes ascribes to the ego that thinks – the status of *res cogitans*, a thinking thing.[141] Descartes defines this thinking thing as a substance: 'I also think that I am a substance',[142] and more generally, the name given to the thinking substance by Descartes is 'mind'.[143] Descartes defines 'substance' as 'a thing capable of existing independently'[144] (as opposed to a mode, a quality, or an attribute, which rely upon a substance), and more importantly, he claims that all substances are 'by their nature incorruptible and cannot ever cease to exist unless they are reduced to nothingness by God's denying his concurrence to them'.[145] Descartes' line of argumentation thus moves from the awareness of thinking itself to the positing of a substantial, constantly presencing, essentially indestructible, *ego* or subject: 'So the *ego* becomes the *subiectum*, i.e., the subject becomes self-consciousness.'[146] As Nietzsche writes:

> 'There is thinking: therefore there is something that thinks': this is the upshot of all Descartes' argumentation. But that means positing as 'true *a priori*' our belief in the concept of substance – that when there is thought there has to be something 'that thinks' is simply a formulation of our grammatical custom that adds a doer to every deed. In short, this is not merely the substantiation of a fact but a logical-metaphysical postulate.[147]

Georges Dicker calls Descartes' adherence to substance metaphysics 'the most basic assumption involved in the *cogito*'.[148] Heidegger's point is that Descartes, in search of absolute certainty, finds it in the absolutely indubitable and essentially indestructible, constantly presencing substantiality of the mind: 'The subjectivity of the subject is determined out of the certainty of this consciousness.'[149]

As we have seen, for Heidegger, Nietzsche's will to power 'determines beings in their *essentia*'.[150] We are now in a position to understand the two ways in which this is intended by Heidegger: (1) The will to power posits itself, its preservation, and the conditions necessary for that preservation, as a necessary value. In thus positing itself, the will to power ensures its own stabilisation and permanentising, thereby determining itself, or, in Heidegger's language, bringing itself to presence; (2) at the same time, in so far as it is also the evaluative eye, the will to power represents to itself everything else that it encounters. Representation, we recall from Leibniz, is a striving or an *appetitus* that seeks to secure the certainty of that which it represents to itself. In representing, it freezes the thing in its becoming, stopping the flow of time, as it were. It is only at this point that the will to power 'simultaneously justifies the necessity of such securing in all beings'.[151]

The will to power lies at the essence of everything that is, and seeks to stabilise and permanentise itself and every object of its representative gaze. In this sense, the will to power denotes the very same subjective certainty that Descartes sought in the cogito, the difference being that the will to power deposits this subjectivity right at the heart of being itself. The 'subjectivity of the subject'[152] is no longer the self-conscious substance of the ego, but an inscrutable and inaccessible subject – a drive – hidden deep within the body. As Eugen Fink says, referencing Heidegger's Nietzsche readings: 'The subject is will and representation. The driving force of the representation is the will. Representation is an objectification. Representation as such is a violating will to power. Nietzsche brings this hidden basis into view. The subject's own experience of itself becomes the ontological essence.'[153]

Nietzsche therefore reverses the Cartesian subject, shifting the grounding certainty of the subject from the mental or spiritual to the bodily, and in reversing Descartes, he also reverses Platonism. Platonism is the tradition that posits the highest values of humankind in the supersensuous domain of the forms, and the history of that tradition is the gradual devaluation of those values over a period spanning two millennia. Christianity, or 'Platonism for "the people"',[154] continues the tradition, putting the forms in the mind of God. Descartes then shifts the ideas from the mind of God to the mind of the thinking subject. Thus, by explicitly resituating the point of view of value, from heaven to earth, from death to life, and from mind to body, Nietzsche re-establishes value in a way that is no less substantial and no less supersensuous than were Plato's forms. Finally, by determining the essence of being as 'will to power', Nietzsche makes explicit the essence of modern philosophy, beginning with Descartes' infinitude of the will and the insatiable desire for the stabilising certainty of the cogito. Nietzsche therefore positions himself (on Heidegger's reading) at the end of the modern period, the end of the metaphysical tradition, which has culminated in humankind's enframing within the throes of power, the tradition that Heidegger refers to as nihilism. Thus we could say, putting this in the language of the history that *we* are describing, that, according to Heidegger, Nietzsche attempts but does not accomplish the decentring of the philosophical tradition.

Difference as the decentred centre

The philosophy of difference picks up where Heidegger's criticisms leave off. There are a few important points to be gleaned from our historical narrative of philosophy as the oscillation between the centring and decentring of thought. First, the more radical the effort of centring, the more radical and abrupt the counter-movement of decentring. As Nietzsche writes, 'Extreme positions are not succeeded by moderate ones but by extreme positions of the opposite kind.'[155] Descartes is responding to the cultural explosions of scepticism and the scientific revolution; Hegel to the Kantian noumenon-phenomenon divide; Edmund Husserl and phenomenology to the 'crisis of foundations'.[156] Each recentring, more radical than its predecessor, is followed in turn by a movement of decentring, decreasing in time elapsed and increasing in intensity, as the history progresses. Barely more than a century separates the Cartesian demand for absolute certitude and the triumph of Humean scepticism. Less than a century separates Nietzsche from Hegel; and the momentum of the phenomenological tradition of Husserl, whose thought Derrida referred to as 'metaphysics in its most modern, critical, and vigilant form',[157] is still alive and well when Deleuze and Derrida are active.

Second, the further thought goes in the direction of decentring, the closer it dances to what is no longer philosophical, inasmuch as the philosophical has always been understood as the search for the universal, or for what we have referred to as the 'centre'. This demand, established by Parmenides and codified by both Plato and Aristotle, has defined the Western philosophical tradition for two and a half millennia. A purely decentred thought would be a pure empiricism, recognising only 'this', 'that', 'these', 'those', 'here', and 'now', and it is little wonder that, when thinkers have focused on 'thises' (Duns Scotus), or on empiricist foundations of knowledge (Locke and Hume), philosophy has moved in the direction of decentring. But a pure decentring – shunning any notion of the centre – would be a purely non-philosophical mode of thought. This is incontestably not where Deleuze and Derrida operate.

For both Derrida and Deleuze, the problem will be that of the *constitution* of the centre, the genetic conditions that make the centre possible, and in that sense, their philosophies comprise an even more radical and fundamental thinking of the centre than any others we have encountered along our path. For Derrida, this will be the constitution of ideality within the phenomenological sphere of immanence. For Deleuze, it will be the incapacity of the thought of identity to truly grasp the thing itself in its singularity, the inability of substantialist ontology to adequately think being. However, for both philosophers, this thought of the *conditions* of the centre is *so* radical and *so* fundamental that it dislodges and disrupts the notion of the centre as we have hitherto defined it – as an absolute kernel of stasis and identity. They are still thinkers of the centre, inasmuch as they are in pursuit of the fundamental conditions, and as such, they are philosophers. But the centre they pursue is not static and immobile, but one always decentred and decentring; it is essentially multiple, while its multiplicity nevertheless remains 'the centre'.

This language appears numerous times throughout the writings of Derrida and especially of Deleuze. Derrida refers to 'the science of writing' as a 'necessary decentering',[158] writing that 'the necessary decentering cannot be a philosophic or scientific act as such, since it is a question of dislocating, through access to another system linking speech and writing, the founding categories of language and the grammar of the *epistemè*'.[159] Deleuze, as we have seen, points to a 'monocentering of circles in the case of Hegel',[160] arguing that 'representation fails to capture the affirmed world of difference' because it 'has only a single center',[161] and that Nietzschean eternal return is a 'constantly decentred, continually tortuous circle which revolves only around the unequal'.[162] Genuine movement, he says, 'for its part, implies a plurality of centers, a superposition of perspectives, a tangle of points of view, a coexistence of moments which essentially distort representation'.[163] The philosophy of difference is the thought of the decentred centre.

Conclusion

We can thus bring to a conclusion our introduction to the task at hand, and address the questions we laid out at the beginning of this chapter. First, the philosophy of difference is not a new-fangled project, unique to the 1960s French tradition. Its precursors lie in the deepest recesses of the Western philosophical tradition itself, in Parmenides and Heraclitus, and in Plato, who despite himself formulated a thought of the different that nearly threatened the entirety of the tradition bearing the name 'Platonism'. We have caught glimmers of it in Duns Scotus and Ockham, in the revolutions of the sciences and in the philosophies of Hume and Nietzsche. Difference has been an ongoing concern of the tradition since its inception.

Secondly the philosophy of difference maintains the thought of what I called the centre, a kernel of identity or the universal, in search of which the Western philosophical tradition in its entirety has been conceived. The philosophy of difference seeks to destabilise notions of identity and rethink the very concept of the foundation on a differential ground, or an ungrounding, or a decentred centre, but a centre nonetheless. It is therefore not non-philosophical or even, strictly speaking, anti-foundationalist, but rather, seeks *even more radically and more fundamentally* the foundation in question, but in so doing comes face to face with the differential basis of the foundation.

Finally, at stake in the philosophy of difference is a critique of representational thinking, the meaning of identity, and the nature and task of philosophy itself; all of which are perennial concerns in the history of philosophy. Therefore, we can assert that the philosophy of difference speaks to the tradition and its problems, offers a fundamental critique of representation, and attempts to formulate new trajectories for philosophy itself. The thought of the centre has always danced with the thought of its own decentring, and it is this decentred centre that is at stake in the philosophies of Derrida and Deleuze. Thus, we can assert unequivocally the value in their respective projects, and its continuity with the tradition writ large.

We now embark upon our investigation. Derrida and Deleuze both formulate their respective philosophies of difference in the triangulation of argumentation found in the Hegel-Nietzsche-Heidegger triad. Both Derrida and Deleuze will argue that Hegel conceives a notion of difference in the context of the dialectic, but both will find some flaw in his concept of difference. Both will reject Heidegger's criticisms of Nietzsche,[164] and locate in Nietzsche a way of thinking difference that moves beyond the faults they find in Hegelian dialectical difference. However, in every way, the progression through this triad will differ between Derrida and Deleuze, and will open onto an ostensible difference in their understandings of the task of philosophy itself. This triad thus dictates to us the progression of chapters in this project. In Chapter 3, we shall begin the exploration of their engagements with Hegel, by looking at the Hegelian system as one of the two pillars of deconstruction, the other being Heidegger's critique of ontotheology.

Notes

1. May, *Reconsidering Difference: Nancy, Derrida, Levinas, and Deleuze*, 1.
2. Ibid., 3.
3. *WD*, 278.
4. Gorman, *The Undecidable: Jacques Derrida and Paul Howard*, 9.
5. DK22B30 (all DK references refer to the Diels-Kranz numbering system).
6. DK22B31a
7. DK22B76
8. *NP*, 29.
9. DK22B12
10. DK22B49a
11. DK22B56
12. DK22B123
13. DK22B53
14. DK22B8
15. DK22B50
16. DK28B6
17. DK28B3
18. DK28B4.2
19. DK28B8.19–21
20. DK28B1.29
21. *DR*, 59.
22. See *Republic*, 5.476e–479a.
23. For a discussion of the traditionally accepted dating of Plato's works, see Kraut, 'Introduction to the Study of Plato', in *The Cambridge Companion to Plato*, 1–50. A rival account, ordered by the dramatic development of the characters in the dialogues, is Zuckert, *Plato's Philosophers*.
24. See *Republic*, 7.523e.
25. See, for example, *Theaetetus* 186a; *Parmenides* 143b, 146b, and 153a; and *Sophist* 254e, 257b, and 259a.
26. *Sophist*, 248a.
27. *Sophist*, 247e.
28. 'Do you then want us to assume two kinds of existences, the visible and the invisible?' Plato, *Phaedo*, 79a–b.

29. 'In any case, you have two kinds of thing, visible and intelligible.' Plato, *Republic*, 6.509d.
30. *Sophist*, 248e–249a.
31. *Sophist*, 249b.
32. *Sophist*, 252b.
33. Plato's reasoning for this point is as follows: we have established that being, rest, and change all participate in both the same and the different. Each is the same as itself, and different from the other two. This being the case, if we subsequently assert that either the same or the different is coextensive with any of the other three, then in so far as the two of the three remaining original forms (being, change, rest) participate in both the same and the different, we are forced into the unhappy conclusion that things that are, we think, different, are in fact the same. Let us suppose, for instance, that rest *just is* the same. Then in so far as change participates in the same, in that it is the same as itself, it would follow that change is also rest, because the same would be coextensive with or synonymous with rest. But, as change and rest are contraries, they cannot blend with each other, according to Plato.
34. See *Republic*, 7.523e.
35. *Sophist*, 255e.
36. Ibid.
37. See *Republic*, 6.509b.
38. *DR*, 29.
39. See Aristotle, *Metaphysics*, X.1.
40. *Metaphysics*, V.6.
41. *Metaphysics*, X.3.
42. Augustine of Hippo, *Eighty-Three Different Questions*, q. 46, 1–2.
43. Augustine of Hippo, *Confessions*, IV.25.
44. The Islamic philosophers, such as Al-Fārābī and Ibn Sīnā, were even closer to the absolute centrality of Plotinus than was Augustine.
45. Copleston, SJ, *A History of Philosophy, Volume III: Ockham to Suárez*, 49.
46. I treat this discussion much more thoroughly in Chapter 7.
47. See the classic study by Arthur Lovejoy, *The Great Chain of Being*.
48. Sextus Empiricus, *Outlines of Skepticism*, xi.
49. For both Leibniz and Malebranche, Descartes had severely compromised orthodox religious doctrine, thereby challenging the absolute centre that the divine holds for many thinkers of this period. Both worried about the possibilities of human freedom in the midst of Descartes' apparently entirely mechanistic physics and, going along with this, both worried about the role of divine providence. Finally and in a related way, they worried about the famous mind-body problem of Descartes' dualistic ontology. Malebranche responded to the problem with the doctrine of occasionalism. With philosophical precursors in the early Arabic philosophers such as Al-Ghazālī, occasionalism maintains the absolute and unassailable providence of the divine by holding that all human 'causes' are merely 'occasional' opportunities for God's intervening causality. When the mind wills to do X, and the body does X, it is not because the mind has caused the body to do so, but rather, because God, assenting to the mind's will, causes the body to do so. Malebranche, also discomforted by Descartes' epistemology, attempts to reinstate Augustinian illuminationism. Leibniz responds with his doctrine of pre-established harmony. Worried by (but also somewhat seduced by) Spinoza's substance monism, Leibniz posits what we might call a substance infinitism, an ontology consisting of an infinity of individual substances which each expresses, from its own limited perspective, the entire cosmos. Not unlike Malebranche's occasionalism, Leibniz's pre-established harmony holds that there is no causal interaction between the individual substances (which he would later christen with the term 'monad', lifted from Lady Anne Conway's *The Principles of the Most Ancient and Modern Philosophy*). Rather, the totality of the monads, established

by God in the creation, expresses in a perfectly coordinated way the appearance of causal interaction between the monads, thereby accounting for Descartes' apparently mechanistic universe, solving the mind-body problem, and salvaging human freedom while at the same time restoring divine providence. What is important to note in this, however, is that in its most robust manifestations (besides Spinoza), rationalism is constantly attempting to restore the thought of the centre.

50. I'm stressing 'robust' in order to distinguish most rationalist strains from the philosophy of Spinoza, to whom I've always had trouble ascribing the 'rationalist' moniker.

51. Locke, *An Essay Concerning Human Understanding*, Book II, Chapter XXIII.

52. Ibid., Book II, Chapter XXVII.

53. Ibid., Book IV, Chapter X.

54. Hume, *A Treatise of Human Nature*, xvi.

55. Ibid., 415.

56. Hume, *An Enquiry Concerning Human Understanding*, 13.

57. 'But tho' these two ideas of identity, and a succession of related objects be in themselves perfectly distinct, and even contrary, yet 'tis certain, that in our common way of thinking they are generally confounded with each other. That action of the imagination, by which we consider the uninterrupted and invariable object, and that by which we reflect on the succession of related objects, are almost the same to the feeling, nor is there much more effort of thought requir'd in the latter case than in the former. The relation facilitates the transition of the mind from one object to another, and renders its passage as smooth as if it contemplated one continu'd object. This resemblance is the cause of the confusion and mistake, and makes us substitute the notion of identity, instead of that of related objects.' Hume, *A Treatise of Human Nature*, 253–4.

58. The treatments of Nietzsche and Hegel given here are admittedly brief; both figures will be treated with greater depth in subsequent chapters.

59. The 'history of philosophy' for Hegel is very narrowly and problematically conceived as strictly Greek-Roman-German, we should note. This point is problematised by both Derrida and Deleuze. 'What remains common to Heidegger and Hegel is having conceived of the relationship of Greece and philosophy as an origin and thus as the point of departure of a history internal to the West, such that *philosophy necessarily becomes indistinguishable from its own history*.' WP, 95. See Chapter 9, note 40.

60. *PH*, 11.

61. *PH*, 10.

62. *PH*, 10.

63. *DR*, 49.

64. *NP*, 7.

65. *Z*, 226.

66. *WTP*, 656.

67. *WTP*, 655.

68. Nietzsche, *The Antichrist*, in *The Portable Nietzsche*, 586.

69. *TI*, 563.

70. *WTP*, 617.

71. *WTP*, 55.

72. See, for example, Kaufmann, *Nietzsche: Philosopher, Psychologist, Antichrist*, 307–33; Schacht, *Nietzsche*, 253–66.

73. *DR*, 242.

74. The Nietzsche lectures were published as Heidegger, *Nietzsche*, 2 Vols (1961), translated into English by David Farrell Krell in four volumes: *Nietzsche, Volume I: The Will to Power as Art*; *Nietzsche, Volume II: The Eternal Recurrence of the Same*; *Nietzsche, Volume III: The Will to Power as Knowledge and Metaphysics*; *Nietzsche, Volume IV: Nihilism*. These four individual translations were later compiled and published together as *Nietzsche, Volumes I and II: The Will to Power as Art; The*

Eternal Recurrence of the Same, and *Nietzsche, Volumes III and IV: The Will to Power as Knowledge and as Metaphysics*.

75. Schrift, *Nietzsche and the Question of Interpretation*, 13.
76. Søren Kierkegaard's name appears only three times in *Being and Time*, and only in endnotes, never in the body of the text. Scholars now know the great extent to which Kierkegaard's analyses, specifically of *angst*, authenticity, and conscience, play a central role in *Being and Time*.
77. Heidegger, *Being and Time*, 308.
78. Aschheim, *The Nietzsche Legacy in Germany: 1890–1990*, 263.
79. I do not wish to enter here into the ongoing debate on Heidegger's affiliations with the Nazi party, or on the extent to which Heidegger agrees and disagrees with Bäumler. For a more thorough examination of the relation between Heidegger and Bäumler, see David Farrell Krell's discussion in the insightful 'Analysis' sections appended to his translations of Heidegger's Nietzsche lectures: *Nietzsche, Volume I: The Will to Power as Art*, 241; *Nietzsche, Volume II: The Eternal Recurrence of the Same*, 256–7; *Nietzsche, Volume III: The Will to Power as Knowledge and as Metaphysics*, 268–74; *Nietzsche, Volume IV: Nihilism*, 269–72.
80. Steigmann-Gall, *The Holy Reich: Nazi Conceptions of Christianity, 1919–1945*, 105.
81. Cited in Müller-Lauter, *Heidegger und Nietzsche: Nietzsche-Interpretationen III*, 17. The statement initially came from Hans-Georg Gadamer, who allegedly heard it second-hand from one of Heidegger's family members.
82. Aschheim, *The Nietzsche Legacy in Germany*, 263–4.
83. The terms 'metaphysics' and 'ontology' are employed quite liberally by all the figures in question – Hegel, Nietzsche, Heidegger, Fink, Derrida, and Deleuze – and it is not clear that they are always using the term in the same sense. What *metaphysics* and *ontology* mean for Derrida and Deleuze, and what they mean for us, is the topic of Chapter 9 of this book.
84. *OBT*, 173.
85. *OBT*, 157–99.
86. *OBT*, 158.
87. *OBT*, 157.
88. I am aware of the apparent redundancy in this formulation. I am making the distinction between the 'history of philosophy' as an ongoing dialogue with a more or less accepted canon out of which everyone works, and the 'historical' understanding – a totalising and organic reading – of that history.
89. *OBT*, 159.
90. Heidegger, *Nietzsche, Volume IV: Nihilism*, 4.
91. *FW*, 279.
92. *WP*, 55.
93. Heidegger, *Nietzsche, Volume IV: Nihilism*, 4.
94. Nietzsche famously called Christianity 'Platonism for "the people"'. See *BGE*, 193.
95. *OBT*, 160.
96. *OBT*, 163.
97. For a full discussion of this concept, see Heidegger, 'The Question Concerning Technology', in *The Question Concerning Technology and Other Essays*, 3–35.
98. Ibid.
99. *OBT*, 163–4.
100. 'Besides, I cannot complain that the will or freedom of choice which I received from God is not sufficiently extensive or perfect, since I know by experience that it is not restricted in any way . . . It is only the will or freedom of choice, which I experience within me to be so great that the idea of any greater faculty is beyond my grasp; so much so that it is above all in virtue of the will that I understand myself to bear in some way the image and likeness of God. For although God's will is incomparably greater than mine, both in virtue of the knowledge and power that accompany it and

make it more firm and efficacious . . . nevertheless it does not seem any greater than mine when considered as will in the essential and strict sense.' Descartes, *Meditations on First Philosophy*, in *The Philosophical Writings of Descartes, Volume II*, 39–40.
101. Heidegger, 'Overcoming Metaphysics', in *The End of Philosophy*, 92.
102. As in Tolstoy's *The Kingdom of God is Within You*.
103. *FW*, 182.
104. *WTP*, 19.
105. *OBT*, 167.
106. *OBT*, 167.
107. *GM*, 117–18.
108. *OBT*, 169.
109. *WTP*, 14.
110. *WTP*, 380, translation modified. For reasons that will become clear in what follows, Heidegger emphasises two key elements of this passage: (1) It is a 'point of view'. Value has to do with a 'looking at'. The German word *Gesicht* is most adequately translated into English as 'face', which connotes a look. Kaufmann's translation of *Gesichtspunkt* as 'standpoint', though adequate, does not quite capture what Heidegger sees as important. (2) Heidegger points out that Nietzsche does not separate the words 'preservation' and 'enhancement', as Kaufmann's translation does. The German reads, and Heidegger is correct about this, 'Erhaltungs-Steigerungs-Bedingungen', or 'Preservation-enhancement-conditions'. Nietzsche, *Nachgelassene Fragmente*, Volume 13 of *Kritische Studienausgabe Herausgegeben*, 36.
111. *OBT*, 171.
112. Leibniz, *On Nature Itself*, in *Philosophical Essays*, 162–3.
113. *OBT*, 172.
114. Heidegger, *Nietzsche, Volume II: The Eternal Recurrence of the Same*, 199–200.
115. *WTP*, 369.
116. *OBT*, 172.
117. See note 110 above.
118. *OBT*, 171.
119. *Z*, 227.
120. *TI*, 522.
121. *BGE*, 211.
122. *GM*, 52.
123. *FW*, 291–2.
124. Mayr, *What Evolution Is*, 88.
125. *OBT*, 174.
126. *OBT*, 177.
127. *OBT*, 175.
128. Heidegger, *Nietzsche, Volume II: The Eternal Recurrence of the Same*, 202–3.
129. *OBT*, 177.
130. 'They [the Stoics] hold that after the conflagration all the same things recur in the world numerically, so that even the same peculiarly qualified individual as before exists and comes to be again in that world, as Chrysippus says in his books *On the world*.' Alexander, *On Aristotle's Prior Analytics*, cited in Long and Sedley (eds), *The Hellenistic Philosophers, Volume I*, 309.
131. *FW*, 273.
132. Nietzsche, 'To Peter Gast, Sils Maria, August 14, 1881', in *Selected Letters of Friedrich Nietzsche*, 178.
133. Heidegger, *Nietzsche Volume III: The Will to Power as Knowledge and as Metaphysics*, 164–5.
134. *OBT*, 177.
135. Heidegger, *Nietzsche, Volume II: The Eternal Recurrence of the Same*, 203.
136. *OBT*, 178.

137. Descartes, *Meditations on First Philosophy*, in *The Philosophical Writings of Descartes, Volume II*, 16.
138. Ibid., 18.
139. 'For a lifespan can be divided into countless parts, each completely independent of the others, so that it does not follow from the fact that I existed a little while ago that I must exist now, unless there is some cause which as it were creates me afresh at this moment – that is, which preserves me. For it is quite clear to anyone who attentively considers the nature of time that the same power and action are needed to preserve anything at each individual moment of its duration as would be required to create the thing anew if it were not yet in existence. Hence the distinction between preservation and creation is only a conceptual one, and this is one of the things that are evident by the natural light.' Descartes, *Meditations on First Philosophy*, in *The Philosophical Writings of Descartes, Volume II*, 33. Also, 'For the nature of time is such that its parts are not mutually dependent, and never coexist.' Descartes, *Principles of Philosophy*, in *The Philosophical Writings of Descartes, Volume I*, 200.
140. *OBT*, 178.
141. Descartes, *Meditations on First Philosophy*, in *The Philosophical Writings of Descartes, Volume II*, 18.
142. Ibid., 30.
143. Descartes, *Objections and Replies*, in *The Philosophical Writings of Descartes, Volume II*, 114.
144. Ibid., 30.
145. Ibid., 10.
146. *OBT*, 178.
147. *WTP*, 484.
148. Dicker, *Descartes: An Analytical and Historical Introduction*, 50.
149. *OBT*, 178.
150. *OBT*, 172.
151. *OBT*, 178.
152. *OBT*, 178.
153. Fink, *Nietzsche's Philosophy*, 171.
154. *BGE*, 193.
155. *WTP*, 55.
156. For a discussion of this historical moment, see Cisney, *Derrida's* Voice and Phenomenon: *An Edinburgh Philosophical Guide*, 15–56.
157. *P*, 5.
158. *OG*, 76.
159. *OG*, 92.
160. *DR*, 49.
161. *DR*, 55.
162. *DR*, 55.
163. *DR*, 55, 56. For further discussion in Deleuze of the monocentricity of Hegel and of representation generally, and the decentred circle of the eternal return, see also *DR*, xxi, 22, 47, 48, 50, 53, 62, 68, 69, 91, 105, 115, 128, 192, 209, 255, 259, 261, 263, 264, 273, 274, 278, 281, 283, 288, 292, 293, 298–304.
164. Although Heidegger's famous Nietzsche lectures were not published until 1961, two of his most well-known (and most mature) critical pieces on Nietzsche, 'The Word of Nietzsche: "God is Dead"', and his famous 1951 and 1952 lectures were in publication by the mid-1950s. 'The Word of Nietzsche: "God is Dead"' appears in *Holzwege*, translated into English in *Off the Beaten Track*; the 1951–2 lectures were published as *Was heißt Denken?*, translated into English in *What is Called Thinking?*

Part II
The Tremendous Power of the Negative

Chapter 3

The Two Pillars of Deconstruction

Part II of the book performs the critical tasks of this project. Both Derrida and Deleuze cite Hegel's conception of difference, specifically in the form of the *Aufhebung*, as the background *against which* their own concepts of difference are formulated. Deleuze famously cites a 'generalized anti-Hegelianism',[1] an intellectual spirit that is practically ubiquitous in 1960s French thought.[2] But anti-Hegelianism can be difficult to execute, as Hegel has surreptitiously woven into his system every conceivable possibility of antithesis and opposition. As Michel Foucault famously notes, 'to truly escape Hegel involves an exact appreciation of the price we have to pay to detach ourselves from him. . . . We have to determine the extent to which our anti-Hegelianism is possibly one of his tricks directed against us, at the end of which he stands, motionless, waiting for us.'[3] The question of what it means to escape Hegel comes down, in some senses, to the ways in which one understands Hegel's significance in the history of philosophy more generally. It is in the context of these questions and responses that sharp distinctions emerge between Derrida and Deleuze. Each rejects specific aspects of Hegelian difference. For Deleuze, the rejection is predicated upon his rejection of the negative more generally, while Derrida's rejection of Hegelian difference is that its negativity is *insufficient*. As we shall see, *différance* for Derrida is understood as a *negativity so negative* that it forever eludes the traditional, Hegelian understanding of the negative. In this chapter, we explore what Derrida sees as impossible attempts to *break* with Hegel, positing Hegel's thought as one of the two pillars of deconstruction, the other being Heidegger's critique of ontotheology.

Though it is a popular stereotype for French philosophy in the 1960s, the characterisation of 'anti-Hegelianism' is certainly not a comfortable fit when it comes to the philosophy of Jacques Derrida. Derrida repeatedly casts his project, explicitly and in practice, as an extended engagement with Hegel's thought: 'We will never be finished with the reading or rereading of Hegel and, in a certain way, I do nothing other than attempt to explain myself on this point.'[4] In his preface to Catherine Malabou's important work, *The Future of Hegel*, Derrida claims that 'nothing in the world can be in this way determined or pre-determined, for almost two centuries . . . that does not entertain some sort of relation with the living tradition embodied by Hegel'.[5] *Différance* 'took its place within metaphysics', according to Derrida, 'with Hegel',[6] and *différance* 'makes it possible to translate Hegel at . . . an absolutely decisive point in his discourse – without further notes or specifications'.[7] Furthermore, despite 'maintaining relations of profound affinity with Hegelian discourse', such that it is 'up to a certain point, unable to break with that discourse', the task of *différance* is to 'operate a kind of infinitesimal and radical displacement of it'.[8] Derrida's project is an explicit renegotiation with and reassessment of Hegel's thought, and it is precisely in marking the ruptures between himself and Hegel that Derrida formulates the 'non-concept'[9] of *différance*.

The apparent impossibility of breaking with Hegel's discourse is a theme that occupies much of Derrida's early thought; and as John Protevi writes, 'his confrontation with Hegel is instructive'.[10] Therefore we must investigate: (1) what Derrida understands to be essential to Hegel's discourse; (2) why, for Derrida, a radical break from Hegel in any form of anti-Hegelian philosophy is impossible; (3) how Derrida's concept of *différance* is to be understood as operating a displacement, both infinitesimal and radical, of Hegel's discourse. This investigation will proceed primarily through readings of two of Derrida's early essays: 'Cogito and the History of Madness', a lecture delivered in 1963 and published in 1964; and 'Violence and Metaphysics: An Essay on the Thought of Emmanuel Levinas', published in 1964. My readings deal with these three points, focusing specifically on the moments where these concerns are addressed. In these two early essays, written during the formative period of Derrida's thinking before he had completely found the voice of deconstruction, we find Derrida battling seriously, in his negotiations with other thinkers, with the significance of Hegel, and with these thinkers' purported efforts to formulate anti-Hegelian philosophies. It is here that we see the central role that Hegel plays for Derrida's thinking, as the thinker who consummates the philosophical tradition. This is a position, one of the two pillars of deconstruction, that Derrida never abandons, even in the later, more mature phases of his career.

'Cogito and the History of Madness'

Michel Foucault, in his ground-breaking first work, *Folie et Déraison: Histoire de la folie à l'âge classique*, claims that the task of his work is to 'write the history of madness',[11] to reconstitute 'the experience of madness',[12] to 'draw up the archaeology of that silence'[13] against which reason constitutes itself by separating itself from its other. According to Foucault, 'Classical' reason – the reason of modernity – in accordance with a logic reminiscent of Nietzsche's 'slave morality',[14] has determined itself as reason by negating its other, un-reason or madness. Proclaiming itself the sole legitimate bearer of meaning and of truth, reason sees itself as qualified and obliged to intern, study, manipulate, and manage madness. As a result of being spoken only through the language of reason, madness has been prohibited from giving voice to its own experience from the depths of that experience itself. Foucault's project is to subvert the totalising force of reason, and enable this monologue. Derrida, as is well-known, studied under Foucault in the seminars that went into the preparation of this work.[15] It is in response to Foucault's efforts to speak the history of madness that Derrida's criticisms in 'Cogito and the History of Madness' take shape. These criticisms are revelatory in understanding Derrida's relation to what he considers to be the legacy and significance of Hegelianism.

Derrida's criticisms of Foucault extend along multiple trajectories. First, the project of writing an 'archaeology of silence', as Foucault intends, is in its very formulation a problematic endeavour, 'the very infeasibility of his book'.[16] Foucault's text is pervaded by the exigency that madness be allowed to express itself apart from the conceptual web within which classical reason has it ensnared. For this reason, Foucault at times rejects entirely the language of the psychiatrist. But because Foucault determines the founding of psychiatric reason as historically contemporaneous with the Cartesian moment, the language of psychiatry is simultaneously the Cartesian language of self-certainty and the foundation of modern philosophy, the very language of structure and order. The language of madness's captor *is* language itself, the language of Western thought. In so far as any history or archaeology will require the use of language, any attempt to articulate a history of silence, in the way that Foucault prescribes, is doomed from its inception. One may *ignore* the silence, thus preventing its contamination by the language of its captor, or one may *become* silent, but writing a *history* of that silence is impossible, Derrida claims.

This structural impossibility reveals the inevitable consequence that the very awareness of the problem, the 'perception that aims to apprehend them in their wild state necessarily belongs to a world that has captured them already'.[17] The conscious awareness that madness has been interred can only be constituted within the reason of the one for whom madness is, already, its other. Madness itself – the silence of reason – lacks the language to articulate its imprisonment. As Foucault claims, it is *'the absence of an œuvre'*.[18] The investigator thus faces a paradox: she seeks to give voice to the unique experience of madness in its wild and primitive state; but both the realisation of this need, as well as the tools by which the vocalisation would be conducted, are the property of the very reason that has exorcised and excluded it.

The language of Foucault's archaeology must therefore be neither the wild silence of the mad, nor the determined form of Classical reason, but rather, the language of their decisive collision. This reveals, according to Derrida, a second project in Foucault's text, in some ways at odds with the first. The historical moment of exorcism, which Foucault calls the *Decision*, must become the object of analysis. To enable the monologue of madness requires in fact a dialogue between reason and madness – the restoration of a more basic or primitive or primordial reason, in which the otherness of madness has not yet attained its polarity: 'a reason more profound than the reason which issued forth during the classical age',[19] or to speak with Foucault, 'a language more original, much rougher, and much more matutinal than that of science'.[20]

But as Foucault notes, the dialogue between reason and un-reason *is* the dialogue of history itself, out of which is constituted the very possibility of meaning, and without which no history of any sort would be possible: '*The necessity of madness* throughout the history of the West is linked to that decisive action that extracts a significant language from the background noise and its continuous monotony.'[21] History, archaeology, genealogy, philosophy – all are impossible without the clear distinction of reason from un-reason, sense from nonsense, on which the 'meaningful' and the 'non-meaningful' are established. The expulsion of madness from reason is a necessary and essential feature of reason itself, according to Foucault. Derrida agrees, but then finds all the more puzzling the fact that Foucault cites the Cartesian moment as the defining moment of the historical Decision.[22] For there to have been a history that made possible the Cartesian moment, reason and un-reason must already have been separated. As Derrida notes in a manner that is 'strictly Foucauldian',[23] as soon as reason speaks, and as a condition of its speaking, the Decision is already made.

Hegel has by now made his appearance in Derrida's essay. 'The revolution against reason', Derrida claims, 'can be made only within it, in accordance with a Hegelian law . . . in Foucault's book, despite the absence of any precise reference to Hegel.'[24] This 'Hegelian law' in question is the articulation of a negation, contradiction, or an opposition, aimed at the subsumption and elevation of this contradiction within a higher, dialectical identity, the movement that in Hegel's thought is known as the *Aufhebung*. Foucault allegedly seeks to write a history of madness itself, a history in which voice is given to the silence of reason that constitutes madness. But such a history is possible only by the employment of a more primordial reason, one that contains within itself both the classical reason of modernity, and the un-reason that it will establish as its other, that is, madness. In a move designed to challenge the (Hegelian) totalitarian authority of reason, Foucault challenges merely a particular historical determination of reason, leaving untouched the totalising force of the possibility of meaning itself. Foucault subsumes the opposition that proceeds from the Decision within the unity of an all-encompassing reason in a 'reappropriation of negativity',[25] thereby running the 'risk of being totalitarian'.[26] Madness, falling under the 'rubric of *negativity*'[27] as the bipolar opposite of Classical reason, is united by Foucault with Classical reason beneath the banner of a more primordial reason, from which the Decision then appears as a fallenness or deficient form of knowledge. In attempting to escape Hegel, Foucault has merely employed Hegelian negation in pursuit of an originary moment of presence, 'thereby confirming metaphysics in its fundamental operation'.[28] However much Derrida might appreciate the necessity of Foucault's project of giving voice to un-reason, it is a necessity that can only ever be paradoxical. Through the very movement by which he sought escape, Foucault repeats Hegel, and thereby falls prey to the totalising trap he has so carefully set.

'Violence and Metaphysics'

In this early engagement with Emmanuel Levinas, Derrida addresses many themes and questions similar to those in the 'Cogito' piece – the relation of reason to un-reason, of philosophy to non-philosophy, and of self to other. Moreover, Derrida begins to emerge into his own voice in this essay, defining the contemporary philosophical landscape precisely in terms of the relation between philosophy and non-philosophy: 'It may even be that these questions are not *philosophical*, are not *philosophy's* questions. Nevertheless, these should be the only questions today capable of founding the community, within the world, of those who are still called philosophers.'[29] These questions are of the so-called 'death of philosophy' – the relation of the Western philosophical tradition to its own undoing or demise – and the way in which this demise is constitutive of and essential to the history of Western philosophy itself. The phenomenological tradition – of Husserl, Heidegger, and Levinas – is relevant to this inquiry thanks to its ever-renewed search for a rigorous foundation of philosophy itself. According to Derrida, such a foundation *of* philosophy cannot itself *be* philosophical, strictly speaking. Thus as a condition of its rigorous exercise, philosophy must always interact with what is not philosophy. The paradoxical necessity that marked the 'Cogito' essay is here made explicit and will establish itself as the hallmark of deconstruction, held fast by the twin pillars of Hegel's completion of metaphysics and Heidegger's critique of ontotheology.

Levinas's thought resides in the intellectual juncture of Edmund Husserl and Martin Heidegger, revolving around three points of concurrence: (1) The originariness of the Greek experience of thought as forming the roots of philosophy's history. However differently they may construe this originariness, Husserl and Heidegger agree in their conviction that anything passing as 'philosophy' must trace its origins to the concepts and problems first instituted by Plato.[30] (2) The reduction of metaphysics. Heidegger's call for the *Destruktion* of the history of ontology, as well as his later critique of ontotheology are well-known. In addition, Husserl's 'principle of principles' in *Ideas I* dictates that metaphysical speculation must be bracketed to focus on the apodicticity of the phenomenality of consciousness itself, to the extent that Husserl famously understood his own project as sharing features with the 'radical empiricism' of William James. (3) The dissociation of ethics from metaphysics. Without this separation, ethics would become a mere sub-field of ontology and thereby lose its ethical specificity. These three points, the shared tasks and presuppositions of Husserl and Heidegger, mark the inheritance of the Western philosophical tradition. This inheritance, and the security it provides, are not 'in the world: rather they are the possibility of our language and the nexus of our world'.[31] The truths that they seek to realise – for Husserl, philosophy as a rigorous science; for Heidegger, the primordial thought of Being – have a common origin: the Greek logos that founds the history of the West. These three elements will, point by point, be opposed by Levinas.

Levinas characterises *Totality and Infinity* as a work of metaphysics but in a precise sense, emphasising the notion of transcendence embedded within the Greek prefix 'meta'. It is a thought of otherness that seeks to engender an experience of rupture or breach – a disturbance of the Parmenidean monism that, Levinas holds, has dominated the entirety of Western thought. According to Levinas, 'metaphysics arises and is maintained in this alibi. It is turned toward the "elsewhere" and the "otherwise" and the "other."'[32] Contrary to Husserl and Heidegger, Levinas will not bend to the demands of an inherited tradition, instead calling for a 'dislocation of the Greek logos, . . . a dislocation of our identity, and perhaps of identity in general'.[33] To the Greek origin, Levinas will counterpose what he considers to be the 'other' foundational voice of the West, the Hebraic. This is not to establish a theological foundation, but simply to open the inheritance of the Greek tradition to the thought of radical alterity, offered by Judaic religion in the concept of creation: 'The great force of the idea of creation such as it was contributed by monotheism is that this creation is *ex nihilo*.'[34] Greek philosophy and its successors, bound by Parmenidean monism, are incapable of thinking the *ex nihilo* – nothing truly new is possible, because anything that comes to be would have already been contained as an element of necessity within the totalising force of Being. The radicality of the thought of creation *ex nihilo* is that the creator remains absolutely distinct from creation, thus opening thought 'toward a pluralism that does not merge into unity':[35] 'The absolute gap of separation which transcendence implies could not be better expressed than by the term creation, in which the kinship of beings among themselves is affirmed, but at the same time their radical heterogeneity also, their reciprocal exteriority coming from nothingness.'[36]

The 'metaphysical' desire, constitutive of the self for Levinas, is the desire for transcendence – to escape the self with no longing for return. This will be made possible in the ethical relationship – 'a nonviolent relationship to the infinite as infinitely other, to the Other – as the only one capable of opening the space of transcendence and of liberating metaphysics'.[37] In the thought of the Other, Greek monism is breached, executing the 'parricide' of Parmenides. But to be complete, 'the metaphysical relation cannot be properly speaking a representation, for the other would therein dissolve into the same'.[38] Representational thought is a problematic avenue of relating to the other, for two reasons: (1) it is founded on the basis of a horizon relative to a thinking subject – *my experience* of the other; (2) it is filtered through universal concepts, thereby reducing the singularity of the other to what is familiar. Thus Husserl's solution to the phenomenological problem of intersubjectivity – his notion of analogical apperception[39] – is entirely inadequate for Levinas. The other, likewise, cannot be understood as a negation, 'other than myself': for this too centralises alterity in a point relative to myself. Therefore, at stake in this endeavour is a thought of the other that does not rely upon negation, representation, or conceptualisation. It is a thought of infinity, in that every other is infinitely other, but a positive infinity as opposed to an infinity derived from a negation of the self. It is an infinity that pushes toward a 'multiplicity not united into a totality'.[40] 'This hollow space', Derrida claims, 'is not an opening among others. It is opening itself, the opening of opening, that which can be enclosed within no category or totality, that is, everything within experience which can no longer be described by traditional concepts, and which resists every philosopheme.'[41] Metaphysics is the thought of transcendence, and hence, the thought of alterity. The thought of alterity is not separate from the ethical, as in Husserl and Heidegger; rather, it is the very opening of the ethical. At this point, Derrida's analysis – part critique, part deconstruction – commences: (1) Levinas's thought must take place within language (as all thought does, for Levinas), but the project as he announces it is one that must use language in such a way as to destroy its own relationship to language, thus making the project impossible. (2) As Levinas's discourse unfolds, it reveals three essential characteristics of all conceptuality and language according to Derrida: (a) spatiality; (b) binarity; (c) equivocality. These three elements will make unthinkable the alterity of the positive infinity, according to Derrida. Let us now look at these two points in turn.

(1) The otherness Levinas seeks is not locatable within the ipseity of one's subjectivity. That is to say, there is no 'I' within the self that is other *to* itself. In earlier texts, Levinas had allowed for an alterity within the individual subjectivity, but in *Totality and Infinity* he reduces ipseity to identity, the self to the same. He thus does not repeat the move of Kierkegaard, who breaks with the thought of Hegelian totality in favour of individual subjectivity as a proper self-relation; rather Levinas moves 'simultaneously against Hegel and against Kierkegaard'.[42] In Levinas's words, 'It is not I who resist the system, as Kierkegaard thought; it is the other.'[43] The essence of the subject for Levinas is precisely this breach toward the other.

As Derrida notes, however, Kierkegaard does not espouse an existential solipsism or empirical egoism. 'I', for Kierkegaard, is a placeholder, a 'pseudonym', Derrida claims, 'for subjective experience in general'.[44] It is not 'I' alone, for Kierkegaard, but subjective experience itself, that resists the totalisation of the dialectic. In Silentio's words, 'there is an interiority that is incommensurable with exteriority'[45] – the 'there is' signifies an anonymous, universal and essential structure of subjective life such that Kierkegaard can claim to his readers, 'to love yourself in the right way and to love the neighbor correspond perfectly to one another: fundamentally they are one and the same thing'.[46] However strenuously Levinas may resist any conceptualisation of the other, the other must at the very least be understood as a subject in order to function as the ground of a Levinasian ethics. 'The other is not myself . . . but it is *an* Ego, as Levinas must suppose in order to maintain his own discourse.'[47] The final words in this sentence, 'to maintain his own discourse', have a double sense for Derrida: (i) On the one hand, *Totality and Infinity* grapples with the question of 'hospitality'[48] in the ethical relation. But this question of welcoming the other at the very least presupposes that the other can in some sense be thought. Thus, to maintain his own *discourse* as an ethics, Levinas must presuppose the subjectivity that he decries in Kierkegaard. (ii) On the other hand, in order to maintain *his* own discourse, Levinas must assume the philosophical stance of himself, Emmanuel Levinas, as the one maintaining the discourse. Put otherwise, Levinas must presuppose his own subjective existence, if *his* discourse is to be sustained. To avoid a Kierkegaardian refusal of Hegel, Levinas must reject the quiddity of subjective existence. But to do so, according to Derrida, is to throw off one's *own* right to any philosophical discourse whatsoever, thereby making this thought impossible. This for Derrida reveals the essential paradox of Levinas's thought: that it seeks to break with philosophical discourse in a way that uses that discourse as its medium:

> And, if you will, the attempt to achieve an opening toward the beyond of philosophical discourse, by means of philosophical discourse, which can never be shaken off completely, cannot possibly succeed *within language* – and Levinas recognizes that there is no thought before language and outside of it – except by *formally* and *thematically* posing *the question of the relations between the belonging and the opening*, the *question of closure*. Formally – that is by posing it in the most effective and most formal, the most formal-ized way possible: not in a *logic*, in other words in a philosophy, but in an inscribed description, in an inscription of the relations between the philo-sophical and the nonphilosophical, in a kind of unheard of *graphics*, within which philosophical conceptuality would be no more than a *function*.[49]

The possibility of thought and the necessity of language are coextensive. How then does one formulate a thought that, of necessity, must dispense with its own discourse? One may do so only by dancing in the space between the philosophical and the non-philosophical, at the site where both are made possible. In Levinas's words, the metaphysical relation 'is prior to the negative or affirmative proposition; it first institutes language, where neither the no nor the yes is the first word'.[50] Yet he also says of the metaphysical relation that it 'is language',[51] and furthermore that 'thought consists in speaking'.[52] Within Levinas's text there is an apparent tension that Levinas himself seems only to partly recognise and express: 'But it belongs to the very essence of language, which consists in continually undoing its phrase by the foreword or the exegesis, in unsaying the said, in attempting to restate without ceremonies what has already been ill understood in the inevitable ceremonial in which the said delights.'[53] This paradoxical exigency of thought, which Levinas does not directly address, reveals for Derrida an 'indestructible and unforeseeable resource of the Greek logos', an 'unlimited power of envelopment',[54] that always traps the one seeking escape.

(2) Levinas reinstates a concept of exteriority, asserting all the while that it is not to be understood spatially. The Levinas of *Time and the Other* had excluded the concept of exteriority from that of alterity, writing it only under erasure: 'The other's entire being is constituted by its exteriority, or rather its alterity, for exteriority is a property of space.'[55] The concept of space is reductive, from this point of view. 'Exteriority' would be outside of the inside, but both outside and inside indicate an even greater, all-encompassing spatial medium, and in that sense, even the outside would be inside. This, for Levinas, does not go far enough toward the alterity of the other.

But in *Totality and Infinity* (subtitled *An Essay on Exteriority*), Levinas reintroduces the concept of exteriority, only to once again write it under erasure by insisting that it should not be understood in spatial terms: 'The void of space is not the absolute interval from which the absolutely exterior being can arise.'[56] While attempting to exclude spatiality, Levinas employs the concept of exteriority – a term inconceivable without some notion of space. This highlights for Derrida another essential element of language – that the moment one speaks, one necessarily employs an inside/outside structure. It is why, for Derrida, despite Levinas's protestation to the contrary, he can only characterise alterity in terms of exteriority (even if '*true* exteriority' is 'non-*exteriority*'[57]), or why he can only speak of infinity as that which *ex*-ceeds totality, or why one of the key terms that dominates the entirety of his discourse from beginning to end – transcendence – is itself spatially charged, characterising a 'beyond'. 'All this means, perhaps', Derrida says, 'that there is no philosophical logos which must not *first* let itself be expatriated into the structure Inside-Outside.'[58] Language is essentially metaphorical; a necessity imposes itself on Levinas's language such that, try as he may, he cannot speak of a non-spatial alterity *except* by way of spatial language.

Furthermore, the inside/outside structure that opens the possibility of language is a two-term structure, revealing for Derrida an essential binarity to language in which one term of each binary is given privilege over the other. Because of this essential binarity, we cannot exclude one term of any given opposition without at the same time expelling the other. 'The meanings which radiate from' the oppositional terms (light/night, inside/outside, presence/absence, etc.) 'do not only inhabit the proscribed words; they are embedded, in person or vicariously, at the very heart of conceptuality itself'.[59] To say that this binarity is essentially spatial is *not* to suggest that these oppositional concepts *occupy* space, as though space were an abstract medium or field in which the concepts have meaning. Thought in this way, 'space' would itself be a concept prior to the essential binarity of concepts that Derrida has articulated. This would return us to the 'bad' exteriority feared by Levinas, an exteriority reduced to a larger interiority. Space does not precede language; rather, language is spatial at its origin, and it functions essentially within the originary rupture of inside and outside, not unlike the 'Decision' separating reason from un-reason.

Finally, it is noteworthy that despite his desire for a 'positive' infinity, Levinas cannot articulate the infinite as such. It is expressible only as what is 'not finite'. This inability on the part of language to appropriate the infinite indicates for Derrida an essential finitude at the heart of language. This essential finitude entails that language can never provide its own ultimate ground, and thus, it can never purify itself absolutely of its nonspeculative ancestry – the cultural and historical ambiguities that birthed it. Philosophical language is an amalgam, a codification and rigidification of inherited syntax and concepts; its lineage arises from historical languages, which bring with them 'a certain equivocality',[60] an essential ambiguity and metaphoricity accompanying all speculative concepts. Unable to purge itself entirely of this ambiguity, 'perhaps philosophy must adopt it, think it and be thought in it, must accommodate duplicity and difference within speculation, within the very purity of philosophical meaning. No one, it seems to us, has attempted this more profoundly than Hegel.'[61] Faced with an irreducible contamination that haunts all language, the *purity* of philosophical language must then reside in the accommodation, engendering, and exploration of this ambiguity. Here Derrida invokes the Hegelian *Aufhebung*, which contains the dual sense of preservation and destruction.

Levinas, we recall, wants to formulate a non-negative concept of alterity. A negative alterity would make the otherness of the other relative to a self, hence excluding its status as a genuine alterity. However, given that, as we have seen, Levinas's infinity cannot enter into language, except through terms that are (a) spatial, and (b) negative, the infinity of absolute alterity cannot, it seems, be truly positive. A truly positive infinity would be all-consuming, and thus could not tolerate any alterity. That it is *infinitely other* means that its otherness is limitless, despite whatever efforts I may impose upon it, despite whatever conceptual violence I may carry out upon it – it is irreducibly other. 'As soon as one attempts to think Infinity as a positive plenitude (one pole of Levinas's non-negative transcendence), the other becomes unthinkable, impossible, unutterable. Perhaps Levinas calls us toward this unthinkable-impossible-unutterable beyond (tradition's) Being and Logos. But it must not be possible either to think or state this call.'[62] To speak in Foucauldian terms, one may only speak to madness in the voice of its captor.

Derrida and Hegel

We are now in a position to situate Derrida's understanding of Hegel, his significance, and the position that he occupies with respect to the history of philosophy. The ways in which Derrida critiques Foucault and Levinas reveal his commitments. There are three major assertions that we shall list and discuss. First, language, whenever and wherever it operates, does so in accordance with a necessary structure of inclusion and exclusion. Second, the thought of what is outside the system can only ever come from within the system – the implication being that one may never think beyond the system itself, despite one's best efforts. Lastly, and most importantly, 'Hegel' is the designator of the thought that closed the Western system, and subsumed all previous and future metaphysics beneath the logic of his dialectic.

First, we look at the inside/outside structure. Foucault had argued in his preface for a 'necessity of madness' in the history of the West. Language, he claimed, required a 'Decision', one that silences the clamour and extracts significance without which no reason, history, science, or philosophy could get underway. Foucault recognises, and Derrida agrees, that there is an originary inscription of distinction within the functioning and the language of reason. Whenever reason speaks, the Decision separating reason from madness is already made. In speaking, it must recognise as a matter of structural necessity what is inside and what is outside the system. Even if Foucault nevertheless argues for a more polarising Decision in the Cartesian moment, he seems to acknowledge this necessary structure of inclusion and exclusion, running through the history of Western thought, that would have preceded even the Decision of the Classical moment.

Levinas, on the other hand, employs the *exteriority* of the other while insisting that this exteriority is not spatial. Nevertheless, that he is unable to explain his concept without relying upon language of spatiality is crucial, for Derrida, especially given that for Levinas 'thought consists in speaking'.[63] If thought consists in speaking, speaking requires language, and his language cannot avoid the inside/outside structure, then Levinas's thought cannot avoid the irruption of spatiality. This reveals a point similar to the one made in the 'Cogito' essay, that language always operates under a necessary binary structure of inside and outside, however strenuously we may try to avoid it.

Secondly, any movements against the system of language must originate within the system and thus are inevitably doomed to failure. Foucault's philosophical movement against the imprisonment of madness, as Foucault acknowledges, could only come from within the language of the captors. Moreover, Foucault sought to put into words the very experience of madness, knowing all the while that the language with which one would do so is the property of reason. He is thus only able to give voice to madness on the assumption that reason, as determined in the Classical age, is not the most basic reason, but a fallen and deficient reason that exists only by excluding an essential element. For Derrida, these commitments amount to a 'reappropriation of negativity' in pursuit of an 'originary presence'. They amount to the subsumption of an historically determined contradiction beneath the unity of a higher, synthetic identity. Hence in attempting to articulate the voice of reason's other and subvert the totalising force of reason, Foucault himself enacts this force with the spectre of Hegel.

Levinas, for all his efforts, also fails to break with Hegel. Even more aggressively and explicitly than Foucault, Levinas seeks to think beyond the reduction imposed by a totalising system. He attempts to formulate the exteriority of the other while at the same time explicitly rejecting an all-encompassing, reductive space in which self and other are situated. He sought to enable the positive experience of the infinitely other, but in the end was incapable of doing so except in the language of the negation of the same. Derrida thus makes a bold claim: 'Levinas is very close to Hegel, much closer than he admits, and at the very moment when he is apparently opposed to Hegel in the most radical fashion. This is a situation he must share with all anti-Hegelian thinkers.'[64] The more one struggles against Hegel's totalising force of reason and history, the more indelibly one is trapped. The most ardent anti-Hegelianism is in fact the most insidious re-enactment of Hegel.

Hegel's thinking, for Derrida, is the completion and consummation of Western metaphysics. It comprehends the mechanisms by which 'the language' of the West operates. 'Language' in this case is left deliberately singular, and the definite article deliberately applied. Across all their differences, Western languages operate in accordance with the same logical structure. Hegel's thought sees and articulates this structure, unfolding throughout the history of metaphysics, and along with it, the history of art, morality, freedom, and history itself. He constructs a comprehensive system of Western thought, taking into itself all of its progressions and apparent contradictions and negations. This structure permits Derrida to say that 'there is only one discourse, it is significative, and here one cannot get around Hegel'.[65] All of metaphysics is 'expanded and rethought in him'.[66] But this entails, according to Derrida, that there is little hope of escaping the system by way of philosophy. Philosophy is structured by language, and Hegelianism, he claims, 'is only this language [the language of Western philosophy] coming into absolute possession of itself'.[67] One cannot speak against the system, because to speak is to confirm, and to negate, where Hegel is concerned, is to affirm.

Derrida is therefore committed to the position that Hegel completes and consummates the system of Western metaphysics. Hegel marks the 'closure' to which Derrida refers in *Voice and Phenomenon*: 'In this sense, *within* the metaphysics of presence, of philosophy as the knowledge of the presence of the object, as knowing's being-nearby-itself in consciousness, we believe quite simply in absolute knowledge as the *closure* if not the end of history. We believe in it literally – *and that such a closure has taken place.*'[68] However, if this were the end of the story, we would merely have shown that Derrida is merely repeating Hegel, which is not only obviously false but is also not terribly interesting. Above I alluded to the 'twin pillars of deconstruction'. The first is Hegel's closure of metaphysics. The second is Heidegger's critique of ontotheology, to which I now turn.

The critique of ontotheology

Heidegger formulates his famous critique of ontotheology in an essay entitled 'The Onto-theo-logical Constitution of Metaphysics', written as the conclusion to a seminar on Hegel. This essay is collected, along with 'The Principle of Identity', in the volume, *Identity and Difference*. We cannot track the full complexity of the line of thinking that threads together these two essays, but must focus on those aspects relevant to the movement of Derrida's thinking. The Aristotelian inception from whence 'metaphysics' derives its name marks the history of metaphysics as 'ontotheological'. Aristotle characterises metaphysics as the science of being – both in the most universal, general sense (ontology, the 'science which investigates being as being'[69]), and being as generative ground or the first cause ('theology, since it is obvious that if the divine is present anywhere, it is present in things of this sort' [immaterial and immovable][70]). Metaphysics is thus concerned with the domains of both ontology and theology, according to Aristotle.

Aristotle's 'first mover', 'which moves while itself unmoved', is 'separate from sensible things', but nevertheless, as the living divine, it is not inactive; rather, 'God's essential actuality is life most good and eternal'. Given that God is immaterial, the life and activity in which it engages must also be immaterial. The only immaterial activity is thinking, and since the divine (as unchangingly good) can only think about the highest object of thought, God thinks the divine nature itself: 'therefore, it must be itself that thought thinks (since it is the most excellent of things), and its thinking is a thinking on thinking'.[71] Given that 'God' is synonymous with thought, and that the highest thought is self-identical, Heidegger notes that the principle of identity, A = A, is considered the 'highest principle of thought'.[72] The principle of identity is incontrovertible, the truest thought that thought can think, and hence the core and foundation of all philosophical thinking.

In the philosophy of Hegel, this Aristotelian foundation reaches its dialectical completion. Aristotle's self-thinking thought is Being, as 'absolute idea'.[73] Of this 'Absolute', or 'the Divine',[74] Hegel repeatedly and explicitly speaks in theological terms. In his lectures on the philosophy of history, Hegel writes that 'history is the unfolding of God's nature in a particular, determinate element'.[75] In *The Science of Logic* he claims, 'and *God* has the absolutely undisputed right that the beginning [of philosophy] be made with him'.[76] But for Hegel, the beginning is also the end: 'of the Absolute it must be said that it is essentially a *result*, that only in the *end* is it what it truly is; and that precisely in this consists its nature, viz. to be actual, subject, the spontaneous becoming of itself'.[77] That thought should think itself requires that thinking is both subject and object of the act of thinking. What begins in the Aristotelian 'simple immediacy' of the self-thinking thought must become completed knowledge, which requires the mediation of difference at the heart of identity: 'Through this progress, then, the beginning loses the one-sidedness which attaches to it as something simply immediate and abstract; it becomes something mediated, and hence the line of the scientific advance becomes a circle.'[78] The full weight of the 'highest principle of thought' is realised only when the 'sameness' of being is no longer conceived as simple identity, 'the night in which . . . all cows are black',[79] but as an active and ongoing 'self-externalization'[80] that maintains its difference within its sameness: 'thinking comes to itself only in the process of its speculative development, thus running through stages of the variously developed, and hence of necessity previously undeveloped, forms'.[81] The history of metaphysics, culminating in Hegel, is this movement from simple to complex identity, in which the movement of thought progressively constitutes its object as radically other, only to recognise in this insuperable difference the identity of the self. The highest thought that thought can think is completed not in the form of A = A, but rather in the form of A *is* A, where the 'is' is understood as a mediating, differential term. 'In the merely identical, the difference disappears. In the same the difference appears, and appears all the more pressingly.'[82] This complex identity, consummating the history inaugurated by Plato and Aristotle, Hegel calls 'God'. As Deleuze writes, 'this Hegelian infinite remains the infinitely large of theology, of the *Ens quo nihil majus*'.[83]

This theological impulse functions in tandem with the determination of Being, 'its original meaning, as presence',[84] with God being understood as the maximal conception of Being, 'that being than which none greater can be conceived'.[85] As early as *Being and Time* Heidegger claims that Being has been historically determined in terms of beings, which are present or lying before us in the present moment: 'entities are grasped in their Being as "presence"; this means that they are understood with regard to a definite mode of time – the *"Present"*'.[86] Heidegger will continue to work out the implications of this for the remainder of his life. Being has always been determined as presence in two senses – spatially as the proximity of the object of thought and temporally as the privileging of the temporal 'now'. Truth and knowledge are most properly understood as the representational appropriations of this absolute presence, with the divine as the telos. In seeking to grasp this absolute presence, the history of metaphysics amounts to 'statements of representational thinking about God',[87] while 'the Being of God gets interpreted ontologically by means of the ancient ontology' as '*ens infinitum*', '*ens increatum*', or '*ens perfectissimum*'.[88] Thus, as Being is always interpreted in the light of present beings, what is distinctive about Being itself is overlooked or forgotten, in what Heidegger calls the '*oblivion*' of Being.[89]

The task outlined in *Being and Time* is to think the meaning of Being in its primordiality, and Heidegger begins this undertaking through the analysis of Dasein:

> But here our ontological task is to show that when we choose to designate the Being of this entity [Dasein] as 'existence' [Existenz], this term does not and cannot have the ontological signification of the traditional term '*existentia*'; ontologically *existentia* is tantamount to *Being-present-at hand*, a kind of Being which is essentially inappropriate to entities of Dasein's character.[90]

What is required is thus to think Being through the existence of that being for whom its existence is a concern, and whose Being can never be understood in terms of presence. Through the analysis of what he calls Dasein's 'care structure' – the structure by which Dasein cares for its Being, informed by its past with an eye toward its future – Heidegger demonstrates that presence (in the form of the present moment) is always both undermined *and* constituted by absence or difference.

Shortly after *Being and Time*, the anthropocentrism of Dasein will drop from Heidegger's focus, replaced explicitly by the question of difference. For Heidegger, 'we think of Being rigorously only when we think of it in its difference with beings, and of beings in their difference with Being. The difference thus comes specifically into view.'[91] Hegel, according to Heidegger, in consummating the history of metaphysics, incorporates an essential moment of mediation, movement, or difference, but ultimately subsumes this concept of difference beneath the structural movement of the *Aufhebung* – 'the cold march of necessity'[92] – which is ontotheological because it privileges the moment of completion and full realisation of the absolute self-proximity of Being as presence. In place of the *Aufhebung*, which characterises the history of thought, Heidegger thus proposes the engagement with the 'unthought' that hides in the history of thought:

> For us, the character of the conversation with the history of thinking is no longer *Aufhebung*, but the step back. *Aufhebung* leads to the heightening and gathering area of truth posited as absolute, truth in the sense of the completely developed certainty of self-knowing knowledge. The step back points to the realm which until now has been skipped over, and from which the essence of truth becomes first of all worthy of thought.[93]

The *Aufhebung* completes but remains within the history of metaphysics, while what Heidegger here calls 'the step back' initiates thought beyond the system, which, on account of its being beyond, can at last characterise the essence of that history, hitherto inaccessible. Hence, 'The difference between beings and Being is the area within which metaphysics, Western thinking in its entire nature, can be what it is. The step back thus moves out of metaphysics into the essential nature of metaphysics.'[94] Hegel recognises the importance of difference, but ultimately subordinates it to the ontotheological presence of the *Aufhebung*.

This is what Derrida means when he speaks of Heidegger's critique of ontotheology. It is important to note that Derrida himself almost completely accepts the critical aspects of Heidegger's project: 'what I have attempted to do would not have been possible without the opening of Heidegger's questions . . . without the attention to what Heidegger calls the difference between Being and beings, the ontico-ontological difference such as, in a way, it remains unthought by philosophy'.[95] In *Of Grammatology*, he writes, 'this proposition of transgression, not yet integrated into a careful discourse, runs the risk of formulating regression itself. One must therefore go by way of the question of being as it is directed by Heidegger and by him alone, at and beyond onto-theology, in order to reach the rigorous thought of that strange nondifference and in order to determine it correctly.'[96] Finally, in the famous 1968 lecture, '*Différance*', Derrida claims 'one can delimit such a closure today only by soliciting the value of presence that Heidegger has shown to be the ontotheological determination of Being'.[97] We have already claimed that Derrida is not, despite his many affinities with Hegel, a Hegelian. But we would be equally ill-advised to assert without qualification, as Simon Critchley appears to, that 'Derrida is a Heideggerian'.[98] Derrida himself rejects the 'analogizing confusion' of 'reducing, using no other procedure, grammatological deconstruction to a pre-fabricated Heideggerianism',

citing such reduction as '*completely misunderstood*'.[99] Much has been written discussing the relations between Derrida and Heidegger, and this is
not the context in which such a comparison belongs.[100] Nevertheless, we
can briefly sketch a trajectory of Derrida's appropriation and later criticism of Heidegger.

His early works reveal that Derrida is quite taken with, and arguably
almost entirely convinced by, Heidegger's project. In his 1953/4 thesis on
Husserl, he writes that 'it is only from Husserl on, if not explicitly with
him, that the great dialectical theme which animates and motivates the
most powerful philosophical tradition, from Platonism to Hegelianism,
can be renewed, or if not renewed then at least rounded, authenticated,
and completed'.[101] Through the course of the thesis, however, he goes on to
argue that 'in spite of the immense philosophical revolution that Husserl
undertook, he remains the prisoner of a great classical tradition: the one
that reduces human finitude to an accident of history, to an "essence of
man" that understands temporality against a background of possible or
actual eternity in which it has or could have participated'.[102] The problem
of originary finitude is one with which Husserl cannot reckon, and for
which Heidegger serves as the corrective in Derrida's thinking: 'the dialectic is exclusively "phenomenological" in Husserl and . . . the transcendental idealism of the latter will always prevent him from founding it in an
ontology of temporality or in a temporality of being – which Heidegger
will mean to begin by doing'.[103] Again, he writes:

> this is the whole difference separating Husserl from Heidegger. The tran-
> scendental subject is originarily existential for the latter; which allows him
> to describe an origin of negation that is neither psychological nor logical. It
> is the very nothing which allows negation . . . In this sense, [Husserl] is very
> far behind Hegel and Heidegger, who give an originary sense to negation
> and found it, not on an attitude or on an operation but on nothingness.[104]

A decade later, in 'Violence and Metaphysics', in the final section titled
'Of Ontological Violence', Derrida spends a great deal of time defending
Heidegger against the ethical charges of Levinas: 'Not only is the thought
of Being not ethical violence, but it seems that no ethics – in Levinas's
sense – can be opened without it.'[105] Elsewhere, 'the best liberation from
violence is a certain putting into question, which makes the search for an
archia tremble. Only the thought of Being can do so, and not traditional
"philosophy" or "metaphysics."'[106]

From the mid-1960s, however, Derrida begins to locate in Heidegger's
discourse some of the same ontotheological tendencies that Heidegger
himself had so vigorously identified and attempted to overcome in the
tradition. These tendencies are already present in *Being and Time*. In ¶44

of *Being and Time*, Heidegger formulates his theory of truth as *aletheia* or unconcealment, in opposition to the traditional definition of truth as a correspondence between a proposition and its purported state of affairs. Alethetic truth, on the contrary, discloses beings as they are: '*The most primordial phenomenon of truth is first shown by the existential-ontological foundations of uncovering.*'[107] The 'truth' of a thing is the thing showing itself as it is in itself. This applies to 'things' in the world in a derivative or secondary sense: what is 'primarily "true" – that is, uncovering – is Dasein'.[108] This sets the stage for the movement into Division II of *Being and Time* where the task is the extrication of Dasein from its *fallenness*, understood as its immersion in the world and in the dispersion of what Heidegger calls '*das Man*', and which Macquarrie and Robinson translate as '*the "they"*'.[109] According to Heidegger, 'to Dasein's state of Being belongs *falling*'.[110] This presupposes, however, and the entire text of *Being and Time* bears this out, a falling away from a primordially 'authentic' (*eigentlich*) state. Heidegger's conception of truth as disclosing or unconcealing becomes a methodology by which Dasein's authentic Being may be revealed. To be sure, Heidegger attempts a thought of originary finitude in his concept of 'Being-towards-death', but nevertheless, for the later Derrida, he does so for the sake of an originary presence. The finitude that Heidegger conceives does not go all the way down. There remains a presupposition of a fullness in which this originary finitude is understood, a moment of completion, perfection, or purity which, even if it is never fully attainable, nevertheless serves as a guide or a regulative ideal for the entirety of the project.

As we have seen, shortly after *Being and Time* and specifically after 1929's 'What is Metaphysics?',[111] Heidegger will almost completely drop the voluntaristic and anthropocentric language of Dasein. But the language indicating a commitment to a moment of purity never leaves Heidegger's discourse. In the essay entitled 'Language', for instance, what Heidegger calls the 'oldest natural cast of language',[112] that which gives rise to the possibility of speaking, is '*the peal of stillness*'.[113] Pure language is silence – language bereft of its execution – as the execution of language contaminates it with empirical accidents not proper to the essence of language itself. He speaks elsewhere of the thought of Being and of language in terms of 'salvation', when, for instance, he says of German poet, Georg Trakl, that his poetry 'sings of the destiny which casts mankind in his still withheld nature – that is to say, *saves mankind*'.[114] We can also cite the famous *Der Spiegel* interview in which Heidegger says, 'philosophy will not be able to bring about an immediate transformation of the present condition of the world. This is true not only of philosophy but of all merely human thought and endeavor. Only a god can save us now.'[115]

Even if the Dasein-laden language of 'fallenness' and 'authenticity' has by now disappeared, their place in Heidegger's thinking – the place of salvation, purity, and primordiality – has not. As Gayatri Spivak writes in her now-canonical 'Translator's Preface' to *Of Grammatology,* "'It was within concepts inherited from metaphysics that Nietzsche, Freud, and Heidegger worked."[116] Heidegger came close to undoing them, "destroying" them (Heidegger's word), but gave in to them as well.'[117] Thus, from the mid-1960s onward, Derrida will begin reading Heidegger more critically: 'But despite this debt to Heidegger's thought, or rather because of it, I attempt to locate in Heidegger's text . . . the signs of belonging to metaphysics, or to what he calls onto-theology.'[118] In another interview, he cites a *'departure* from the Heideggerian problematic', claiming that 'this departure is related particularly to the concepts of *origin* and *fall*,'[119] and he even suggests that 'the Heideggerian problematic is the most "profound" and "powerful" defence of what I attempt to put into question under the rubric of the *thought of presence*'.[120] Derrida thus begins a path of critical engagement with the questions of Heidegger's project, one that will occupy him on and off throughout the rest of his career.[121]

Conclusion

Derrida's project of deconstruction thus rests upon the twin pillars of Hegel's consummation of the history of metaphysics, coupled with Heidegger's critique of ontotheology. Hegel completes the language and logic of the West, but, as Heidegger recognises, Hegel ultimately subordinates the essential mediating mechanism of the system to the ontotheological presence of the *Aufhebung.* As Derrida writes, 'for Hegelian idealism consists precisely of a *relève* of the binary oppositions of classical idealism, a resolution of contradiction into a third term that comes in order to *aufheben,* to deny while raising up, while idealising, while sublimating into an anamnesic interiority (*Errinnerung*), while *interning* difference in a self-presence'.[122] Heidegger too, despite his cautious efforts, succumbs to the same ontotheological temptations, with his tireless search for authenticity, fallenness, gathering, purity, and so on. Together, Hegel and Heidegger reveal the difficulty of thinking a concept of difference without the subordination to presence or non-difference, or its congealing within the pre-existing framework of the system. Any philosophy that attempts a shift outside the system is forced to do so by way of the language and the logic of the system itself, thereby confirming the very system from which it seeks escape. This is the error that Derrida locates first in Foucault and then in Levinas, but ultimately, in 'all anti-Hegelian thinkers'.[123] The more virulently one tries to escape, the more inextricably one is bound. It is perhaps little wonder that in the famous '*Différance*' essay of 1968, the first and last proper names to appear are, respectively, Hegel and Heidegger. The beating heart of deconstruction resides in the tension between the two: how does one formulate a thought beyond the system of presence, when the system of presence has already thought everything that can be thought, and spoken everything that can be spoken?

In the next chapter, we shall look in detail at three specific criticisms of Hegelian difference as offered by Deleuze. These three criticisms are that: (1) negation is *less* than difference in itself; (2) conceptualising difference as negation expresses a nihilistic spirit of *ressentiment* – being is inconceivable without a fundamental *not*; (3) conceived as contradiction, difference merely collapses into identity. Where Derrida understands Hegel as *the* force to be reckoned with, Deleuze understands Hegel as an enemy, whose conception of difference marks the antithesis of philosophy and of life itself.

Notes

1. *DR*, xix.
2. There have been excellent works dedicated specifically to this question. See Baugh, *French Hegel: From Surrealism to Postmodernism*; and Butler, *Subjects of Desire: Hegelian Reflections in Twentieth-Century France*.
3. Foucault, 'The Discourse on Language', in *The Archaeology of Knowledge and The Discourse on Language*, 235.
4. *P*, 77.
5. 'Preface by Jacques Derrida', in Malabou, *The Future of Hegel*, vii–xlvii. The quote appears on xviii.
6. Derrida, 'The Original Discussion of "Différance"', in Wood and Bernasconi (eds), *Derrida and* Différance, 95.
7. *MP*, 14.
8. *MP*, 14.
9. Famously, Derrida claims that *différance* is 'neither a word nor a concept' (*MP*, 3). Derrida has good reasons, to be examined in what follows, to sometimes speak of *différance* as though it were not a concept. Nevertheless, with the necessary caveats in place (that *différance* is not a signifier that points to a signified presence of meaning), there is no reason not to operate with the terminology of the concept. Indeed, Derrida himself does so as well: 'By means of this double, and precisely stratified, dislodged and dislodging, writing, we must also mark the interval between inversion, which brings low what was high, and the irruptive emergence of a new "concept," a concept that can no longer be, and never could be, included in the previous regime' (*P*, 42). With this in mind, I will move forward speaking of *différance* as a Derridean concept.
10. Protevi, *Political Physics*, 46.
11. Foucault, *History of Madness*, xxxiii.
12. Ibid., xxxiv.
13. Ibid., xxviii.
14. See *GM*, 'First Treatise: "Good and Evil," "Good and Bad"'.

15. *WD*, 31; see also Schrift, *Twentieth-Century French Philosophy*, 126.
16. *WD*, 33.
17. Foucault, *History of Madness*, xxxii.
18. Ibid., xxxi.
19. *WD*, 36.
20. Foucault, *History of Madness*, xxviii.
21. Ibid., xxxii.
22. Moreover, Foucault is wrong in his reading of Descartes, according to Derrida. The Cartesian cogito does not exclude madness. The cogito is valid even if the subject is mad when she utters it.
23. *WD*, 54.
24. *WD*, 36.
25. *WD*, 55.
26. *WD*, 57.
27. *WD*, 41.
28. *WD*, 40.
29. *WD*, 79.
30. This point is problematised by both Derrida and Deleuze.
31. *WD*, 82.
32. Levinas, *Totality and Infinity*, 33.
33. *WD*, 82.
34. Levinas, *Totality and Infinity*, 63.
35. Levinas, *Time and the Other*, 42.
36. Levinas, *Totality and Infinity*, 293.
37. *WD*, 83.
38. Levinas, *Totality and Infinity*, 38.
39. See *CM*, Fifth Meditation.
40. Levinas, *Totality and Infinity*, 104.
41. *WD*, 83.
42. *WD*, 110.
43. Levinas, *Totality and Infinity*, 40.
44. *WD*, 110. Derrida himself explores the 'meaning' of the 'I' in *VP*, particularly chapter 7.
45. Kierkegaard, *Fear and Trembling*, 69.
46. Kierkegaard, *Works of Love*, 22.
47. *WD*, 110.
48. Levinas, *Totality and Infinity*, 27, 300.
49. *WD*, 110–11.
50. Levinas, *Totality and Infinity*, 42.
51. Ibid., 39.
52. Ibid., 40.
53. Ibid., 30.
54. *WD*, 111–12.
55. Levinas, *Time and the Other*, 75–6.
56. Levinas, *Totality and Infinity*, 191.
57. *WD*, 112.
58. *WD*, 112.
59. *WD*, 113.
60. *WD*, 113.
61. *WD*, 113.
62. *WD*, 114.
63. Levinas, *Totality and Infinity*, 40.
64. *WD*, 99.
65. *WD*, 261.

66. *WD*, 119.
67. *WD*, 119.
68. *VP*, 87.
69. *Metaphysics*, Bk. IV, ch. 1.
70. *Metaphysics*, Bk. VI, ch. 1.
71. *Metaphysics*, Bk. XII, ch. 7, 9.
72. *ID*, 23.
73. *ID*, 43.
74. *PH*, 11.
75. Hegel, *Lectures on the Philosophy of World History, Introduction: Reason In History*, 42.
76. *GL*, 78.
77. *PH*, 11.
78. *GL*, 71–2.
79. *PH*, 9.
80. *ID*, 44.
81. *ID*, 45.
82. *ID*, 45.
83. *DR*, 45.
84. *ID*, 31.
85. Anselm of Canterbury, *The Proslogion*, ch. 2, in Anselm of Canterbury, *The Major Works*.
86. Heidegger, *Being and Time*, 47.
87. *ID*, 54.
88. Heidegger, *Being and Time*, 74, 46, 125.
89. *ID*, 50.
90. Heidegger, *Being and Time*, 67.
91. *ID*, 62.
92. *PH*, 5.
93. *ID*, 49.
94. *ID*, 51.
95. *P*, 9.
96. *OG*, 23.
97. *MP*, 16.
98. See, 'No Exit For Derrida: Jeremy Butman interviews Simon Critchley', *Los Angeles Review of Books*, https://lareviewofbooks.org/interview/exit-derrida.
99. *P*, 55.
100. See, for example, Donkel, *The Understanding of Difference in Heidegger and Derrida*; Wood (ed.), *Of Derrida, Heidegger, and Spirit*; Marrati, *Genesis and Trace: Derrida Reading Husserl and Heidegger*; Hodge, *Derrida on Time*; Kates, *Essential History: Jacques Derrida and the Development of Deconstruction*; Sallis, *Delimitations: Phenomenology and the End of Metaphysics*; Sallis, *Echoes: After Heidegger*; Clark, *Derrida, Heidegger, Blanchot: Sources of Derrida's Notion and Practice of Literature*; Behler, *Confrontations: Derrida/Heidegger/Nietzsche*; Rapaport, *Heidegger and Derrida: Reflections on Time and Language*; Protevi, *Time and Exteriority: Aristotle, Heidegger, Derrida*; Stellardi, *Heidegger and Derrida on Philosophy and Metaphor: Imperfect Thought*.
101. Derrida, *The Problem of Genesis in Husserl's Philosophy*, xxi.
102. Ibid., 5.
103. Ibid., 198n.39.
104. Ibid., 205n.47.
105. *WD*, 137.
106. *WD*, 141.
107. Heidegger, *Being and Time*, 263.
108. Ibid.

109. Ibid., 164.
110. Ibid., 264.
111. Heidegger, 'What is Metaphysics?', in *Pathmarks*.
112. Heidegger, 'Language', in *Poetry, Language, Thought*, 191.
113. Ibid., 205.
114. Heidegger, 'Language in the Poem: A Discussion on Georg Trakl's Poetic Work', in *On the Way to Language*, 196.
115. Heidegger, 'Only a God Can Save Us: *Der Spiegel's* Interview (September 23, 1966)', in Stassen (ed.), *Philosophical and Political Writings*, 38.
116. This quotation is Spivak's translation of a passage found in *WD*, 281.
117. Spivak, 'Translator's Preface', *OG*, ix–lxxxvii; xxxviii.
118. *P*, 10.
119. *P*, 54.
120. *P*, 55.
121. See Derrida, *Aporias*; Derrida, '*Geschlecht* I: Sexual Difference, Ontological Difference', *PIA*, 7–26; Derrida, 'Heidegger's Hand (*Geschlecht* II)', *PIA*, 27–62; Derrida, *Of Spirit: Heidegger and the Question*; Derrida, '*Ousia and Grammē:* Note on a Note from *Being and Time*', *MP*, 29–68; Derrida, 'The Ends of Man', *MP*, 109–36.
122. *P*, 43.
123. *WD*, 99.

Chapter 4

Deleuze and Hegelian Difference

Much more than in the case of Derrida, the characterisation of 'anti-Hegelian' fits comfortably with the philosophy of Gilles Deleuze. In reflecting upon his education in the philosophical tradition, Deleuze famously said, 'I could not stand Descartes, the dualisms and the Cogito, or Hegel, the triad and the operation of the negation',[1] and, 'what I detested most was Hegelianism and dialectics'.[2] Deleuze's 1962 work *Nietzsche and Philosophy* is explicitly anti-Hegelian in scope: 'If we do not discover its target the whole of Nietzsche's philosophy remains abstract and barely comprehensible . . . the concept of the Overman is directed against the dialectical conception of man, and transvaluation is directed against the dialectic or appropriation or suppression of alienation. Anti-Hegelianism runs through Nietzsche's work as its cutting edge',[3] and as we have already cited, Deleuze regards the entire modern problematic as arising from out of a 'generalized anti-Hegelianism'.[4] From the 1954 review of 'Jean Hyppolite's *Logic and Existence*' through 1991's *What is Philosophy?*, written with Félix Guattari, Deleuze's work bears the explicit markings of anti-Hegelian thinking.

However, as in Derrida's case, the meaning of this opposition is not as simple as it is sometimes cast, and will depend upon how Deleuze understands Hegel and his relation to the philosophy of difference.[5] What this avowed anti-Hegelianism amounts to or why Deleuze so vehemently commits himself to it is not obvious, because Deleuze himself, though offering many direct and indirect jabs at Hegelian dialectics, never undertakes a clear and consistent engagement with Hegel's thought. In her essay, 'Who's Afraid of Hegelian Wolves?', Catherine Malabou rightly notes that for Deleuze, 'No outline of Hegelian philosophy is drawn, if by "outline" we understand what *What is Philosophy?* calls the "plane" of someone's thinking. This plane, constitutive of each particular philosophy, is a complex play of movements.'[6] Even in *Nietzsche and Philosophy*, Deleuze's most ardently anti-Hegelian book, Hegel plays more the role of a foil than an interlocutor, a character against whom Nietzsche's *Übermensch* emerges, rather than an object of extended critique. Deleuze offers us a possible reason for this omission in an interview with Jeanette Colombel. Regarding his 'merciless' aversion to Hegel, Deleuze says, 'If you don't admire something, if you don't love it, you have no reason to write a word about it.'[7] One need not waste one's time writing on one's enemies, unless, as in the case of Spinoza and Nietzsche, 'whose critical and destructive powers', Deleuze claims, 'are without equal', one is critiquing in order to recreate, redefine, or reconstruct the object of critique. Clearly, however, Deleuze is not completely opposed to writing on enemies, as elsewhere he claims, 'My book on Kant's different; I like it, I did it as a book about an enemy that tries to show how his system works, its various cogs.'[8] Later in her essay Malabou writes, 'At the same time this extreme reaction amounts to an exceptional treatment for no other philosopher meets this fate in Deleuze's work',[9] and she appears to be correct. On the figures of Hume, Leibniz, Spinoza, Nietzsche, Proust, Sacher-Masoch, even 'the enemy' Kant, Deleuze writes careful monographs in order to utilise particular elements of their thinking for the construction of his own philosophical system.

What then can explain the omission of any extended treatment of Hegel? What distinguishes Deleuze's other enemies – Kant, for instance, or Plato, on whom Deleuze writes in *The Logic of Sense*, or Husserl, whose concept of the transcendental ego Deleuze relentlessly attacks, but whose work lies in the background of much of Deleuze's philosophy[10] – from Hegel, whom Deleuze says he cannot stand?[11] What explains the 'privileged treatment'[12] that Deleuze accords to Hegel, in overlooking an engagement with his thought? Given everything that Deleuze has stated regarding Kant, Hegel, and the relationship to one's enemies, we can proffer a reasonable estimation: If Deleuze writes on Kant, it is because Deleuze actualises a positive virtuality that Kant does not quite recognise – Deleuze is critiquing in order to affirm, as he does in the case of Plato and in the case of Husserl as well; if he does *not* write on Hegel, perhaps it is not because Hegel is the '*single* figure of the thinker of identity',[13] as Malabou suspects (as clearly Deleuze is critical of the entire philosophical tradition on this point – Hegel is not unique in this regard), but rather because there is a tendency in Hegel's thinking, according to Deleuze, that pollutes the entire system, such that there is nothing positive or affirmative to draw out of it. As Deleuze writes, 'There is no possible compromise between Hegel and Nietzsche.'[14] Kant is an enemy, but an enemy can be a valuable foil and source of inspiration. Deleuze cannot critique Hegel, because he cannot affirm Hegel, and for Deleuze, this comes down to the fact that for Hegel, the work of creation and affirmation take place through the work of the negative: 'But that an accident as such, detached from what circumscribes it, what is bound and is actual only in its context with others, should attain an existence of its own and a separate freedom – this is the tremendous power of the negative; it is the energy of thought, of the pure "I" '.[15]

Negation is the engine that drives the machinery of the Hegelian system. In the words of Jean Hyppolite, 'Hegel's philosophy is a philosophy of negation and negativity.'[16] In *The Science of Logic*, Hegel writes, 'Difference as such is already *implicitly* contradiction; for it is the unity of sides which are, only in so far as they are *not one* . . . But the positive and the negative are the *posited* contradiction because, as negative unities, they are themselves the positing of themselves, and in this positing each is the sublating of itself and the positing of its opposite.'[17] Since Aristotle, philosophy has represented difference as an empirical difference between things that are, in some sense, identical, and hence it has subordinated difference to identity. But no one, quite so explicitly as Hegel, goes so far as to designate difference as negation and contradiction, and to conceive of creation or production in these terms. This tendency is at the heart of Hegel's thought, and it is this tendency with which Deleuze takes issue, for three reasons: (1) Difference as contradiction is *less than* difference itself. That is to say, contradiction is difference pushed to its extremity, but this extremity would not be possible without the primary relation that is difference itself. (2) Difference as contradiction is an indication of a thinking rooted in what Nietzsche calls *ressentiment*. *Ressentiment*, on Deleuze's appropriation of Nietzsche, is the state in which reactive forces overtake active forces such that active forces become incapable of acting on their own – in this condition, the being cannot affirm or express the self without first negating its other. (3) Difference, when pushed to the point of contradiction, ultimately collapses into identity and, hence, is not really difference at all. So in order to understand why and how Deleuze rejects Hegel, we shall have to carry out an operation that is somewhat similar to the one carried out with Derrida: we shall have to reconstruct a picture from the various bits that Deleuze leaves us in his works on other figures.

Negation as *less than* difference

Above, we noted that the entirety of Deleuze's corpus bears the explicit marks of anti-Hegelian thinking. However, this statement is a bit misleading, as these *marks* themselves are not monolithic. They assume an increasingly virulent form, as Deleuze begins to read and publish on Bergson and Nietzsche more closely, and ultimately culminate in the unbridled onslaught of 1962's *Nietzsche and Philosophy*. In the book on Hume, for instance – 1953's *Empiricism and Subjectivity: An Essay on Hume's Theory of Human Nature* – the name 'Nietzsche' never appears, but the name 'Hegel' does, and in an almost reverent light: 'We shouldn't, of course, present Hume as an exceptional victim, who more than others has felt the unfairness of constant criticisms. The case is similar for all great philosophers. We are surprised by the objections constantly raised against Descartes, Kant, Hegel, etc.'[18] Hegel, in this early text, is one in a group of 'great philosophers' who face the 'unfairness of constant criticisms', along with, we should note, Descartes and Kant, two figures whose philosophies, as we have seen, Deleuze later claims to detest and oppose.

By 1954, a subtly formulated criticism of Hegel begins to emerge, in the context of Deleuze's review of Jean Hyppolite's *Logic and Existence*. For Hyppolite, the determination of any given thing entails its negative relationality with the whole of Being: 'The complete distinction of a thing reconnects it to the whole Universe, reduces differences to essential and internal difference, to the difference between a thing or a determination and its *other*.'[19] Deleuze's charge against Hyppolite (but by proxy, against Hegel himself), is that difference understood as negation or contradiction is in fact *less profound than* difference in itself, as opposed to the most complete form of difference.

In *Logic and Existence*, Hyppolite writes, 'The transition from diversity to opposition can be shown in two ways.'[20] First, in the knowing subject: 'Letting things subsist in their unaltered positivity, thought takes upon itself the movement of comparison.'[21] The subject experiences individual things in terms of categories, and formulates categories in terms of a thing's similarities and dissimilarities with other things. In so far as a thing, x, is similar to other x's, it is dissimilar to things that are not x; and reciprocally, in so far as it is dissimilar to things that are not x, it can be similar to other x's and can hence be categorised as an x. The similar relies upon the dissimilar (the *not*) for its own characterisation, and likewise the dissimilar relies upon the similar.

According to Hegel, then, even in the mode of empirical comparison, thought does not do away with the necessity for contradiction as a category; it simply pushes contradiction into the subjective: 'in this way the contradiction is not resolved but merely shifted elsewhere, into subjective or external reflection generally'.[22] In this case, thought does not grasp the thing itself, but merely poses a relation of thought to the thing. In so far as it is a purely subjective contradiction, the reflection in which this contradiction is posited does not reflect back upon the self. The relation is one of a reflecting subject, thinking *about* a substance external to it.

But one of the chief goals of Hegel's thought is to overcome the twin dangers of the Cartesian problematic – the radical distinction between thought and being. The first of these dangers is the Humean danger, a scepticism that to a large extent denies the possibility of knowledge. The second is the Kantian transcendental move, which reinstates knowledge, but at the expense of Being itself, placing Being (the noumenon) forever out of the reach of experience. To avoid these problems, thought, for Hegel, must be reinscribed at the heart of Being itself: 'In my view, which can be justified only by the exposition of the system itself, everything turns on grasping and expressing the True, not only as *Substance*, but equally as *Subject*.'[23] In like manner, Hyppolite writes, 'Thought is no longer a game about or around the content for which skepticism always lies in wait; it is the very thought of the *Thing*',[24] and 'Hegelian Logic starts with an identification of thought and the thing thought'.[25] Being and subjective reflection become, for Hegel, synonymous. The contradiction of similar and dissimilar, formerly understood as a mere subjective association, must become now the internal, essential contradiction at the heart of Being itself. Invoking Leibniz, Hyppolite expands on this point, speaking of the 'absolute characteristic' of a thing, 'that by which it is made to be what it is . . . in so far as it is discernible from *all the others*'.[26] Likewise, 'This difference (found within them) is essential difference, because it is the difference posited in the identity of the thing; this difference is what puts the thing in opposition to *all the rest*.'[27] A is what it is because it is not what it is not, because it is not Not-A. In this way, the diversity we encounter, comprised of a myriad of singularities exemplifying a multitude of differences, becomes a vast sea of contradiction, with each thing related to every other by a negational relation. So, Hyppolite affirms Hegel's claim that 'Difference as such is already *implicitly* contradiction.'[28]

It is precisely against this affirmation that Deleuze's first criticism of Hegel is formulated: 'But there is one point in *all* this where Hyppolite shows his Hegelian bias: Being can be identical to difference only in so far as difference is taken to the absolute, in other words, all the way to contradiction. Speculative difference is self-contradictory Being.'[29] In this early piece, Deleuze offers both a criticism and an indication of his own imminent trajectory of thought. Contradiction, he claims, is *less than* difference. It is only on the basis of a more fundamental difference that two things can be said, after the fact, to be *opposed*. It is only *because* two things differ that they can contradict. Difference is primary; contradiction secondary or derivative. As Anne Sauvagnargues writes, 'Hegelianism approaches difference only in its actualized mode, and thus misses its becoming.'[30] Elsewhere Deleuze writes, speaking this time of Bergson, 'In Bergson, thanks to the notion of the virtual, the thing differs from itself *first, immediately*. According to Hegel, the thing differs from itself because it differs first from everything it is not, and thus difference goes as far as contradiction.'[31] For Hegel, internal difference, intrinsic difference, lies at the heart of Being, constituting the thing as what it is, *because* it is constituted by its distinction from everything that it is not. In the words of Hyppolite, 'If identity suits things, dissimilarity or intrinsic difference also suits them, since they must be distinguished or differentiated in themselves from all the others.'[32] Hegel identifies the thing with the thought of the *not*, and thus conceptualises internal difference first and foremost as contradiction.

On the contrary, Bergson formulates a concept of difference internal to the thing itself, wherein the thing differs primarily from itself, and only on the basis of this self-difference and differentiation is the thing constituted and is it possible for the thing to oppose and contradict other things: 'The opposition of two terms is only the actualization of a virtuality that contained them both: this is tantamount to saying that difference is more profound than negation or contradiction.'[33] What Deleuze here calls 'actualization' is very close to what he calls 'expression' in his review of *Logic and Existence*, asking, 'does not Hyppolite establish a theory of expression, where difference is expression itself, and contradiction, that aspect which is only phenomenal?'[34] Hyppolite defines philosophy as 'the expression of being in concepts or in discourse'.[35] The central thesis of Hegel's *Phenomenology*, Hyppolite writes, is 'the establishment of absolute knowledge on the basis of the whole of human experience'.[36] Knowledge is grounded on the relation between consciousness and thing, but knowledge is also what makes consciousness itself possible, and establishes the community of consciousnesses for whom the thing is an object of knowledge. Language makes possible the category that thinks the thing, but it also makes possible the characterisation of the 'I' who thinks it, without which there could be, properly speaking, no knowledge of the thing at all. Hyppolite thus claims, 'It has to be the case that human discourse be simultaneously the discourse of being and the discourse of a universal self-consciousness.'[37] Discourse, he says, is 'the reflection of being into itself',[38] the self-awareness of being itself. To say, however, that Being *expresses* itself is not to say, according to Deleuze, that Being *contradicts* itself. Expression engenders differences, rather than contradictions. An individual is an *expression* of a virtuality, of *tendencies* in tension with each other.[39] This tension at the heart of the virtual is difference in itself, prior to the contradiction of the thing against everything that it is not. Hegel's contradictory difference is predicated upon this internal difference, difference in itself; thus, Hegel's difference is *less than* difference. As Joe Hughes writes, contradiction 'is a product of genesis and cannot therefore be the motor of genesis'.[40] This first criticism is best summed up with Deleuze's claim in *Difference and Repetition*: 'The negative and negativity do not even capture the phenomenon of difference, only the phantom or epiphenomenon.'[41]

Negation as a symptom of *ressentiment*

Moving from the mid-1950s to the early 1960s, the criticism just formulated will don a more aggressive visage. Rather than simply a *less profound* concept of difference, difference as contradiction will, in 1962's *Nietzsche and Philosophy*, be portrayed as an indication of a nihilistic spirit, a symptom of *ressentiment*, of a system of thought wherein 'Life takes on a value of nil.'[42] In one of Nietzsche's more famous passages, he writes:

> The slave revolt in morality begins when *ressentiment* itself becomes creative and gives birth to values: the *ressentiment* of beings denied the true reaction, that of the deed, who recover their losses only through an imaginary revenge. Whereas all noble morality grows out of a triumphant yes-saying to oneself, from the outset slave morality says 'no' to an 'outside,' to a 'different,' to a 'not-self': and *this* 'no' is its creative deed.[43]

Let us now look to the way in which Deleuze appropriates Nietzsche's concept of *ressentiment* in his rejection of Hegel.

Nietzsche conceives the health of the individual as a proper relation between its active and reactive forces. Deleuze formulates definitions for these concepts:

> In the normal or healthy state the role of reactive forces is always to limit action. They divide, delay or hinder it by means of another action whose effects we feel. But, conversely, active forces produce a burst of creativity: they set it off at a chosen instant, at a favorable moment, in a given direction, in order to carry out a quick and precise piece of adjustment. In this way a *riposte* is formed.[44]

Active forces are outwardly directed, discharging in the relation between the body and the world – in conquest, aggression, creativity, love, and so forth. Active forces *do*. On the other hand, reactive forces are restraining, limiting, inhibitive, and calculative. In the healthy individual, active forces dominate over the reactive, and the mode of comportment of the active type generally is one of expressivity. But it must not be overlooked that reactive forces are necessary even for the healthy type. For the healthy type will sometimes be required to react to a stimulus, particularly in the case of a threat. The dominance of active over reactive forces dictates that when something would seek to limit the entity, to inhibit its capacity for action in whatever way, its reactive forces are called upon and determine the precise moment to strike. When the moment is right, the being acts, discharging her reaction outwardly; the reaction, thus acted, is finished, and the forces, thus discharged, are satisfied. 'The active type therefore includes reactive forces but ones that are defined by a capacity for obeying or being acted.'[45]

According to Nietzsche, when one can no longer act her reaction, when she has been deprived, as Nietzsche says, of the true reaction, then the reaction becomes an *imaginary revenge*, perceived and felt inwardly rather than acted outwardly. If the state of health is defined as the proper relation between active and reactive forces, then the state of sickness is understood as an improper relation between the two, a state in which reactive forces dominate over the active. But reactive forces are essentially and intrinsically incapable of overpowering active forces; thus they cannot, strictly speaking, dominate over active forces: 'reactive forces do not triumph by forming a force greater than that of active forces'.[46] The only way in which active forces can be subdued is for the reactive forces to *cease to be acted*, thereby depriving the active forces of their proper role. Let us examine this further.

In the Second Treatise of the *Genealogy of Morality*, Nietzsche discusses forgetfulness as a positive, affirmative, and necessary component in the life of the healthy individual:

> Forgetfulness is no mere *vis inertiae* as the superficial believe; rather, it is an active and in the strictest sense positive faculty of suppression, and is responsible for the fact that whatever we experience, learn, or take into ourselves enters just as little into our consciousness during the condition of digestion (one might call it 'inanimation') as does the entire thousand-fold process through which the nourishing of our body, so-called 'incorporation', runs its course. To temporarily close the doors and windows of consciousness; to remain undisturbed by the noise and struggle with which our underworld of subservient organs works for and against each other; a little stillness, a little *tabula rasa* of consciousness so that there is again space for new things, above all for the nobler functions and functionaries, for ruling, foreseeing, predetermining (for our organism is set up oligarchically) – that is the use of this *active forgetfulness*, a doorkeeper as it were, an upholder of psychic order, of rest, of etiquette: from which one can immediately anticipate the degree to which there could be no happiness, no cheerfulness, no hope, no pride, no *present* without forgetfulness.[47]

Forgetfulness is affirmative in that it enables the organism to ever anew receive, interpret, and react accordingly to, the constantly fresh stream of incoming stimuli. Forgetting is not a lack or a passive deficiency, but an active, positive impulse; a *doing*. Deleuze reads forgetfulness as a function of the proper relation between active and reactive forces. The calculative and interpretive roles of the reactive forces will dictate their jurisdiction as everything having to do with the reception or retention of stimuli. This is what Deleuze calls the 'reactive apparatus'.[48] Characterising Freud's *topical hypothesis*, Deleuze claims that 'the same system could not at one and the same time faithfully record the transformations which it undergoes and offer an ever fresh receptivity'.[49] But both functions – receiving and recording – are necessary. An impression, once made, does not simply go away. It becomes the object of reactive forces in the form of unconscious traces. But 'adaptation would never be possible if the reactive apparatus did not have another system of forces at its disposal . . . a system in which reaction is not a reaction to traces but becomes a reaction to the present excitation or to the direct image of the object'.[50] So the reactive apparatus is bifurcated into the conscious and unconscious systems: 'Nietzsche distinguishes two systems within the reactive apparatus: the conscious and the unconscious.'[51]

The task of consciousness is to interpret the present, incoming stimuli, in order to determine whether or not each stimulus demands a reaction. In most cases, they do not, and hence they are immediately transformed into unconscious traces. But if the stimulus presents itself as an indication of something that may limit or harm the individual, then conscious reactive forces act their reaction, discharging the will associated with them. The impression is then transformed into a trace in the unconscious, and is, hence, *forgotten*. As Deleuze interprets Nietzsche's ontology, in the state of health active forces govern the operation of the reactive apparatus, with the net result of a healthy forgetfulness. This for two reasons: (1) Conscious memory has no *need* to hang onto the traces any longer. The reaction has been discharged; the matter has been settled. It bears no ill will or no ill memory simply because it does not need to do so. As Aristotle says in the *Nicomachean Ethics*: 'it is not characteristic of a great-souled person to harbor memories, especially of evils, but rather to overlook them'.[52] (2) It is necessary. Deleuze writes: 'the traces must not invade consciousness'.[53] The job of consciousness is to evaluate the present, incoming excitation in order to determine the appropriate response. If consciousness turns its focus, and begins to chew endlessly instead on traces, it can no longer do what it should be doing – the apparatus begins to break down. 'Let us suppose that there is a lapse in the faculty of forgetting: it is as if the wax of consciousness were hardened, excitation tends to get confused with its trace in the unconscious and overruns it. *Thus at the same time as reaction to traces becomes perceptible, reaction ceases to be acted.*'[54] When consciousness is incapacitated, when it is incapable of *acting* its reaction, there is a rupture, a breach in the apparatus. Once the organism is deprived of its capacity to act its reaction, the reaction manifests itself in the form of a conscious feeling of the reaction, an imagination of the reaction, in a word, *ressentiment*. 'We rediscover the definition of *ressentiment*: *ressentiment* is a reaction which simultaneously becomes perceptible and ceases to be acted.'[55] It '*ceases to be acted in order to become something felt (senti)*'.[56]

This is how reactive forces come to prevail over active forces within the individual. How then do reactive *types* eventually prevail over active *types*? By the same mechanism. Reactive forces must separate active forces from their capacities, and in so doing, turn active forces into reactive forces. Deleuze refers to this mechanism as 'the paralogism of *ressentiment*: *the fiction of a force separated from what it can do*. It is not sufficient for them to hold back from activity: they must also reverse the relation of forces, they must oppose themselves to active forces and represent themselves as superior.'[57] This presumed superiority stems from a primary negation. The paralogism develops in three moments: (1) the moment of causality; (2) the moment of substance; (3) the moment of reciprocal determination.

In the moment of causality, 'the same happening is posited first as cause and then once again as its effect'.[58] We say that 'lightning flashes', as though there were an entity, lightning, distinct from its flashing, when in fact the lightning *just is* the flashing. The doer *just is* the deed, according to Nietzsche. In the moment of causality, *ressentiment* imaginatively splits force into two components: force itself as cause, and manifestation of force as effect. In the second moment, the moment of substance, 'force is neutralized',[59] substantialised, assigned a quiddity or an essence, and projected into a substance, a substratum, a subject, 'free to manifest it or not'.[60] We are then left with an abstract notion of subjectivity who bears forces, and who is equally capable of either manifesting, or not, a particular force. On this model, every concrete subject is a token of this abstract type – *every* subject is equally capable of manifesting, or not, its forces. This is akin to what Heidegger in *Being and Time* calls the '"levelling down" [*Einebnung*] of all possibilities of Being' for Dasein,[61] in that it reduces all human beings to neutral beings who possess the same general forces in an abstract, potential state. The weak then become equally 'strong' with the strong. Put otherwise, the weak individual *can*, if it chooses to do so, *act* in the same manner that the so-called *strong* does. Likewise, the strong *could* choose *not* to act in the way that it does. In the third moment of the paralogism, the moment of reciprocal determination, 'the force, thus neutralized, is moralized'.[62] Once it has been divested of its necessity for manifestation, and cast into a seemingly neutral subject, the force is assigned a moral weight, and the subject is thereby conceived as having a moral determination: she is morally blameworthy if she allows her forces to manifest, and praiseworthy if she does not. 'It is therefore assumed that one and the same force is effectively held back in the virtuous lamb but given free rein in the evil bird of prey.'[63]

In the language of Kant, *ressentiment* engenders its own illusion, namely, freedom of the will. In this way, the servile come to assert their superiority over the noble. In positing the illusion of the *free will*, the weak create an evaluative criterion by which they are permitted to deem as *evil* the noble; the strong are evil because they actualise their forces though they are 'free' to not do so. The actualisation of their forces produces as its by-products the oppression and harm of the weak. This same evaluative criterion thereby gives to the weak his conviction that *he* himself is good, in so far as he is, by his own 'free' choice, *not* like the evil one. 'He has conceived of "the evil enemy," "*the evil one*," and this indeed as the basic concept, from which he now also thinks up, as reaction and counterpart, a "good one" – himself!',[64] and '"whoever is as little as possible a bird of prey but rather its opposite, a lamb, – isn't he good?"'[65] The Nietzschean slave is the slave, because he requires the master in order to affirm himself; the master is deemed *evil* – this is the first moment of negation. The slave is *not* like the master – this is the second moment of negation. Then comes the affirmation – 'therefore, I, the slave, am good'. The slave's *good* is the negation of *evil*, itself a negation; the slave's affirmation is in fact a double negation. The evil of the master is primary. Only in a secondary and negational way is the slave deemed good.

The distinction between noble and servile, according to Nietzsche, is that the primary moment of the noble is a moment of creation and affirmation.[66] The master, on Nietzsche's understanding, is the master because she first affirms herself as good. 'Out of this *pathos of distance* they first took for themselves the right to create values, to coin names for values.'[67] According to Deleuze, Nietzsche 'substitutes the pathos of differ- ence or distance (the differential element) for both the Kantian principle of universality and the principle of resemblance dear to the utilitarians.'[68] The master is the master because he affirms himself in his difference; he affirms his difference as the basis of his height, his superiority – difference, not negation. The *high* and the *low*, the *noble* and the *servile*, are, for Nietzsche, not bipolar, contradictory terms. They are not opposites: '*high and low, noble* and *base*, are not values but represent the differential ele- ment from which the value of values themselves derives'.[69] The difference is what gives the master the *right* to affirm himself as good, 'the noble one, who conceives the basic concept "good" in advance and spontaneously, starting from himself that is, and from there first creates for himself an idea of "bad"!'[70] As Deleuze puts it, 'In the master, everything positive is in the premises.'[71] Likewise, everything in the premises is positive. Only secondarily does the master assert its other as bad, but *this* negation is predicated upon a primary affirmation of difference. In Nietzsche's words, 'The reverse is the case with the noble manner of valuation: it acts and grows spontaneously, it seeks out its opposite only in order to say "yes" to itself still more gratefully and more jubilantly – its negative concept "low" "common" "bad" is only an after-birth.'[72]

What distinguishes Nietzsche's master-slave dialectic from Hegel's is that Hegel's *master* requires the slave in order to be master; Nietzsche's does not. The master's dependence upon the slave entails that Hegel's master is, in fact, a slave, according to Deleuze. This is representative of a larger trend of *ressentiment* running through the entirety of Hegel's work, according to Deleuze, and this is indicated by Hegel's characterisation of difference in terms of negation and contradiction. Above we saw that Deleuze defined *ressentiment* as the state in which reactive forces come to dominate over the active, such that any given reaction ceases to be acted and is instead merely felt. The being is incapacitated; it becomes incapable of acting and affirming on its own. It manifests in the morality of the slave, which cannot affirm itself as good without first negating the master's ethic as evil. To expand this principle, a system of thought that has as its primary motor negation is, for Deleuze, fundamentally incapable of being genuinely creative, it is always reactive. Just as the master cannot be thought without the slave, no positivity in Hegel's thinking is possible without a primary negativity; no affirmation without a primary negation. Hyppolite writes:

> This internal sublation is the genuine affirmation of the Absolute, the one which is no longer immediate; affirmation is negativity or the negation of the negation. Hegel's philosophy is therefore a philosophy of negation in a double sense. On the one hand, it deepens Spinoza's theme 'which is of infinite importance': *all determination is negation*; it apprehends the lack or insufficiency of what is presented as positive. On the other hand, it exhibits, at the very heart of this negation, a repetition of negation, a negation of the negation which alone constitutes authentic positivity.[73]

According to Hyppolite, Hegel cannot conceive the singularity of the being *except* in terms of negation. On Deleuze's view, conceived as negation, difference can only ever become a burden for the thinker. Even if it is eventually characterised as *affirmation*, it is so only in so far as it takes up within itself at the same time all that it denies:

> It may well be that two negations are not too many to produce a phantom of affirmation. But how would affirmation result from negation unless it conserved that which is denied? Accordingly, Nietzsche indicates the terrifying conservatism of such a conception. Affirmation is indeed produced, but in

order to say yes to all that is negative and negating, to all that *can be denied.* Thus Zarathustra's Ass says yes, but for him to affirm is to bear, to assume or shoulder a burden.[74]

Thus, according to Deleuze, Hegel's negational concept of difference is indicative of a nihilistic tendency of thought. 'Nihil *in "nihilism" means negation as quality of the will to power.*'[75] It is a thought of negation and death, as opposed to a philosophy of life. For Hegel, life discovers itself in and struggles constantly against death which is, in some sense, primary: 'This is why death is the beginning of the life of spirit, because, at the level of nature, the Absolute (substance) appears as life as well as death, and this cycle is endless. The singularity of sensible things, and of mortal living beings which are modes of the Absolute, present this Absolute in its annihilation.'[76] On the contrary, Nietzsche, according to Deleuze, 'emphasizes the fact that force has another force as its object. But it is important to see that forces enter into relations with other forces. Life struggles with *another kind* of life.'[77] Deleuze and Guattari's definition of philosophy from *What is Philosophy?* is well-known: 'philosophy is the art of forming, inventing, and fabricating concepts'.[78] Elsewhere Deleuze provides a definition or description of philosophy that is less well-known but which complements and completes the more famous of the two: 'Spinoza or Nietzsche are philosophers whose critical and destructive powers are without equal, but this power always springs from affirmation, from joy, from a cult of affirmation and joy, from the exigency of life against those who would mutilate and mortify it. For me, that is philosophy itself.'[79] Philosophy, according to Deleuze, is necessarily creative, and creativity is necessarily tied to affirmation and to life. As Claire Colebrook writes, Deleuze 'releases us from this subjection to systems and transcendence and does so through an affirmation of "life" '.[80] Fundamental to Deleuze's thinking is the conviction that, 'In its essence, difference is the object of affirmation or affirmation itself. In its essence, affirmation is itself difference.'[81] Thus, Hegel's difference, conceived in terms of negation, is representative for Deleuze of everything that philosophy opposes.

The collapse into identity

In *Difference and Repetition*, Deleuze lays out his mature criticisms of Hegel's concept of difference. In addition to the incorporation of the two previous criticisms, a third one emerges. Deleuze will here distinguish between two modes of representation: *organic* and *orgiastic.* Of organic representation, he writes, 'Difference is "mediated" to the extent that it is subjected to the fourfold root of identity, analogy, opposition, and resemblance. On the basis of a first impression (difference is evil), it is proposed to "save" difference by representing it, and to represent it by relating it to the requirements of the concept in general.'[82] The *fourfold root* of organic representation unfolds in: (1) identity in the form of the undetermined concept (the concept 'human' is identical to, or *just is*, what it is to be human); (2) analogy, in the relation between ultimate determinable concepts ('There are many senses in which a thing may be said to "be" '[83]); (3) opposition in the relations between determinations in the concept itself ('corporeal' and 'incorporeal' are determinations of 'substance'); (4) resemblance in the determined object of the concept itself (particulars organised under a concept *resemble* each other). *Organic* representation, as found in Aristotle, 'has form as its principle and the finite as its element'.[84] It makes finite, delimits, and demarcates, breaking Being into more comprehensible bits. Subordinating things to universals, Aristotle's ontology focuses on wholes, categories, parts, sub-categories, and sub-parts.

In Hegel, Deleuze sees an example of what he calls 'orgiastic representation',[85] evoking the Dionysian imagery of revelry, intoxication, and excess. Hegel himself says of 'the True' that it is 'the Bacchanalian revel in which no member is not drunk'.[86] Unlike organic representation, orgiastic representation posits 'within itself the limits of the organized; tumult, restlessness, and passion underneath apparent calm. It rediscovers monstrosity.'[87] Replacing Aristotle's finite concept (form) as the principle is the concept of the Whole. To think the whole requires a grappling with 'determination in all its metamorphoses'.[88] But in order to think the oppositional relations of determination, the differences must not be purely arbitrary or relative. This is why the infinite is, according to Deleuze, the principal of selection in Hegel's thought – it eliminates the arbitrariness of the differential relation. 'It is the infinite which renders determination conceivable and selectable.'[89] In place of relative difference, Hegel posits the *absolute* difference of the infinite. The infinite enters Hegel's notion of difference in the form of contradiction. The telos of determination is the space of infinity between the determination and its opposite.

With contradiction, the opposition of self and other is pushed to the point of infinite distance. As Deleuze writes, this use of the infinite 'entails the identity of contraries, or makes the contrary of the Other a contrary of the Self'.[90] As stated, for Hegel, difference is always already *implicitly contradiction*. The *telos* of difference is the infinite extension of that difference, in the form of contradiction. The one finds its identity, its *essence*, in the negation of its other. But because its identity is wholly determined by what it is not, the 'what it is not' is fundamental to its own identity.

The self reflects upon the self by reflecting upon the other, which Hegel characterises as '*Pure* self-recognition in absolute otherness'.[91] With this, the negation of the contradiction is attained, and the contradiction is overcome. The very notion of difference as contradiction requires at the same time the overcoming and resolution of the contradiction, and hence of difference itself, in the form of the *Aufhebung*, in which the difference is subordinated to a higher comprehension. Difference is cancelled out precisely at the moment it is reached, and moreover, its *cancellation* is the primary *telos* of its positing – to which Hegel refers as 'self-*restoring* sameness',[92] which is the 'ground and soil of Science or *knowledge in general*'.[93] The negative is the greatest difference, but is also, by design, the cancellation of difference. For Deleuze then, contradiction still ultimately subordinates difference to identity.

Conclusion

Deleuze's thinking, from beginning to end, is marked with a thorough distaste for what he understands as Hegelianism. This distaste is specifically directed against the Hegelian understanding of difference as negation and contradiction. For Deleuze, difference conceived as contradiction is *less profound* than difference itself. Things must first differ in order to oppose or contradict one another, making difference more basic and more fundamental: 'It is not difference which presupposes opposition but opposition which presupposes difference.'[94] Moreover, to conceive of difference as contradiction from all that the thing is *not*, what Kant called 'complete determination', is to define the self in purely negative terms. This, for Deleuze, is indicative of a nihilistic tendency of thought. To base a philosophy on the 'tremendous power of the negative'[95] is to admit the inability to think being in positive, affirmative terms – reaching affirmation only through a double negation. Finally, in attaining the status of contradiction – which, we remind ourselves, *every* difference *is* 'implicitly' according to Hegel – we reach also the negation and sublation of that contradiction, the cancellation of that difference, via the *Aufhebung*. The telos of difference is contradiction, and the telos of contradiction is the cancellation of that difference. Hegel's *Aufhebung* is shot through with the presuppositions of identity, a nihilistic view of life, and the inability to truly grasp the nature of the thing. 'It is said that difference is negativity, that it extends or must extend to the point of contradiction once it is taken to the limit. This is true only to the extent that difference is already placed on a path or along a thread laid out by identity.'[96] Though Deleuze never writes a protracted engagement with the thinking of Hegel, his criticisms of Hegel are subtle, nuanced, varied, and woven throughout multiple texts over many years. Hence, I cannot agree with Catherine Malabou's assessment that 'The Deleuzian discourse which sees in Hegel's dialectics a principle of repetition that does not produce difference, is itself, from one end of his work to the other, univalent and univocal.'[97]

Let us now turn to a comparison and contrast of the ways in which Derrida and Deleuze engage with Hegel's *Aufhebung*. As we have seen, both Derrida and Deleuze reject the Hegelian *Aufhebung* as a model of difference. Moreover, both view it as the *cancellation* of the very difference that it purports to have discovered in thought. Nevertheless, Derrida and Deleuze *differ* with respect to their *reasons* for viewing it in this way. For Derrida, the crucial problem in the Hegelian *Aufhebung* is that the contradiction is ultimately resolved; for Deleuze, the problem is that Hegel thinks that difference must be thought as contradiction at all. We shall pursue this contrast through a discussion of the ways in which Hegel, Derrida, and Deleuze understand the concept of force.

Notes

1. *Dialogues*, 14.
2. *N*, 6.
3. *NP*, 8.
4. *DR*, xix.
5. Indeed, the ascription of 'anti-Hegelian' as it applies to Deleuze is complicated. In recent years, more work has been undertaken to disrupt this story. One is Henry Somers-Hall, *Hegel, Deleuze, and the Critique of Representation*. Another is a collection edited by Karen Houle and Jim Vernon, *Hegel and Deleuze: Together Again for the First Time*. See also Daniel W. Smith, 'Deleuze, Hegel, and the Post-Kantian Tradition', in his *Essays on Deleuze*, 59–71. Here Smith persuasively argues that Deleuze's relation to Hegel should not be carelessly characterised as anti-dialectical, when in fact one of Deleuze's central aims is to formulate a dialectics of difference rather than one of negation and contradiction; he thus situates Deleuze's anti-Hegelianism in the context of Deleuze's larger project, as one of reconceiving the post-Kantian tradition along the lines of critiques offered by Salomon Maimon.
6. Malabou, 'Who's Afraid of Hegelian Wolves?', in Patton (ed.), *Deleuze: A Critical Reader*, 116. For Deleuze's discussion of the plane of immanence, see *WP*, specifically chapters 1 and 2.
7. *DI*, 144.
8. *N*, 6.
9. Malabou, 'Who's Afraid of Hegelian Wolves?', in Patton (ed.), *Deleuze: A Critical Reader*, 120.
10. For an extended discussion of this relation, see Hughes, *Deleuze and the Genesis of Representation*. See also Hughes, *Deleuze's* Difference and Repetition: *A Reader's Guide*.
11. For 'Plato and the Simulacrum', see *LS*, 253–66.
12. Malabou, 'Who's Afraid of Hegelian Wolves?', in Patton (ed.), *Deleuze: A Critical Reader*, 120.
13. Ibid., 115.

14. *NP*, 195.
15. *PH*, 19.
16. *LE*, 105.
17. *GL*, 431–2.
18. Deleuze, *Empiricism and Subjectivity*, 105.
19. *LE*, 115.
20. *LE*, 116.
21. *LE*, 116.
22. *GL*, 423.
23. *PH*, 9–10.
24. *LE*, 118.
25. *LE*, 3
26. *LE*, 118
27. *LE*, 119.
28. *GL*, 431–2.
29. *DI*, 18.
30. Sauvagnargues, 'Hegel and Deleuze: Difference or Contradiction?', in Houle and Vernon (eds), *Hegel and Deleuze*, 50.
31. *DI*, 42.
32. *LE*, 119.
33. *DI*, 43.
34. *DI*, 18.
35. *LE*, 10.
36. *LE*, 10.
37. *LE*, 10–11.
38. *LE*, 12.
39. This will be the subject matter of Chapters 6 and 7, how difference in itself functions for Deleuze, as opposed to *différance* for Derrida.
40. Hughes, *Deleuze's* Difference and Repetition*: A Reader's Guide*, 48.
41. *DR*, 52.
42. *NP*, 147.
43. *GM*, 47.
44. *NP*, 111.
45. *NP*, 111.
46. *NP*, 114.
47. *GM*, 35.
48. *NP*, 112.
49. *NP*, 112.
50. *NP*, 112–13.
51. *NP*, 112.
52. Aristotle, *Nicomachean Ethics*, IV.3.
53. *NP*, 113.
54. *NP*, 114.
55. *NP*, 114.
56. *NP*, 111.
57. *NP*, 123.
58. *GM*, 25
59. *NP*, 123.
60. *NP*, 123.
61. Heidegger, *Being and Time*, 165.
62. *NP*, 124.
63. *NP*, 123.
64. *GM*, 21.
65. *GM*, 25.

66. This must not be overlooked. What Nietzsche describes as 'master' and 'slave' morality has nothing, essentially, to do with de facto masters and slaves. Rather, it has to do with the way in which individuals and types comport themselves toward life and the cosmos. The primary question is: does one's fundamental mode of comportment derive from a position of self-mastery, or from a position of psychic, emotional, physiological subservience. De facto slaves – Epictetus, for instance – are absolutely capable of being Nietzschean masters; while *most* of today's politicians, Wall Street traders, and CEOs (our 'masters') would incontestably be Nietzschean 'slaves'.
67. *GM*, 10.
68. *NP*, 2.
69. *NP*, 2.
70. *GM*, 21.
71. *NP*, 120.
72. *GM*, 19.
73. *LE*, 106.
74. *DR*, 53.
75. *NP*, 147.
76. *LE*, 15.
77. *NP*, 8.
78. *WP*, 2.
79. *DI*, 144.
80. Colebrook, *Deleuze and the Meaning of Life*, 26.
81. *DR*, 52.
82. *DR*, 29.
83. Aristotle, *Metaphysics*, IV.2.
84. *DR*, 43.
85. *DR*, 42.
86. *PH*, 27.
87. *DR*, 42.
88. *DR*, 42.
89. *DR*, 43.
90. *DR*, 44.
91. *PH*, 14.
92. *PH*, 10.
93. *PH*, 14.
94. *DR*, 51.
95. *PH*, 19.
96. *DR*, 49–50.
97. Malabou, 'Who's Afraid of Hegelian Wolves?', in Patton (ed.), *Deleuze: A Critical Reader*, 115.

Chapter 5

The Tremendous Power of the Negative

We must now look at Derrida and Deleuze side by side as they relate to the Hegelian conception of difference. Deconstruction, as we have characterised it, lives and breathes in the tension between two recent, fundamental, and inescapable moments in the history of Western thought: (1) Hegel's closure of Western metaphysics; and (2) Heidegger's critique of ontotheology. Heidegger revealed the ontotheological determination of Being as presence lying at the heart of all metaphysical thinking up to and including Hegel. But all efforts to *escape* the system, including Heidegger's, have failed and must always fail because they inevitably employ the language, logic, presuppositions, and concepts of the tradition in order to execute thought against the system. In using these concepts, they affirm the very system from which they seek escape. '[A]ll anti-Hegelian thinkers', we recall, are 'very close to Hegel', the more so at precisely the moments they seem most radically opposed.[1]

Deconstruction does not therefore seek a radical escape from the system, but rather, to locate and agitate the moments of imbalance within the system, whereby its desired completion disrupts itself. For this reason, deconstruction operates precisely *within* and at the limits of the system of Western thought, and makes absolutely no pretensions to the contrary. In Derrida's words: 'The movements of deconstruction do not destroy structures from the outside. They are not possible and effective, nor can they take accurate aim, except by inhabiting those structures. Inhabiting them *in a certain way*, because one always inhabits, and all the more when one does not suspect it.'[2] According to Derrida, this strategic inhabitation is to be the task of the philosopher for the foreseeable future: 'The movement of this schema will only be able, for the moment and for a long time, to work over from within, from a certain inside, the language of metaphysics.'[3]

Like Heidegger (and not *unlike* Deleuze), Derrida understands Hegel's *Aufhebung* in terms of the ontotheological emphasis on presence – the *Aufhebung* raises up (*relever*) the two contradictory terms into a higher unity, resolving the difference that subsists between them. As Deleuze says, 'Of all the senses of *Aufheben*, none is more important than that of "raise up." '[4] This *raising up* into 'the completely developed certainty of self-knowing knowledge',[5] is the ontotheological moment of presence in Hegel's discourse.

Deleuze as well critiques Hegel's notion of the *Aufhebung* for the fact that it cancels difference at the precise moment at which it is attained. Deleuze and Derrida are no doubt using different terminology to formulate their critiques – Deleuze does not speak in terms of 'ontotheology' or 'the metaphysics of presence', and Derrida does not speak in the language of *ressentiment*. Nevertheless, on at least this one criticism, that Hegel's *Aufhebung* cancels difference, the two thinkers seem to concur: with this, it would appear as though we have reached a point of commonality rather than one of distinction. Yet it is precisely at this juncture that the distinction between the two becomes most salient – not in this problem itself, but in the *meaning* of this problem.

On Deleuze's approach, the cancellation of difference is the third and final criticism in the group of three that Deleuze poses to Hegel. The three criticisms that Deleuze levels against Hegel are ultimately utilised in the service of the larger, overall critical view that negation, difference conceived as a *not*, is a derivative or deficient mode of difference through and through. It is nihilistic, less profound than difference itself, and oriented from start to finish by the presuppositions of representation and identity. That it ultimately cancels difference in the subsumption under a higher unity is one aspect of this problem, but not the entirety of it. We cannot, however, say the same where Derrida is concerned.

We must bear in mind that, although Derrida expresses a 'nearly total affinity' with Deleuze, nevertheless, on the concept of *différance*, he is, by his own explicit admission, not far from Hegel:

> You asked me when the word *différance* or the concept of *différance* took its place within metaphysics. I would be tempted to say: with Hegel, and it is not by chance that it is precisely the interest which Hegel took in the thought of *différance*, at the moment when philosophy was closing itself, completing itself, or, as we say, accomplishing itself, which obliges us today to connect the thought of the end of metaphysics and the thought of *différance*. It is not by chance that Hegel is fundamentally the one who has been the most systematically attentive within metaphysics to difference. And perhaps – but this is a question of reading – there is a certain irreducibility of *différance* in his text. That would be my provisional response to your last question.[6]

We might wonder whether a response that is, in Derrida's own words, 'provisional', ought to be taken as decisive in the matter. Nevertheless, passages such as this are not difficult to find in Derrida's published writings. In *Of Grammatology*, immediately after offering a detailed characterisation of deconstruction, Derrida writes:

> Hegel was already caught up in this game. *On the one hand*, he undoubtedly *summed up* the entire philosophy of the logos. He determined ontology as absolute logic; he assembled all the delimitations of philosophy as presence; he assigned to presence the eschatology of parousia, of the self-proximity of infinite subjectivity . . . Yet, all that Hegel thought within this horizon, all, that is, except eschatology, may be reread as a meditation on writing. Hegel is *also* the thinker of irreducible difference . . . the last philosopher of the book and the first thinker of writing.[7]

In this passage, we see Derrida reiterating his view that Hegel's system marks the closure of Western metaphysics, while at the same time arguing that, with the exception of the teleological components of Hegel's thought, Hegel is, one and a half centuries prior to Derrida, the thinker of grammatology and of 'irreducible difference'. Elsewhere, Derrida writes, 'Pure difference is not absolutely different (from nondifference). Hegel's critique of the concept of pure difference is for us here, doubtless, the most uncircumventable theme. Hegel thought absolute difference, and showed that it can only be pure by being impure.'[8] Hegel's difference is, according to Derrida, very close to *différance*.

For Deleuze, on the other hand, Hegel's concept of difference is so abhorrent that he labels Hegel the 'traitor' of philosophy, whose task is to '"burden" life, to overwhelm it with every burden, to reconcile life with the State and religion, to inscribe death in life – the monstrous enterprise to submit life to negativity, the enterprise of *ressentiment* and unhappy consciousness'.[9] Difference as negation and contradiction is such a *treasonous* concept that Deleuze forgoes any extended engagement with Hegel precisely because Hegel's thinking is so anathema to affirmation that there is nothing for Deleuze to affirm, and critique without affirmation is merely an exercise of *ressentiment*, according to Deleuze. Clearly, on this point, Derrida and Deleuze could not be further apart. How, then, are we to make sense of these paradoxically close yet simultaneously distant readings of Hegel? Let us investigate a bit more closely, and in so doing discuss in more detail the aforementioned imbalances targeted by deconstruction.

Force, understanding, and thought[10]

To do so requires that we look at what Derrida and Deleuze would understand as Hegel's mischaracterisation of 'force'.[11] To begin, let us look to
the definitions of force provided by Hegel, Derrida, and Deleuze:

> Hegel: 'In other words, the "matters" posited as independent directly pass
> over into their unity, and their unity directly unfolds its diversity, and this
> once again reduces itself to unity. But this movement is what is called
> *Force*.'[12]
> Derrida: 'The meaning of meaning is Apollonian by virtue of everything in
> it that can be seen . . . Force is the other of language without which language
> would not be what it is.'[13]
> Deleuze: 'Difference in quantity is the essence of force and of the relation
> of force to force.'[14]

Hegel's definition of force is found in the final chapter of the 'Consciousness'
section of the *Phenomenology of Spirit*, titled 'Force and the Understanding'.
Jean Hyppolite famously characterises Hegel's *Phenomenology* as 'the itin-
erary of the *soul* which rises to *spirit* through the intermediary of *consciousness*', casting it in the tradition of the '*Bildungsromanen* of the time'.[15] The
text is laid out in three major sections: (1) Consciousness (of 'external'
objects); (2) Self-Consciousness; and (3) an untitled section, constituting
almost three quarters of the text, consisting of the four subsections of
(a) Reason (b) Spirit (c) Religion, and (d) Absolute Knowing. To make
sense of the role of force in Hegel's concept of understanding, we should
first briefly address the first two chapters of the 'Consciousness' section,
respectively, 'Sense-Certainty' and 'Perception'.

The knowledge that pertains to sense-certainty is, Hegel writes, 'a
knowledge of the immediate or of what simply *is*'.[16] Sense-certainty would
wish to grasp the purity of the 'this' in the immediate presence of the 'here'
and 'now'. However, as Hegel notes, echoing the beautiful analyses of time
in St Augustine's *Confessions*, 'The Now is pointed to, *this* Now. "Now";
it has already ceased to be in the act of pointing to it.'[17] We can only ever
identify the *now* as the *has been*. In the mere act of *pointing* toward the
present, it has already become the past. But, what *has been*, we might note,
is no more; it now *lacks* being, according to Hegel. So the 'now' that we
have identified as the 'this' of our sense-certainty by our pointing it out,
we also acknowledge *lacks being*. In this recognition, we therefore 'negate
the negation of the "Now", and thus return to the first assertion, that
the "*Now*" *is*'.[18] The 'now' that truly *is*, however, is not *this* or *that* 'now',
but the abstract, 'absolute plurality of Nows'.[19] The truth of the now,
therefore, is that it is a universal. This highlights the broader sense of the

inadequacy of sense-certainty, according to Hegel: sense-certainty would wish to grasp the pure individuality of the 'this', but the moment that one wishes to *say* 'this', one is necessarily employing universals. All of the terms whereby we would wish to express absolute singularity – 'I', 'This', 'Here' – can only be understood, like the 'Now', as absolute pluralities of all 'I's', all 'thises', and all 'heres'. Likewise, sense-certainty would wish to grasp the 'this' in its simple immediacy, but 'in sense-certainty, pure being at once splits up into what we have called the two "Thises", one "This" as "I", and the other "This" as object'.[20] Its desired immediacy, in other words, dissolves into mediation.

In passing from the desire to apprehend the 'this' to the affirmation of the universal, knowledge moves from sense-certainty to what Hegel calls 'perception'. The purportedly *immediate* object of sense-certainty is here unfolded in the light of mediation – the 'I' and the 'this' complicate into 'the movement of pointing-out or the *act of perceiving*' and 'the same movement as a simple event or the *object perceived*'.[21] In this relation, the object shows itself as the essential moment, in so far as knowledge is still, at this point in the *Phenomenology*, anchored in the external world. The constitutive significance of the 'I' has not yet been made manifest, and will not be so until it reaches the stage of the understanding.

The object, in accordance with perception's principle of the universal, reveals itself no longer as the simple 'this', but as the *'thing with many properties'*,[22] each cognised as logically independent of the others. Hegel's exemplar, the grain of salt, is white, and cubical, and tart, and has a specific weight. But to each of these properties belongs a specificity, apart from the rest. The white is *not* the cubical, is *not* the tart, is *not* the weight, etc., 'for only perception contains negation, that is, difference or manifoldness, within its own essence'.[23]

The cognition of the object of perception can focus either on the *properties* that characterise the thing, or on the *thing* that unites the properties, as either the 'also' or the 'one'. On the one hand, qua universals, the properties of the thing are indifferent to each other. Thought on their own, 'white' is white, 'tart' is tart, 'cubical' is cubical, etc., but each of these properties is logically independent of, and hence, essentially indifferent to, the rest. The tartness does not affect the whiteness of the salt. They 'interpenetrate, but without *coming into contact* with one another'.[24] This interpenetration has the character of an 'also', grounded loosely in the universality of 'thinghood', with the thinghood being nothing more than the abstract medium holding together the properties. 'This salt is a simple Here, and at the same time manifold; it is white and *also* tart, *also* cubical in shape, of a specific gravity, etc.'[25] Moreover, as 'properties strictly speaking' require the 'addition of a further determination'[26] (to be a property means to be a property *of* a specific thing), they are not, strictly speaking, properties at all, but what Hegel calls 'determinacies'[27] or 'matters'.[28]

On the other hand, determination requires the distinction from or the negation of everything that one is not, as we have seen. *Omnis determinatio est negatio.*[29] The 'determinacies' are not therefore, strictly speaking, determinacies, unless they '*differentiate* themselves from one another, and *relate* themselves *to others* as to their opposites'.[30] The whiteness is *not* the tart, it is *not* the cubical, etc. The being of the medium that holds them together cannot, in this moment, be thought of as merely the abstract universality of the 'also', for if it were, the properties, in so far as each negates and opposes the others, would disband, and the 'thinghood' whereby they are held together would dissolve. The medium must therefore assert its essential unity, its own essential determinateness, which entails its own type of negation, 'a *One* as well, a unity which *excludes* an other. The One is the *moment of negation*.'[31]

The object, therefore, is understood as a dynamic relation of the moments of the 'also' and of the 'one', 'the point of singular individuality in the medium of subsistence radiating forth into plurality'.[32] However, given that the 'true' in the mode of perception lies on the side of the *object*, as opposed to the side of consciousness, it would appear that there must be a fact of the matter about *which* of these two moments essentially defines the object, and 'it can happen that consciousness apprehends the object incorrectly and deceives itself'.[33] Consciousness, therefore, tries in vain to isolate the would-be *essential* moment of the two, 'but in each single moment it is conscious only of this *one determinateness* as the truth, and then in turn of the opposite one'.[34] The problem resides in the failure of consciousness to affirm its own constitutive role in cognition, a problem that will be remedied in the mode of understanding.

In transitioning from the mode of perception to the mode of understanding, thought encounters what Hegel calls the 'unconditioned universal'.[35] 'Unconditioned' in this context is an English rendering of the German word '*unbedingt*', literally, 'un-thing-ed'. Hyppolite notes that 'this universal is the concept which combines in it the contradictory moments that perceiving consciousness posited alternately in the subject and in the object: the moment of indifferent thingness *expressing* itself in a multitude of subsisting differences'.[36] The thought of the unconditioned universal *combines* these contradictory moments of the 'one' and the 'also' in the abstract sense of the 'object', but not yet in accordance with the explicit unity of these two moments. In Hegel's words, 'consciousness has not yet grasped the Notion of the unconditioned as *Notion*'.[37] Hegel's sense of the Notion, we may think of as 'thought in motion': 'Through this movement the pure thoughts become *Notions*, and are only now what they are in truth, self-movements, circles, spiritual essences, which is what their substance is.'[38]

To rise to the recognition of the unity of the contradictory moments in the unconditioned universal therefore requires the insertion of *movement* into the object; consciousness must see its own movements reflected into the object itself, recognising that 'what is posited' of these contradictory moments is 'only their transition into one another'.[39] Consciousness thereby affirms its own constitutive role in the knowledge of the object. As Hegel writes, 'this movement is what is called *Force*'.[40]

Hegel treats the concept of force in terms that are first singular and then dual. Initially he conceives of force in terms of the distinction between 'Force *proper*' and the '*expression* of Force'.[41] Force proper is the movement in thought to the unity of the 'one', while the expression of force is the movement to the diversity of the 'also'. But we must note that 'the Force which is driven back into itself *must* express itself; and secondly, it is still Force remaining *within itself* in the expression, just as much as it is expression in this self-containedness'.[42] Expression is intrinsic to the nature of force, even within the simplicity of force proper, just as, even in the mode of *expression*, the nature of force proper abides.

However, the very fact that there is a difference between force proper and force as expression indicates an independence of these two, and this independence is conceived by Hegel as the dual relationality of not one, but *two* forces. But this does not compromise the point that each is the other's reflection. As Hyppolite says, 'their interplay reveals their interdependence',[43] and so in this sense their *independence* must be balanced by this essential interdependence. 'Here, these two sides are moments of Force; they are just as much in a unity, as this unity, which appears as the middle term over against the independent extremes, is a perpetual diremption of itself into just these extremes which exist only through this process.'[44] Force, thus conceived, is the *unity* of these two moments, but it is just as well the independent moments themselves, each conceived now as *forces* in their own right. Hegel conceives the relationality between the two as one of 'solicitation'.

As force proper is *essentially* force as expression, it is force as expression that solicits, or calls forth, the expression of force proper. Reciprocally, given that it is in the nature of force as expression to summon forth from its self-containedness force proper, force as expression is in turn solicited by force proper. 'The interplay of the two Forces thus consists in their being determined as mutually opposed, in their being for one another in this determination, and in the absolute, immediate alternation of the determinations.'[45] In positing the essential duality and reciprocity of all relationships of force, Hegel is here echoing Kant: 'Thus, without repulsive forces, and by mere approach, all parts of matter would approach one another without hindrance . . . until no distance existed between them; that is, they would coalesce in a mathematical point, and the space would be empty . . . Matter is accordingly impossible by mere attractive forces, without repulsive.'[46] As Hyppolite writes, 'Each force, then, presupposes another force and is presupposed by it.'[47] Regarding each of these determinations, Hegel writes that 'their being has really the significance of a sheer *vanishing*',[48] in so far as the *being* of each is to solicit and give way to the other.

It is not difficult to recognise, within this description of Hegel's conception of force, the basic structure of the *Aufhebung* itself. What we see is a germinal moment (though even in the germinal the end is already in play), called into relation by its 'other', which is already presupposed by the 'one'. Both of these moments are the logical and ontological reflections of each other; and we see this ongoing dual and reciprocal solicitation maintained within the dynamism of a vital and mobile unity. We can push this even further, in that 'these moments are not divided into two independent extremes offering each other only an opposite extreme: their essence rather consists simply and solely in this, that each *is* solely through the other, and what each thus is it immediately no longer is, since it *is* the other'.[49] Each is therefore the *negative* of the other: 'This play of Forces is consequently the developed negative.'[50] Indeed our explication of force began with the one (force proper), gave way to the *other* (force as expression), and united both within the reciprocally oscillating, dialectical movement (force as the 'whole'[51]). It is little wonder, then, that at precisely the moment that Hegel introduces his concept of Force, he characterises the interpenetration of each of the moments using a form of the German word *Aufhebung*.[52]

The structure and operation of the *Aufhebung*, therefore, is predicated upon a play of forces. These forces subsist in a purely oppositional, which is to say, *negative*, relationship. Each *is* solely through its other, each is the reflection of the other, each is the *negative* of the other. In so far as they are, as we have seen, 'mutually opposed',[53] they solicit each other with equal strength – put otherwise, they are equal forces, and it is their reciprocal, symmetrical interdependence that maintains the dynamic homeostasis of the whole, which amounts to what both Derrida and Deleuze characterise as the cancellation of difference in Hegel's thought. With that, let us now turn back to Deleuze and Derrida because, to repeat what was said at the beginning of this chapter, the distinction between Derrida and Deleuze lies not in the problem itself, but in the meaning of the problem.

Deleuze and Derrida on force

As we have seen, both Derrida and Deleuze critique Hegel's *Aufhebung* on the point that it cancels difference, raising it up and subordinating it beneath the auspices of a higher unity or identity. Now that we have analysed Hegelian force, we can also see exactly where this cancellation of difference goes wrong. Both Derrida and Deleuze would agree with Hegel on the broad point that the play of forces is the constitutive and genetic condition of thinking. As we saw with Derrida, 'Force is the other of language without which language would not be what it is.'[54] Elsewhere, 'We no longer know therefore whether what we call the old names of force and *différance*, is not more "ancient" than the "originary."'[55] Likewise, Deleuze writes, 'What becomes established with the new is precisely not the new. For the new – in other words, difference – calls forth forces in thought which are not the forces of recognition, today or tomorrow, but the powers of a completely other model, from an unrecognized and unrecognizable *terra incognita*.'[56] But for both Derrida and Deleuze, Hegel's key misunderstanding of the nature of force lies in his assumption, following Kant, that every force is essentially counterbalanced by an equal and opposite force. The *Aufhebung* is predicated upon a symmetrical, reciprocal independence and interdependence of two 'mutually opposed' forces. The nature of force, according to both Derrida and Deleuze, rests not in *equality*, but in difference in *quantity*: 'There would be no force in general without the difference between forces; and here the difference of quantity counts more than the content of the quantity, more than absolute size itself.'[57] At precisely this point in the '*Différance*' essay, Derrida also cites Deleuze as a kindred thinker and inspiration: '*Quantity itself is therefore inseparable from difference in quantity.* Difference in quantity is the essence of force and of the relation of force to force. To dream of two equal forces, even if they are said to be of opposite senses is a coarse and approximate dream, a statistical dream in which the living is submerged but which chemistry dispels.'[58] The *Aufhebung* is misguided, according to both Derrida and Deleuze, because it cancels difference, and it cancels difference because it assumes that forces in play with each other are of equal magnitude. Forces, according to Derrida and Deleuze, are *never* equal. As Deleuze writes, 'All force is appropriation, domination, exploitation of a quantity of reality.'[59] Yet again, it appears that we have reached a point of 'nearly total affinity' between these two philosophers. But it is precisely at this point that the difference between the two becomes salient.

Derrida provides many denotative formulations for *différance* throughout his writings, but one of the most explicit is found in the collection of interviews titled *Positions*: 'If there were a definition of *différance*, it would be precisely the limit, the interruption, the destruction of the Hegelian *relève wherever* it operates.'[60] This is not surprising, given everything that we have said about Derrida's interpretation of Hegel's significance in the tradition, as well as his disagreement with Hegel over the nature of force. But again, the important point is not the *destruction itself*, but *why* and *how*.

> I have attempted to distinguish *différance* . . . from Hegelian difference, and have done so precisely at the point at which Hegel, in the greater *Logic*, determines difference as contradiction *only in order* [my emphasis] to resolve it, to interiorize it, to lift it up . . . into the self-presence of an onto-theological or onto-teleological synthesis . . . this conflictuality of *différance* . . . can never be totally resolved.[61]

There is no point at which the philosophical difference between Derrida and Deleuze is more evident than this. Deleuze rejects Hegel's notion of difference *because* it is negational and oppositional – difference, for Hegel, is a *not*. For Derrida, on the other hand, Hegel's notion of difference is *insufficiently* negative; it is *not negative enough*, precisely because it *cancels* the opposition. As Judith Butler writes, for Derrida, '*Aufhebung* is nothing other than a strategy of concealment, not the incorporation of difference into identity, but the denial of difference for the sake of positing a fictive identity.'[62] Contradiction and conflictuality – this cannot be overstated – are precisely what are engendered or exposed by the operation of *différance*, and this conflictuality, this oppositional nature, is irreducible and cannot be overcome. Derrida is repeatedly explicit on this point:

> Thus, *différance* is the name we might give to the 'active,' moving *discord* [my emphasis] of different forces, and of differences of forces, that Nietzsche sets up against the entire system of metaphysical grammar, wherever this system governs culture, philosophy, and science.[63]

> Now, wherever, and in the extent to which, the motif of contradiction functions effectively, in a textual work, outside speculative dialectics, and taking into account a new problematic of meaning . . . I agree.[64]

> But as for the kernel, or rather the interval which constitutes the concept and the effects of contradiction (*différance* and conflict, etc.), what I have written seems to me entirely explicit.[65]

> *Scarpetta*: . . . Does not this practice of shaking, of excess, of destruction seem to you to derive from a logic of contradiction, released from its speculative investments?
> *Derrida*: Yes, why not? Provided that one determines the concept of contradiction with the necessary critical precautions, and by elucidating its relationship or non-relationship to Hegel's *Logic*.[66]

For Derrida, Hegel is *right* in his understanding of difference as oppositional and conflictual. Indeed, in *Of Grammatology*, he explicitly characterises difference as opposition.[67] Hegel is *wrong*, however, in his conviction that these oppositional poles counterbalance each other with equal force, thereby sustaining each other in a dynamic homeostasis that, in effect, *cancels* the difference.

It is in this way that Hegel is, for Derrida, both 'the last philosopher of the book and the first thinker of writing'.[68] For Derrida, Hegel, aside from his misconception on the essential reciprocity of force, stands right on the cusp of *différance*. This is precisely why, as we noted at the outset of this chapter, deconstruction seeks not a radical escape from the system of Western thought, but rather to occupy and agitate the moments of imbalance within the system. These imbalances are found in the interactions between the binary groupings that categorise Western thought, and they are bound up with Derrida's insight that 'in a classical philosophical opposition we are not dealing with the peaceful coexistence of a *vis-à-vis*, but rather with a violent hierarchy. One of the two terms governs the other (axiologically, logically, etc.), or has the upper hand.'[69] One, in other words, operates with *more force* than the other. In order to effectively synthesise its oppositions and consummate its system, the logic of the history of Western metaphysics, as consummated by Hegel, demands that these imbalances are wilfully suppressed and masked, even forgotten, in a countervailing balancing act of the forces of sense whereby they are constituted. The task of deconstruction is to expose these hidden imbalances, to 'shape or shift the play of presence or absence',[70] in order to provoke disruption and dislocate the fulcrum around which they turn, opening new strategies for thinking what was hitherto impossible. It also institutes essential slippages of force whereby the voices of the subaltern and the oppressed may be lit up, opened, and empowered. Hence, at precisely the moments when the security of their bipolarities appears complete, deconstruction uses 'the strengths of the field to turn its own stratagems against it, producing a force of dislocation that spreads itself throughout the entire system, fissuring it in every direction and thoroughly *delimiting* it'.[71] The effect of this fissuring is characterised in stark terms in the endnotes to 'Cogito and the History of Madness':

> It is necessary, and it is perhaps time to come back to the ahistorical in a sense radically opposed to that of classical philosophy: not to misconstrue negativity, but this time to affirm it – silently. It is negativity and not positive truth that is the nonhistorical capital of history. In question then would be a *negativity so negative* [my emphasis] that it could not even be called such any longer. Negativity has always been determined by dialectics – that is to say, by metaphysics – as *work* in the service of the constitution of meaning.

To affirm negativity in silence is to gain access to a nonclassical type of dissociation between thought and language.[72]

This *negativity* so negative is described in more detail elsewhere:

> The blind spot of Hegelianism, *around* which can be organized the representation of meaning, is the *point* at which destruction, suppression, death and sacrifice constitute so irreversible an expenditure, so radical a negativity – here we would have to say an expenditure and a negativity *without reserve* – that they can no longer be determined as negativity in a process or a system. In discourse (the unity of process and system), negativity is always the underside and accomplice of positivity . . . To go 'to the end' both of 'absolute rending' and of the negative without 'measure,' without reserve, is not progressively to pursue *logic* to the point at which, *within discourse*, the *Aufhebung* (discourse itself) makes logic collaborate with the constitution and interiorizing memory of meaning, with *Erinnerung*. On the contrary, it is convulsively to tear apart the negative side, that which makes it the reassuring *other* surface of the positive; and it is to exhibit within the negative, in an instant, that which can no longer be called negative. And can no longer be called negative precisely because it has no reserved underside, because it can no longer permit itself to be converted into positivity, because it can no longer *collaborate* with the continuous linking-up of meaning, concept, time and truth in discourse . . .[73]

Différance amounts to a *negativity so negative* that the term 'negative' cannot even encapsulate it, abolishing as it does any hope of conversion or restoration into positivity. It unleashes the fullness of Hegel's *tremendous power of the negative*, freeing it from the speculative assumption of the equality of forces, whereby that negativity, on Derrida's reading, is limited. It is difficult to imagine a view of difference more distant from that of Deleuze, who treats the negative as the nihilistic antithesis of the philosophy of difference: 'This is what the philosophy of difference refuses: *omnis determinatio negatio*. . .'.[74]

Finally, that Derrida understands difference as oppositional entails that, just as for Hegel, the forces in relation are interdependent, and thus, the relations of forces are, using this word with the utmost care, essential. As Hegel writes, 'their essence rather consists simply and solely in this, that each *is* solely through the other, and what each thus is it immediately no longer is, since it *is* the other'.[75] Each force is expressed as the other to the other, as the mirror reflection of the other, and hence, each force, and the term of which it is the expression, may be understood only through its other. Derrida echoes this understanding:

> The same, precisely, is *différance* (with an *a*) as the displaced and equivocal passage of one different thing to another, from one term of an opposition to the other. Thus one could reconsider all the pairs of opposites on which

philosophy is constructed and on which our discourse lives, *not in order to see opposition erase itself* [my emphasis] but to see what indicates that each of the terms must appear as the *différance* of the other, as the other different and deferred in the economy of the same.[76]

Each term *must* appear as the *différance* of the other because, given the oppositional nature of *différance* itself, these specific forces subsist necessarily in precisely these relations. *Différance* is the productive relationality that *constitutes* the opposition, and hence, it also allows for the fluidity that enables the passage between the two terms. But what does not change is the 'all or nothing'[77] – the either/or, the 'binarity', if I may permit myself the use of such a controversial term – of each particular signifying relation, predicated as it is on Derrida's oppositional understanding of *différance*.

On these two points – the *conflictuality* of difference and the essential interdependency of specific relations of forces – Deleuze and Derrida could not be further apart; and both are rooted in Derrida's oppositional understanding of *différance*. For Deleuze difference is not essentially oppositional, and hence, 'we affirm the relation of *all* forces'.[78] This is not to say that each force *in fact* relates to every other force, as though all were woven together on a continuum: 'all forces do not enter into relations all at once on their own account. Their respective power is, in fact, fulfilled by relating to a small number of forces.'[79] Rather, that forces are not essentially oppositionally related for Deleuze means that they are *not* interdependent, and there is nothing essentially preventing any given force from interacting with any other force. These interactions and encounters Deleuze refers to as 'concrete parts of chance ... alien to every law'.[80] Citing Nietzsche, Deleuze argues that the differences in *quantity* of force amount to differences in *quality* as well. Forces in relation with each other beget changes in the magnitude of each, but these changes – though understood quantitatively – amount to changes in the *nature* of each as well. The difference between the Nietzschean 'master' and the Nietzschean 'slave' is not simply one of degree – *they are rather different types of animals*. To see this more clearly, we may note that the same type of event – conflict, for example – may produce in the 'master' an intensification of her power, while in the 'slave' it may engender a further diminishment. Hence, 'we can not abstractly calculate forces. In each case we have to concretely evaluate their respective quality and the nuance of this quality.'[81] But in any given case, one of the 'terms' may break off from its relations and enter into new relations. Each, for Deleuze, is therefore something different and something more than the *différance* of its 'other'.

Then, the oppositional nature of *différance* entails an essentially *conflictual* understanding of the relations of forces, as we have seen extensively.

Deleuze too, in a discussion of Freud, explicitly connects the conflictual understanding of the relations of forces to the oppositional (or dualistic) conception of difference: 'For Freud, it is not only the theory of repression but the dualism in the theory of drives which encourages the primacy of a conflictual model.'[82] In rejecting the oppositional understanding of difference, Deleuze therefore denies the essential conflictuality of relations of force. Forces may be in tension, dynamically related, but this tension is not necessarily *conflictual*. Forces frequently enter into relations of mutual assistance and symbiotic benefit; for instance, I could not live without the trillions of microbes that populate my body, inside and out. More fundamentally, *my body* itself is a relationship of forces: 'every relationship of forces constitutes a body'.[83] This is not, of course, to deny that forces often do enter into relationships of conflict; it is merely to deny the point that this conflict is ontologically primary. What is more significant for Deleuze is that forces are only able to enter into relations *at all* – whether of cooperation or of conflict – because they first differ: 'the conflicts are the result of more subtle differential mechanisms (displacements and disguises). And if the *forces* naturally enter into relations of opposition, this is on the basis of differential elements which express a more profound instance.'[84]

Conclusion

We are now in a position to summarise the results of Part II. In Chapter 3, we analysed the two pillars of deconstruction: Hegel's completion of the history of Western metaphysics, coupled with Heidegger's famous critique of ontotheology. For Derrida, Hegel completes the system of Western metaphysics, thinking the irreducible difference that functions at the heart of language itself. This irreducible difference enables Hegel to think the *trace* of alterity in every moment of presence in the development of the history of Western thought. For Hegel and for Derrida both, this difference is oppositional or negational. On Derrida's view, it engenders, of necessity, the oppositional terms of the binary logic of Western metaphysics. To this point, Derrida agrees with Hegel. The problem, according to Derrida (following Heidegger), is that the oppositional terms that Hegel thinks are themselves *Aufgehoben*, they are lifted, elevated, subsumed into a higher unity, such that the 'conflictuality' is cancelled out, ultimately in another moment of presence. To think beyond ontotheology, the difference as conflict and opposition must never be resolved – given what we have discussed, it would appear that for Derrida this will take the form of an engendering of contradictions with no resolution, but this is the subject of Chapter 6. What we have shown is that, for Derrida, Hegel's concept of difference is a truth that demands reckoning, in the sense of an acute awareness of just how *right* Hegel was,[85] and that, ultimately, this difference demands surpassing. For Deleuze, on the contrary, Hegel's concept of difference is deficient, derivative, in some cases, pernicious. It is an error, anathema to true philosophy, and as such, must be corrected, or better still, left behind entirely. The way in which Derrida and Deleuze attempt to formulate their concepts of difference in light of their respective readings of Hegel, the way, that is, in which *différance* and difference in itself are thought to overcome whatever problems Hegel poses, is the topic of Part III.

Notes

1. *WD*, 99.
2. *OG*, 24.
3. *VP*, 44.
4. *DR*, 53.
5. *ID*, 49.
6. Derrida, 'The Original Discussion of "*Différance*"', in Wood and Bernasconi (eds), *Derrida and* Différance, 95.
7. *OG*, 25–6.
8. *WD*, 320n91.
9. *DI*, 144.
10. I would like to thank Anindya Bhattacharyya, whose blog was positively indispensable to me as I tried to wade through the dense forests of Hegel's thought on this concept. See https://bat020.com/2011/05/20/force-and-understanding-in-hegels-phenomenology-of-spirit.
11. I am indebted to John Protevi for this reference to Derrida and Hegel on the question of 'force'. See Protevi, *Political Physics*, 45–71.
12. *PH*, 81.
13. *WD*, 26–7.
14. *NP*, 43.
15. *GS*, 11.
16. *PH*, 58.
17. *PH*, 63.
18. *PH*, 63.
19. *PH*, 64.
20. *PH*, 59.
21. *PH*, 67.
22. *PH*, 67.
23. *PH*, 67.
24. *PH*, 68.
25. *PH*, 68.
26. *PH*, 68.
27. *PH*, 68.
28. *PH*, 69.
29. See Spinoza, 'Letter 50', in *Complete Works*, 891. See also *DR*, 52: 'This is what the philosophy of difference refuses: *omnis determinatio negatio.*'
30. *PH*, 69.

31. *PH*, 69.
32. *PH*, 69.
33. *PH*, 70.
34. *PH*, 78.
35. *PH*, 79.
36. *GS*, 119.
37. *PH*, 79.
38. *PH*, 20.
39. *PH*, 81.
40. *PH*, 81.
41. *PH*, 81. It is worth noting here that, although the name Hegel rarely appears in Nietzsche's *Genealogy*, Nietzsche nevertheless takes explicit issue with the conceptual distinction between 'force' and 'expression': 'For just as common people separate the lightning from its flash and take the latter as a *doing*, as an effect of a force called lightning, so popular morality also separates strength from the expressions of strength as if there were behind the strong an indifferent substratum that is free to express strength – or not to. But there is no such substratum; there is no "being" behind the doing, effecting, becoming; "the doer" is simply fabricated into the doing – the doing is everything. Common people basically double the doing when they have the lightning flash; this is a doing-doing: the same happening is posited first as cause and then once again as its effect. Natural scientists do no better when they say "force moves, force causes," and so on . . .' (*GM*, 25).
42. *PH*, 81.
43. *GS*, 83.
44. *PH*, 82–3.
45. *PH*, 84.
46. Kant, *The Metaphysical Foundations of Natural Science*, Second Division, Proposition 6, Demonstration, in *Kant's Prolegomena and Metaphysical Foundations of Natural Science*, 185.
47. *GS*, 123.
48. *PH*, 85.
49. *PH*, 86.
50. *PH*, 87.
51. *PH*, 82.
52. '*Aufgehobensein*', Hegel, *Phänomenologie des Geistes*, 110.
53. *PH*, 84.
54. *WD*, 26–7.
55. *VP*, 88–9.
56. *DR*, 136.
57. *MP*, 17.
58. *NP*, 43.
59. *NP*, 3.
60. *P*, 40.
61. *P*, 44.
62. Butler, *Subjects of Desire*, 183.
63. *MP*, 18.
64. *P*, 74.
65. *P*, 76.
66. *P*, 76.
67. *OG*, 62.
68. *OG*, 25–6.
69. *P*, 41.
70. *OG*, 167.
71. *WD*, 20.

72. *WD*, 308n4.
73. *WD*, 259–60.
74. *DR*, 52.
75. *PH*, 86.
76. *MP*, 17.
77. *LI*, 116.
78. *NP*, 44.
79. *NP*, 44.
80. *NP*, 44. The mention and rejection of 'law' by Deleuze in this passage reinforces that this is an explicit rejection of Hegel's understanding of force, as the last half of the 'Force and the Understanding' chapter focuses extensively on *law* as the outcome of Hegel's discussion of force. 'This difference is expressed in the *law*, which is the *stable* image of unstable appearance' (*PH*, 90).
81. *NP*, 44.
82. *DR*, 106.
83. *NP*, 40.
84. *DR*, 106.
85. See *WD*, 251.

Part III
Thinking Difference Itself

Chapter 6

Traces and Ashes

While Hegel served as our touchstone through Part II, Nietzsche, read through the lenses of Heidegger, serves as our touchstone for Part III. Both Derrida and Deleuze will cite Nietzsche as the figure whose thinking carries us beyond Hegelian difference, and both will explicitly read him against and beyond Heidegger. According to Derrida, Heidegger regards Nietzsche, 'with as much lucidity and rigor as bad faith and misconstruction, as the last metaphysician'.[1] Given that their respective understandings of Hegel's contribution to the philosophy of difference were divergent, we can expect that the ways in which Derrida and Deleuze understand Nietzsche to liberate difference from Hegelian trappings will be different also. Nevertheless, both recognise a certain Nietzscheanism as the inspiration for a non-Hegelian conception of difference. An analysis of these Nietzschean strains of thought thus cannot but assist us in our investigation – here the distinction between Derrida and Deleuze fully emerges.

As we saw in Chapter 3, according to Derrida, though Heidegger rightly characterises the history of metaphysics in ontotheological terms, he nevertheless remains trapped in the very tradition from which he seeks escape. Thus:

> Now, among these holds, the ultimate determination of difference as the ontico-ontological difference – however necessary and decisive this phase must be – still seems to me, in a strange way, to be in the grasp of metaphysics. Perhaps then, *moving along lines that would be more Nietzschean than Heideggerian* [my emphasis], by going to the end of this thought of the truth of Being, we would have to become open to a *différance* that is no longer determined, in the language of the West, as the difference between Being and beings.[2]

Indeed, as we saw in Chapter 5, Derrida on one occasion explicitly defines *différance* as a Nietzschean invention: 'Thus, *différance* is the name we might give to the "active," moving discord of different forces, and of differences of forces, that *Nietzsche sets up against the entire system* [my emphasis] of metaphysical grammar, wherever this system governs culture, philosophy, and science.'[3] Likewise, Deleuze, after critically lauding the concepts of univocity and immanence found in Duns Scotus and Spinoza, says of Nietzsche in *Difference and Repetition*:

> That identity not be first, that it exist as a principle but as a second principle, as a principle *become*; that it revolve around the Different: such would be the nature of a Copernican revolution which opens the possibility of difference having its own concept, rather than being maintained under the domination of a concept in general already understood as identical. *Nietzsche meant nothing more than this by eternal return* [my emphasis].[4]

Referring to Heidegger, Deleuze asks, 'But does he effectuate the conversion after which univocal Being belongs only to difference and, in this sense, revolves around being? Does he conceive of *being* in such a manner that it will be truly disengaged from any subordination in relation to the identity of representation?' To this question he answers, 'It would seem not, *given his critique of the Nietzschean eternal return*' (my emphasis).[5] For Deleuze then, that Heidegger is not able to think Being as difference is most salient in his critique of Nietzsche's eternal return. Both Deleuze and Derrida therefore recognise Nietzsche as an inspiration for the overcoming of Hegelianism, but where Derrida understands Nietzsche's achievement as the 'liberation of the signifier from its dependence or derivation with respect to the logos',[6] claiming at the same time that Nietzsche must not be read as an ontological thinker, Deleuze will claim that Nietzsche constructs an ontology that effects the overcoming of Platonism, demanding the thought of internal difference in the form of eternal return.

The task of Part II was negative and critical – it was necessary to highlight the ways in which, for both Derrida and Deleuze, difference had *not yet* been thought. This came to the fore most readily in their criticisms of Hegel. The task of Part III, on the basis of the criticisms of the previous chapters, is to formulate their respective philosophies of difference in light of the affirmative things each says about Nietzsche's contribution to such a philosophy. For Derrida, *différance* is conceived in the context of a 'Hegelianism without reserve', a dialectics in which nothing is held back, a *negativity so negative* that opposition and conflictuality are not overcome, but celebrated, liberated, and disseminated. For Deleuze, on the contrary, difference in itself (*la différence en elle-même*) is pure, non-negational relation, in a 'prior field of individuation',[7] wherein pre-individual singularities emerge, and relate in such a way that individuals become.

Derrida and *différance*

Derrida writes, 'If words and concepts receive meaning only in sequences of differences, one can justify one's language, and one's choice of terms, only within a topic [an orientation in space] and an historical strategy.'[8] In this spirit, we would be remiss were we to assert that what we hope to offer is a once-for-all *definition* of this most elusive of Derridean concepts, *différance*. This is especially true given that Derrida himself offers numerous definitions of *différance*, often within a single line of argumentation. To synthesise and summarise, we might say that *différance* is the differing-deferring becoming-time-of-space and becoming-space-of-time. Such a definition, however, gets us no closer to understanding what *différance* is or how it operates. Rodolphe Gasché identifies five specific definitions, while admitting, at the same time, 'The list of these incommensurable and heterogeneous kinds of differences is, for structural reasons, open; their synthesis as *différance* is not complete, for such a synthesis necessarily defers its own closure.'[9] *Différance* only *is* in its operations, it is true. Nevertheless, and with Derrida, we can hope to isolate what he calls the '*general system of this economy*',[10] the basic structural movements characteristic of its various operations. We begin by tracing further the thread that we began in the previous chapter. Derrida's questions begin from and are made possible by Heidegger's questions: 'What I have attempted to do would not have been possible without the opening of Heidegger's questions.'[11] Deconstruction, we said, functions at the heart of a fundamental tension: how to speak or think beyond or outside the system of presence when all that can be said and thought, including its every rejection and rebellion, is already accounted for in the system?

As we have hinted, the answer to this question lies in a certain Nietzscheanism: 'Nietzsche, far from remaining *simply* (with Hegel and as Heidegger wished) *within* metaphysics, contributed a great deal to the liberation of the signifier from its dependence or derivation with respect to the logos.'[12] In order to get to this point, however, we must look at Derrida's deconstruction of consciousness, for in *Of Grammatology* Derrida writes: 'This deconstruction of presence accomplishes itself through the deconstruction of consciousness, and therefore through the irreducible notion of the trace (*Spur*), as it appears in both Nietzschean and Freudian discourse.'[13] Echoing Heidegger, Derrida notes that since Descartes the metaphysics of modernity has privileged consciousness, particularly self-consciousness, as the guarantor and guardian of presence and hence of truth. This is no less the case for the empiricists, for Kant, for Hegel, or for Husserl. The self-presence of subjectivity, however, is only ever present to itself through an experience of time. The subject's experience of time, through which its experience of self is constantly mediated, undercuts any presumption to a full experience of certainty. Thus, *différance* appears in the context of those thinkers the entirety of whose projects vigorously sought to establish presence at the core of what was most undeniably certain, the consciousness of the self. The salient example for Derrida is Husserl, whose radicalised Cartesianism Derrida characterised as 'metaphysics in its most modern, critical, and vigilant form'.[14]

The discovery of *différance*

In the introduction to his landmark text, *La voix et le phénomène*, Derrida writes: 'Let us note, however, in order to specify our intention here, that phenomenology appears to us to be tormented if not contested, from the inside, by means of its own descriptions of the movement of temporalization and of the constitution of intersubjectivity.'[15] The relation in Husserl between the subject and its experience of time will stand to complicate and forestall the desire for presence at the core of Husserl's philosophy of consciousness. Derrida goes on to say: 'At the greatest depth of what connects these two decisive moments of the description together, one sees an irreducible non-presence recognised as a constituting value, and with it a non-life or a non-presence of the living present, a non-belonging of the living present to itself, a non-originarity that cannot be eradicated.'[16] This is the discovery of *différance*. Let us lay out, despite all of Derrida's warnings, a formulation for *différance*, before tracing out how the concept unfolds in this work: *différance is the non-originary constituting-disruption of presence*. For the sake of clarity, let us briefly dissect the meaning of this formulation. *Différance* is the constituting of presence – this means that it is the play of *différance* that makes possible all of the binary categories in accordance with which philosophy has, since Plato, conducted itself: intelligible/sensible, form/matter, spirit/flesh, subject/object, soul/body, good/evil, voice/writing, etc. As we saw in Chapter 5, *différance* is the play of forces that makes these possible, and in this sense, *différance* is constitutive. 'Constitutive', however, cannot be understood as originary without qualification. To speak in terms of origin implies a primordial purity or stasis, a presence from which meaning has somehow fallen away: 'To say that *différance* is originary is simultaneously to erase the myth of a present origin. Which is why "originary" must be understood as having been *crossed out*, without which *différance* would be derived from an original plenitude. It is a non-origin which is originary.'[17] While *différance* is constitutive, it does not stand for a moment of originary purity. It is an origin, but is, *at* the origin, already contaminated; hence it is a non-originary origin.

At the same time, because *différance* as constitutive play ever underlies the functioning of philosophical concepts, it likewise prevents their fully securing the operations that the author intends. Thus, even as it constitutes the terms, making philosophy possible, it denies the full presence of meaning that they (the concepts or the author) *want* to say.[18] This constituting-disruption is the source of one of Derrida's more famous descriptions of the deconstructive project: 'But this condition of possibility turns into a condition of impossibility.'[19] *Différance* makes possible, but also forbids, presence. As we saw in Chapter 3, presence is understood in two forms of absolute proximity: (1) spatial – the absolute proximity of the object of intuition to consciousness, or of meaning to itself; and (2) temporal – the absolute proximity of the present moment as the landscape of clear intuition. Both of these senses of presence are made explicit in Husserl's '*principle of all principles*':

> that every originary presentive intuition is a legitimizing source of cognition, that *everything originarily* (so to speak, in its 'personal' actuality) *offered* to us in 'intuition' is to be accepted simply as what it is presented as being, but also, only within the limits in which it is presented there . . . Every statement which does no more than confer expression on such data by simple explication and by means of significations precisely conforming to them is . . . actually an *absolute beginning* called upon to serve as a foundation, a *principium* in the genuine sense of the word.[20]

Différance attenuates and mediates these two senses of presence: spatially, it *differs*, produces differences, ruptures, and spaces, rather than absolute proximities; temporally, it *defers*, it delays *presence* from ever being fully attained, 'putting off until later', 'taking into account', 'taking account of time and of the forces of an operation that implies an economical calculation, a detour, a delay, a relay, a reserve'.[21] Derrida happily capitalises on the 'two motifs of the Latin *differre*'.[22] Let us now look to Derrida's discovery of *différance* in Husserl's philosophy, in order that we may more fully and completely understand exactly how *différance* functions for Derrida, and how this differs from Deleuze's concept of difference in itself.

The first three chapters of *Voice and Phenomenon* together form an expository account of Husserl's theory of meaning as found in the *Logical Investigations*. In the opening chapter of the first Logical Investigation, titled 'Essential Distinctions', Husserl writes, 'The terms "expression" [*Ausdruck*] and "sign" [*Zeichen*] are often treated as synonyms, but it will not be amiss to point out that they do not always coincide in application in common usage. Every sign is a sign for something, but not every sign has "meaning" [*Bedeutung*], a "sense" [*Sinn*] that the sign "expresses."[23] For in addition to expressions, *indications* (*Anzeichen*) also signify. The distinction between expressions and indications is that an indication, properly speaking, signifies without pointing to a sense or a meaning. Indications signify by pointing us to other things, as a fever points to an illness in the body. The illness is not the *meaning* of the fever, but it is brought to our attention by way of the fever. An expression, on the other hand, 'is a sign charged with *Bedeutung*',[24] 'a purely linguistic sign'.[25] There are countless types of signs – animal tracks point to the recent presence of life, certain scents may indicate particular foods, facial expressions indicate certain emotions – but expressions are linguistic signs that are themselves meaningful.

Derrida then problematises this distinction: 'The difference between indication and expression appears very quickly, over the course of the description, as a difference more *functional* than *substantial*.'[26] Depending upon the context, an indication can function as an expression, and conversely, expressions are almost always indicative. One might see, for instance, on a sheet of paper a collection of written scribbles which, at first glance, appear to be random, purposeless, and meaningless. Nonetheless, these scribbles serve as indications that someone was here, and that she wrote something on the piece of paper. The shapes and contours of the marks, their illegibility, may be indications of a hurried or frantic act of writing. Further investigation may reveal that the marks are, in fact, Latin letters, forming English words. The marks persist in their status as indications, in all the senses we discussed, but beyond their indicative function (*someone wrote this*), they have also become expressions.

Conversely, nearly all expression, 'in communicative discourse',[27] is indicative. In communication, the signs that we use with one another point toward empirical states of affairs, physical entities, psychological states, and so on, hopefully to be received and understood on the part of the listener. In so pointing, expressions are also indicative:

> We therefore already know that, *in fact*, the discursive sign and consequently the meaning <*le vouloir-dire*> is *always* entangled, *gripped* within an indicative system. The expressive and logical purity of the *Bedeutung* that Husserl wants to grasp as a possibility of the *Logos* is gripped, that is, contaminated – *in fact and always* (*allzeit verflochen ist*) in so far as the *Bedeutung* is gripped within a communicative discourse.[28]

Nonetheless, even if, *in fact*, expressions are always caught up in indication, Husserl maintains his conviction that this has nothing to do with the 'essential distinction' between the two types of sign. 'The whole analysis

will move forward therefore in this hiatus between fact and right, existence and essence, reality and the intentional function.'[29] If expressions
are meaningful signs, while indications point elsewhere, the object of
Husserl's pursuit will be the sign that is eminently meaningful, hence
purely expressive, and will thus necessitate the divorce of the expression
from its indicative function. But this is not an easy task, for as we have seen
already, '*All discourse, in so far as it is engaged in a communication and in so
far as it manifests lived-experiences, operates as indication.*'[30] In communication, a speaker attempts to embody an internal and personal experience by
animating audible or visible signs, invested with meaning, for the purpose
of manifesting that experience or that meaning in the consciousness of
another. The meaning or the experience is thereby irreducibly mediated
through the use of the signs, such that, however carefully and thoroughly
the speaker may articulate her experience, however numerous and precise
the signs she uses to enrich the description, the experience itself can never
be perfectly recreated in the mind of the listener: 'In effect, when I listen to
another person, his lived-experience is not present to me "in person" and
originally.'[31] Some measure of meaning is always lost in the communicative function of expression. This is as a result of the empirical nature of
the expression's *going forth* into the world. To isolate the core essence of
expression entails that we must suspend the *going forth* of the expression:
'In order to reduce indication in language and attain once more finally
pure expressivity, it is therefore necessary to suspend the relation to others.
Then I would no longer have to pass through the mediation of the physical
side or through any appresentation in general.'[32] This is accomplished in
the soliloquy of the inner life of consciousness.

In our interior monologue, there is nothing empirical, and hence,
nothing indicative. The signs themselves are not sensible; they have only
ideal, as opposed to real, existence: 'In imagination a spoken or printed
word floats before us, though in reality it has no existence.'[33] Likewise, the
signs of the interior monologue do not indicate in the way that expressive
signs do. Communicative expressions point us to states of affairs or the
internal experiences of others, in short, empirical events. The expressions
of interior monologue indeed *point us to* things, but the things to which
they point are not external, empirical realities, but 'the sense seems the
thing aimed at by the verbal sign and meant by its means: the expression
seems to direct interest away from itself towards its sense, and to point
to the latter'.[34] Thus, for Husserl, the purest, most meaningful form of
expression (*ex-pression*, literally, *pressing out*), is precisely the expression in
which nothing is expressed to anyone: 'it is necessary to track down the
unmarred purity of expression. Through a strange paradox, the meaning
<*le vouloir-dire*> would isolate the concentrated purity of ex-pressivity only

when the relation to a certain *outside* would be suspended.'[35] This is the internal voice of consciousness, immediately present to the subject in the interior life of thought.

Nonetheless, one might ask, is it not the case that in the internal monologue we are expressing or articulating a meaning *to ourselves*? Husserl responds in the negative. The signs of soliloquy are not indicative – they do not make manifest to the self across a space of mediation a content that was previously inaccessible to the self. The sense of the expression is fully and unmistakably present in the consciousness of the individual: 'It is immediately present to itself. It is living consciousness.'[36] In the interior monologue, 'the word', Husserl writes, 'comes before us as intrinsically indifferent, whereas the sense seems the thing aimed at by the verbal sign and meant by its means'.[37] The word, the sign, is *intrinsically indifferent*, essentially non-essential, while the beating heart of the interior soliloquy is the sense itself. But the sense is not conveyed *from* the self *to* the self, 'since such indication would be quite purposeless. For the acts in question are themselves experienced by us at that very moment [*im selben Augenblick*].'[38] For this reason, the punctuatedness and discreteness of the present moment will play for Husserl a foundational role. Without it, Derrida claims, Husserl's ability to maintain the *essential distinction* between indication and expression – which, Derrida will claim, 'rigorously order all the later analyses',[39] and mark 'the germinal structure of all of Husserl's thought'[40] – collapses.[41] The hinge of Derrida's analysis is thus found in chapter 5 of *Voice and Phenomenon*, his deconstruction of Husserl's *living present*, entitled 'The Sign and the Blink of an Eye'.

The thrust of Derrida's analysis revolves around the two foundational and irreducible elements of Husserl's notion of the living present: (1) the emphasis on the *primal impression*, understood as the now-point, the point of contact with the immediacy of experience; and (2) the halo of retention and protention surrounding every moment of primal impression, comprising together the 'living present', the structure of time-consciousness. The primal impression is in constant motion, perpetually displaced by a new primal impression. However, this does not prevent Husserl from referring to the moment of the primal impression in the atomistic terms of a *point*: 'First of all, we emphasize that the running-off modes of an immanent temporal object have a beginning, a source-point, so to speak.'[42] The source-point serves as the ground zero from which the modes of retention derive their content. The sense stamped in the impression is retained in the various running-off points of retention, becoming a continuing perception of what *was* a now-point, but is *now* moving further and further from the primal impression. The primal impression is the 'source-point',[43] the 'head attached to the comet's tail of retentions',[44] a 'punctual phase . . . present as now'.[45] Derrida thus notes: 'Nevertheless this spreading-out [of the living present] is still thought and described on the basis of the self-identity of the now as point, as a point, as "source-point." '[46] The source-point of the primal impression is the 'non-displaceable center, an eye or living nucleus' of temporality.[47]

Likewise, for both Heidegger and Derrida, this foundational status of the present is one of the irreducible grounds of Western metaphysics. It grounds the form/matter distinction in Plato, in that the forms, unlike any particulars in the world, remain eternally unchanging through each newly present moment, while particulars in the world are in a constant state of flux. Hence, knowledge can only be grounded in the *forms*, because the *world* is not so rooted to the eternal present.[48] It lies at the heart of the Cartesian cogito, and is no less important for the rest of the modern period, up to and including Husserl himself. Here in the context of this grounding presence (of the present moment), and even though he has yet to introduce the neologism itself, Derrida begins to motion toward what *différance* does and how it functions:

> Moreover, there is no possible objection, within philosophy, in regard to this privilege of the present-now. This privilege defines the very element of philosophical thought. It is *evidentness* itself, conscious thought itself. It governs every possible concept of truth and of sense. We cannot raise suspicions about it without beginning to enucleate consciousness itself from an elsewhere of philosophy which takes away from discourse all possible *security* and every possible *foundation*.[49]

The philosophical tradition is defined by its emphasis on the present, and hence, to call it into question is to shift one's vantage point from one that is, strictly speaking, philosophical, to one that inhabits the space between philosophy and non-philosophy, which, as we demonstrated in Chapter 3, is the direction to which Derrida motions.

This calling into question arises in the second point of Husserl's temporal structure, that every primal impression is ensconced in an essential relation with a structure of retention and protention, without which the primal impression never occurs. Husserl's criticism of Brentano's understanding of time is that Brentano is incapable of making a distinction between the two irreducible modes of memory: on the one hand, *Representation*, the intentionally conjured imagination of a past event, such as a song I heard last week; and on the other hand, the *Retention* of a moment still fresh to consciousness. For Husserl, these two types of memory are essentially and qualitatively distinct. Thus, Husserl will ascribe to retention the status of a perception, of a *Presentation*, as opposed to a *Re-presentation*:

> Up to this point, the consciousness of the past – the primary consciousness of the past, that is – was not <called> perception because perception was taken as the act that originally constitutes the now. But the consciousness of the past does not constitute a now; it rather constitutes a 'just past,' something that has preceded the now intuitively. But if we call perception the *act in which all 'origin' lies*, the act that *constitutes originally*, then *primary memory* is *perception*. For only in primary memory do we *see* what is past, only in it does the past become constituted – and constituted presentatively, not re-presentatively. The just past, the before in opposition to the now, can be directly seen only in primary memory; it is its essence to bring this new and original past to primary, direct intuition, just as it is the essence of the perception of the now to bring the now directly to intuition.[50]

Primary memory is not the present, in the way that the primal impression is. Nevertheless, primary memory (retention) is still vitally attached to the moment of the now. It is a *direct intuition* of the just passed, fully seen in the moment of the now, as opposed to *represented* memory, which is not. Furthermore, though the primal impression gives us the now, it presents it in the mode of constantly passing away, and this impression only becomes substantively accessible in the mode of retention: 'Temporal objects – and this pertains to their essence – spread their matter over an extent of time, and such objects can become constituted only in acts that constitute the very differences belonging to time.'[51] In this sense, we can say that for Husserl, the present only truly becomes present in the mode of retention, which is decidedly *not* the present, indeed, is the 'antithesis of perception',[52] paradoxically a perceived non-perception that accompanies and constitutes every single perception, according to Husserl.

The continual accommodation of the present of primal impression to the non-presence of retention entails the admission of an alterity into the self-present now-moment of experience, thus undermining Husserl's claim that there is no indication involved in the expression of the interior soliloquy.[53] This requires further explanation. We must recall that the reason for which Husserl claims that we do not indicate to ourselves in expression is that 'such indication would there be quite purposeless. For the acts in question are themselves experienced by us at that very moment [*im selben Augenblick*].'[54] There is no multiplicity, no otherness, no hiatus, in the self-experience of interiority, such that there is nothing separating the self from the self. The presence of the self is immediately experienced by the self, and for this reason, the self does not indicate any sense to itself. If alterity were to become the constituting necessity of the subject, as Derrida is here suggesting, Husserl's position would be threatened.

The question then is, what is the status of this alterity? At the very least we can say that Husserl would not want to consider *retention* to be an 'other' to perception. Let us look again at his two fundamental commitments: (1) On the one hand, 'the living now is constituted as the absolute perceptual source only in continuity with retention as non-perception'.[55] Every moment of inner-time consciousness is a living present, and primal impression is never present without retention. The primal impression, moreover, is an *ideal* limit: 'The apprehensions continuously blend into one another here; they terminate in an apprehension that constitutes the now, but which is only an ideal limit.'[56] There is not and cannot be a radical distinction between primal impression and retention; they are continuous. (2) On the other hand, 'the source of certitude in general is the originarity of the living now'.[57] The primordial truth for the phenomenologist is Husserl's principle of principles, '*that every originary presentive intuition is a legitimizing source of cognition . . . to be accepted simply as what it is presented as being*, but also, *only within the limits in which it is presented there*'.[58] This being the case, and because retention resides on a continuum with primal impression, retention must be considered under the banner of primordial certitude, and as essentially distinct from memory as representation.

Nevertheless, the common root, what makes both retention and representation possible, is the 'possibility of re-petition in its most general form, that is, the trace in the most universal sense'.[59] The *trace* is the imprint of alterity in the interiority of ipseity, 'the relation of intimacy of the living present to its outside, the openness to exteriority in general, to the non-proper, etc.'[60] As Derrida here defines it, the trace is the structural possibility of repetition, without which retention would not be guaranteed as a structural component of the living present. Retention, we said, is a non-presence, but one still continuous with the present now itself. This is only possible, for Derrida, because the primal impression, the *im selben Augenblick*, is traced with exteriority. That this is the case is not an accidental or empirical fact about the nature of time; the structure of repetition constitutes the very possibility of the primal impression itself:

> The ideality of the form (*Form*) of presence itself implies consequently that it can be repeated to infinity, that its return, as the return of the same, is to infinity necessary and inscribed in presence as such; that the re-turn is the return of a present that will be retained in a *finite* movement of retention; that there is originary truth, in the phenomenological sense, only in so far as it is enrooted in the finitude of this retention; finally that the relation to infinity can be instituted only in the openness to the ideality of the form of presence as the possibility of a re-turn to infinity.[61]

In other words, the very structure of presence itself demands that the experience in question attains a fullness, a stasis, a quiddity, a constitution *as* experience, such that it is repeatable, now and infinitely again. The name that Derrida gives to this possibility is the *trace* because the infinite iterability of the present requires that, structurally and essentially, it possess the possibility of repetition *in the absence of its presence*. It thus follows that the trace, the mark of alterity and openness to exteriority, is a structural component of the present itself. The ideality of the present is constituted, according to Derrida, by what is not present. For this reason Derrida writes, 'this intimacy of non-presence and alterity with presence cuts into, at its root, the argument for the uselessness of the sign in the self-relation'.[62]

At last, *différance* is introduced: 'the trace in the most universal sense, is a possibility that not only must inhabit the pure actuality of the now but must constitute it by means of the very movement of the *différance* that the possibility inserts into the pure actuality of the now'.[63] The constitutive force of the trace introduces *différance* in that it is only on the basis of a fundamental structure of *movement* – that of repetition – that the present as such is possible. *Différance* is the name of this movement:

> In all of these directions, the presence of the present is thought beginning from the fold of the return, beginning from the movement of repetition and not the reverse. Does not the fact that this fold in presence or in self-presence is irreducible, that this trace or this *différance* is always older than presence and obtains for it its openness, forbid us from speaking of a simple self-identity 'im selben Augenblick'?[64]

Further, 'Must we not say that the concept of pure solitude – and of the monad in the phenomenological sense – is *split open* by its own origin, by the very condition of its self-presence: "time" rethought beginning from the *différance* in auto-affection, beginning from the identity of identity and non-identity in the "same" of the *im selben Augenblick*?'[65] There is a fundamental blindness constituting the certainty of the phenomenological vision, 'a duration to the blink of an eye, and the duration closes the eye'.[66]

In his effort to radicalise the Cartesian project, to ground with even greater certainty the *cogitations* as the foundation and exhaustion of truth, Husserl establishes a model of time consciousness that, contrary to Descartes, does not find temporality in the linear time of the objective world, but as the very constitution of subjectivity itself. It is here that Derrida first discovers *différance*. The dominance of the now, he claims, 'therefore prescribes the place of a problematic that puts phenomenology into confrontation with every thought of non-consciousness that would know how to approach the genuine stakes and profound agency where the decision is made: the concept of time'.[67] The thinkers whom Derrida cites as sensitive to this problem, as thinkers of the trace? Freud, and Nietzsche.

The inadequacy of Freud's trace

In *Of Grammatology*, Derrida writes that the 'deconstruction of presence accomplishes itself through the deconstruction of consciousness'. This is the operation that we have now seen opened by way of his analysis of Husserl, which is why he continues, 'and therefore through the irreducible notion of the trace (*Spur*), as it appears in both Nietzschean and Freudian discourse'.[68] In the '*Différance*' essay Derrida claims:

> Before being so radically and purposely the gesture of Heidegger, this gesture was also made by Nietzsche and Freud, both of whom, as is well known, and sometimes in very similar fashion, put consciousness into question in its assured certainty of itself. Now is it not remarkable that they both did so on the basis of the motif of *différance*? *Différance* appears almost by name in their texts, and in those places where everything is at stake.[69]

Derrida later claims: 'And the concept of the trace, like that of *différance* thereby organises, along the lines of these different traces and differences of traces, in Nietzsche's sense, in Freud's sense, in Levinas's sense – these "names of authors" here being only indices – the network which reassembles and traverses our "era" as the delimitation of the ontology of presence.'[70] Nietzsche and Freud, the great thinkers of the unconscious, of consciousness as the mere epidermal expression or effect of the forces of the unconscious, mark the thought that anticipated the deconstruction of presence, via a deconstruction of consciousness, which, according to Derrida, marks the contemporary 'era'.

'Freud and the Scene of Writing' was originally a lecture delivered at the Institut de Psychanalyse in 1966. Though it is difficult to say with any precision which text *came first* in terms of composition, it is contiguous, both thematically and chronologically, with *La voix et le phénomène*, and it seems likely that they were composed at about the same time. Indeed, Derrida himself relates the two texts, by citing 'Freud and the Scene of Writing' in *Voice and Phenomenon*,[71] thus once again tying together inextricably the deconstruction of phenomenology – the most vigilant form of metaphysics – with the thought of the trace, as found in the texts of Freud and Nietzsche.

In his 1925 essay, 'A Note Upon the "Mystic Writing-Pad"', Freud outlines in brief fashion a model of the mind, one based by way of analogy upon 'a small contrivance that promises to perform more than the sheet of paper or the slate',[72] perform more, that is, in the sense of prosthetic memory. The name of this device is the *Wunderblock*, or the Mystic Writing-Pad. 'If I distrust my memory . . . I am able to supplement and guarantee its working by making a note in writing',[73] Freud says. There are two possible methods by which this is accomplished: (1) permanent markings on a spatially limited surface – paper; or (2) temporary markings on a surface which provides an ever-fresh receptivity for new markings – slate. The latter method suffers from its lack of permanence; the former from its limited receptivity.

The *Wunderblock* is unique in that it provides both infinite receptivity and permanence of the traces committed thereto. Freud's vivid description bears a complete citation:

> The Mystic Pad is a slab of dark brown resin or wax with a paper edging; over the slab is laid a thin transparent sheet, the top end of which is firmly secured to the slab while its bottom end rests upon it without being fixed to it. This transparent sheet is the more interesting part of the little device. It itself consists of two layers, which can be detached from each other except at their two ends. The upper layer is a transparent piece of celluloid; the lower layer is made of thin translucent waxed paper. When the apparatus is not in use, the lower surface of the waxed paper adheres lightly to the upper surface of the wax slab.
>
> To make use of the Mystic Pad, one writes upon the celluloid portion of the covering-sheet which rests upon the wax slab. For this purpose no pencil or chalk is necessary, since the writing does not depend upon material being deposited upon the receptive surface. It is a return to the ancient method of writing upon tablets of clay or wax: a pointed stilus scratches the surface, the depressions upon which constitute the 'writing.' In the case of the Mystic Pad this scratching is not effected directly, but through the medium of the covering-sheet. At the points which the stilus touches, it presses the lower surface of the waxed paper on to the wax slab, and the grooves are visible as dark writing upon the otherwise whitish-grey surface of the celluloid. If one wishes to destroy what has been written, all that is necessary is to raise the double covering-sheet from the wax slab by a light pull, starting from the free lower end. The close contact between the waxed paper and the wax slab at the places which have been scratched (upon which the visibility of the writing depended) is thus brought to an end and it does not recur when the two surfaces come together once more. The Mystic Pad is now clear of writing and ready to receive fresh notes.[74]

A stylus inscribes upon the sheet of waxed paper, forming a temporary bond between the waxed paper and surface of the wax or resin, thus creating the epidermal effect of a visible inscription of the mark traced on the surface. To 'erase' the mark, one need only 'break' the bond between the waxed paper and the resin, by lifting the sheet from the surface of the resin. From this, Freud draws four analogically important elements:

(1) Infinite receptivity – the dual-layered transparent sheet bears no permanent mark upon its surface. The moment the bond is broken with the resin, the surface is once again pure, 'ideal virginity'.[75]

(2) Permanence of traces – Freud notes a peculiar fact about the structure of the *Wunderblock*:

> The analogy would not be of much value if it could not be pursued further than this. If we lift the entire covering-sheet – both the celluloid and the waxed paper – off the waxed slab, the writing vanishes and, as I have already remarked, does not re-appear again. The surface of the Mystic Pad is clear of writing and once more capable of receiving impressions. But it is easy to discover that the permanent trace of what was written is retained upon the wax slab itself and is legible in suitable lights.[76]

In spite of the infinite receptivity of its surface, nevertheless the depth of the wax slab permanently bears the marks of inscription made by the stylus. The *Wunderblock* therefore provides a model for thinking the system characterised by 'unlimited receptive capacity and a retention of permanent traces'.[77] As early as *The Interpretation of Dreams* (1900), Freud had advanced what would come to be called the *topographical hypothesis*: 'we shall therefore ascribe these two functions to two different systems. We assume that an initial system of this apparatus receives the stimuli of perception but retains nothing of them – that is, it has no memory; and that behind this there lies a second system, which transforms the momentary excitation of the first into lasting traces.'[78]

(3) Protection for the receptive surface – Freud notes that if one carefully separates the transparent celluloid sheet from the translucent sheet of waxed paper, taking care not to separate the wax paper from the wax, the marks are just as visible on the wax sheet itself, 'and the question may arise why there should be any necessity for the celluloid portion of the cover. Experiment will then show that the thin paper would be very easily crumpled or torn if one were to write directly upon it with the stilus.'[79] The thickness and durability of the celluloid sheet provides a protective buffer for the fragility of the receptivity of the waxed paper. In *Beyond the Pleasure Principle* (1920), Freud writes, 'This little fragment of living substance is suspended in the middle of an external world charged with the most powerful energies; and it would be killed by the stimulation emanating from these if it were not provided with a protective shield against stimuli.'[80]

(4) The dependence of consciousness upon the unconscious – without the cooperation and participation of the wax, there is no perception. The fragile sheet of wax paper alone is incapable of bearing the marks of the stylus. Freud writes:

> My theory was that cathectic innervations are sent out and withdrawn in rapid periodic impulses from within into the completely pervious system Pcpt.-Cs.[81] So long as that system is cathected in this manner, it receives

perceptions (which are accompanied by consciousness) and passes the excitation on to the unconscious mnemic systems; but as soon as the cathexis is
withdrawn, consciousness is extinguished and the functioning of the system
comes to a standstill. It is as though the unconscious stretches out feelers,
through the medium of the system Pcpt.-Cs., towards the external world
and hastily withdraws them as soon as they have sampled the excitations
coming from it.[82]

The image thus offered is one of the unconscious pulsing forth into and
out of contact with consciousness, such that contact is repeatedly made
and broken, made and broken; the sheet, as it were, is lifted repeatedly.
This provides the fresh receptivity of consciousness while permanently
depositing the traces into the unconscious. Freud goes on to say, 'I further
had a suspicion that this discontinuous method of functioning of the
system Pcpt.-Cs. lies at the bottom of the origin of the concept of time.'[83]

Freud's thought of the trace thus challenges much of what is held as
true by the tradition with respect to consciousness, to time, to perception,
to agency, etc. Derrida draws from Freud's model of the *Wunderblock*
implications not explicitly made by Freud himself. First, the temporality
of the *Wunderblock* is inseparable from its spatial operations; time is not
a secondary characteristic or quality of the machine. When Descartes
questions the nature of the piece of wax in the second Meditation, he
tests whether its nature consists of all the characteristics that we receive
through the senses: the smell, the feel, the shape, the colour, etc. Each of
these qualities, however, can change given alterations in temperature; but
we recognise it as the same wax. The essence of the wax thus has nothing
to do with the sensory qualities which are subject to the flow of time, 'and
here is the point, the perception I have of it is a case not of vision or touch
or imagination . . . but of purely mental scrutiny'.[84] Descartes, then, 'can
reduce its essence to the timeless simplicity of an intelligible object'.[85] The
physical operation of the writing pad, however, is unthinkable without a
structure of time, which thus complicates any metaphysical, puncti-linear
model of time, according to which time would be that *through which* we
pass, or *in which* we are. 'Temporality as spacing will be not only the
horizontal discontinuity of a chain of signs, but also will be writing as
the interruption and restoration of contact between the various depths of
psychical levels: the remarkably heterogeneous temporal fabric of psychical work itself.'[86] Time is inseparable from the functioning of the psychical
apparatus. This functioning is not a smooth, linear temporality. Rather it is
the discontinuous, ruptured, breached 'economy of a system of writing'.[87]

Secondly, that the model of the *Wunderblock* relies upon a multiplicity
of agencies without which the machine is inconceivable fractures and
fragments the Classical, self-enclosed subject. The final line of Freud's

essay reads, 'If we imagine one hand writing upon the surface of the Mystic Writing-Pad while another periodically raises its covering sheet from the wax slab, we shall have a concrete representation of the way in which I tried to picture the functioning of the perceptual apparatus of our mind.'[88] The two hands metaphorically depict a manifold system of relations and coordinated operations. That Freud cannot conceive the functioning of the machine without coordinated effort is indicative of a structural impossibility. The ever-fresh receptivity of consciousness is only possible on the basis of a structured, organised, hence 'memorised' coordination between the systems. First, the impression of the trace is engendered by erasure. 'Traces thus produce the space of their inscription only by acceding to the period of their erasure.'[89] We might say that the condition of possibility for the trace is the erasure of the trace, in that the receptivity of perception is impossible without the assurance that the trace will be deleted. Moreover, 'writing is unthinkable without repression. The condition for writing is that there be neither a permanent contact nor an absolute break between strata: the vigilance and failure of censorship.'[90] Permanent contact between the surface and the depth, between Pcpt.-Cs. and unconscious, is impossible because in a short time, the *surface* of consciousness would be saturated. The inscription of perception requires the periodic break at which time the trace becomes unconscious. But the break cannot be absolute or permanent because, as we said, perception as writing requires the contact between the two strata. Thus, in the same sense that the fragile surface of consciousness is ever prepared anew for fresh perception, the unconscious is constantly in the mode of repressing traces. Thus, 'repetition and erasure, legibility and illegibility',[91] mark the origin of the trace.

The active participation of the unconscious with the world and with consciousness, its ongoing pulsation forth into the world, entails that there is no such thing as a *pure* perception, a *pure* receptivity of a *pure* subject. 'The subject of writing is a *system* of relations between strata: the Mystic Pad, the psyche, society, the world. Within that scene, on that stage, the punctual simplicity of the classical subject is not to be found.'[92] The subject is always *many*. Nevertheless, at this point, the image breaks down, according to Freud: 'There must come a point at which the analogy between an auxiliary apparatus of this kind and the organ which is its prototype will cease to apply. It is true, too, that once the writing has been erased, the Mystic Pad cannot "reproduce it" from within; it would be a mystic pad indeed if, like our memory, it could accomplish that.'[93] Unlike the psychic apparatus, once the celluloid has been lifted from the surface of the resin, the trace – though forever impressed upon the resin's surface – is also forever divorced from the celluloid, never again reaching or influencing the surface. In Derrida's words, this is because 'The machine is dead',[94] a mere representation of a living system – not itself alive.

For Derrida, this thought of the machine as synonymous with death puts Freud in line with Platonic themes: 'the Freudian concept of the trace must be radicalized and extracted from the metaphysics of presence which still retains it'.[95] Rather than embodying a death that would be the antithesis of the 'life' of the psyche, the machine for Derrida signifies the finitude of the so-called mnemic spontaneity itself, 'death and finitude within the psyche'.[96] This requires explanation. The psychic trace is the only active, living trace – the only spontaneous, *vital*, system. In this sense, the machine acts as a mere supplement, dead in itself as compared to the life of the psychic memory. Nevertheless, the machine as a supplement would not be necessary were it not for the fact that the spontaneity of memory is itself finite. Indeed, despite Freud's characterisation, we supplement memory constantly: calendars, day planners, smartphones, grocery lists, errand lists, etc. Our prostheses are an essential component of our memory. The *Wunderblock* may go a long way toward aiding in comprehension of the psychic apparatus, but the very existence of the physical *Wunderblock*, and hence Freud's ability to use it for illustrative purposes, depends upon the *fact* of writing as a metaphor for the operation of memory in the psyche. 'This resemblance – i.e., necessarily a certain Being-in-the-world of the psyche – did not happen to memory from without, any more than death surprises life. It founds memory.'[97] Writing, in the sense of permanent inscription, is not the supplement of memory, it is rather the very possibility of memory. It unites memory as life and memory as death, '*technē* as the relation between life and death'.[98] Death therefore lies at the heart of this life. The machine, as death, is necessary for the proper functioning of the psychic apparatus, as life. Thus, although Freud did not fully examine the implications of his discoveries, his writing opens itself to an analysis and an interrogation of writing itself.

Despite all of his breakthroughs, Freud remains bound in the metaphysics of presence, according to Derrida, in two ways: (1) He thinks the functioning of the psyche in the classical terms of the ego-subject, which, for Derrida, necessarily commits him to a substance metaphysics. The unconscious in Freud, though a powerhouse of force and trace, is substantialised as the double of consciousness itself: 'The concept of a (conscious or unconscious) subject necessarily refers to the concept of substance – and thus of presence – out of which it is born.'[99] (2) Traces for Freud are permanent. The trace, Derrida says, must not be thought as permanent, must possess no *being* of its own: 'The trace is the erasure of selfhood, of one's own presence, and is constituted by the threat or anguish of its irremediable disappearance, of the disappearance of its disappearance. An unerasable trace is not a trace, it is a full presence, an immobile and uncorruptible substance, a son of God, a sign of parousia and not a seed, that is, a mortal gem.'[100] Freud thinks the trace as a permanent inscription,[101] and he projects it into a substantial ego or subject. These two elements are essentially bound together and are united by Freud's inability to think the death at the core of the living. For this reason, the trace is not thought through to its completion, it is not thought radically enough. For that, we turn to Nietzsche.

The trace as production, metaphoricity, and play: Nietzsche

At long last, we have reached our destination. Though the names 'Freud' and 'Nietzsche' frequently appear together in Derrida's texts, as thinkers of the trace – whose thinking preemptively carries out the deconstruction of presence via the deconstruction of consciousness – nevertheless these two are not one. Despite all of his innovations, Freud, as we have just seen, fails to radically think the trace. Nietzsche, however, enjoys a peculiar status in Derrida's texts. Hegel, as we saw in Chapters 3 and 5, thinks *différance*, Derrida says, but subordinates it to an ontotheological moment with the *Aufhebung*. Heidegger opens the very questions that mark the entirety of Derrida's project. Nevertheless, Derrida claims, 'I have marked quite explicitly, in *all* the essays I have published, as can be verified, a *departure* from the Heideggerian problematic. This departure is related particularly to the concepts of *origin* and *fall* of which we were just speaking.'[102] Elsewhere, in the interview with Houdebine and Scarpetta, Derrida says 'that the Heideggerian problematic is the most "profound" and "powerful" defence of what I attempt to put into question under the rubric of the *thought of presence*'.[103] Despite Derrida's nearly two decades of work on Husserl, despite his admission as to the urgency of fidelity to Husserl, nevertheless, Husserlian phenomenology remains 'the most radical and most critical restoration of the metaphysics of presence'.[104]

Among all the myriad Derridean influences and interlocutors, Nietzsche occupies a unique status: 'Perhaps then, moving along lines that would be more Nietzschean than Heideggerian, by going to the end of this thought of the truth of Being, we would have to become open to a *différance* that is no longer determined, in the language of the West, as the difference between Being and beings.'[105] Derrida bypasses the Heideggerian moment, returning to the Nietzschean critique of truth and being. Put otherwise, he re-enacts a Nietzschean discovery *in light of* the Heideggerian reading. As Spivak writes of those *concepts inherited from metaphysics*: 'But Nietzsche cracked them apart and then advocated forgetting that fact!'[106]

We recall from Chapter 2 the three main points of Heidegger's criticism of Nietzsche: (1) Heidegger reads will to power in a substantialist way, as having a quiddity or an 'essence'; (2) in so doing, he is able to isolate the will and characterise it as such, as what is essential about *a* will to power, which is its ever-expanding desire for more power, demanding the attendant securing of presence; (3) Nietzsche thus reverses metaphysics – he drives the subjectness of the subject out of the 'spiritual', in the form of the conscious subject, and into the 'bodily' in the form of the will to power lying at the heart of all life. In place of soul, body; in place of heaven, earth; in place of God, man. Nietzsche therefore reverses the structure; but any reversal, Heidegger claims, remains mired in what it reverses. Heidegger reads Nietzsche explicitly as a metaphysical thinker who thinks essence as will to power, and existence as eternal return.

Derrida takes issue on the first of these three criticisms: 'So that, let it be said in parenthesis, in wishing to restore a *truth* and an originary or fundamental *ontology* in the thought of Nietzsche, one risks misunderstanding, perhaps at the expense of everything else, the axial intention of his concept of interpretation.'[107] Elsewhere, he asks, 'is it perhaps hasty to make Nietzsche out to be a metaphysician, albeit the last one?'[108] Then again in *Of Grammatology*, he writes:

> To save Nietzsche from a reading of the Heideggerian type, it seems that we must above all not attempt to restore or make explicit a less naïve 'ontology,' composed of profound ontological intuitions acceding to some originary truth, an entire fundamentality hidden under the appearance of an empiricist or metaphysical text. The virulence of Nietzschean thought could not be more completely misunderstood.[109]

A *less naïve* ontology would be one that purports to more fundamentally grasp 'the sense of being'[110] or the 'logos *of* being',[111] but Nietzsche's is a thought that demonstrates that sense, even the sense of 'being', is always *produced*, under specific historical and genealogical conditions. Again:

> Nietzsche has *written what* he has written. He has written that writing – and first of all his own – is not originarily subordinate to the logos and to truth. And that this subordination has *come into being* during an epoch whose meaning we must deconstruct. Now in this direction (but only in this direction, for read otherwise, the Nietzschean demolition remains dogmatic and, *like all reversals* [my emphasis], a captive of that metaphysical edifice which it professes to overthrow. On that point and in that *order of reading*, the conclusions of Heidegger and Fink are irrefutable).[112]

Nietzsche is not, according to Derrida, an ontological thinker. Nietzsche's thought embarks upon an experiment of writing, a strategy of writing that loosens his thought from any presupposition to 'truth' or to 'being'. That he *has written what he has written* means that, for Derrida, Nietzsche writes in accordance with the structure of archē-writing (of originary writing as highlighting that sense is always produced and never stable, that its origins are never pure or simple[113]) that Derrida is attempting to articulate: 'Reading, and therefore writing, the text were for Nietzsche "originary" operations . . . with regard to a sense that they do not first have to transcribe or discover.'[114] This means that Nietzsche writes only in the simultaneous effacement and cancellation of what he writes: he *has written what* he has written. Nietzsche's thought lives and breathes in the air of exchange, metonymy, metaphor, rupture, and contradiction.

In a now-famous posthumously published early essay, Nietzsche writes: 'What then is truth? A movable host of metaphors, metonymies, and anthropomorphisms: in short, a sum of human relations which have been poetically and rhetorically intensified, transferred, and embellished, and which, after long usage, seem to a people to be fixed, canonical, and binding. Truths are illusions which we have forgotten are illusions.'[115] A 'truth' is a seemingly congealed metaphor, according to Nietzsche, whose slippages of meaning we ignore or suppress.

The first words of Nietzsche's *Beyond Good and Evil* put this suggestion into motion: 'Supposing truth is a woman – what then? Are there not grounds for the suspicion that all philosophers, in so far as they were dogmatists, have been very inexpert about women?'[116] On this passage, Derrida writes:

> the credulous and dogmatic philosopher who *believes* in the truth that is woman, who believes in truth just as he believes in woman, this philosopher has understood nothing of truth, nor anything of woman. Because, indeed, if woman *is* truth, *she* at least knows that there is no truth, that truth has no place here and that no one has a place for truth. And she is woman precisely because she herself does not believe in truth itself, because she does not believe in what she is, in what she is believed to be, in what she thus is not.[117]

Nietzsche's strange question sets the tone for everything that he says throughout *Beyond Good and Evil* regarding the relations between men and women, philosophers and truth, such that, by way of a barely perceptible metonymic exchange, we get assertions such as this:

> Philosophers [men] have so far treated truths [women] like birds who had strayed to them from some height: as something more refined and vulnerable, wilder, stranger, sweeter, and more soulful – but as something one has to lock up lest it fly away . . . A philosopher, on the other hand, who has depth, in his spirit as well as in his desires . . . must conceive of truth as a possession, as property that can be locked, as something predestined for service and achieving its perfection in that.[118]

Truth does not come ready-made, once and for all. 'They have not fallen from the sky fully formed',[119] says Derrida. Truths operate in particular relations under particular circumstances at particular times, and at bottom, truth is nothing but these veils: 'From the beginning, nothing has been more alien, repugnant, and hostile to woman than truth – her great art is the lie, her highest concern is mere appearance and beauty.'[120] 'Woman', in this context, is a metaphor for the concern with veils, with appearances and dissimulations. Truth as woman presents itself only in veils, and behind its veils lie only more veils. As Derrida writes, 'There is no such thing as a woman, as a truth in itself of woman in itself . . . For just this reason then, there is no such thing either as the truth of Nietzsche, or of Nietzsche's text . . . Indeed there is no such thing as a truth in itself. But only a surfeit of it.'[121] That this is what Nietzsche intends with this metaphor is evidenced by an earlier passage from *The Gay Science*:

> 'Is it true that God is present everywhere?' a little girl asked her mother; 'I think that's indecent' – a hint for philosophers! One should have more respect for the bashfulness with which nature has hidden behind riddles and iridescent uncertainties. Perhaps truth is a woman who has reasons for not letting us see her reasons? Perhaps her name is – to speak Greek – *Baubo*?
>
> Oh, those Greeks! They knew how to live. What is required for that is to stop courageously at the surface, the fold, the skin, to adore appearance, to believe in forms, tones, words, in the whole Olympus of appearance. Those Greeks were superficial – *out of profundity*.[122]

It also makes it possible to consistently interpret some of the more perplexing and appalling claims that Nietzsche makes regarding women:

> Science offends the modesty of all real women. It makes them feel as if one wanted to peep under their skin – yet worse, under their dress and finery.[123]

> Women are considered profound. Why? Because one never fathoms their depths. Women aren't even shallow.[124]

The unsettling and superficiality of truth is a constant theme throughout the entirety of Nietzsche's writings, from beginning to end. As late as *On the Genealogy of Morality* (1887), Nietzsche writes: 'what meaning would *our* entire being have if not this, that in us this will to truth has come to a consciousness of itself *as a problem*?'[125] *This* is the Nietzsche that, for Derrida, thinks difference beyond Hegel, thinks *différance* without reconciliation. Nietzsche's strategy liberates 'the signifier from its dependence or derivation with respect to the logos'.[126] The genealogical method thinks truths as constituted, as the effects of imperceptible differentials of forces. For this reason, Derrida writes:

> Therefore, rather than protect Nietzsche from the Heideggerian reading, we should perhaps offer him up to it completely, underwriting that interpretation without reserve; in a *certain way* and up to the point where, the content of the Nietzschean discourse being almost lost for the question of being, its form regains its absolute strangeness, where his text finally invokes a different type of reading, more faithful to his type of writing.[127]

If Nietzsche is an ontological thinker, Derrida claims, Heidegger's criticisms succeed. If Nietzsche is thinking a logos of being, then will to power must be understood substantially, and results in the Heideggerian reversal which leaves intact the structure and remains ensnared in the metaphysical tradition. To *give Nietzsche up* to Heidegger's reading means to follow Heidegger through these stages, culminating in the reversal of the tradition, but precisely at the moment when it looks as though we have merely performed an inversion and have stood metaphysics on its head, everything that Nietzsche has said – about identity, about subjectivity, about the ephemeral nature of consciousness, about truth, about Being – intervenes and does not permit the inversion, *as* simple inversion, to stand. By giving Nietzsche up to Heidegger, while remaining faithful to Nietzsche, we invert the structure, only to mark the space and the gesture that gave rise to the structure to begin with. These two moves prefigure the two moments of deconstruction exactly:

> Therefore we must proceed using a double gesture, according to a unity that is both systematic and in and of itself divided, a double writing, that is, a writing that is in and of itself multiple . . . On the one hand, we must traverse a phase of *overturning* . . . to recognize that in a classical philosophical opposition we are not dealing with the peaceful coexistence of a *vis-à-vis*, but rather with a violent hierarchy . . .
>
> That being said – and on the other hand – to remain in this phase is still to operate on the terrain of and from within the deconstructed system. By means of this double, and precisely stratified, dislodged and dislodging, writing, we must also mark the interval between inversion, which brings low what was high, and the irruptive emergence of a new 'concept,' a concept that can no longer be, and never could be, included in the previous regime.[128]

Or, in Nietzsche's words, 'The true world – we have abolished. What world has remained? The apparent one perhaps? But no! *With the true world we have also abolished the apparent one.*'[129] The destruction of the *true world* in Nietzsche's understanding brings with it the destruction of the *apparent world* as well, because the world was only established as *apparent* in opposition to a presumed *truth* that lay in the suprasensuous. In breaking down the one, the overall structure collapses, pointing the way to *a philosophy of the future*. This new concept is the non-concept that, in

Derrida's writings, goes under the name of, at various points, *différance*, archē-writing, trace, supplement, etc.[130] We are now in a position to see how *différance* functions for Derrida, and we shall do so by looking at his own formulations and complementing, or supplementing, them with what we have seen in his readings of Husserl, Freud, and Nietzsche.

Différance and trace: inversion and ashes

Above, I offered a brief formulation for what *différance* is, piecing together a few elements of the more commonly expressed recurrent themes whenever Derrida himself offers such a formulation: *différance is the non-originary constituting-disruption of presence*. We are now in a position to see how it operates, and to think through the implications of this operation. *Différance* exposes itself at work in a text precisely at the moment when the author would least desire, in accordance with a 'logic of supplementarity': 'The question is of an originary supplement, if this absurd expression may be risked, totally unacceptable as it is within classical logic.'[131] In the classical, philosophical binaries, hierarchically structured as we saw above, one of the terms is always suppressed or repressed in an attempt to valorise and purify the other. But the suppressed term always returns in the form of a supplement, an 'addition' meant to bolster or undergird the would-be primary term. Derrida's logic of the supplement demonstrates that if the primary term *needs* to be supplemented, it must itself suffer from an originary lack. What the philosophical author sees as a sickness (the deficient term) is in fact the only cure for the insufficiency of the primary term they originally sought to isolate and valorise. Thus the primary term, despite the intentions of the author, is conceptually and structurally 'infected' from its origin by the 'contamination' of the secondary term. For example, as we saw, Husserl's demand for the most *meaningful* sign required the exclusion of the indicative function of the sign, focusing solely on expression as the voice of the inner soliloquy. This was complicated by Husserl's *living present*, the structure of which infected every present (where the apodicticity of subjectivity would be secured) with non-presence, and infected every presentation of the primal impression with a primary structure of repetition, introducing a hiatus into the self-presence of consciousness, thus requiring the indicative function of the sign to supplement the expressive.

Likewise, Freud, as we saw, sought to think memory in terms of life, and the machine – the prosthetic memory of the *Wunderblock* – in terms of death. Nevertheless, the fact that living memory requires a prosthesis is an indication that memory itself is finite, or, put otherwise, that death infects it. Memory requires the supplement of a prosthesis. Rousseau, Saussure, and Husserl too, sought to suppress writing (death), in favour of the voice, the form of signification closest to the soul. In so doing, they are being faithful to an ancient, Aristotelian impetus: 'Now spoken sounds are symbols of affections in the soul, and written marks symbols of spoken sounds. And just as written marks are not the same for all men, neither are spoken sounds. But what these are in the first place signs of – affections of the soul – are the same for all; and what these affections are likenesses of – actual things – are also the same.'[132] The spoken signs are closest to the soul, closest to the living itself. Nevertheless, the insufficiency of the living voice is that it dies in the very moment it is spoken – the very characteristic that makes it most alive also makes it most mortal. The written sign thus supplements the living voice, allowing the sign to be preserved forever, even beyond the death of the speaker. However, even in the act of verbal communication, the speaker and listener mutually rely upon a semi-permanent system of meaning, *inscribed* within the linguistic culture of which they are a part. This inscription entails an ideality and iterability of the signs that would *seem* to belong more properly to the *written* sign, as opposed to the *vocal* sign. This is the logic of supplementarity: the supplement is originary – it belongs to and in some senses conditions the primary term, to which it is meant to be subordinate. This is the meaning of deconstruction's stage of *inversion*.

By inverting the structure, however, what comes to the fore is the essential complicity of the terms of any binary in the system. In Chapter 5, we saw that the oppositional nature of *différance* amounted to the interdependency of specific relations of forces, which entailed that in any given binary, 'each of the terms must appear as the *différance* of the other, as the other different and deferred in the economy of the same'.[133] The two terms are spawned together; the fall, if you will, has already happened in the garden. This indicates that something more fundamental is at work – the movement of *différance*.

Différance is an originary 'play of difference' which 'is the condition for the possibility and functioning of every sign'.[134] It is not a thing, not a being (for, recall, Being has been determined historically as presence). It is 'neither a word nor a concept',[135] as a *word* names a *thing* and a *concept* denotes an essentiality. It is not a name, which would be a 'pure nominal unity',[136] outside the movements of signification which would thereby be, as all names are, metaphysical. It is the '"productive" movement of differences',[137] and the productive play of forces. These terms *movement of differences* and *play of forces* are in some sense synonymous, as force itself is but a play of difference, according to Derrida. Citing Deleuze, he writes, 'Force itself is never present; it is only a play of differences and quantities.'[138] Forces, then, have no stasis, and as we saw in Chapter 5, there *are* no equal forces; forces have their being only in their differential relations.

Moreover, Derrida rejects the conceptualisation of *différance* as a *differentiation*. Differentiation would suggest a logically independent operation which would occur upon a more primordial 'one', such as in the cosmology of Anaxagoras. As Derrida says, differentiation 'would have left open the possibility of an organic, original, and homogeneous unity that eventually would come to be divided, to receive difference as an event'.[139] In one definition, '*Différance* is the non-full, non-simple, structured and differentiating origin of differences.'[140] But these differences are not to be understood as static relations between static entities, but rather, 'these differences are themselves effects'[141] of the plays of forces. These constituted differences are what we defined above as traces, the mark of absolute exteriority: 'This principle compels us not only not to privilege one substance . . . but even to consider every process of signification as a formal play of differences. That is, of traces.'[142]

Traces are thus the effects, the differences produced by the play of *différance*. The trace, we recall, is the *openness upon exteriority in general*. In its production, it has, strictly speaking, no *identity* of its own, no *presence*. Freud mistakenly thought the trace as permanent, but 'an unerasable trace is not a trace, it is a full presence, an immobile and uncorruptible substance, a son of God'.[143] The trace is produced only in its essential complicity and relatedness to its opposites, or to the other traces in the system. The logic of the supplement exposes the 'displaced and equivocal passage of one different thing to another, from one term of an opposition to the other'.[144] The trace is thus produced as a presence, only in a qualified sense, as the *presence of an absence*, the experience of a fundamental lack: 'But the movement of the trace is necessarily occulted, it produces itself as self-occultation. When the other announces itself as such, it presents itself in the dissimulation of itself.'[145] The terms in any relation or in any system thus possess no identity in themselves. They *are* only in terms of what they are *not*: the trace *is* but a trace of other traces. 'There are only, everywhere, differences and traces of traces.'[146] Here we must be absolutely clear – the trace, the constituted effect and presupposition of *différance*, like Nietzsche's *mobile army of metaphor*, subsists only as the apparition of all its related, absent traces. 'But at the same time, this erasure of the trace must have been traced in the metaphysical text. Presence, then, far from being, as is commonly thought, *what* the sign signifies, what a trace refers to, presence, then, is the trace of the trace, the trace of the erasure of the trace. Such is, for us, the text of metaphysics, and such is, for us, the language which we speak.'[147] Every trace is thus a nexus of negation, a

'Cinder as the house of being. . .'.[148] In *Cinders*, Derrida explicitly ties the notion of the trace to that of ash,[149] and writes:

> I understand that the cinder is nothing that can be in the world, nothing that remains as an entity [*étant*]. It is the being [*l'être*], rather, that there is – this is a name of the being that there is but which, giving itself (*es gibt ashes*), is nothing, remains beyond everything that is (*konis epekeina tes ousias*), remains unpronounceable in order to make saying it possible although it is nothing.[150]

As Derrida writes in *Of Grammatology*, 'The trace *is nothing*.'[151] The trace gives itself, but *is* itself, nothing. 'It remains *from* what is not, in order to recall at the delicate, charred bottom of itself only nonbeing or nonpresence.'[152] It is, like Plato's form of the good, beyond being, *epekeina tes ousias*.

Indeed the same holds true of *différance* itself. *Différance*, as we have shown, precedes and conditions the binaries of Western metaphysics, each as the *différance* of the other. Among these binaries are the terms of Heidegger's ontico-ontological difference: Being and beings: 'Since Being has never had a "meaning," has never been thought or said as such, except by dissimulating itself in beings, then *différance*, in a certain and very strange way (is) "older" than the ontological difference or than the truth of Being . . . There is no maintaining, and no depth to, this bottomless chessboard on which Being is put into play.'[153] *Différance*, then, is older than Being; it is, in a certain sense, beyond Being, according to Derrida.

Like Plato's form of the good, *différance* for Derrida concerns the very possibility of thought itself, but in such a way as to effect a certain fracturing (not to say a reversal) of the Platonic structure. One of the effects of Platonism, the inauguration of the tradition of Western metaphysics, is the 'blockage of passage among opposing values'.[154] The force of thought, Derrida claims, must escape its imprisonment in the binary system. This is precisely what *différance* does for Derrida – it opens passage between opposing values:

> Such a radicalisation of the *thought of the trace* (a *thought because it escapes binarism and makes binarism possible* on the basis of *nothing* [my emphasis]), would be fruitful not only in the deconstruction of logocentrism, but in a kind of reflection exercised more positively in different fields, at different levels of writing in general, at the point of articulation of writing in the current sense and of the trace in general.[155]

This is why Derrida commences his famous January 1968 lecture with the proclamation: 'And I must state here and now that today's discourse will be less a justification of, and even less an apology for, this silent lapse in spelling, than a kind of insistent intensification of its play.'[156] There *is*, strictly speaking, no defence for *différance*, as any such defence would have to be rooted in the argumentative logic of the West, the very structure that *différance* disrupts. *Différance* only *is* in its operations and relations, such that there can be no justification for *différance* as such. Because it surfaces only in 'originary reading', to think *différance* is to *read* it, it is to *participate* in its play. For this reason the thought of *différance* amounts to the *insistent intensification of its play*.

If the play of *différance* exposes the trace as a trace of traces, a nexus of negations or a presence of absences, then the intensification of this play would result in the multiplication and amplification of these negations and oppositions. As we saw in Chapter 5, Derrida is always reticent with respect to the notion of *contradiction*, but only because it is a notion so thoroughly imbued with Hegelian tones: 'Now, wherever, and in the extent to which, the motif of contradiction functions effectively, in a textual work, outside speculative dialectics, and taking into account a new problematic of meaning . . . I agree.'[157] Shortly thereafter, as we also saw earlier, Guy Scarpetta asks of Derrida: 'Does not this practice of shaking, of excess, of destruction seem to you to derive from a logic of contradiction, released from its speculative investments?', to which Derrida responds, 'Yes, why not? Provided that one determines the concept of contradiction with the necessary critical precautions, and by elucidating its relationship or non-relationship to Hegel's *Logic*.'[158] To avoid Hegelian contradiction means, as we saw in the last chapter, to avoid the resolution of the contradiction. To intensify the play of *différance*, then, is to multiply its oppositions and negations, to free them from the resolution of the *Aufhebung*, in which they would be suppressed. It is to put truth into motion, as a *mobile army of metaphor and metonymy*, just as Nietzsche had done. It is to enter the value of truth into what Derrida elsewhere calls 'a Hegelianism without reserve', a 'difference as the affirmative elusion of presence',[159] as the '*indefinite* destruction of value'.[160] The results are new concepts 'that can no longer be, and never could be, included in the previous regime'.[161]

Conclusion

In this chapter we have shown that it is a certain Nietzscheanism that, for Derrida, enables us to think difference beyond the trappings of Hegel. Nietzsche's thought is characterised by

> the systematic mistrust as concerns the entirety of metaphysics, the formal vision of philosophical discourse, the concept of the philosopher-artist, the rhetorical and philological questions put to the history of philosophy, the suspiciousness concerning the values of truth ('a well applied convention'),

of meaning and of Being, of the 'meaning of Being,' the attention to the economic phenomena of force and of the difference of forces.[162]

Nietzsche's thought, for Derrida, takes us beyond the difference of Hegelianism, 'difference in the service of presence'.[163] It does so not by merely reversing Platonism, as any reversal remains ensnared in that which it reverses. Rather, Nietzsche thinks difference by liberating the signifier from any presumption to truth or to Being. He thereby exposes the *trace* as the ghost, the cinder, or the ash of its other. In so doing, Nietzsche, almost a century prior to Derrida, carries out the double gesture of deconstruction, revealing the genealogical element of *différance* that always eludes presence.

In Chapter 7 we shall examine Deleuze's appropriation of Nietzsche. For Deleuze, Nietzsche provides the clearest possible articulation of the univocity of being, with his notion of eternal return. We shall begin by discussing the task of modern philosophy as laid out by Nietzsche – the reversal of Platonism. For Deleuze, this reversal does not merely invert a binary structure (as it would for Heidegger and for Derrida). Rather, the reversal of Platonism highlights a suppressed term in the Platonic paradigm – the simulacrum from Book X of the *Republic*. The simulacrum is understood by Deleuze as founded upon an internal *difference*, as opposed to an internal *resemblance* (as when the particular *copy* in the world *resembles* its form). This internal difference will be the fundamental concept of Deleuze's ontology. It is made thinkable by Nietzsche's notion of eternal return, which we explore in three distinct but related senses: (1) the affirmation of chance; (2) the affirmation of the disjunctive synthesis; (3) the selective and unthinkable heartbeat of time.

Notes

1. *WD*, 281.
2. *P*, 10.
3. *MP*, 18.
4. *DR*, 40–1.
5. *DR*, 66.
6. *OG*, 19.
7. *DR*, 38.
8. *OG*, 70.
9. Gasché, *The Tain of the Mirror*, 204, and 194–205.
10. *MP*, 3.
11. *P*, 9.
12. *OG*, 19.
13. *OG*, 70.
14. *P*, 5.
15. *VP*, 6.

16. *VP*, 6.
17. *WD*, 203.
18. *VP*, 16.
19. *OG*, 74.
20. *IPP*, 44.
21. *MP*, 8.
22. *MP*, 8. Derrida notes that the duality of senses in the Latin word is carried over into the French *differer*, and he is sensitive to this as early as his 1962 Introduction to Husserl's 'Origin of Geometry'. See Derrida, *Edmund Husserl's Origin of Geometry: An Introduction*, 153.
23. *LU*, 183.
24. *VP*, 27.
25. *VP*, 16.
26. *VP*, 17.
27. *VP*, 17.
28. *VP*, 17–18.
29. *VP*, 18.
30. *VP*, 32.
31. *VP*, 32.
32. *VP*, 34.
33. *LU*, 191.
34. *LU*, 191.
35. *VP*, 19.
36. *VP*, 37.
37. *LU*, 191.
38. *LU*, 191. This translates, literally, as 'in the same blink of the eye'. The German word *Augenblick*, which is the word translated as 'moment', literally means 'blink of an eye'.
39. *VP*, 3.
40. *VP*, 3.
41. This due to the fact that the essential distinction between indication and expression demands that there be nothing indicative about the expression. This is only the case if it is in fact true that the self is immediately present to the self, which thus requires the punctual, discrete, now-point of self-presence.
42. *PCT*, 29.
43. *PCT*, 30.
44. *PCT,* 30.
45. *PCT*, 40.
46. *VP*, 52.
47. *VP*, 53.
48. See Plato's Divided Line, *Republic*, Bk. VI.
49. *VP*, 53.
50. *PCT*, 43.
51. *PCT*, 41.
52. *PCT*, 41.
53. See Cisney, *Derrida's* Voice and Phenomenon, 123–39, for a detailed discussion of this passage.
54. *LU*, 191.
55. *VP*, 57.
56. *PCT*, 41.
57. *VP*, 57.
58. *IPP*, 44.
59. *VP*, 58.
60. *VP*, 73.

61. *VP*, 58.
62. *VP*, 57.
63. *VP*, 58.
64. *VP*, 58.
65. *VP*, 59.
66. *VP*, 56.
67. *VP*, 53.
68. *OG*, 70.
69. *MP*, 17.
70. *MP*, 21.
71. *VP*, 54n. 'Freud and the Scene of Writing' is the only text of Derrida's *not* centred on Husserl that is cited in *Voice and Phenomenon*.
72. Freud, 'A Note upon the "Mystic Writing-Pad" ', in *General Psychological Theory*, 209.
73. Ibid., 207.
74. Ibid., 209–10.
75. *WD*, 226.
76. Freud, 'A Note upon the "Mystic Writing-Pad" ', in *General Psychological Theory*, 210–11.
77. Ibid., 208.
78. Freud, *The Interpretation of Dreams*, in *The Basic Writings of Sigmund Freud*, 489.
79. Freud, 'A Note upon the "Mystic Writing-Pad" ', in *General Psychological Theory*, 210.
80. Freud, *Beyond the Pleasure Principle*, 30.
81. Perception-Consciousness – this is Freud's term for the system that receives perceptions.
82. Freud, 'A Note upon the "Mystic Writing-Pad" ', in *General Psychological Theory*, 211–12.
83. Ibid., 212.
84. Descartes, *Meditations on First Philosophy*, in *The Philosophical Writings of Descartes, Volume II*, 21.
85. *WD*, 225.
86. *WD*, 225.
87. *WD*, 226.
88. Freud, 'A Note upon the "Mystic Writing-Pad" ', in *General Psychological Theory*, 212.
89. *WD*, 226.
90. *WD*, 226.
91. *WD*, 226.
92. *WD*, 226–7.
93. Freud, 'A Note upon the "Mystic Writing-Pad" ', in *General Psychological Theory*, 211.
94. *WD*, 227.
95. *WD*, 229.
96. *WD*, 228.
97. *WD*, 228.
98. *WD*, 228.
99. *WD*, 229.
100. *WD*, 230.
101. Derrida is not being entirely fair to Freud here, as Freud says explicitly that the trace is permanent, 'even though not unalterable'. Freud, 'A Note upon the "Mystic Writing-Pad" ', in *General Psychological Theory*, 208.
102. *P*, 54.
103. *P*, 55.

104. *OG*, 49.
105. *P*, 10.
106. Spivak, 'Translator's Preface', *OG*, xxxviii.
107. *OG*, 286–7.
108. Derrida, 'Interpreting Signatures (Nietzsche/Heidegger): Two Questions', 260.
109. *OG*, 19.
110. *OG*, 22.
111. *OG*, 20.
112. *OG*, 19–20.
113. 'This complicity of origins may be called archē-writing' (*OG*, 92).
114. *OG*, 19.
115. Nietzsche, 'On Truth and Lies in a Nonmoral Sense', in *Philosophy and Truth*, 84.
116. *BGE*, 192. I do not wish to enter into the complex debate over Nietzsche's philosophical treatment of women in his writings, nor do I make excuses for the blatantly misogynistic language in his corpus. But I suspect that, like most concepts in Nietzsche's works, the concept of gender is likely not as simple as it may seem. Nietzsche's emphasis on *birthing* throughout his works is worth noting. In *On the Genealogy of Morality*, for instance, the philosopher is described as having a '"motherly" instinct, the secret love of that which grows in him' (*GM*, 78). For an exceptionally nuanced engagement with this question, see Ormiston, 'Traces of Derrida: Nietzsche's Image of Woman'. See also Irigaray, *Marine Lover of Friedrich Nietzsche*; Oliver, *Womanizing Nietzsche: Philosophy's Relation to the 'Feminine'*; Oliver and Pearsall (eds), *Feminist Interpretations of Friedrich Nietzsche*; and *SNS*.
117. *SNS*, 53.
118. *BGE*, 356–7.
119. *MP*, 11.
120. *BGE*, 353.
121. *SNS*, 101–3.
122. *FW*, 38.
123. *BGE*, 277.
124. *TI*, 470.
125. *GM*, 117.
126. *OG*, 19.
127. *OG*, 19.
128. *P*, 42.
129. *TI*, 486.
130. This is not to say that these are all synonymous, even though Derrida frequently uses them interchangeably.
131. *OG*, 313.
132. Aristotle, *De Interpretatione*, 16a1.
133. *MP*, 17.
134. *MP*, 5.
135. *MP*, 7.
136. *MP*, 26.
137. Derrida, 'The Original Discussion of "*Différance*"', in Wood and Bernasconi (eds), *Derrida and* Différance, 85.
138. *MP*, 17.
139. *MP*, 13.
140. *MP*, 11.
141. *MP*, 11.
142. *P*, 26.
143. *WD*, 230.
144. *MP*, 17.
145. *OG*, 47.

146. *P*, 26.
147. *MP*, 66.
148. *C*, 23.
149. *C*, 25.
150. *C*, 55.
151. *OG*, 75.
152. *C*, 21.
153. *MP*, 22.
154. *D*, 98.
155. *WD*, 230.
156. *MP*, 3.
157. *P*, 74.
158. *P*, 76.
159. *WD*, 263.
160. *WD*, 271.
161. *P*, 42.
162. *MP*, 305.
163. *WD*, 263.

Chapter 7

Deleuze, Plato's Reversal, and Eternal Return

Like Derrida, Deleuze will reject Heidegger's reading of Nietzsche, and will find in Nietzsche's thought a way of thinking difference beyond Hegelian difference. In the case of Derrida, we saw that he rejected the first of Heidegger's three criticisms, the substantiality of will to power, on the basis of his understanding that Nietzsche is not formulating an ontology. If he *were* an ontological thinker, then not only would the first of Heidegger's criticisms work (inasmuch as any *logos* of *being* will always be bound up with the demand for presence), but the subsequent two follow as well, from which it follows that Nietzsche reverses Platonism, but in so reversing it, remains ensnared by it.

On the contrary, Deleuze will affirm Nietzsche as an ontological thinker, rejecting however that the Being he thinks is the self-presencing substantiality of the will as Heidegger conceives it. Nietzsche indeed reverses Platonism, but does so by freeing up a marginalised category in the Platonic subtext, *the simulacrum*, thinking the simulacrum in terms of its own internal difference, as its constitutive, essential truth. When the *simulacra* are thought on their own terms, rather than as degraded copies, what results is a model of difference in which the returning of the Same is in fact the returning of the different, identity is displaced and secondary, and the negative is abolished. The affirmation of the *simulacra* destroys both model and copy, in favour of the thought of the selective character of Being, the eternal return, the play of chance and destiny, and the dual affirmation of both.

Nietzsche and the reversal of Platonism

Nietzsche, Derrida says, cannot be carrying out a reversal of Platonism, for 'all reversals', he claims, remain 'a captive of that metaphysical edifice which it professes to overthrow'.[1] Deleuze, on the contrary, unapologetically says, 'What does it mean "to reverse Platonism"? This is how Nietzsche defined the task of philosophy or, more generally, the task of the philosophy of the future',[2] elsewhere calling this reversal, 'the task of modern philosophy'.[3] Moreover, in response to Derrida's concern about remaining 'captive' to a system that one reverses, Deleuze appears uninterested: 'That this overturning should conserve many Platonic characteristics is not only inevitable but desirable.'[4] 'Plato' marks the moment that Western philosophy first finds its voice, but as such, the *decisions* of the Platonic moment, which will govern the tasks and goals of the history of philosophy into the present, are made in the context of a soil that is still itself undecided. As we saw in Chapter 2, Plato flirts dangerously close to a form of the different that would undermine the entirety of his metaphysics, or, to quote Deleuze, 'the Heraclitean world still growls in Platonism'.[5] The Platonic 'decisions' are made upon the soil of the pre-Platonic, and for this reason any so-called reversal of the structure cannot but retain certain elements of the structure itself. This does *not* entail, however, that the elements themselves or the relations between the elements remain the same, if only in an inverse reflection, as Heidegger seems to think. It all depends upon the way in which one understands the structure to begin with. In the context of the Heidegger-Derrida reading of the reversal of Platonism, we find a somewhat standard interpretation of the tradition that goes by the name 'Platonism', as a binary distinction between sensible and intelligible, and as we have seen in Derrida, that its effect is the 'blockage of passage among opposing values'.[6] For Heidegger, Nietzsche reverses Platonism in that he shifts the point of view of value from the transcendent to the immanent, from the spiritual to the bodily – this reversal, however, leaves the structure, and its groundedness in the suprasensuous, intact. For Derrida, Nietzsche's thought *beyond good and evil* is to be understood in the sense that, by carrying out the inversion to which Heidegger refers, while simultaneously cancelling out any presuppositions with respect to being or truth (thus leaving behind any presumptions to ontology), Nietzsche in fact shifts beyond the binary structure, beyond the true and the apparent, to the space between that made the binary structure possible in the first place. Derrida thus tacitly agrees with Heidegger's estimation of Platonism,[7] but disagrees with Heidegger's understanding of Nietzsche as an ontological thinker who merely reverses the tradition.

On the contrary, Deleuze expressly rejects the straightforwardly dualistic reading of the Platonic system (and hence, the significance of its reversal): 'The formula seems to mean the abolition of the world of essences *and* of the world of appearances. Such a project, however, would not be peculiar to Nietzsche. The dual denunciation of essences and appearances dates back to Hegel or, better yet, to Kant. It is doubtful that Nietzsche meant the same thing.'[8] In place of the standard binary interpretation, Deleuze introduces a third tier into the standard historical analysis. Like our analysis of the form of the different in Chapter 2, Deleuze locates within Plato's thinking a virtuality which, if unleashed, possesses the potential to disrupt the entire Platonic edifice. As Ronald Bogue says in his *Deleuze and Guattari*, 'Deleuze's strategy in overcoming Platonism is not, as one might expect, simply to invert the hierarchy of essence and appearance, but to extract from Plato's texts a marginalized category that subverts both models and copies, both essence and appearance – that of the simulacrum.'[9] In reversing Platonism, Deleuze claims, Nietzsche allows the simulacra to rise to the surface, liberating them from their oppressive subordination to form and its copies. According to Deleuze, the problem with any so-called 'standard' or 'traditional' interpretation of Platonism is that it presumes to know, without justification or explanation, the nature of Plato's goal: 'it leaves the motivation of Platonism in the shadows'.[10]

Plato introduces the dialectical method into philosophy, but his dialectic is of a different stripe than that of Aristotle: 'Our mistake lies', Deleuze claims, 'in trying to understand Platonic division on the basis of Aristotelian requirements.'[11] The task of Plato's dialectic is to divide and to collect, to split into groups, to make distinctions.[12] It is a method of division, but not of dividing genera into species; rather, it is a method of distinguishing the true from the false, the 'Participants'[13] from the false suitors, which Deleuze calls the *simulacra*. The exhaustive taxonomy of angling in the *Sophist*, for instance, serves as a mere preparatory exercise in the *hunt* for the Sophist: 'But it isn't the easiest thing in the world to grasp the tribe we're planning to search for – I mean, the sophist – or say what it is. But if an important issue needs to be worked out well, then as everyone has long thought, you need to practice on unimportant, easier issues first.'[14] Likewise, throughout the dialogues, when Socrates seeks an answer to the question, *what is?*, it is always with the motivation of identifying the *true* participant and distinguishing it from the false, as in the *Euthyphro*, when he says, 'Tell me then what this form itself is so that I may look upon it, and using it as a model, say that any action of yours or another's that is of that kind is pious, and if it is not that it is not',[15] or in the *Gorgias* when Socrates says, 'Or rather, Gorgias, why don't you tell us yourself what the craft you're knowledgeable in is, and hence, what we're supposed to call you?'[16]

Thus, the task of the Platonic system is not to separate originals from copies, but to *know* the originals (the forms), *so that* one may divide and distinguish true copies[17] from false copies, or what Plato calls 'appearances that aren't likenesses'.[18] Deleuze says, 'it has to do with selecting among the pretenders, distinguishing good and bad copies or, rather, copies (always well-founded) and simulacra (always engulfed in dissimilarity)'.[19] Distinguishing the copy (the icon) from the simulacrum is the extent of its resemblance to (based upon its participation in) the form itself. In Book X of the *Republic*, Plato provides us with an example, that of a couch: 'There turn out, then, to be these three kinds of couches: one that *is* in nature . . . one that the carpenter produced . . . and one that the painter produced.'[20] The one that *is* in nature is the form of the couch, produced, Socrates surmises, by a god. The carpenter too, Socrates claims, is a 'craftsman of a couch', but the couch he crafts is not 'the being but something that is like the being' of the couch.[21] The craftsman's couch resembles the god's couch; it copies it well. The painter, however, possesses no knowledge of the couch that *is* in nature. The painter merely imitates 'the works of the craftsmen'.[22] Its imitation is not an imitation of the 'truth' of the couch. If the craftsman's couch is a copy of the couch that *is* in nature, the painter's couch, inasmuch as the painter possesses no knowledge of the couch that *is* in nature, is a copy of the craftsman's couch – a copy of a copy, reproducing the *look* of the couch. This copy, however, is mere shadow and reflection: 'Therefore, imitation is surely far from the truth; and, as it seems, it is due to this that it produces everything – because it lays hold of a certain small part of each thing, and that part is itself only a phantom [εἴδωλον].'[23] The simulacrum lays hold of an illusory image of the thing.

For Deleuze, however, to define the simulacrum as a 'copy of a copy'[24] is to miss the essential, constitutive nature of the simulacrum, that which causes it to differ in nature from the icon, the *true* copy. 'The copy', Deleuze says, 'is an image endowed with resemblance, the simulacrum is an image without resemblance.'[25] But clearly, the simulacrum *must* demonstrate *some* resemblance, or it would not easily fool the observer. The skilled painter, Socrates advises, can imitate in such a way as to convince the foolish into thinking that they are looking at something real. Indeed the devil himself, we are told, comes not as the *opposite* of God, but *in the image* of God, 'for Satan himself masquerades as an angel of light'.[26] How then are we to understand this resemblance and this dissimilarity? Plato says that the distinction is between an imitation based upon the *look* and one based upon *truth*.[27] The carpenter's couch resembles the couch that *is* in nature by way of an internal resemblance. The painted depiction of the couch has the outward appearance of the couch, but internally and essentially lacks in every way the *being* of the couch. In Deleuze's terminology then, the icon resembles in that its imitation is based upon truth, the knowledge of the form, upon the 'veritable production ruled by the relations and proportions constitutive of the essence',[28] whereas the simulacrum lacks this resemblance. Its phantom image is 'an *effect* of resemblance; but this is an effect of the whole, completely external and produced by totally different means than those at work within the model'.[29]

The nature of the simulacrum is thus deception and dissimulation. What is most terrifying, however, is that the simulacrum exposes us to an image that is unmasterable, subject neither to the conditions of knowledge, nor even of right opinion. In the *Republic*, Plato outlines a triad of levels of knowledge: 'For each thing there are these three arts – one that will use, one that will make, one that will imitate.'[30] The user, Plato claims, will possess the highest level of knowledge, in so far as 'the virtue, beauty, and rightness of each implement, animal and action' are 'related to nothing but the use for which each was made, or grew naturally'.[31] Take the example of the guitar. The guitar-maker no doubt possesses great knowledge when it comes to the proper proportions and materials that a well-made guitar should bear. However, it is the guitar player who best knows which woods respond in which ways to certain temperatures, which strings produce the best sounds under which conditions and why, how far away from the neck the strings should be to provide a balance of ease of playing and quality of sound, etc. In other words, the user knows the form of the thing in a way that even the producer does not, and in fact it is the user who reports back to the producer with advice for improvement of her craft. The imitator, however, regarding his imitations, will not 'have knowledge of whether they are fair and right or not, or right opinion due to the necessity of being with the man who knows'.[32]

Thus the imitator's art is 'an art of the encounter that is outside knowledge and opinion',[33] operating through creation of impressions of 'huge dimensions, depths, and distances that the observer cannot master'.[34] In so far as it creates the illusion of depth and dimension that eludes our capacities for measurement, its power relates to the part of the soul furthest from the rational, calculative part. We understand, Plato says, that a thing can look different at different distances, from different perspectives, in or out of water, and so on – this is a result of a constitutional flaw in our makeup. Measurements, weights, and calculations thus necessarily come to our rescue, so that 'we are not ruled by a thing's looking bigger or smaller or more or heavier; rather we are ruled by that which has calculated, measured, or, if you please, weighed'.[35] The imitator, however, *relies* upon these constitutional, cognitive flaws when creating the simulacrum. As Plato says, 'it is impossible for the same thing to opine contraries at the same time about the same things'.[36] When observing a painting of a couch, the skilled artist can make us believe that we are *actually* looking at a couch. We thus *opine* that it is a couch of such and such approximate measurements. The measurements themselves, however, would yield results entirely incompatible. Nevertheless, a part of our soul will insist on opining, *this is a couch*, bearing certain approximate measurements. Thus, Plato claims, 'imitation keeps company with the part of us that is far from prudence, and is not comrade and friend for any healthy or true purpose'.[37] The observer *becomes* a simulacrum herself. As Deleuze says, 'this simulacrum includes the differential point of view; and the observer becomes a part of the simulacrum itself, which is transformed and deformed by his point of view'.[38] The unmasterable depths and measurements of this deception, which draw the observer into the production of its dissimulation, reveal a 'becoming-mad, or a becoming-unlimited',[39] according to Deleuze. The decisive moment in Platonism revolves around the subordination of this becoming: 'such is the aim of Platonism in its will to bring about the triumph of icons over simulacra'.[40] This means that in the Platonic hierarchy of intelligible-sensible, being-becoming, etc., the simulacra are not at the lowest level of the hierarchy; rather they are beneath even this.

To *reverse* Platonism, as Nietzsche (and Deleuze, following him) proposes, does not merely entail a shift from the soul to the body, from being to becoming, from death to life; nor does it entail a mere shift to the *space between*. Rather, it 'means to make the simulacra rise and to affirm their rights among icons and copies'.[41] It has nothing to do with the mere reversal of the form-particular, model-icon structure, because the sheer affirmation of the simulacra destroys this representational model of thinking. On Plato's system, the simulacrum is a third-rate copy, a copy of a copy. To affirm simulacra *as* simulacra, however, means to think the nature of the simulacrum *as such*, not as a degraded copy. The simulacrum, Deleuze says, 'harbors a positive power which denies *the original and the copy, the model and the representation*'.[42] The icon is based upon internal resemblance, whereas in the case of the simulacrum, the resemblance is an external effect, an effect of an internal difference, 'an internalized dissemblance'.[43]

This internal difference is the same that Deleuze introduces as early as his 1954 review of Hyppolite's *Logic and Existence*, where he first mentions the notion of 'an ontology of pure difference', one 'that would not go all the way to contradiction, since contradiction would be less and not more than difference'.[44] It is difference internal to Being itself. Deleuze's crucial 1956 essay, 'Bergson's Conception of Difference', not only charts the seminal beginnings of an ontology of pure difference, but more importantly outlines an argument for difference conceived in this way: 'If philosophy has a positive and direct relation to things, it is only in so far as philosophy claims to grasp the thing itself, according to what it is, in its difference from everything it is not, in other words, in its *internal difference*.'[45] A concept of difference is for Deleuze a matter of ontological precision. In Bergson he finds the impulse to renew the search for the concept that reaches to the individual: 'What he rejects is a distribution that locates cause or reason in the genus and the category and abandons the individual to contingency, stranding him in space. Reason must reach all the way to the individual, the genuine concept all the way to the thing, and comprehension, all the way to "this."'[46] Aristotle had tried: his notion of the 'primary substance' is an effort to think 'the individual man or horse'.[47] However, for reasons to be discussed, Aristotle's equivocity of being, as demonstrated in the oft-cited formulation, *being is said in many ways*,[48] will reveal cracks in Aristotle's ontology that will, according to Deleuze, disallow him a proper thought of Being, difference, *or* the individual.

Aristotle and analogy

Aristotle says, 'There is a science which investigates being as being and the attributes which belong to this in virtue of its own nature.'[49] This is the philosophical science, metaphysics. This science is 'not the same as any of the so-called special sciences',[50] in that none, other than metaphysics, treats exclusively of the subject of being *qua* being. Also distinguishing metaphysics from the rest of the sciences is the fact that, although metaphysics, like *all* sciences, deals with universals, it is unique in that the universals it deals with are neither genera nor species. In dealing with being *qua* being, being as Aristotle conceives it cannot be a genus, 'for the differentiae of any genus must each of them both have being and be one, but it is not possible for the genus taken apart from its species (any more than for the species of the genus) to be predicated of its proper differentiae'.[51] A genus is predicated of its *species*, but not of its *differences*. In his famous commentary on Aristotle's *Categories*, the *Isagoge*, Porphyry defines a difference in this sense as 'what is of a nature such as to separate items under the same genus – rational and non-rational separate man and horse, which are under the same genus, animal'.[52] The genus *animal* then consists of numerous species, among them humans, horses, oxen, cows, goats, etc. The differentia that distinguishes humans from all other animals is rationality. Rationality then is not a *species* of animal, but one of the differentiae that separates *one* species of animal from *other* species of animals. (Other examples would be quadrupedal vs. bipedal, and so on). 'Differences *are*',[53] however – rationality *is*; bipedalism *is*. If Being is a genus, according to Aristotle, it is divisible into species (which would be species *of* Being, hence Being would be predicated of them), and yet, if differences *are*, if they *have Being*, as Aristotle has said they do, then Being must also be predicated of the differentiae by which its species are determined. As Smith writes, 'it would mean that the genus "Being" would have to be predicated twice: once to its species and once to its own differentiae'.[54] Thus Being is not a genus, according to Aristotle.

This leads us to an apparent problem. Philosophy is the science of being *qua* being, sciences concern themselves with genera or species, but being is neither. Thus it would seem, at least on the surface, as though a science of being *qua* being is impossible:

> Since the science of the philosopher treats of being *qua* being universally and not in respect of a part of it, and 'being' has many senses and is not used in one only, it follows that if the word is used equivocally and in virtue of nothing common to its various uses, being does not fall under one science (for the meanings of an equivocal term do not form one genus); but if the word is used in virtue of something common, being will fall under one science.[55]

In the *Categories*, Aristotle defines equivocity and univocity thusly: 'Things are said to be named "equivocally" when, though they have a common name, the definition corresponding with the name differs for each . . . On the other hand, things are said to be named "univocally" which have both the name and the definition answering to the name in common.'[56] 'Being' is named equivocally, says Aristotle. Being is not a genus, and hence, does not apply univocally to all the things of which it is predicated, though all may be said *to be*, in some sense. What then remains as an object of study for the one who studies the science of being *qua* being? Much like the mathematician, who studies number *qua* number, the philosopher studies being by way of abstraction:

> As the mathematician investigates abstractions . . . the same is true with regard to being. For the attributes of this in so far as it is being, and the contrarieties in it *qua* being, it is the business of no other science than philosophy to investigate . . . therefore it remains that it is the philosopher who studies the things we have named, in so far as they are being. Since all that is is said to 'be' in virtue of something single and common, though the term has many meanings . . . and things of this sort can fall under one science, the difficulty we stated at the beginning appears to be solved.[57]

The difficulty in part derives from the use of the Latin word 'qua', as in the expression, 'being *qua* being'. 'Qua' is almost always translated with the English word 'as', to such an extent that we use these terms almost interchangeably. 'Qua', however, is a Latin transliteration of the Greek word, 'ἦ' which, though it may indeed be translated as 'as', is more appropriately translated as 'in so far as'. In this sense, the science of being *qua* being is more appropriately understood as the science of what is, in so far as it is said to be. For Aristotle, the primary mode of this *in so far as* is the notion of substance: 'But everywhere science deals chiefly with that which is primary, and on which the other things depend, and in virtue of which they get their names. If, then, this is substance, it will be of substances that the philosopher must grasp the principles and the causes.'[58] Again, 'And those who study these properties err not by leaving the sphere of philosophy, but by forgetting that substance, of which they have no correct idea, is prior to these others.'[59] Finally, 'Obviously then it is the work of one science to examine being *qua* being, and the attributes which belong to it *qua* being, and the same science will examine not only substances but also their attributes.'[60] *This*, then, is the object of study for the philosopher. Of the various *ways* in which being is said, substance is unique, in that it is logically and ontologically prior – remaining the same – while everything else we may say of it is posterior to it. Of all the ways in which being is said, substance says being most fully and completely. The science of the philosopher then is the study of substance and its attributes. We must now look briefly to the *Categories*.

Being is said in many ways, as we have seen, 'equivocally and in virtue of nothing common to its various uses'.[61] The ways in which being is said make up the categories, which are the simple (non-composite) expressions, in and of themselves admitting of neither affirmation nor negation: substance and those things predicated of it – quantity, quality, relation, time, place, position, state, action, and affection. Since being is not a genus, the categories are not species of being. They are related to each other, Aristotle thinks, analogically: 'There are many senses in which a thing may be said to "be", but all that "is" is related to one central point (πρὸς ἕν), one definite kind of thing, and is not said to "be" by a mere ambiguity.'[62] Take, for example, the term, 'healthy'. We might say, for instance, that the act of walking is healthy, that a salad is healthy, that a portion size is healthy, that a family is healthy, or that this specific man is healthy. 'Everything that is healthy is related to health.'[63] Health is, in this sense, the singular starting point on the basis of which all other things are, to greater and lesser degrees and in different ways, related to health. In the case of being, substance is primary being, and of substance are predicated various qualities and attributes, which themselves *are*, but they *are* in an analogical fashion, in that they could not *be* without the substance that bears them: 'Thus everything except primary substances is either predicated of primary substances, or is present in them, and if these last did not exist, it would be impossible for anything else to exist.'[64] The red of the wagon could not *be* without the being of the wagon.

Thus, as Deleuze notes, analogical being has two senses in Aristotle: a distributive common sense and a hierarchical good sense.[65] 'This concept of Being . . . has no content in itself, only a content in proportion to the formally different terms of which it is predicated.'[66] Though philosophy is the science of being *qua* being, being itself, for Aristotle, only *is* as an object of study in its proportional distribution in the categories, each of which has an '*internal* relation'[67] to being. Being is hierarchical in that there are greater and lesser degrees to which a thing may be said *to be*. In this sense, analogical being is a natural bedfellow with the theological impetus, in that it provides a means of speaking and thinking about God that does not flirt with heresy, that is, does not fall into either of these two traps: (1) believing that a finite mind could ever possess knowledge of an infinite being; (2) thinking that God's qualities, for example, his love or justice, are to be understood in like fashion to our own.[68] Analogical being easily and naturally allows the scholastics to hierarchise the *great chain of being*, thus creating a space in language and thought for the ineffable. This is why Deleuze claims 'analogy has always been a theological vision, not a philosophical one, adapted to the forms of God, the world, and the self'.[69]

Problems with analogical being

Above, we briefly alluded to three specific problems with Aristotle's ontology, according to Deleuze: it disallows Aristotle a genuine concept of Being, of difference, or of the individual: 'However, this form of distribution commanded by the categories seemed to us to betray the nature of Being (as a cardinal and collective concept) and the nature of the distributions themselves (as nomadic rather than sedentary and fixed distributions), as well as the nature of difference (as individuating difference).'[70] Elsewhere Deleuze writes: 'What is missed at the two extremities is the collective sense of being [*être*] and the play of individuating difference in being [*étant*].'[71] Deleuze here identifies two sides or aspects of the concept of Being: collective and cardinal, and the two senses are typically distinguished in *Difference and Repetition* by way of a lower-case letter 'b' for the collective, and an upper-case letter 'B' for the cardinal.[72] The collective sense of being for Deleuze is something like the totality of *what is* – 'all things being divided up within being in the univocity of simple presence (the One – All)';[73] while the cardinal sense is the fundamental and constitutive sense of Being, the genetic factors that constitute an individual and make it what it is, the engine of the system. This is clearly outlined in the following passage:

By contrast, when we say that univocal being is related immediately and essentially to individuating factors, we certainly do not mean by the latter individuals constituted in experience, but that which acts in them as a transcendental principle: as a plastic, anarchic and nomadic principle, contemporaneous with the process of individuation, no less capable of dissolving and destroying individuals than of constituting them temporarily.[74]

These *individuating factors* are what Deleuze means by the cardinal sense of Being.

Thus, being is essentially and immediately related to Being; the whole of *what is* to the fundamental, constitutive principle of individuation (which is also a principle of dissolution), the most universal to the most particular. Again, 'If "being" is above all difference and commencement, Being is itself repetition, the recommencement of being.'[75] This 'being' is what Deleuze elsewhere calls '"that which is."'[76] He thus attempts an ontology in which the concept of being is both collective (in the sense of 'that which is') and constitutive (in the sense of the constitutive and individuating factors of 'that which is'). As we saw, however, from Aristotle's own metaphysics, Being is not a genus, and 'it has no content in itself, only a content in proportion to the formally different terms of which it is predicated'.[77] Thus his ontology does not allow a genuine concept of Being.

Secondly, analogical being cannot provide a genuine account of the individual. As we said above, Aristotle's ontology had included *some* notion of the individual: the 'primary substance', as we have discussed it, is an effort to think 'the individual man or horse'.[78] However, as demonstrated by the discussion of the *four causes* in the *Physics* and the outline of the categories in the *Categories*, what constitutes the essence of *this* individual man, this primary substance, is the contingent and accidental fact that he, and no other, is comprised of this conglomerate of matter (itself a universal concept) in these and those spatiotemporal relations, bearing these and those qualities (themselves accidental and universal). Such blockages will infect *any* effort to representationally formulate a concept of the individual, and indeed, Aristotle himself appears to recognise, indeed affirm, this point: 'For it is by stating the species or the genus that we appropriately define any individual man; and we shall make our definition more exact by stating the former than by stating the latter. All other things that we state, such as that he is white, that he runs, and so on, are irrelevant to the definition.'[79] As Deleuze notes, this relation of being to individual provides no ontological account for how *this* particular man is different from *that* particular man: 'It is henceforth inevitable that analogy falls into an unresolvable difficulty: it must essentially relate being to particular existents, but at the same time it cannot say what constitutes their individuality. For it retains in the particular only that which conforms to the general (matter and form).'[80] We can compound concepts as much as we like in characterising a thing (human, female, fair-skinned, tall, brown-haired, etc.), but in the end, the individual, though she may indeed *be* all these things, is also irreducibly *different* from all these things as well. Her singularity will forever elude whatever conceptual apparatuses we may attempt to overlay them with. Though the individual is what it is, what most characteristically *makes* it what it is (and not another of its kind), is that it differs from those things, its qualities and categories, as well; in other words, it differs internally, from itself. This is the internal difference that Deleuze seeks: 'we already know that internal difference exists, *given that there exist differences of nature between things of the same genus*'.[81]

This brings us to the third problem in Aristotle's ontology, namely, that it cannot account for a true formulation of difference. As we saw in Chapter 2, rather than providing us with a concept *of* difference, Aristotle thinks difference within the boundaries of the concept (representational, hence subordinated to the requirements of identity) itself. Aristotle distinguishes difference from simple otherness: 'the other and that which it is other than need not be other in some definite respect (for everything that is existent is either other or the same), but that which is different is different from some particular thing in some particular respect, so that there must be something identical whereby they differ'.[82] Difference, then, as Aristotle conceives it, is different only in so far as it is grasped in the synthesis of a higher category (in the loose sense), be it a substance, a species, a genus, or a category (in the strict sense). 'Afternoon' is other than, but not different than, 'man', because 'afternoon' and 'man' are derivatives of separate categories. On the other hand, 'man' differs from 'horse' by way of differences, such as 'rational/non-rational', 'bipedal/quadrupedal', and so on, but only because both belong to the category of 'substance' and to the genus of 'animal'. As Porphyry says, 'a difference is what is of a nature such as to separate items under the same genus', in so far as it 'contributes to their being and which is a part of what it is to be the object'.[83] The *being* in question, the being of the thing for Aristotle (even in the case of the primary substance), is most properly formulated in terms of its genus and species, and more truly of the species than of the genus, because the species most properly bears all the differentiae that get us as close as possible to the thing itself. Even if the thing itself is constituted by subtle differences, accidental and/or material, that cause it to, in some sense, *differ* from these categorial determinations, nevertheless, these subtle differences are not part of what make up its essential being. This 'essential being', however, is determined in advance as according with the requirements of identity and representation. The differentiae that constitute the essential being of the thing are therefore differences empirically determined by the faculty of judgement as contrarieties under higher groupings of identity. Put otherwise, 'specific difference, therefore, in no way represents a universal concept (that is to say, an Idea) encompassing all the singularities and turnings of difference, but rather refers to a particular moment in which difference is merely reconciled with the concept in general'.[84] It does not provide a 'differenciator of difference which would relate, in their respective immediacy, the most universal and the most singular'[85] – being and the particular, existent being. It cannot think being in the sense of the whole, nor can it properly think the individual, and these deficiencies derive from its inability to think difference. This third criticism thus unites the previous two.

The univocity of being

Analogical being, according to Deleuze, can only ever offer a hierarchical and distributive ontology, one that is theological through and through, and thus one that is incommensurate with the most pressing tasks of ontology. For this reason, ontology must forever dispense with analogical notions of being and affirm the univocity of being: 'Philosophy merges with ontology, but ontology merges with the univocity of Being',[86] and, 'There has only ever been one ontological proposition: Being is univocal.'[87] That Being is univocal does not mean that every being is the same, or equal, but rather that Being itself, in both the collective and constitutive senses of the term, is said in a single sense *of* that of which it is said. That Being is univocal entails that we think the whole of that which is, on the basis of the individuating factor(s), difference, which is the same for all that is (the same in so far as it is in each case the Different), thus reconciling the thought of the whole to the thought of the individual.

Univocity, however, immediately opens onto a problem, in that it seems, once we abolish fixed, categorical borders within being, we are left with only the pure, undifferenciated abyss. Univocity of Being will thus require a reformulation of the concepts of limit, distribution, hierarchy, and the individual. In univocal Being, hierarchy and distribution persist, but they are no longer left to the whims of a faculty of judgement, nor are they subject 'to what maintains the thing under a law'.[88] Deleuze distinguishes sedentary from nomadic distributions, and limitational from transgressive hierarchies. With respect to distributions, Deleuze writes, 'To fill a space, to be distributed within it, is very different from distributing the space.'[89] In analogical being, *being is said in many ways*, and these ways are the categories. Being is distributed in greater and lesser proportional degrees, among the categories which, taken together, are exhaustive. Distribution in this sense assigns limits, 'fixed and proportional deter-minations'[90] which, once established by the dictates of judgement, are immutable. Nomadic distribution is understood otherwise. In this mode of distribution, Being (as difference) is distributed within being (the whole of what is) – it *fills the space*. But it does so in various networks and series, consisting of relations and singularities, which relate to each other in different ways at different times and different intensities, all of which are themselves constituted by the various plays of difference itself. Being is thus distributed, filling the space of *that which is*, but its distributions are fluid, mobile, and nomadic.

Hierarchy persists as well, but in an altogether different sense. In ana-logical being, the limitations of sedentary distribution in accordance with representational concepts of identity dictate that beings are evaluated and comprehended in terms of their fixed limits, against established principles, whether generic, specific, or moral. In univocal being, these limits and hierarchical principles are jettisoned, but this does not leave us in 'the undifferenciated abyss, the black nothingness, the indeterminate animal in which everything is dissolved'.[91] The only remaining evaluative criteria are variations of intensities and degrees of power. Deleuze writes:

> There is a hierarchy which measures beings according to their limits, and according to their degree of proximity or distance from a principle. But there is also a hierarchy which considers things and beings from the point of view of power: it is not a question of considering absolute degrees of power, but only of knowing whether a being eventually 'leaps over' or transcends its limits in going to the limit of what it can do, whatever its degree.[92]

The 'limit', as he describes it here, is not an imposition formed on the basis of an outside rule, principle, or dictate of judgement. Rather, the limit is the fluid and mobile border at which a thing has deployed the maximum of its power. 'Things reside unequally in this equal being',[93] in so far as beings are constituted by greater and lesser degrees of power, but in so far as a thing goes to and transgresses its limit, *'the smallest becomes equivalent to the largest'*.[94] Nothing – quality, quantity, substance, genus, fruit fly, man, or God – participates more or less in being. Yet hierarchy persists in terms of differences of power: 'Being is said in a single and same sense of everything of which it is said, but that of which it is said differs: it is said of difference itself.'[95] There are three key moments in the history of the univocity of being: John Duns Scotus, Benedict de Spinoza, and Friedrich Nietzsche. Let us now look at each of these in turn.

Duns Scotus

The first of these three moments is represented by John Duns Scotus, the thirteenth-century Scottish philosopher and priest, whose *Opus Oxoniense* Deleuze called 'the greatest book of pure ontology'.[96] As we mentioned in Chapter 2, Scotus' argumentation is oriented by a defence of humanity's natural knowledge of God. Here, in one of the clearer expositions of this form of argumentation, he makes his case:

> In the present life no concept representing reality is formed naturally in the mind except by reason of those factors which naturally motivate the intellect. Now these factors are the active intellect, and either the sense image or the object revealed in the sense image. No simple concept, then, is produced naturally in our mind except that which can arise in virtue of these factors. Now, no concept could arise in virtue of the active intellect and the sense image that is not univocal but only analogous with, or wholly other than, what is revealed in the sense image. In the present life, since no other such analogous concept could arise in the intellect naturally, it would be simply impossible to have any natural concept of God whatsoever. But this is false.[97]

Any argument that draws a conclusion about the being of God on the basis of some fact about his creatures (and all 'proofs' in some sense do) presupposes, Scotus thinks, the univocal expression of the term 'being'. If the being of God is wholly other, or even only analogous to, the being of humankind, the proposition 'God exists' loses its significance, in so far as the existence in question is of a different kind than any other existence with which we are familiar. Thus, he claims, 'God is conceived not only in a concept analogous to the concept of a creature, that is, one which is wholly other than that which is predicated of creatures, but even in some concept univocal to Himself and to a creature.'[98] This situates Scotus in a precarious position. As we saw above, the language of analogy gave the scholastics a handy tool for characterising the being of God as in some sense accessible in the understanding of humankind, but without falling into the dual heretical temptations of thinking that God's being is the same as humanity's being, or that the finite mind of human beings is capable of *comprehending* God's existence. As Deleuze says, 'Here one feels that if the equivocists already had such a possible sin in themselves, the univocists were thinkers who told us: of everything which is, being is said in one and the same sense – of a chair, of an animal, of a man or of God.'[99] Duns Scotus, however, in order to salvage the very ability of human beings to access the divine, abolished analogy in favour of univocity. But as Deleuze notes, in the effort to avoid heresy of a *different* sort, namely pantheism, he had to neutralise univocal being: 'In order to neutralize the forces of analogy in judgment, he took the offensive and neutralized being itself in an abstract concept.'[100] This abstract concept of being precedes and conditions the division (of being) into the categories of 'finite' and 'infinite', a division that precedes even the distribution of finite being into Aristotle's categories. Thus, even if being is univocal in the abstract, God's being is nevertheless distinguished from humanity's in terms of its infinity. This, however, affords Duns Scotus the possibility of the natural knowledge of God (in so far as all the predicates of infinite being are contained virtually in the notion of being itself, distinguished only by their infinity) which does not at the same time fall into a pantheistic conflation of God and man. Nevertheless, being, for Deleuze, is not abstract and indifferent, but creative, expressive, and in this sense, affirmative. For this reason, Duns Scotus did not *live* univocal being, 'he only *thought* univocal being'.[101]

Spinoza

'With the second moment', according to Deleuze, 'Spinoza marks a considerable progress.'[102] Spinoza unfolds an elaborate ontology of expression, consisting of substance, attributes, and modes. There is but one substance, God or Nature (*Deus sive Natura*);[103] that substance is eternal, self-caused, existing necessarily, and absolutely infinite, 'consisting of infinite attributes, each of which expresses eternal and infinite essence'.[104] An attribute is conceived through itself, and understood as constituting the essence of a substance, while a mode is an affection of substance, 'or, that which is in something else, through which it is also conceived'.[105] That is to say, a mode cannot be conceived apart from its status as an expression of substance itself. Substance is indivisible (because if it were divisible, its divisions would themselves be substances, which Spinoza rejects), and hence, unlike in the Cartesian paradigm, for Spinoza, there is really only one *thing*.[106] This means that God's status as creator is not one of the *creation ex nihilo*, in which God brings into being something outside of himself which, formerly, was not there. Rather, 'God is the immanent but not the transitive cause of all things.'[107] What we casually call 'beings' are really only modes or expressions of God's immutable and eternal nature, so that, 'In Nature there exists nothing contingent, but all things have been determined by the necessity of the divine nature to exist and operate in a certain way.'[108] 'The power of God', says Spinoza, 'is his essence',[109] because it is in the necessary nature of God to exist, which means that God is self-caused (Part I, d1), which means that God is the cause both of himself and of all things which are merely modal expressions of himself. Conversely then, *the essence of God is power*, such that the modal expressions thereof are themselves expressions of distributions of that power. Deleuze writes, 'Here again the reduction of creatures to the status of modes appears as the condition of their essence being a power, that is, of being an irreducible part of God's power. Thus modes are in their essence expressive: they express God's essence, each according to the degree of power that constitutes its essence.'[110] The univocal being of Spinoza is not the neutral, indifferent being of Duns Scotus,[111] in that Spinoza thinks being as a pure expression of power, without any sense of negation, and thereby 'makes it an object of pure affirmation',[112] a step that Duns Scotus was not willing to take.

However, for Deleuze, Spinoza does not quite go far enough, in that, as Spinoza says, 'Substance is prior in nature to its affections.'[113] Substance, Spinoza says, is 'that which is in itself and is conceived through itself; that is, that which does not need the concept of another thing, from which concept it must be formed'.[114] There is, in this sense, a definitional distinction between Substance and the modes, and as a result, an ontological priority of Substance *over* modes. Substance can be conceptualised on its own, apart from the modes, while the converse cannot be said of the modes themselves. For Deleuze, however, 'substance must itself be said *of* the modes and only *of* the modes'.[115] Spinoza ultimately maintains an essential unity or identity of the one substance, which for Deleuze does not sufficiently free up *difference in itself*. This transition is made possible only by Nietzsche's notion of eternal return. As Foucault says, 'For Deleuze, the noncategorical univocity of being does not directly attach the multiple to unity itself (the universal neutrality of being, or the expressive force of substance); it puts being into play as that which is repetitively expressed as difference.'[116] This is the transformation in thought made possible by Nietzsche's concept of the eternal return.

Nietzsche and eternal return

With Nietzsche, the univocity of being assumes its fullness in the notion of the eternal return, which Deleuze characterises as 'the affirmation of all chance in a single moment, the unique cast for all throws, one Being and only for all forms and all times, a single instance for all that exists, a single phantom for all the living, a single voice for every hum of voices and every drop of water in the sea'.[117] In eternal return, identity fully and completely becomes subordinated to difference, and the same to the different. 'Returning', Deleuze claims, 'is the becoming-identical of becoming itself . . . the only identity, but identity as a secondary power; the identity of difference, the identical which belongs to the different, or turns around the different. Such an identity, produced by difference, is determined as "repetition."'[118] Thus in eternal return, we see the dual unfolding of the two objectives of the entirety of *Difference and Repetition*: *'these concepts of a pure difference and a complex repetition'*,[119] which, Deleuze claims, are 'the same thing'.[120] To explicate Deleuze's interpretation of eternal return, the 'effective realization'[121] of univocity, will require examination from the following three aspects: (1) the ideal game – the affirmation of all chance, all at once; (2) the affirmation of the disjunctive synthesis; and (3) the essential becoming of time itself – repetition, which provides the single and sole form of identity in any properly formulated philosophy of difference.

The dicethrow and the ideal game: all of chance, all at once

Deleuze says, 'The ultimate origin was always assimilated to a solitary and divine game. There are several ways to play, however, and collective and human games do not resemble the solitary divine game.'[122] According to Leibniz, on the gameboard of being, God plays by specific rules, according with the principle that a skilled player will not use more moves than he must in order to accomplish his goal: 'Yet there is a definite rule by which a maximum number of spaces can be filled in the easiest way.'[123] Heraclitus, on the other hand, says, 'Time [αἰών] is a game played by a child moving pieces on a board; the kingly power is a child.'[124] Being is child's play. These two theories of the game will be opposed to one another by Deleuze: the rule-oriented division of chance versus the eternality of ideal play. Eternal return is, in the first sense, the great game of being, or the anarchic rule of the game. In *Nietzsche and Philosophy*, Deleuze calls it 'the dicethrow';[125] in *Difference and Repetition*, the 'divine game',[126] which is synonymous with the 'ideal game'[127] of *The Logic of Sense*. In characterising the ideal game, Deleuze outlines four specific characteristics, counterpoised in every sense against the human game: (1) Whereas in the human game, there is a pre-existing set of inviolable rules governing the progression of play, in the ideal game, 'each move invents its own rules'.[128] (2) In the human game, the rules act to partition and apportion chance, formulating the hypotheses of loss and gain (if x happens, then y . . .), while in the ideal game, all throws of the dice affirm chance, 'and endlessly ramify it with each throw'.[129] (3) The throws in the human game are really and numerically distinct, each attempting to redeem chance by giving it a 'fresh start' each time, each bringing about a fixed distribution of results; they 'never affirm the whole of chance, since they assign this or that loss or gain as though it were necessarily tied to a given hypothesis',[130] whereas in the ideal game, the throws are 'qualitatively distinct, but are the qualitative forms of a single cast which is ontologically one'.[131] And finally, (4) in the human game, the accumulated results of the throws dictate winners and losers, whereas in the ideal game, the innocence of being and of chance reigns, a game without responsibility, without winners and losers, a game wherein being is no longer required to justify itself before a tribunal, no longer a 'theodicy, but a cosmodicy',[132] where the creative play of being itself serves as its own justification.

The heart of the 'ideal game' is actually one of the more perplexing points that Deleuze makes: the distinction between multiple dicethrows, coupled with the assertion of a 'unique cast', which is 'ontologically one'.[133] At first glance, these two principles appear to be in direct opposition to one another, so we must work this out more carefully. When Deleuze talks about the ontologically one unique cast, he means the affirmation of all of chance, as such, all at once. Chance never gets a 'fresh start' or a 'do-over', as it were. There are no radically disconnected or discrete breaches or ruptures in the whole game of chance, such that the player would ever have or hope for *another turn*.

This singular cast, however, is infinitely and eternally distributed, placed, and displaced throughout the whole, in what Deleuze calls the 'throws'. Above we discussed Deleuze's notion of the nomadic distributions of being. That being is distributed nomadically entails that it constitutes varying syntheses, various series, consisting of groups of relations and points. These series relate and diverge from each other at different points, at different times, and at varying degrees of intensity, modifying themselves, forming new series and disbanding old ones, in fluid and ever-changing configurations. The 'throws' are the infinitesimally small pulsations of chance, communication, and differentiation impacting specific series at specific moments in time. Chance is constantly coursing throughout the entirety of the system, and though all of the series are in one way or another connected (a series not in any way in communication with some part of the whole of being would be a transcendent series), the throws are themselves successive and in some sense localised. This is what it means to say that each throw endlessly 'ramifies' chance. To ramify is to disperse, to send branching forth into new directions and along new paths. As chance pulses through the system, it displaces particular series, but does so in such a way that with each pulsation, they are once again opened anew to the governance of chance, new combinations and relations, new displacements and differences. This does not signify a fresh injection of chance into the system, but 'each necessarily winning throw entails the reproduction of the act of throwing under another rule which still draws all its consequences from among the consequences of the preceding throw'.[134] A tornado, when it collides with a structure, may level the structure to the ground, it may change course, or it may begin to disperse, diminish, and dissolve. It may, moreover, result in some combination of these outcomes. At each moment along its path, it is subject to a new set of conditions – constitutive, environmental, and oppositional – which it 'interprets' accordingly, and to which it reacts – new conditions which engender new possibilities, but conditions which were always destined to be part of its series and part of its communication.

> Destiny never consists in step-by-step deterministic relations between presents which succeed one another according to the rule of a represented time. Rather, it implies between successive presents non-localisable connections, actions at a distance, systems of replay, resonance and echoes, objective chances, signs, signals and roles which transcend spatial locations and temporal successions.[135]

From this principle, the rest follow. There are, strictly speaking, no abiding rules in the ideal game. If 'game' is understood in the sense of structured play, then the 'ideal game' is the game of pure play, wherein each move introduces its own new set of rules. There is structure, to be sure, but the structure is constantly itself in play – the rules are ever changing. There is thus no division of chance; distribution, perhaps, but each point of the distribution is in tensile communication with, ultimately, the whole. The whole of chance is 'endlessly displaced throughout all series'. In the human game, the rules come, strictly speaking, from outside the immanent play of the game itself, and they declare what is just and unjust, what is allowed and what is not, what is fair and what is not, and finally, they declare the winner and the loser. Even Leibniz's omnipotent chess-playing God acts in accordance with a principle, that of perfection, which is at least conceptually distinct from God himself. In Deleuze's ideal game, whatever rules there are, are immanent to the game itself; they are creations of chance and are in constant states of transformation. Thus there is no external standard by which being must be evaluated, or by which one may be said to 'win' and another to 'lose'. Being, being subject to the rule of chance, no longer demands or requires a justification in accordance with a transcendent notion of the Good or the Just. 'When chance is sufficiently affirmed the player can no longer lose, since every combination and every throw which produces it is by nature adequate to the place and the mobile command of the aleatory point.'[136] Eternal return as the ideal game is the *Amor fati* of which Nietzsche speaks, 'the highest affirmation . . . the affirmation of all chance in a single moment'.[137]

The disjunctive synthesis

The throws impact and impart the disparate series, we said, 'ramifying' chance, communicating it throughout various series at various points. 'What does it mean, therefore, to affirm the whole of chance, every time, in a single time? This affirmation takes place to the degree that the disparates which emanate from a throw begin to resonate, thereby forming a problem.'[138] We must therefore address now the synonymy whereby Deleuze equates the univocity of Being as eternal return with 'the positive use of the disjunctive synthesis which is the highest affirmation'.[139] The *disjunctive synthesis*: this paradoxical formulation involves the differential communication between two or more divergent series, forming a system. For the eternal return constitutes systems.[140] But what are the natures of these systems? What are their constitutive elements and functions? It is here that we find the *in itself* of *difference in itself* for Deleuze. For difference in itself is not given as such: 'Difference is not diversity. Diversity is given, but difference is that by which the given is given, that by which the given is given as diverse. Difference is not phenomenon but the noumenon closest to the phenomenon.'[141] Eternal return is the being of the phenomenon.

Being is eternal return; Being is the whole; Being is the intensive *spatium*; and Being is problematic – these four proclamations say the same thing. The phenomenon is diversity; not *difference*, but differenc*es*, different things, limits, alliances, oppositions, and so on. For Deleuze, such a 'crucial experience of difference . . . presupposes a swarm of differences, a pluralism of free, wild, or untamed differences; a properly differential and original space and time'.[142] The planar effects of limitations and oppositions presuppose a sub-phenomenal play of constitutive difference – a pure depth. 'Depth and intensity are the same at the level of being, but the same in so far as this is said of difference. Depth is the intensity of being, or vice versa.'[143] It is sub-phenomenal, hence imperceptible. But its imperceptibility is not an accidental feature, a result of its being *too small*, but rather, 'it is simultaneously the imperceptible and that which can only be sensed'.[144] In so far as it is the being *of* the sensible it is not, strictly speaking, sensible; it is, nevertheless, that on the basis of which the sensible is sensible, and hence, it 'defines the proper limits of sensibility',[145] and is, in this sense that which can only be sensed. The *spatium* is 'space as a whole',[146] but space understood only in terms of its intensive character, 'that preexists every quality and every extension'.[147] The *spatium* is 'not an extension but a pure *implex*',[148] a depth, folded inward upon itself, which is not first extended in any sense, an inward fold without a primary or originary length or width. It is the 'virtual continuum'[149] in which difference, singularities, series, and systems relate and interact.

'A system', Deleuze says, 'must be constituted on the basis of two or more series, each series being defined by the differences between the terms that compose it.'[150] A series contains terms, but those terms are thought only by the relations that constitute and engender them: 'Each of these series is constituted by terms which exist only through the relations they maintain with one another.'[151] The series is thus essentially constituted by its differences. Its elements are its differences, and 'these are intensities, the peculiarity of intensities being to be constituted by a difference which itself refers to other differences'.[152] We can think of these intensities as Deleuze's differential elements, or elemental differences.

'Intensities are implicated multiplicities, "implexes," made up of relations between asymmetrical elements',[153] understood according to three characteristics. First, an intensity is 'the uncancellable in difference of quantity',[154] a relation that cannot be equalised, a bare and elemental asymmetry. Secondly, inasmuch as it is positively characterised by its essential asymmetry, this means that it is 'constructed on at least two series, one superior and one inferior, with each series referring in turn to other implicated series'. Though it is the differential element, there could be no such thing as an intensity *as such*, and so each intensity is nestled within and between distinct series. It therefore '*affirms* difference'; inasmuch as intensity is expressive and generative, and is expressive precisely in terms of its essential asymmetry, it thus affirms its own difference, even the lowness of the low.[155] It is, essentially, 'energy in terms of the difference buried in this pure intensity and it is the formula "difference of intensity" which bears the tautology, but this time the beautiful and profound tautology of the Different'.[156] The third characteristic assimilates the first two: 'intensity is an implicated, enveloped, or "embryonized" quantity'.[157] Intensity is essentially implicated, an internalising and internalised essential imbalance. It is both folding and folded: an essential, elemental asymmetry, folded inward, enveloping its own internal 'distance', which, in this case, does not describe an extensivity of any sort, but rather a relation 'between series of heterogeneous terms'.[158]

This term *embryonized* is not accidental. Deleuze is famous for some of his odd formulations, and among these is one, playing on an ancient myth, that 'The entire world is an egg.'[159] But all oddity aside, Deleuze is making a crucial point: 'Embryology already displays the truth that there are systematic vital movements, torsions and drifts, that only the embryo can sustain: an adult would be torn apart by them. There are movements for which one can only be a patient, but the patient in turn can only be a larva',[160] and 'Embryology shows that the division of an egg into parts is secondary in relation to more significant morphogenetic movements: the augmentation of free surfaces, stretching of cellular layers, invagination by folding, regional displacement of groups.'[161] An intensity is an embryonic quantity in that its own internal resonance, which is constitutive of higher levels of synthesis and actualisation, pulsates in a pure speed and time that would devastate a constituted being; it is for this reason that qualities and surface phenomena can only come to be on a plane in which difference is aborted: 'For difference, to be explicated is to be cancelled or to dispel the inequality which constitutes it',[162] even as the ground continues to rumble underneath.

These intensities are the elements of the various series. A system is formed whenever two or more heterogeneous series communicate. In so far as each series is itself constituted by differences, the communication that takes place between the two heterogeneous series is a difference relating differences, a second-order difference, which Deleuze calls the 'differenciator',[163] in that these differences relate to each other, and in so relating, differenciate what he calls first-order differences. The differenciator thus constitutes, according to Deleuze, 'a differenciation of difference'.[164] In order that this relation can be established, a path is required, which Deleuze calls the 'dark precursor',[165] comparing it to the negative path cleared for a bolt of lightning: 'Thunderbolts explode between different intensities, but they are preceded by an invisible, imperceptible, dark precursor, which determines their path in advance but in reverse, as though intagliated.'[166]

Once the communication between series is established, however, the system explodes: 'coupling between heterogeneous systems, from which is derived an internal resonance within the system, and from which in turn is derived a forced movement the amplitude of which exceeds that of the basic series themselves'.[167] Deleuze understands 'qualities' as extensive manifestations of an intensive difference, which 'cancel' the difference (in their manifestations, though the intensive, constitutive difference remains). Thus, the compounding of these series and relations are the introduction of spatio-temporal dynamisms, which are themselves the sources of qualities and extensions:

> Spatio-temporal dynamisms fill the system, expressing simultaneously the resonance of the coupled series and the amplitude of the forced movement which exceeds them. The system is populated by subjects, both larval subjects and passive selves: passive selves because they are indistinguishable from the contemplation of couplings and resonances; larval subjects because they are the supports or the patients of the dynamisms.[168]

The communication takes place, we said, by way of a dark precursor, which Deleuze also christens with the name 'the disparate'.[169] Recall that above we cited Deleuze as saying that the disparate is what emanates from the throw of the dice.[170] He also claims that 'each throw emits singular points', or 'singularities'.[171] Singularities are points of interest in the series, 'turning points and points of inflection; bottlenecks, knots, foyers, and centers; points of fusion, condensation, and boiling; points of tears and joy, sickness and health, hope and anxiety, "sensitive" points'.[172] Thus we see the internal connectedness of these concepts. The pulsation of chance through the system, which we called the 'dicethrows', are the openings of pathways, *disparates*, between heterogeneous series of varying intensities, whereby these series may communicate. In so communicating, the series form new series, and new systems, de-enlisting and redistributing singular points of interest and their constitutive and corresponding relations, which are themselves implicating, and conversely, explicated in the phenomenal realm. The opening of the disparate is the dicethrow of chance. Deleuze, moreover, equates affirmation with the resonance of the disparates, which, through their resonance, form a *problem*.

A problem, according to Deleuze, is an Idea, and 'every idea is a multiplicity or a variety'.[173] Multiplicity, for Deleuze, is not the *unity* of the multiple, but the inherent organisation of the multiple as multiple. 'An Idea is an n-dimensional, continuous, defined multiplicity',[174] 'a multiplicity constituted of differential elements, differential relations between those elements, and singularities corresponding to those relations'.[175] There are three characteristics whereby Deleuze formulates the notion of the multiplicity as an Idea: (1) The elements of the Idea are virtual (not actual), and hence neither conceptually determinable nor phenomenally sensible. (2) The elements are determined by reciprocal relations 'which allow no independence whatsoever to subsist'.[176] Any change in the elements can only be accompanied by a change in the overall metric and structure of the multiplicity itself. (3) The differential relations are actualised in spatio-temporal relationships simultaneous with the explication of the elements themselves. 'The Idea is thus defined as a structure . . . a "complex theme" . . . which is incarnated in real relations and actual terms.'[177]

The 'disjunctive synthesis' is the affirmative employment of the creativity brought about by the various plays of differences. Leibniz had defined the perfection of the cosmos in terms of the structural compossibility of all its individual substances (or monads). The perfection of the cosmos dictates that *all* of the individual substances throughout the cosmos, throughout all eternity, subsist at each moment in perfectly balanced states of expression and inhibition. Like a precisely tuned, perfectly balanced but constantly varying puzzle, the infinite monads grow and diminish in power and in expression in perfect harmony with each other. The disjunctive synthesis, against Leibniz's compossibility, affirms *in*compossibility:

'Incompossibility is now a means of communication.'[178] The disjunctive synthesis brings about the communication and cooperative *disharmony* of divergent and heterogeneous series; it does not, thereby, cancel the differences between them, as the system is in constant modes of tension, which resolve and ramify into new tensions, and so on. 'It is not that the disjunction has become a simple conjunction.'[179] Where incompossibility for Leibniz was a means of exclusion – an infinity of *possible worlds* being excluded from reality on the basis of their incompossibility – in the hands of Deleuze it becomes a means of opening the 'thing' to the possible infinity of events. It is in this sense that 'The univocity of Being merges with the positive use of the disjunctive synthesis which is the highest affirmation.'[180]

The selective heartbeat of time

With that we turn now to the final sense in which Nietzsche's eternal return serves for Deleuze as the subordination of identity to difference: eternal return as the essential becoming of time itself, the centrifugal, selective, expulsive heartbeat of repetition. With respect to the game of chance, one of the distinguishing features between the unique, ontological cast and the individual throws is their temporality:

> each throw is itself a series, but *in a time much smaller than the minimum* of continuous, thinkable time . . . But the set of throws is included in the aleatory point, a unique cast which is endlessly displaced throughout all series, *in a time greater than the maximum* of continuous, thinkable time. These throws are successive in relation to one another, yet simultaneous in relation to this point.[181]

It is thus clear that the affirmation of all of chance all at once and the disjunctive synthesis require a rethinking of the very being of time itself, which is the third sense of eternal return. 'The great discovery of Nietzsche's philosophy', Deleuze writes,

> which marks his break with Schopenhauer and goes by the name of the will to power or the Dionysian world, is the following: no doubt the I and the Self must be replaced by an undifferenciated abyss, but this abyss is neither an impersonal nor an abstract Universal beyond individuation. On the contrary, it is the I and the self which are the abstract universals. They must be replaced, but in and by individuation, in the direction of the individuating factors which consume them and which constitute the world of Dionysus.[182]

In *Nietzsche and Philosophy*, Deleuze defines the will to power as 'the genealogical element of force, both differential and genetic'.[183] Here, will to power appears as a synthetic principle, bringing forces into asymmetrical and hierarchical relations with one another. In this sense, the will to power as Deleuze describes it here closely resembles the thunderbolt in *Difference and Repetition*, communicating by way of the disparate between two heterogeneous series: 'The will to power is the flashing world of metamorphoses, of communicating intensities, differences of differences, of *breaths*, insinuations and exhalations: a world of intensive intentionalities, a world of simulacra or "mysteries." '[184] Will to power is the explosive differential principle, the being of which is the eternal return: 'Eternal return is the being of this world, the only Same which is said of this world and excludes any prior identity therein.'[185] Again, 'If difference is the in-itself, then repetition in the eternal return is the for-itself of difference.'[186] Let us look at the sense in which eternal return is, he says, the 'consequence'[187] of will to power.

'Repetition', he claims, 'necessarily flows from this play of difference in two ways.'[188] As we just saw, intensity *as such* is an uncancellable difference, an essential asymmetry. But intensity *as such*, according to Deleuze, inasmuch as it *is* difference, requires other differences in order to be explicated, and is unthinkable without them. The communications between these series take place through a discharge of signals through the disparate, forming a system, a multiplicity, or an Idea. Thus, in the play of difference, a series *explicates* itself, manifesting spatio-temporal dynamisms, qualities, extensions, etc., only by way of *implicating* other series, in a mutual, and mutually constitutive, relation between the two (or more) series. In this multiplicitous communication, each series *explicates itself* only by implicating others, which are, in turn, themselves only explicated by way of the implication of the former. In this mutually implicating communication, taking place in a pure time much smaller than the minimum of continuous, thinkable time, what we have then is the *bare repetition* of self to self, and the *clothed repetition* of self in other. In other words, the series repeats in virtue of its *back and forth* communications with other series. The nature of this *self* is not the nature of the same, or rather, it is the very rethinking of the same in the order of the different, for as the differential relation between differential elements relates them one to another, it at the very same time differenciates them – the constitutive relations comprising the system cannot but change the elements that they relate, and vice versa. The *same* is now rethought as a 'same' which is itself different.

In a second sense, the simulacra, which Deleuze here defines as 'systems in which different relates to different *by means of* difference itself', also return, in the same sense as the former. The dicethrows, recall, are not numerically, but merely formally distinct from one another, which means that 'all the outcomes are included in the number of each [throw] according to the relations between implicated and implicator just referred to, each returning in the others in accordance with the formal distinction of throws, but also always returning to itself in accordance with the unity of the play of difference'.[189] Chance is redistributed endlessly, not by way of a fresh start, but rather each redistribution provides the conditions for new encounters, where new negotiations will occur, and from which new redistributions will arise. Thus, though chance reigns, it is not in the form of radically discrete moments of chance, but as one cast, endlessly dispersed, dislocated, and displaced. Just as series communicate with series, constituting systems, those differential systems communicate with each other, returning to self, and from self to other, altering self and other in the same differential movement.

Moreover, the eternal return in this third sense is *selective*, tending toward the 'becoming-active' of reactive forces. In Chapter 4, we analysed the Nietzschean mechanism whereby reactive forces come to dominate active forces, and reactive types come to dominate active types. The thought of the eternal return transmutes reactive forces, by *repeating* in the name of a primary affirmation the negativity associated with them, turning the will to negation against itself. 'Only the eternal return can complete nihilism *because it makes negation a negation of reactive forces themselves*. By and in the eternal return nihilism no longer expresses itself as the conservation and victory of the weak, but as their destruction, their *self-destruction*.'[190] This is what, in *Difference and Repetition*, Deleuze characterises as 'a No which results from affirmation'.[191] In this way, 'reactive forces are themselves denied and led to nothingness'.[192]

We must, however, be absolutely clear about the distinction between this Nietzschean-Deleuzian *negation of the negative*, as opposed to that of Hegel. In Hegel, the primary motor of the system is itself 'the tremendous power of the negative'.[193] Affirmation then, according to Deleuze, is but a secondary epiphenomenon, constituted only by way of a movement of double negation. This, for Deleuze, is but a 'phantom of affirmation',[194] taking up within itself and maintaining in a negative and oppositional, homeostatic relation all that it has already denied: '*this kind of affirming is nothing but bearing, taking upon oneself*, acquiescing in the real as it is, taking reality as it is upon oneself'.[195] With the notion of eternal return, 'the motor is changed',[196] and in place of the *negative*, the primary motor *is* affirmation itself. The notion of eternal return constitutes a *repetition* of that affirmation, which at the same time *affirms* also the negative, amounting to a *repetition* of the negative, but in the service of that primary affirmation: 'In and through the eternal return negation as a quality of the will to power transmutes itself into affirmation, it becomes an affirmation of negation itself, it becomes a power of affirming, an affirmative power.'[197] The repetition of the affirmation amounts to a 'double affirmation',[198] while the affirmative repetition of the negative amounts to the abolition or the 'transmutation'[199] of the negative. It is the difference between Hegel's 'phantom' of affirmation that *results* from the 'negation of the negation',[200] and Nietzsche's negative of the negative that *results* from primary affirmation when reactive forces bubble to the surface. It is the difference between Hegel's 'positivity of the negative' and Nietzsche's 'negativity of the positive',[201] the source of Nietzsche's 'critical and destructive powers',[202] and the source of Deleuze and Guattari's 'Destroy, destroy'.[203] As Deleuze writes, 'Zarathustra opposes pure affirmation to the buffoon: *affirmation is necessary and sufficient to create two negations, two negations form part of the powers of affirming which are modes of being of affirmation as such.*'[204]

Eternal return thus constitutes the only Same of the Different, the being of the becoming, the Parmenidean stamp upon the Heraclitean world.

> The eternal return is itself the Identical, the similar and the equal, but it pre-supposes nothing of itself in that of which it is said. It is said of that which has no identity, no resemblance and no equality. It is the identical which is said of the different, the resemblance which is said of the pure *disparate*, the equal which is said only of the unequal and the proximity which is said of all distances.[205]

It is the pure and empty form of time, the ceaseless unfolding of the future, which perpetually displaces and reconstitutes identities, dissolves and reformulates selves, and consumes past and present as mere dimensions of its eternal synthesis. It 'constitutes the only Same of that which becomes',[206] and 'has an essential relation with the future . . . because the future is the deployment and explication of the multiple, of the different and of the fortuitous, for themselves and "for all times"'.[207] It is selective, abolishing that which would find itself most resistant to the sense of the eternal return: namely, the negative, and the identical, the *not*, and any presumption to presence: 'The eternal return has no other sense but this: the absence of any assignable origin – in other words, the assignation of difference as the origin, which then relates different to different in order to make it (or them) return as such.'[208] It is the Being of being and the Being of difference, which abolishes all notions of identity and presence, and is itself the only pure presence.

Conclusion

To conclude our discussion of Deleuze's notion of difference in itself, we return to our point of departure: namely, Nietzsche and the reversal of

Platonism. Deleuze understands Platonism as the oppressive subordination of the simulacra beneath the hierarchy of model and icon. 'So "to
reverse Platonism" means to make the simulacra rise and to affirm their
rights among icons and copies',[209] to think the simulacrum, not as a
degraded copy, but rather on its own, positive terms, on the basis of its
essential, internal dissimilarity, its internal difference, which we revealed
most fully in the three aspects of the eternal return for Deleuze:

> Between the eternal return and the simulacrum, there is such a profound
> link that the one cannot be understood except through the other. Only the
> divergent series, in so far as they are divergent, return: that is, each series in
> so far as it displaces its difference along with all the others, and all series in
> so far as they complicate their difference within the chaos which is without
> beginning or end. The circle of the eternal return is a circle which is always
> excentric in relation to an always decentered center.[210]

For Deleuze, Nietzsche reverses Platonism, formulating a thought of difference in itself, the fullest possible expression of the univocity of Being,
in the form of eternal return: 'It is the eternal return itself, or – as we have
seen in the case of the ideal game – the affirmation of all chance in a single
moment, the unique cast for all throws, one Being and only for all forms
and all times, a single instance for all that exists, a single phantom for all
the living, a single voice for every hum of voices and every drop of water
in the sea.'[211]

In Chapter 8, we shall look more directly at the ways in which Deleuze
and Derrida engage with Heidegger's influential reading of Nietzsche.
While Deleuze *agrees* with Heidegger's basic assessment that Nietzsche is
formulating an ontology, Deleuze rejects that this in any way commits him
to the three claims (and errors) that Heidegger diagnoses. That Nietzsche
offers an ontology does *not* indicate a substantiality or 'essence' to the
notion of will to power, and hence, the other two Heideggerian charges
do not hold either. For Derrida, on the contrary, if it *were* in fact the case
that Nietzsche were formulating an ontology, as Heidegger suspects (and
Deleuze agrees), then he would indeed fall prey to the Heideggerian criticisms. On this Derrida is unequivocal. However, *against* both Heidegger
and Deleuze, Derrida argues that Nietzsche is not formulating an ontology
at all, but rather, a reconceptualisation of the notion of the sign, liberated
from any pretence to *truth* or *presence*. Sense, Derrida argues, is always
produced, by way of the oppositional play of force that creates signifying
spaces or *intervals* whereby meanings coalesce. For Deleuze, difference is
not oppositional.

Notes

1. *OG*, 19.
2. *LS*, 253. This essay originally appeared in *Revue de Métaphysique et de Morale* 71, no. 4 (Oct.–Dec. 1966), pp. 426–38, and was revised and reprinted as the first Appendix to *The Logic of Sense*. A translation of the original 1966 version appears as 'Reversing Platonism', trans. Heath Massey, in Lawlor, *Thinking Through French Philosophy*, 163–77. Unless otherwise noted, I will cite from the version in *The Logic of Sense*.
3. *DR*, 59.
4. *DR*, 59.
5. *DR*, 59.
6. *D*, 98.
7. As is usually the case with Derrida, however, the story is much more complicated than this, as he demonstrates in the 'Plato's Pharmacy' essay (in *D*).
8. *LS*, 253.
9. Bogue, *Deleuze and Guattari*, 56.
10. *LS*, 253.
11. *DR*, 59.
12. The Greek word διαλέγω combines the preposition δια, meaning 'through' or 'apart' with the verb λέγω meaning 'to say', 'to gather', or 'to collect'.
13. *DR*, 62.
14. Plato, *Sophist*, 218c.
15. Plato, *Euthyphro*, 6e.
16. Plato, *Gorgias*, 449a.
17. The εἰκών, see *Sophist*, 236a and 236c.
18. *Sophist*, 236c.
19. *LS*, 257.
20. Plato, *Republic*, 597b.
21. *Republic*, 597d, 597a.
22. *Republic*, 598a.
23. Ibid. This word εἴδωλον bears obvious etymological affinities with εἶδος, Plato's word for the form. The primary sense of εἶδος in Greek, according to Liddell and Scott, is the look of a thing, that which is seen, its shape, form, or figure. Related to this, εἴδωλον is an image, a phantom, an appearance that, strictly speaking, *is not*. In Homer it is the word applied to the 'shades' of the dead in Hades. In the New Testament, εἴδωλον is the word for 'image' or 'idol.'
24. *LS*, 257.
25. *LS*, 257.
26. 2 Corinthians 11:14. Likewise, the Greek preface ἀντί (anti), as in the sense of the term 'antichrist' (1 John 2:18, 2 John 1:7), according to Liddell and Scott, while it connotes senses that conform to our traditional understanding of 'against', also connotes primary senses of 'as good as', and 'in the place of'.
27. *Republic*, 598b.
28. *LS*, 258.
29. *LS*, 258.
30. *Republic*, 601d.
31. Ibid.
32. *Republic*, 602a.
33. *LS*, 258.
34. *LS*, 258.
35. *Republic*, 602d.
36. *Republic*, 602e.

37. *Republic*, 603a–b.
38. *LS*, 258.
39. *LS*, 258.
40. *LS*, 259.
41. *LS*, 262.
42. *LS*, 262.
43. *LS*, 258.
44. *DI*, 18.
45. *DI*, 32.
46. *DI*, 36.
47. Aristotle, *Categories*, chap. 5.
48. See, for example: Aristotle, *Metaphysics*, IV.2, V.7, V.11, V.28, VI.2, VII.1, VIII.2, IX.1, IX.10; *Physics* 185a; *On the Soul*, 410a.
49. *Metaphysics*, IV.1.
50. Ibid.
51. *Metaphysics*, III.3.
52. Porphyry, *Introduction*, §3.
53. *DR*, 32.
54. Smith, *Essays on Deleuze*, 39.
55. *Metaphysics*, XI.2.
56. *Categories*, ch. 1.
57. *Metaphysics*, XI.3.
58. *Metaphysics*, IV.2.
59. Ibid.
60. Ibid.
61. *Metaphysics*, XI.2. Aristotle is here summarising elements and criticisms of the thoughts of others, nevertheless, he seems to be in agreement on this point.
62. *Metaphysics*, IV.2.
63. Ibid.
64. *Categories*, chap. 5.
65. *DR*, 33, 269.
66. *DR*, 33.
67. *DR*, 33.
68. 'In the same way, as was said above, all perfections existing in creatures divided and multiplied pre-exist in God unitedly. Hence, when any name expressing perfection is applied to a creature, it signifies that perfection as distinct from the others according to the nature of its definition; as for instance, by this term *wise* applied to a man, we signify some perfection distinct from a man's essence, and distinct from his power and his being, and from all similar things. But when we apply *wise* to God, we do not mean to signify anything distinct from His essence or power or being. And thus when this term *wise* is applied to man, in some degree it circumscribes and comprehends the thing signified; whereas this is not the case when it is applied to God, but it leaves the thing signified as uncomprehended and as exceeding the signification of the name. Hence it is evident that this term *wise* is not applied in the same way to God and to man. The same applies to other terms. Hence, no name is predicated univocally of God and of creatures.' Aquinas, *The Summa Theologica*, Q.13.Art.5. 'Therefore such terms are not predicated altogether equivocally about God and other things, as happens in the case of fortuitous equivocation. Thus they are predicated according to analogy, that is, according to their proportion to one thing.' St Thomas quinas, *Aquinas's Shorter Summa*, chap. 27.
69. *LS*, 179. Univocity of being, as we shall see below, always flirts with the dangers of heresy.
70. *DR*, 269.
71. *DR*, 303.

72. A very clear example of this distinction is found on page 36 of *DR* (page 53 in the French): the distinction between l'être and l'Être, being and Being.
73. *DR*, 37.
74. *DR*, 38.
75. *DR*, 202.
76. *DR*, 199.
77. *DR*, 33.
78. *Categories*, chap. 5.
79. Ibid.
80. *DR*, 38.
81. *DI*, 33.
82. *Metaphysics*, Bk. X, ch. 3.
83. Porphyry, *Introduction*, §3.
84. *DR*, 31–2.
85. *DR*, 32.
86. *LS*, 179.
87. *DR*, 35.
88. *DR*, 37.
89. *DR*, 36.
90. *DR*, 36.
91. *DR*, 28.
92. *DR*, 37.
93. *DR*, 37.
94. *DR*, 37.
95. *DR*, 36.
96. *DR*, 39.
97. Duns Scotus, *Opus oxoniense*, I, dist. III, q. i., in *Philosophical Writings: A Selection*, 22.
98. Ibid., 19.
99. Deleuze, Anti-Oedipus Seminar, 14 January 1974, at https://www.webdeleuze.com/textes/176.
100. *DR*, 39.
101. *DR*, 39.
102. *DR*, 40.
103. Spinoza, *Ethics*, Part I, p14. This famous formulation is found in Part IV, 'Preface', and p4. Descartes as well, on a few occasions, characterises God in this manner. See *Meditations*, VI, AT 80, and *Principles of Philosophy*, Part I.28.
104. *Ethics*, Part I, d6.
105. Ibid., d5.
106. Descartes on this point suffers from an apparent inconsistency, resolved only by his reliance upon an analogical notion of being. In *Principles*, I.51, he defines a substance as 'a thing which exists in such a way as to depend on no other thing for its existence', just before going on to say that, 'there is only one substance which can be understood to depend on no other thing whatsoever, namely God. In the case of all other substances, we perceive that they can exist only with the help of God's concurrence.' Thus, he concludes that 'substance' is a term that does not apply univocally to God and creatures, whereas 'substance' does apply univocally to created substance. For all his hard-fought rejections of Aristotle, without the presuppositions of an analogical understanding of being, Descartes would be unable to maintain this distinction between God and creation; put simply, he would *become-Spinoza*.
107. *Ethics*, Part I, p18.
108. Ibid., p29.
109. Ibid., p34.
110. *EPS*, 199.

111. It is interesting to note that Spinoza himself, so far as I know, never mentions Duns Scotus *or* univocity, and does not enter explicitly into the Medieval debate between apophatic theology, kataphatic theology of analogy, and univocity. Yet Deleuze makes these connections as though they are obvious. See *EPS*, 48–9, 53–68; *SPP*, 63–4. Daniel W. Smith notes: 'To my knowledge, Deleuze is the only commentator to have drawn this link between Duns Scotus and Spinoza on the question of univocity.' *Essays on Deleuze*, 368n9.
112. *DR*, 40.
113. *Ethics*, Part I, p1.
114. Ibid., d3.
115. *DR*, 40.
116. Foucault, 'Theatrum Philosophicum', in *The Essential Works of Foucault: 1954–1984, Volume 2*, 360.
117. *LS*, 180.
118. *DR*, 41.
119. *DR*, xx.
120. *DI*, 142.
121. *DR*, 41.
122. *DR*, 282.
123. Leibniz, 'On the Radical Origination of Things', in *Philosophical Papers and Letters*, 487.
124. Heraclitus, DK 51.
125. *NP*, 25–7.
126. *DR*, 116, 282–4. See also *NP*, 22–9.
127. *LS*, 60. Though in *The Logic of Sense* Deleuze explicitly claims 'It is not enough to oppose a "major" game to the minor game of man, nor a divine game to the human game' (59), and asserts that the game 'cannot be played by either man or God' (60), this coupling of the 'divine' and the 'ideal' is clear, based both upon the structure and the terminological conflation of the 'ideal' and the 'divine' in *DR* (282).
128. *LS*, 59.
129. *LS*, 59.
130. *DR*, 282.
131. *LS*, 59.
132. *NP*, 25.
133. *LS*, 59–60.
134. *DR*, 283.
135. *DR*, 83.
136. *DR*, 198.
137. *LS*, 180.
138. *DR*, 198.
139. *LS*, 179–80.
140. *DR*, 116.
141. *DR*, 222.
142. *DR*, 50.
143. *DR*, 231.
144. *DR*, 230. In the French this reads, 'L'intensité est à la fois l'insensible et ce qui ne peut être que senti.' Deleuze, *Différence et Répétition*, 297.
145. *DR*, 230.
146. *DR*, 230.
147. *DI*, 97.
148. *DI*, 229.
149. DeLanda, *Intensive Science and Virtual Philosophy*, 203.
150. *DR*, 117.
151. *LS*, 50.

152. *DR*, 117.
153. *DR*, 244.
154. *DR*, 233.
155. At this point, Deleuze will claim that the *origin* of the negative is the perspective of difference seen from the low. The high recognises the difference of the low, but *affirms* this difference, whereas the low recognises the difference of the high, and *negates* this difference.
156. *DR*, 240.
157. *DR*, 237.
158. *DR*, 238.
159. *DR*, 216. See also 251.
160. *DR*, 118.
161. *DR*, 214.
162. *DR*, 228.
163. *DR*, 117.
164. *DR*, 117.
165. See Eleanor Kaufman's interesting and atypical reading of Deleuze, titled *Deleuze, The Dark Precursor: Dialectic, Structure, Being*. Kaufman's work explores the important and under-analysed 'disturbing structural-ontological persistence' throughout Deleuze's earlier single-authored works. She argues that 'Deleuze is not simply the positive friend of philosophy and of the concept . . . but he is unsparing to the point of perversity in terms of thinking the quasi-sadistic force of structures and forms' (3). She writes that 'One of the goals of this study is thus to develop the implications of this "dark ontology" that Deleuze himself chose not to undertake . . . Instead it alights on those states – stuckness, disembodiment, isolation, the world as perceived by the immobile underclass that we would generally rather not dwell on and argues that looking at these things in an unflinching fashion may in fact allow the discernment of more positive and in any case less pathologizing modes of perception' (4).
166. *DR*, 119.
167. *DR*, 117.
168. *DR*, 118.
169. *DR*, 120.
170. See, again, *DR*, 198.
171. *LS*, 59.
172. *LS*, 52.
173. *DR*, 182.
174. *DR*, 182.
175. *DR*, 278.
176. *DR*, 183.
177. *DR*, 183.
178. *LS*, 174.
179. *LS*, 174.
180. *LS*, 180.
181. *LS*, 59.
182. *DR*, 258.
183. *NP*, 50.
184. *DR*, 243.
185. *DR*, 243.
186. *DR*, 125.
187. *DR*, 125.
188. *DR*, 300.
189. *DR*, 300.
190. *NP*, 70.
191. *DR*, 54.

192. *NP*, 70.
193. *PH*, 19.
194. *NP*, 196; *DR*, 53–4.
195. *NP*, 181.
196. *NP*, 191.
197. *NP*, 71.
198. *NP*, 24.
199. *NP*, 191.
200. *NP*, 196.
201. *NP*, 180.
202. *DI*, 144.
203. *AO*, 311.
204. *NP*, 180.
205. *DR*, 241.
206. *DR*, 41.
207. *DR*, 115.
208. *DR*, 125.
209. *LS*, 262.
210. *LS*, 264.
211. *LS*, 180.

Chapter 8

Derrida, Deleuze, and Difference

We are now in a position to contrast the differing views of difference as conceived by Derrida and Deleuze. As we have said, their respective uses of Nietzsche in the face of Heidegger's criticisms, along with their respective interpretations of Heidegger's criticisms, reveal the fundamental structure at work in their respective concepts of difference. So we shall begin by summarising Heidegger's criticisms, showing point by point why Deleuze rejects them, before turning to Derrida. Deleuze agrees with Heidegger's basic point that Nietzsche is formulating an ontology, while rejecting the substance of the rest of Heidegger's reading. Derrida, on the contrary, agrees with Heidegger that, *if* Nietzsche *were* an ontological thinker, then Heidegger's criticisms would indeed apply. For Derrida, however, Nietzsche is not a thinker of ontology, but rather, one who has articulated a new conception of the sign, one devoid of any traditional pretences to *truth*.

Deleuze contra Heidegger

By way of introduction, we can say that Deleuze would agree with Heidegger's evaluation that Nietzsche is an ontological thinker, in the sense of one who attempts to formulate an account of being. This, however, is where Deleuze's consonance with Heidegger ends. For Heidegger, in so far as Nietzsche is an ontological thinker, and in so far as *all* ontology determines being as presence, Nietzsche too is a thinker of presence. Thus, when Nietzsche employs the term 'will', as in 'will to power', in order to characterise the fundamental creative, expressive, and expansive impulse underlying all of life, Heidegger unavoidably reads this in a substantialist way, assigning it a quiddity. Conversely, Deleuze says, 'when we posit the unity, the identity, of the will we must necessarily repudiate the will itself'.[1] Deleuze reads will to power in a purely relational way, as the explosive, pulsational communication between two or more divergent series. Moreover, though it is certainly elemental and constitutive in the creation of spatio-temporal dynamisms, in the production of qualities and extensions, it is not the differential element for Deleuze.[2] Rather, this role is occupied by the notion of intensity, an essentially asymmetrical, implicated inequality, a fundamental difference. The will to power is the differential principle.

Secondly, because Heidegger isolates a quiddity to Nietzschean will to power, he is then able to provide an essentialist explication of it, of what *a* will to power *as such* looks like. It is the ever-expanding oscillation between securing greater degrees of presence, and transcending itself in the pursuit of more. It is the will to will, discharging its resources (will itself) in an effort to secure more power. In the case of Deleuze, however, and given his understanding of the overall system, there is no such thing as a will to power *as such*. The will to power never *is*, in the sense of an established presence, and never *is*, except in its relations, different to different, and relations to other manifestations of will to power across other series and systems. Moreover the will to power, on Deleuze's reading, is never the *desire* for power: 'will to power does not at all mean "to want power"'.[3] On the contrary, the desire for power is a mere representation of power, rooted in *ressentiment*, and itself inverted: 'What we present to ourselves as power itself is merely the representation of power formed by the slave.'[4]

Finally, the third of Heidegger's criticisms which we addressed was his diagnosis of the so-called reversal of Platonism that Nietzsche carries out. Since the will to power is understood in a substantialist way, the reversal of Platonism merely inverts the hierarchical structure on which that substantiality is spawned. Instead of eternal life (now revealed as death), life in the fullest sense; instead of heaven, earth; instead of soul, body – the subjectness of the subject, the striving for power, characteristic of all representational models of thinking for Heidegger, is deposed from its centrality in the 'I', and deposited in the ineffable 'I's of the drives in the depths of the body, wills that strive for ever increasing degrees and levels of power.

Against Heidegger, in reading Nietzsche's reversal of Platonism, Deleuze does not merely invert the traditional hierarchy, but rather actualises a suppressed term that is marginalised in most traditional readings of Plato. This term is the 'simulacrum', which simulates by way of dissimulation, an internalised difference. Deleuze thus understands Nietzsche's reversal of Platonism as the establishment of an ontology, but one rooted in systems of differential, though non-negational, relations.

Derrida contra Heidegger: implications of *différance*

Like Deleuze, Derrida rejects Heidegger's reading of Nietzsche, but unlike Deleuze, he also paradoxically accepts it in its entirety. If Nietzsche is formulating an ontology, Derrida claims, then Heidegger's criticisms hold up. However, Nietzsche is *not* attempting an ontology, as any ontology will attempt to formulate a 'logos' or a 'sense' of being, whereas Nietzsche's project in its entirety is dedicated to the demonstration that sense is always produced. Derrida thus proposes that we *give Nietzsche up* to Heidegger's reading, following it through the moment when Heidegger's reversal occurs, but in following this inversion, we note the gestures and the spaces that made the structure possible in the first place. Nietzsche, we saw, 'has *written what* he has written',[5] in Derrida's sense of 'originary writing' attentive to the production of sense. Sense is always *produced* – there is no originary 'sense' toward which our discourse endeavours – and for this reason, Heidegger's reading is rejected. Derrida understands Nietzsche's project as one reformulating the conception of the sign. The Nietzschean sign is absent of any presupposition to truth or being, open to opposition, slippage, and contradiction.

Following Nietzsche's lead, Derrida's notion of *différance* involves the '"active," moving discord of different forces',[6] the productive play of differences, or 'traces', which are themselves the effects of *différance*. But the *positive* identity of the trace is its status as a presence of an absence, which above we characterised as a nexus of negations: the trace is but the trace of the trace. Its constitutive identity is its *not-being-x*. Here we quote Derrida extensively and in various contexts: 'The trace is the erasure of selfhood, of one's own presence, and is constituted by the threat or anguish of its irremediable disappearance, of the disappearance of its disappearance.'[7] The thought of the trace 'makes binarism possible on the basis of *nothing*'.[8] 'Presence, then, far from being, as is commonly thought, *what* the sign signifies, what a trace refers to, presence then, is the trace of the trace, the trace of the erasure of the trace.'[9] 'There is no trace *itself*, no *proper* trace . . . The trace of the trace which (is) difference above all could not appear or be named *as such*, that is, in its presence. It is the *as such* which precisely, and as such, evades us forever'.[10] The trace is a 'Cinder as the house of being. . .'.[11] As he writes in *Of Grammatology*, 'The trace is *nothing*. . .'.[12]

> The play of differences supposes, in effect, syntheses and referrals which forbid at any moment, or in any sense, that a simple element be *present* in and of itself, referring only to itself. Whether in the order of spoken or written discourse, no element can function as a sign without referring to another element which itself is not simply present. This interweaving results in each

'element' – phoneme or grapheme – being constituted on the basis of the trace within it of the other elements of the chain or system . . . Nothing, neither among the elements nor within the system, is anywhere ever simply present or absent. There are only, everywhere, differences and traces of traces.[13]

Derrida employs an interesting turn of phrase in this last passage: *neither* among the elements *nor* within the system, indicating a distinction between the system itself and its elements, as though its elements are not, strictly speaking, within the system, but are rather productions *of* the system. The passage goes on to make the distinction between differences, and the traces of traces. If we take his binary assignation (*neither-nor*) above as our lead, we can infer that the traces of the traces (the productions of *différance*) are the elements, while the differences (or spaces, as he will elsewhere call them) comprise the system itself. The element finds its identity only in its reflection, or rather its negation, in its other (itself also an element), which in turn, but at the same time, is *also* constituted on the basis of its *not* being the former. The identity of the trace is one of lack. It *is* primarily what it *is not*.

Clearly this is a controversial claim. Geoffrey Bennington writes: 'for we must not suppose that because Derrida questions presence, he must therefore be a thinker of absence, emptiness, nothing'.[14] Our evaluation, however, is not made in this way. We do not assume that *because* Derrida questions presence, he is *therefore* a thinker of absence. On the contrary, our estimation is borne out in Derrida's own claims about the status of the trace. Yet, to be sure, Derrida himself struggles to avoid such a conclusion:

The gram as *différance*, then, is a structure and a movement no longer conceivable on the basis of the opposition presence/absence. *Différance* is the systematic play of differences, of the traces of differences, of the *spacing* by means of which elements are related to each other. This spacing is the simultaneously active and passive . . . production of the intervals without which the 'full' terms would not signify, would not function.[15]

Here we have all the components of a differential ontology: primary plays of differences, spaces, and identities constituted on an ongoing basis. Yet everything turns on the way in which these components play out and relate to one another.

Différance is, we have seen, a productive play of forces, but how do these forces play? According to Derrida, these plays of forces create 'intervals' – both spatially and temporally:

It is because of *différance* that the movement of signification is possible only if each so-called 'present' element, each element appearing on the scene of presence, is related to something other than itself, thereby keeping within itself the mark of the past element, and already letting itself be vitiated by the mark of its relation to the future element, this trace being related no less to what is called the future than to what is called the past, and constituting what is called the present by means of this very relation to what it is not: what it absolutely is not, not even a past or a future as a modified present. An interval must separate the present from what it is not in order for the present to be itself . . . In constituting itself, in dividing itself dynamically, this interval is what might be called *spacing*, the becoming-space of time or the becoming-time of space (temporization).[16]

These forces *play*, Derrida suggests, by pressing outwardly against each other, in opposing directions, creating intervals. It is the act of interval-creation which spawns the elemental terms of the system, which subsequently, in so far as still related each to the other, find their truest significance in their respective, reflected others. We can imagine an undifferenciated chaotic mass of signifying materiality, and imagine a duality of forces, bursting outward each against the other (each then is agent and recipient of activity, active and passive), pressing a portion of the signifying materiality into a condensation or crystallisation of meaning. This oppositional play of forces thus constitutes the terms, and in its oppositional play, maintains the terms in their semblance of presence, since 'this conflictuality of *différance* . . . can never be totally resolved'.[17] The identity of each of its terms – its traces – is understood only through the hauntings of the absent traces that it marks. *Différance* reveals a fundamental constitutive structure of absence at the heart of presence, 'the identity of identity and non-identity in the "same" of the *im selben Augenblick*'.[18]

Différance then, as I have characterised it, is a constitutive play of opposition and negation. It is unthinkable and uncharacterisable without reference to its constituted elements, which are the traces. The traces, as we said, mark the spacing of a polar opposition, displaying the dual and irreducible complicity between the two ostensibly opposed terms, thereby revealing the differential play of oppositional forces that gave rise to them. 'Hegelianism without reserve', this *insistent intensification of the play of différance*, that the project of deconstruction enlists, is the intensification of these oppositions, the unapologetic opening of negation, the endless dissemination of oppositions, for the purpose of thinking the space in between, for the purpose of pointing 'toward the unnameable',[19] with an eye toward a thought hitherto unthought and unthinkable.

Derrida contra Deleuze

In this way, the differences between Derrida and Deleuze become manifest. Difference in itself, for Deleuze, is primarily and fundamentally relational, all the way down. The 'elements' in Deleuze's system, as we saw, are not elemental in the sense of *atomic*, constituent components. The elements are themselves infolded, implicated differences, imbalances, intensities. They are themselves *constituted* on an ongoing basis in terms of their relations to other elements, and there is no part of the system that escapes the play of relationality. In their specific relations, the elements reverberate in communication from self to other and back to self, and in so doing, this reciprocal communication cannot but displace once again the dicethrow of chance in the system, dispelling the identical with each pulsation. Each element, and the relations relating them, are in constant transformation.

More importantly, at the level at which we stayed in our analysis, the ontological level of Deleuze's account, we never encountered the oppositional or the negative. We saw flashes, bursts, intensities, and forces, but no *conflictuality*. Unlike Derrida's trace, it is not correct to say that Deleuze's element, the intensity, is constituted as merely the 'trace' of what it is not. The element *is what it is*, an essentially uncancellable inequality, and hence the intensity is, strictly speaking, *indifferent* to the other elements in the system. Its *being* is not defined solely by the *absence* of its related terms; rather, the nexus of relations in which Deleuze's elements inhere continues to reconfigure the relative identities of the intensities. Though an intensity is never found in isolation (essentially so), nevertheless its being, as intensity, is comprehended without *necessarily* referring to its *other*, unlike Derrida's trace which is only ever a trace of absent traces. As we saw in Chapter 5, for Derrida, given the oppositional nature of force, two specific forces are essentially interdependent, just as each of their terms 'must appear as the *différance* of the other'.[20] For Deleuze, on the contrary, 'we affirm the relation of *all* forces'.[21] In Derrida's system, the 'other' is the 'not-I', whereas in Deleuze's system, what serves as the other is always a fluid matter.

Thus we have determined at last what we set out to find in the opening of the question: what difference obtains between the concept of difference in itself for Deleuze and the concept of *différance* for Derrida? Derrida's *différance* is a constitutive but negational concept of difference, while Deleuze's difference in itself is a constitutive but positive or relational conception of difference. In so highlighting their differences, we can thus point to the ways in which they would critique each other.

Deleuze, as we have seen from Chapter 4 on, understands the negative as an inverted image of difference. It is not difference in itself, but difference seen from the perspective of the one who is resentful against life. Less profound than difference in itself, inasmuch as it is only made possible *by* difference in itself, negation is ultimately a subordination of difference to the presuppositions of identity and representation, in that it assumes *a priori* a *this* against which difference is determined, even if this *this* is itself understood only as an absence. The situation is in no way improved if, rather than making the negation primary, we make it secondary, as the result of an *oppositional* play of forces, and this for the same reasons. Opposition is predicated upon the interaction of two or more identities. In order to say that forces *oppose* one another, we must first presuppose an identity to the forces themselves, so that they may relate to each other in an oppositional way. Pure relationality presupposes no identity, but if the fundamental and constitutive principle is one of opposition, then there is already identity in the conditions. Though he does not cite Derrida in this passage, Deleuze speaks with respect to this very issue:

> it is a question of knowing whether it is enough to pluralise opposition or to overdetermine contradiction and to distribute them among different figures which, despite everything, still preserve the form of the negative. It seems to us that pluralism is a more enticing and dangerous thought: fragmentation implies overturning. The discovery in any domain of a plurality of coexisting oppositions is inseparable from a more profound discovery, that of difference, which denounces the negative and opposition itself as no more than appearances in relation to the problematic field of a problematic multiplicity.[22]

On Deleuze's account, it is almost as if Derrida discovered the phenomenal secret, the pluralism of constitutive oppositions, but was unable to make the final turn that abolished the opposition and cast out the negative from his concept of *différance*.

Derrida, on the other hand, would more than likely concede that *différance* is characterised by a negative moment. After all, the very name of his project *is* itself a negative: *DE*-construction is by its very appellation an undoing, an unfolding of the absence at the founding moment of presence. Derrida would no doubt reject any presuppositions to any notion of a *pure* concept, inasmuch as any concept we take up (such as concept, multiplicity, being, Idea, eternal return, will to power, self, subject, difference, virtuality, etc.), precedes our use of it, and is necessarily contaminated by a content that, whether we asked for it or not, it brings with it. Moreover, to invoke *any* presumed purity of a concept, for Derrida, will involve the necessary negation of its opposing term. To say that one's ontology is immanent is to say that it is *not* transcendent, which thereby, whether we like it or not, brings the transcendent into the immanent. We must not forget Derrida's early comment on Hegelian difference: 'Pure difference is not absolutely different (from nondifference).'[23] Moreover, he speaks affirmingly when he cites Hegel as saying 'What differentiates difference is identity.'[24] Inasmuch as the binary terms of the Western philosophical tradition are constituted by way of an irreducible complicity, it is a grandiose act of self-delusion on the part of the one who seeks to utterly purify one of its other. Deleuze, in vain, attempts to formulate 'a *pure* thought of *pure* difference', which Derrida equates with the '*dream*' of empiricism, which 'has ever committed but one fault: the fault of presenting itself as a philosophy'.[25] We shall examine these implied criticisms in greater detail in Chapter 10.

Conclusion

Our discussion, therefore, has brought us to the final question we must address, namely, what is the nature of philosophy for these two thinkers? Derrida has formulated a differential system of thought on the basis of signs – traces – constituted by a fundamental negativity, while Deleuze has sought to formulate an ontology, an account of being, on the basis of relationality. Derrida in this fashion speaks constantly of an overcoming of metaphysics, even if this overcoming is constantly underway, claiming that he writes always in the *margins* of philosophy, while Deleuze dismisses any and all talk of an end to philosophy as empty, idle chatter. What then is the nature of our task, and what is it that these two thinkers are doing? That is the question we shall examine in Chapter 9.

Notes

1. *NP*, 7.
2. This is a complicated point to make. In *NP*, Deleuze explicitly states: 'The will to power is thus added to force, but as the differential and genetic element, as the internal element of its production' (51). In French, 'La volenté de puissance s'ajoute donc à la force, mais comme l'élément differentiel et génétique, comme l'élément interne de sa production' (57–8). The expression, *l'élément différentiel*, is the same that appears in *DR*, and which Paul Patton translates as 'differential element'. In other words, in *NP*, Deleuze explicitly refers to the will to power as the 'differential element' in Nietzsche's thought. It seems, however, that Deleuze is using this term 'element' in slightly different ways in the two texts. In *NP*, he goes on to say that will to power is 'added to force as the internal principle of the determination of its quality in a relation (x+dx) and as the internal principle of the quantitative determination of this relation itself (dy/dx)'. In *NP*, therefore, the 'differential element' appears to be an 'internal principle' of differentiation, not unlike, it would seem, what Deleuze, in *DR*, calls 'the flashing world of metamorphoses' (243), and what I am referring to as the 'differential principle'. In *DR*, on the other hand, 'element' appears to mean something much closer to the standard sense of the word 'element', the most basic 'unit' of difference or 'intensive quantity'. 'The element of this internal genesis seems to us to consist of intensive quantity' (*DR*, 26). However, we must always keep in mind that these words, such as 'element' and 'unit', have to be understood and contextualised within a framework in which there are no self-standing, self-contained, atomistic units of any kind. As Smith and Protevi note, '"Elements" must have no independent existence from the system in

which they inhere.' 'Gilles Deleuze', *The Stanford Encyclopedia of Philosophy*, https://plato.stanford.edu/archives/win2015/entries/deleuze. It is important to note that the terms 'intensity' and 'difference in itself', important technical terms for Deleuze's mature ontology, do not appear in *NP*.

3. *DR*, 8.
4. *NP*, 81. See also *NP*, 10.
5. *OG*, 19.
6. *MP*, 18.
7. *WD*, 230.
8. *WD*, 230.
9. *MP*, 66.
10. *MP*, 66.
11. *C*, 23.
12. *OG*, 75.
13. *P*, 26.
14. Bennington, *Derridabase*, 75–6.
15. *P*, 27.
16. *MP*, 13.
17. *P*, 44.
18. *VP*, 59.
19. *VP*, 66.
20. *MP*, 17.
21. *NP*, 44.
22. *DR*, 204.
23. *WD*, 320n91.
24. *WD*, 320n91. This quote is taken from *Hegel's Science of Logic*: 'Difference in itself is self-related difference; as such, it is the negativity of itself, the difference not of an other, but *of itself from itself*; it is not itself but its other. But that which is different from difference is identity. Difference is therefore itself and identity. Both together constitute difference; it is the whole, and its moment. It can equally be said that difference, as simple, is no difference; it is this only when it is in relation with identity; but the truth is rather that, as difference, it contains equally identity and this relation itself. Difference is the whole and its own *moment*, just as identity equally is its whole and its moment. This is to be considered as the essential nature of reflection and as the *specific, original ground of all activity and self-movement*. Difference and also identity, make themselves into a moment or a positedness because, as reflection, they are negative relation-to-self (*GL*, 417–18).
25. *WD*, 151.

Part IV
Implications and Conclusions

Chapter 9

Deconstruction vs. Constructivism

The previous chapter left us with a question: *What is philosophy?* Derrida and Deleuze reached ostensibly differing understandings regarding the nature of philosophy and the task of the philosopher. We saw this clearly in our articulations of their respective concepts of difference. Derrida, we saw, embraced a Nietzscheanism based upon the divorce of the signifier from its traditional pretention to truth – understanding 'sense' and hence 'truth' as something that is always produced – thus opening the notion of the signifier to the possibility of limitless dissemination of opposition, slippage, and internal contradiction. On the surface, it would therefore seem as though Derrida were providing a differential version of thought situated within the broader framework of what we might think of as philosophy of language. Indeed, consider the opening words in *Of Grammatology*: 'However the topic is considered, the *problem of language* has never been simply one problem among others.'[1] Or the titles and subtitles of his early works: in addition to *Of Grammatology*, we have *Writing and Difference*, containing such essays as 'Force and Signification', 'La parole soufflée', and 'Structure, Sign, and Play in the Discourse of the Human Sciences'; along with *Voice and Phenomenon*, subtitled, *Introduction to the Problem of the Sign in Husserl's Phenomenology*.

For his part, Deleuze reads Nietzsche as formulating a differential ontology of force, will to power, and eternal return, an ontology of pure immanence and univocity of being that implies its own ethical perspective on life. For this reason, we can all too easily be tempted to say that the only *difference* between Derrida and Deleuze regarding their concepts of difference is that Derrida's is motivated by and situated in a differential philosophy of language, while Deleuze is articulating a differential ontology. Indeed, as we have seen, Derrida himself seems to suggest that any differences between him and Deleuze can be understood as strategic or methodological, citing disparities in 'the "gesture," the "strategy," the "manner" of writing, of speaking, of reading perhaps'.[2]

But like Zarathustra's dwarf, we risk making things too easy for ourselves if we rest content with this response. To begin with, whatever else Derrida means when he uses the word 'sign', and despite its ubiquity especially in his early writings, it is clear that for him it is not reducible to a *linguistic* sign, strictly speaking. As he writes in *Of Grammatology*:

> There is not a single signified that escapes, even if recaptured, the play of signifying references that constitute language. The advent of writing is the advent of this play; today such a play is coming into its own, effacing the limit starting from which one had thought to regulate the circulation of signs, drawing along with it all the reassuring signifieds, reducing all the strongholds, all the out-of-bounds shelters that watched over the field of language. This, strictly speaking, amounts to destroying the concept of 'sign' and its entire logic.[3]

When sense and truth are themselves produced, when '*The thing itself is a sign*',[4] and '*The represented* is always already a *representamen*',[5] the traditional definition of the sign – '*anything which, being determined by an object, determines an interpretation to determination, through it, by the same object*'[6] – is expanded to the point of obliteration, and the same is true of any traditional philosophy of language predicated thereupon. As Derrida elsewhere writes, 'the field of oppositions' that deconstruction criticises 'is also a field of nondiscursive forces'.[7]

Moreover, the question, *What is philosophy?*, and the answer that the thinker provides to that question, drives right to the very heart of the nature of being itself. The methodology of the philosopher speaks to and is informed by their understanding of 'the fundamental', inasmuch as *how* they engage with it cannot but implicate *what* they think of it. So to reduce the difference between Derrida and Deleuze to a mere question of strategy or methodology is to risk losing sight of the deeper difference between the two. Derrida claims, regarding Deleuze, 'I have never felt the slightest "objection" arising in me, not even potentially, against any one of his works, even if I happened to grumble a bit . . . about the idea that philosophy consists in "creating" concepts.'[8] This is not surprising, given everything that we have seen about Derrida's understanding concerning the expressions of relations of force. In Chapter 5, we saw that Derrida's understanding of *différance* is oppositional in nature, and hence, specific forces subsist in specific, negational relations. For this reason, in any given logical or ontological binary, 'each term must appear as the *différance* of the other'.[9] We saw this again, more clearly, in Chapter 6, where we discovered that 'The trace is *nothing*'[10] other than 'traces of traces'.[11] Given this understanding, it would stand to reason that for Derrida, the creation of concepts would also accord with this interdependent, binary structure, and indeed, Derrida states this explicitly and unequivocally:

> Every concept that lays claim to any rigor whatsoever implies the alternative of 'all or nothing.' Even if in 'reality' or in 'experience' everyone believes he knows that there is never 'all or nothing,' a concept determines itself only according to 'all or nothing.' . . . It is impossible or illegitimate to form a *philosophical concept* outside this logic of all or nothing. But one can . . . think or deconstruct the concept of concept otherwise, think a *différance* . . . But it is true, when a concept is to be treated as a concept, I believe that one has to accept the logic of all or nothing.[12]

> The 'all or nothing' choice was not 'set up' by me. It is implied in every distinction or every opposition of concepts, which is to say, of idealities.[13]

Thus, Derrida's 'grumbles' about Deleuze's understanding of philosophy are to be expected.

But it must be noted that the idea of philosophy as concept-creation is not an incidental or tangential element in Deleuze's oeuvre. Rather, it guides everything he does from his very first book, *Empiricism and Subjectivity: An Essay on Hume's Theory of Human Nature*, up through his very last, written with Félix Guattari, *What is Philosophy?* Every single one of the monographs he writes in the history of philosophy and of literature is guided by the question, *what concepts did this thinker create?* One cannot therefore say of Deleuze, and in the same breath, that one has no objections to his works, *and* that one disagrees with his formulation of the task of philosophy. These two propositions are mutually exclusive. One cannot 'grumble' about Deleuze's understanding of philosophy without at the same time grumbling about his entire body of work.

It is also important to note that Derrida explicitly rejects the language of ontology, and understands the task of the contemporary philosopher as founding a 'community of the question'[14] pertaining to the fact 'that beyond the death, or dying nature, of philosophy, perhaps even because of it, thought still has a future'.[15] For Derrida, the project of ontology will always seek an unmediated, simple 'sense of being',[16] and philosophy, strictly speaking, is always a thought of presence:

> Moreover, there is no possible objection, within philosophy, in regard to the privilege of the present-now. This privilege defines the very element of philosophical thought. It is *evidentness* itself, conscious thought itself . . . We cannot raise suspicions about it without beginning to enucleate consciousness itself from an elsewhere of philosophy which takes away from discourse all possible *security* and every possible foundation. And it is really around the privilege of the actual present, of the now, that, in the last analysis,

this debate, which resembles no other, is played out between philosophy, which is always a philosophy of presence, and a thought of non-presence, which is not inevitably its opposite nor necessarily a meditation on negative absence.[17]

For Derrida therefore, the task at hand is the opening of new possibilities for thinking itself, which the tradition of Western metaphysics, with its necessary binary structure, essentially restricts. This necessary binarism also entails the necessarily axiological and hierarchical structure of metaphysical thought. This too, Derrida states explicitly:

> The enterprise of returning 'strategically,' ideally, to an origin or to a 'priority' held to be simple, intact, normal, pure, standard, self-identical, in order *then* to think in terms of derivation, complication, deterioration, accident, etc. All metaphysicians, from Plato, to Rousseau, Descartes to Husserl, have proceeded in this way, conceiving good to be before evil, the positive before the negative, the pure before the impure, the simple before the complex, the essential before the accidental, the imitated before the imitation, etc. And this is not just *one* metaphysical gesture among others, it is *the* metaphysical exigency, that which has been the most constant, most profound, and most potent.[18]

However, as is made clear by these passages, the philosophical tradition is *founded* upon the moment of presence. Without it, philosophy *as such* is not. Thus *thought*, as Derrida understands it, must always move, deconstructively, in the space between philosophy and non-philosophy, in 'the margin of the margin',[19] *outside the text of Western metaphysics.*[20] Echoing Heidegger's call for a *Destruktion* of the history of ontology, Derrida claims that 'the supplement is neither a presence nor an absence. No ontology can think its operation.'[21] He speaks of 'a writing that absolutely upsets all dialectics, all theology, all teleology, all ontology',[22] of the 'dream of a writing that would be neither literature nor philosophy',[23] a 'work which produces its reader',[24] and claims that the questions regarding the death of philosophy 'should be the only questions today capable of founding the community, within the world, of those who are still called philosophers'.[25] The task of the philosopher then lies outside of all ontology, which, as a logos of *being*, can only ever be a thought of presence. The task lies in the *spaces* between philosophy and non-philosophy, the *spacing* that gives rise to the tradition itself.

Deleuze, on the contrary, is explicit in his self-characterisation as a metaphysician: 'I feel I am a pure metaphysician', following Bergson 'when Bergson says that modern science has not found its metaphysics, the metaphysics it needs. It is that metaphysics that interests me.'[26] Deleuze affirms Hyppolite's assertion that '*Philosophy must be ontology, it cannot be anything else*', while clarifying that, '*there is no ontology of essence, there is only an ontology of sense'.*[27] The philosopher's ontological project is, for Deleuze, one of *creation*: 'To think is to create – there is no other creation – but to create is first of all to engender "thinking" in thought',[28] and as Derrida has begrudgingly signalled, the philosopher's creative object for Deleuze is that of the concept: 'A book of philosophy should be in part a very particular species of detective novel', in that 'concepts, with their zones of presence, should intervene to resolve local situations'.[29] Again, 'philosophy is the discipline that involves *creating* concepts',[30] and philosophy is 'knowledge through pure concepts',[31] such that, 'so long as there is a time and a place for creating concepts, the operation that undertakes this will always be called philosophy, or will be indistinguishable from philosophy even if it is called something else'.[32] For this reason, Deleuze explicitly claims that 'Philosophy is a constructivism.'[33] The philosopher will of necessity be disruptive and offensive, just as the *detective* is of necessity irksome to those people whom she interrogates: philosophy 'serves no established power. The use of philosophy is to *sadden*. A philosophy that saddens no one, that annoys no one, is not a philosophy.'[34] Its project is one of 'breaking with *doxa*'[35] – the established 'givens' of any particular cultural milieu – and the disruption of the *doxa* will, of its very nature, be offensive, dangerous, and unpopular: 'What is a thought which harms no one, neither thinkers nor anyone else?'[36] Philosophy then, according to Deleuze, is a necessarily disruptive but altogether positive ontological creation of concepts, designed to intervene in localised situations, as a means of thinking the problematic nature of being itself. In this sense, and though he at times may speak of an 'overcoming of philosophy',[37] it is clear that this *overcoming* takes place for Deleuze in a zone immanent to philosophy itself. There is no *end* to metaphysics, for Deleuze: 'In any case, the death of metaphysics or the overcoming of philosophy has never been a problem for us: it is just tiresome, idle chatter',[38] and 'questions that address "the death of philosophy" or "going beyond philosophy" have never inspired me. I consider myself a classic philosopher.'[39]

What is therefore apparent in Derrida and Deleuze is the emergence of two radically distinct and fundamentally opposed conceptions of what the philosopher is and ought to be. *Our* task in this chapter, then, will be to address that most basic of philosophical questions: what is philosophy for Derrida and Deleuze? What is the task of the philosopher for the two of them, how does it differ, and how does it relate to their respective understandings of the nature of difference? In a formulation that I can only defend through the course of this chapter, it is my view that while Deleuze's philosophy offers a positive and relational differential ontology, Derrida's deconstruction is a negative differential ontology.

Origins: Plato and Husserl

Since ours is a question of the *nature* of philosophy for Derrida and Deleuze, it is inseparable from the questions of *origin* and *beginning*. Thus, in posing the question, we proceed by way of thinking *through* origins, two in particular: Plato, as the origin[40] of the Western philosophical tradition generally, and Husserl, as the origin[41] of the philosophical tradition bearing the name 'continental philosophy', in which Derrida and Deleuze are situated. Our questioning must begin on the soil in which philosophy took its first breaths, the Greek landscape, as Derrida notes that 'the founding concepts of philosophy are primarily Greek, and it would not be possible to philosophize, or to speak philosophically, outside this medium',[42] and as Deleuze and Guattari write, 'philosophy was something Greek – although brought by immigrants'.[43] It is Plato who laid out for us what a philosopher *is* and *does*; it is Plato who first outlined for us the questions with which philosophy grapples; and so it is to Plato that we first turn for insight as to the task before us.

Edmund Husserl, our other origin, may seem an odd choice, but this selection is not arbitrary, but rather one of the strictest importance. As Merleau-Ponty notes, we stand and think in the shadow of Husserl.[44] Over a century after the publication of the *Logische Untersuchungen* and of *Ideen I*, perhaps it is still too soon to fully take stock of Husserl's impact. But if, as Hegel claimed, 'the owl of Minerva begins its flight, only with the onset of dusk',[45] we can say with confidence that in the waning moments of twilight, immediately preceding dusk, the shadows cast are at their longest. Husserl's shadow is no different: it encapsulates a broad and diverse assemblage of philosophers and philosophical movements, charting a myriad of problems, schools, and trajectories of thinking. Nevertheless, it is Husserl who made the discoveries and laid the foundations for everything that would follow in continental philosophy, up through the present. It was Husserl who reduced Being to sense – as when Deleuze writes that '*there is only an ontology of sense*'[46] – though not in a resurrection of the Kantian paradigm (which still leaves Nietzsche's *true world* intact, but wholly out of our reach), but rather in a synthetic structure of temporality which simultaneously constitutes subject and object, thereby also reducing sense to Being. (It is in this sense that any distinction between a 'philosophy of language' and an 'ontology of sense' cannot be a real distinction, but merely a formal one.) It was Husserl who made the greatest strides in forever breaking with the traditional, representational, puncti-linear model of time, strides which governed and oriented every single continental philosopher to come after him, including Derrida and Deleuze. To repeat, we stand and think in the shadow of Husserl.

What we shall find is that Plato's philosopher is in a certain sense like Nietzsche's, a *sounder of idols*, who transgresses and disrupts common opinion in search of the fundamental. Husserl, like Plato, in combating commonplace notions (what he calls 'the natural attitude'), formulates a methodology of phenomenological reduction, which exposes a pure field of immanence, pure temporality. Thus, we must carry out a phenomenological analysis of the experience of time, exposing the fundamental structure of futuricity therein. From here, we shall proceed to show how this opens onto the positive task of the philosopher, in the mode of a differential ontology, and finally, we shall conclude by demonstrating that, in this sense, both Derrida and Deleuze are formulating a differential ontology. Taking a lead from Eugen Fink, I shall argue that Derrida articulates a negative differential ontology, while Deleuze formulates a positive differential ontology.

The *doxa*, the natural attitude, and the philosopher

We turn first to Plato. In the *Republic* Socrates asks of Glaucon, 'Must we, therefore, call philosophers rather than lovers of *doxa* [δόξα] those who delight in each thing that is itself?', to which Glaucon responds, 'That is entirely certain.'[47] There are two elements – one positive and one negative – that define the task of the philosopher in this characterisation offered by Plato. First, the negative: the philosopher is *not* an adherent to the *doxa* of their day, whatever it may be. In Greek philosophical parlance,[48] the *doxa* is the common opinion of the masses. Often misguided, it is the understood, established code of *givens* with which an individual, as a citizen living in a specific historical culture, is inculcated. The first characteristic, the negative characteristic, of the philosopher according to Plato is that the philosopher will not be swayed by, and (if we may take Socrates as our example) will even positively disrupt, the *doxa*. From this characteristic, the philosopher derives her irksome reputation for attempting to abolish all cultural presuppositions – religious, political, cultural, scientific – in short, wherever they may be found. As Deleuze claims, 'Where to begin in philosophy has always – rightly – been regarded as a very delicate problem, for beginning means eliminating all presuppositions.'[49]

The second characteristic, this time positive, of the philosopher: the philosopher will seek *each thing that is itself*. In seeking *the thing that is itself*, the philosopher seeks what I shall call the 'fundamental'.[50] In Plato's case, the fundamental is the transcendent form, never given *as such* in particular things, but necessary for thinking them. But we need not accept the transcendent, idealist, metaphysical implications of Plato's philosophy in order to accept his prescribed task for the philosopher. The fundamental, for our purposes, merely indicates *whatever, in whatever sense of the term 'whatever', grounds, or conditions, whatever is*. We make no presumptions at this time about, nor does the term commit us to, an ontological status of the *whatever*. It does not commit us to a substantialist metaphysics, nor does it commit us to the *simple presence or purity of the origin*,[51] or anything of this nature. The fundamental may be a 'how' rather than a 'what', fluid rather than static, relational rather than essential. But with this understanding, we have identified the task of the philosopher as outlined by Plato: the disruption of the *doxa* in pursuit of the fundamental. This *fundamental*, whatever it may come to be, I shall henceforth refer to as *Being*, and the pursuit thereof, *ontology*. As Miguel de Beistegui writes, 'the essence of philosophy is concerned with one thing, and one thing only – "being"'.[52]

For his part, Husserl too laboured arduously against a prevailing *doxa*, a particularly convincing one, which he called 'the natural attitude'. The natural attitude, though implicit in Plato and the tradition generally, reaches its apex only with the inauguration of the Cartesian paradigm. The natural attitude is what we as cognising subjects take for granted, accept as *given*, undeniable, irrefutable, and in no need of defence or even explicit articulation. In the natural attitude, I find a world, a world of objects, consisting of things in pre-established systems of arrangement and value. They just *are*, as they *are*, and they just *mean so and so*, with or without my knowledge of them, or even, with or without *any* knowledge of them, 'corporeal physical things with some spatial distribution or other are *simply there for me, "on hand"* in the literal or the figurative sense, whether or not I am particularly heedful of them and busied with them in my considering, thinking, feeling, or willing'.[53] I at the same time find myself, a passive thinking thing, an embodied *soul*, or a *mind*, which *looks out upon* the world of objects. Being, on the natural attitude, is thus divided into two categories: the objects of the world (what we shall call 'brute being'), and thought, which is conceived as ontologically distinct from brute being, and which mediates all of my encounters with being; brute being and thought-of-being, my representations of being.

Thought, or my representations of being, arises via the intercourse of my sensory faculties with being, along with the transmissions they receive, as interpreted and rendered by the brain. Thus, on this account, it is clear that there is always an irreducible disconnect between being and thought. Perception is always translation, and translation is always alteration, on some level. This puts our thought of being at the mercy of our sensory faculties, which can render things differently based upon the conditions, and based upon their own (the faculties') relative strengths or weaknesses. A person with some form of colour blindness, for instance, will represent being differently (and on the natural attitude, less *truly*) than a person without such colour blindness. Likewise, the same table may appear blue, red, or even purple, depending upon the intensity and hue of the lighting in the room.

Thus, in the natural attitude, philosophy's ontological purpose must subordinate itself to the task of epistemology. Even if we grant that the task of the philosopher is primarily to think Being, we have already taken it as a given that Being is ontologically subdivided into the categories of *brute being* and *thought-of-being*, which more or less closely approximates *brute being* as it in fact *is*. In order to think Being in its entirety then, the philosopher must first make sure her thoughts are true; she must secure for herself a domain of juridicality, where she can be sure that her perceptions and representations are, in fact, grounded and justified. In other words, she must formulate a theory wherein she secures for herself: (1) an evaluation, the evaluative criterion by which she may distinguish between what does and does not count as a true thought or idea, and (2) a method, the means whereby the adequation between her thought of being and being itself is made perfect, the perfection of the faculty of thinking itself.

These two requirements posed by the natural attitude, however, unfortunately present the philosopher with an insuperable paradox: in order to provide an account of Being, I must possess the means or method of thinking, capable of perfecting the adequation between brute being and thought; but in order to *validate* my method, I must already have at my disposal the ability to distinguish between a true and a false idea. The impasse of this paradox can be highlighted by an example. If, for instance, I wish to know if my cleaning solution is properly mixed (if my methodology is sound) I can run a simple test: is the surface on which I have used it now *clean*? But this test only works because I already know the desired outcome; I already know what *clean* means, as opposed to dirty. To continue with our analogy, in the natural attitude, the philosopher knows neither whether the solution is properly mixed, nor does she possess any adequate concept of *clean*. Thought, on the natural attitude, is forever divorced from being, and ontology on this model is forever damned to vain attempts at reconciliation. It is thus no surprise that the radical certainty afforded by the Cartesian cogito in the so-called *way of ideas* terminates in Humean scepticism a mere century later.

Breaking with the *doxa*: the *epoché* and the transcendental reduction

In the face of this paradox, thought is born. Husserl's response (and Deleuze and Derrida's as well) is the return to a field of immanence, in order to evaluate the given as given. This takes the form of Husserl's famous *principle of all principles*: '*that everything originarily . . . offered* to us *in "intuition" is to be accepted simply as what it is presented as being*, but also *only within the limits in which it is presented there*'.[54] His methodology is the absolute suspension of the natural attitude, in the mode of the phenomenological *epoché*: '*We put out of action the general positing which belongs to the essence of the natural attitude*.'[55] Though sharing methodological similarities with Cartesian doubt, the *epoché* does not negate, deny, or doubt the *real* existence of the world; it simply puts it out of play, suspends the judgement that would either affirm *or* deny its existence, and along with it, all the propositions and conclusions of the sciences founded thereupon.

The *epoché* thus fundamentally transforms our understanding of the world and of the things in it. But to be a truly phenomenological account, we must not stop there, but rather, the *epoché* must be radicalised, through the *transcendental reduction*, of which the *epoché* serves as the *condition of possibility*.[56] Through the reduction is discovered the 'universal, absolutely self-enclosed and absolutely self-sufficient correlation between the world itself and world-consciousness'.[57] The reduction reveals the transcendental ego as correlative to the world, that on the basis of which anything like a 'world', meaningful and endowed with value, can appear at all. The *epoché*, radicalised in the reduction, reduces all *things*, including myself, to their status as 'sense'. Thus the sphere of experience opened up takes us to pure immanence, pure phenomenality, to the transcendental, the *origin of the world*, what Zahavi calls the '*expansion* of our field of research'.[58] It thus reveals a plane of pure experience, the constituted poles of which are my subjectivity and the world. Here we discover what Heidegger refers to in *Kant and the Problem of Metaphysics* as pure auto-affection,[59] which is the structure of temporalisation. Thus we must carry out an analysis of the consciousness of time.

The structural experience of time: the living present

Our own analyses of time consciousness will resemble Husserl's in many ways, but will differ in significant ways as well. Husserl's grapplings with time will occupy him repeatedly throughout his career. What follows will most closely resemble Husserl's discussion of the *living present*, as discussed in his 1905 Göttingen lectures on time-consciousness.[60] Reduced to pure phenomenality, our experience is always opened, and opening, temporally. Put otherwise, experience is always in passage. More appropriately, experience always *is* passage. The structure of time-consciousness, for Husserl, is comprised of three *moments*: primal impression, retention, and protention.

The primal impression is the now-point – the constantly born, constantly dying, present *now*. Husserl calls it 'the "source-point" with which the "production" of the enduring object begins',[61] the punctuated centre moment, the core of experience. Retention is *primary memory*,[62] the still *living* consciousness of that which has just passed. Protention is the fundamental structural experience of expectation, endemic to each living present (as when we lead with our heads and shoulders through a doorway because we *expect* that the door is going to open when we casually tap the handle).

Let us explore this experience further, by way of a relevant example. I sit now, typing at my computer. In each moment of my typing, each keystroke marks a close approximation to what we called our 'primal impression'. Each tapping of the keys marks (or seems to mark) an instantaneous, momentary depression of time, akin to the structural element of impression. But this account of the present is not rich enough, and does not capture the present as it is in fact *given*. For in order to cognise the sentence as I type it, in order for me, as thinker and typist, to keep straight in my mind what I am typing, *so that* I can continue thinking and typing, my memory must continue to hang onto what I have just typed. Moreover, if my argument is to have any hope for coherence, memory must hang on, not only to that which has *just* been typed, but all that I have typed in the recent past. This reveals the structural and essential experience of retention in the living present.

To further elaborate, retention (primary memory) must be understood as distinct from another kind of memory, re-production.[63] Reproduction is what we typically think of when we casually use the term 'memory', the bringing back to consciousness, by way of a willed re-presentation, of a previously *present* impression. In each moment, were it necessary to *re-produce*, by an act of will, recently past impressions, I could never effectively cognise the present, precisely because, in each moment, I would be ever anew summoning back to consciousness the immediately preceding moments so that I could contextualise the present one (which of course, by that time, would have also passed). Conscious experience would then be a life lived *always too late*. So memory in the present cannot take the form of reproduction.

But without *some* kind of memory still connected to the present, there would be no comprehensibility of the present, because each and every present moment would *present* itself to consciousness as a discrete, isolated experience, one that dies just as quickly as it is born. Each keystroke would appear in a self-contained moment of time that would be lost as soon as it were lived. Hence, there could be no meaningfully *new* keystroke, because I would never remember which keystrokes had come before. The memory needed must not be *willed* then, but must be endemic to the very structure of conscious life itself, and this form of memory is primary memory, which Husserl calls 'retention'. It is still attached to the present; it has never left consciousness, but in its temporalisation, it *shades off* into the past.

The future is somewhat more difficult, but our typing example will work just as well. As I type this very sentence, begun with a capital letter 'A', or rather, as I end the previous sentence, with a '.', I *anticipate* the next sentence, the capital letter that will have to lead it off, necessitating the operation of the 'shift' key on the keyboard. Thus, as the ring finger of my right hand hits the '.' key, the pinky of my right hand, in anticipation of the imminent beginning, moves toward the 'shift' key, while the pinky of my left hand moves toward the 'A'. Numerous such examples could be adduced. As the bus approaches the stop, I stand up, precisely because I *expect* that it is going to stop at the stop. I lead with my head through the doorway because I *expect* that the door, unlocked, will open when I casually tap the handle. Often, we are not fully *aware* of our expectations, unless and until they are ruptured. The shift key may have a crumb of food beneath it that prevents its depression; the bus may pass the stop without coming to a stop; the door may be locked and I may thus hit my head. Nevertheless, the fact that I stood up, the fact that I hit my head, indicates this structural element of *openness to the future* that constitutes my very experience of the present.

What, then, of this primal impression? It is the *Now*. When is the primal impression *given* to consciousness? Presumably, in the very moment, the *living* moment, that it is happening. Indeed, when else could it be given? Yet, if the structure of time consciousness demonstrates anything, it is precisely that this moment, as such, is never given, it is never made present. The living present, as we have shown, is only ever given as possessing the structure of retention and protention. It is only upon reflection that we assert the *truth* or *reality* of a specific primal impression. I *hit* such and such a key – that happened *in a moment*. I *will hit* such and such a key – it *will happen* in *some future moment*. But what of this moment? It appears only in retention, reproduction, and protention. In short, the atomised moment, as such, never appears. What then, do we make of it?

The present, in its very nature *as* present, *is passing*, or more adequately, is *passage*. If the present moment, the present Now, were a discrete, iso-lated, self-contained kernel of time, and the future Nows were like this as well, the present Now would be forever waiting, and the present would never pass. The present, even at its most abstract, must be *contemporane-ous* with its past, it must be *passing*. Here we call upon Deleuze: 'If the present did not pass of its own accord, if it had to wait for a new present in order to become past, the past in general would never be constituted in time, and this particular present would not pass.'[64] Or as Kierkegaard (in the voice of Haufniensis), says, there is no *foothold* to be found in the passage of time.[65] The present can only become past in so far as the past reaches into the present, as it comes to be, as it becomes. This means that the present can only become past in so far as the past reaches *through* the present, into the future, drawing the future into itself. Likewise, the future can only become past in so far as it at the same time reaches, through the present, into the past. Experience confirms this: though from a reflective standpoint (and, we should add, on the basis of a presupposed tradi-tional, puncti-linear model of time), my keystroke *appears* punctuated, momentary, instantaneous, I in fact know that this is not the case. If I, for instance, slow my typing down, and immerse myself in the awareness of my typing, I find that my keystrokes are continuous, fluid. There is a time that passes as my finger presses the key down to the computer, thereby pushing the relevant button underneath, and releases. All of this is to say that the present, as such, is never *given*. To insist upon the necessity, the structural and essential necessity, of the primal impression, as a punctu-ated now-point or source-point, is to presuppose the very model of time which Husserl's discovery of the living present forbids.[66]

And yet, in another sense entirely, the present is *all* that is given. I cannot *relive* or *remember* my past, except in the present. I cannot make plans, set goals, etc., for the future, *except* in the present. Reflection and expectation can only *take place* in the context of a living, present, moment. As Augustine puts it beautifully in *Confessions*:

> What should be clear and obvious by now is that we cannot properly say that the future or the past exist, or that there are three times, past, present, and future. Perhaps we can say that there are three tenses, but that they are the present of the past, the present of the present, and the present of the future. This would correspond, in some sense, with a triad I find in the soul and nowhere else, where the past is present to memory, the present is present to observation, and the future is present to anticipation.[67]

So as we have already established, the present *as such* is never given, and yet, the present is all that *is*. This presents us with an apparent paradox: the present *is not*, and yet, the present *is all that is*. But it appears as paradoxical only because of the extreme difficulty we have with thinking time in a non-punctuated, non-linear, non-presentist manner – where *time* is understood as a line, comprised of an infinite amount of discrete points, called *moments*, and the past, present, and future are the dimensions of this line of time. On this model, a *present*, whether *now*, *then*, or *to come*, has a self-contained identity as a *point of time*. If this is the case, the present cannot both *be* and *not be*. The paradox that has arisen thus forces us to rethink the present itself. What has made itself apparent is that the present is not given as a punctuated *instant*, but rather, the present *is* nothing more than the relationality of past to future, future to past.[68]

This relationality is not the accidental, *empirical* relation between two pre-established *identities*, a future that *just is*, and a past that *just is*. Rather, this relationality is itself productive. The past reaches into the future in such a way that, as it reaches, it thereby *gives birth* to the future itself. Let us examine, by eidetic variation, our concept of protention. The examples we have used thus far are mundane, everyday examples (awaiting the bus, hitting keys on a keyboard, etc.). But these everyday examples are predicated upon a more basic and fundamental structure of openness, the experience of futurality itself. It is only on the basis of futurality that I can *anticipate* anything at all. But futurality itself is not the expectation of *anything* in particular, but rather the mere expectation of a future, an openness to the new, to the *coming*, that is constituted, lived, indeed birthed, in each present moment, as resulting from its past. The relationality that constitutes the present pro-duces its future, pro-duces this structural experience of openness.

What, then, of the past? On the traditional, puncti-linear model of time, the past is comprised of the *presents* that *are no more*. But on our understanding of the living present, nothing could be further from the truth. The past *is*, and forevermore *shall be*. Let us analyse the experience of memory, the death of a loved one, for instance. When someone we love dies, it is wholly inaccurate to say that this event *is no more*. On the contrary, this event *is*, and *will be*, for the duration of the life of the organism. A painful romance, a heartbreak, a divorce, the birth of a child, a wedding day, *the event*, is not *gone*; it is what is *pro-duced* (from the Latin – 'pro' meaning 'bringing forth' and 'ducere' meaning 'to guide' or 'to lead'), brought forth or led forward, by the future in its coming. The past, *from the future*, perpetually meets consciousness in its present. As the future comes to pass, it produces the past, and this past forever runs simultaneously parallel, and intertwined with, the future in its coming. The past relates to the future in such a way that its events make possible the future as such; and in like manner, the future constitutes the past. Both are intertwined in, and constituted by, the present in its productive relationality.

'The present alone exists',[69] but it exists always and only as the productive relationality constituting simultaneously its dually intertwined dimensions of future and past. This is the structure of what I call 'futuricity'.

A philosophy of the future

Philosophy, as we have traced it out of Plato's thought, is ontology. Philosophy is the attempt to think Being, the fundamental, as we have understood it in the broadest possible sense. Despite its myriad forms, it is forever distinguished from the sciences by its pursuit of the fundamental: philosophy of art is neither art history nor art criticism; philosophy of physics is not physics; political philosophy is not political science; philosophy of film is not film theory. Philosophy's revelations are, according to Husserl, '*metaphysical*, if it be true that the ultimate cognitions of being should be called metaphysical'.[70] The *ultimate cognitions of being* on Husserl's account overcome the traditional dualistic metaphysics that forever damns ontology to the backseat with epistemology at the wheel – because Husserl puts thought at the very heart of being. Being, we realise in the shadow of Husserl, is the fundamental structure of life itself, which we, in agreement with Husserl, identified as essentially temporalising: Being is productive relationality.

What is philosophy, according to Derrida and Deleuze? It is ontology in the very broad sense that we have described. But in its ontological pursuits, it must vigilantly avoid the trappings of traditional essentialist metaphysics, metaphysics of identity, of centrality, of presence, which continually tempts the thinker with its promises of the universal.[71] Philosophy must attempt to think Being in its very *sense* as productive relationality, without compromise, as what fundamentally opens thought to the experience of the new, even in its manifestations as *past*. 'Without compromise', that is to say, *as nothing but compromise*, as compromising is a 'promising together'. In its productive relationality, its difference, Being promises itself in the dual futuricity of past and future. Philosophy, for Derrida and Deleuze, is differential ontology.

'Differential', in this context, is both *de*-scriptive and *pre*-scriptive. A differential ontology is one that attempts to think being on a differential foundation, thinking identity as secondary and essentially relational. In this setting, 'truth' becomes not irrelevant, non-existent, or worse, purely relativistic, but itself essentially constituted and temporalising. It is 'foundational' in a certain sense, but the foundation it thinks is not one of absolute presence, certainty, identity, or centrality. 'Ideas, therefore, are related not to a Cogito which functions as ground or as a proposition of consciousness, but to the fractured I of a dissolved Cogito; in other words, to the universal *ungrounding* which characterizes thought as a faculty in its transcendental exercise.'[72] Differential ontology thinks the ground, but must always think the ground as an *essential ungrounding*. It does not abolish the pursuit of the ground, but perpetually attempts to reformulate the language whereby we address the ground.

This means that its concepts must not be representational. Representation fixes stable and permanent limits, demarcating what *is* from what *is not* the thing in question, establishing atemporal quiddities within beings. This activity thus immobilises and hence corrupts the thinking proper to an ontology of difference. The concepts of a differential ontology must themselves *be* differential in nature. That is to say, whatever concepts a differential ontology formulates must be fluid, mobile, transformational and transforming, in flux, and, as Deleuze says, must 'intervene to resolve local situations'.[73] That they are differential in nature means that when they *intervene* in this way, the networks of relations within which they are situated will necessarily alter them. They will never be the same from one problem to the next, because the relations and structures that define the problem itself will differ from situation to situation.

Indeed, this is what makes it so difficult to *define* what *différance* is and does for Derrida, precisely because the concepts Derrida abstracts from a text (what Gasché calls '*infrastructures*'[74]) derive the extent of their significance from the internal logic of the texts in which they operate. Their *thisness* is more of a 'how' than a 'what'; Derrida's concerns are not with the *essence* of *différance*, but with 'the *general system of this economy*'.[75] Thus it becomes difficult, nearly impossible, to define them in any general or universal sense. Likewise, Deleuze's concepts transform with each manifestation, in each project. Manuel DeLanda writes:

> Gilles Deleuze changes his terminology in every one of his books. Very few of his concepts retain their names or linguistic identity. The point of this terminological exuberance is not merely to give the impression of difference through the use of synonyms, but rather to develop a set of *different* theories on the *same* subject, theories which are slightly displaced relative to one another but retain enough overlaps that they can be meshed together as a heterogeneous assemblage. Thus, the different names which a given concept gets are not exact synonyms but near synonyms, or sometimes, non-synonymous terms defining closely related concepts.[76]

Likewise, Daniel W. Smith writes: 'One of the most obvious features of Deleuze's analytic of concepts lies in the fact that, from a Deleuzian perspective, concepts do not have an *identity* but only a *becoming*.'[77] Though there is indeed continuity to Deleuze's thinking, from the early book on Hume all the way through the later politically motivated works with

Guattari, nevertheless, his concepts transform. The *simulacrum*, which, as we have seen, was so central to his formulation of a philosophy of difference in *both Difference and Repetition* and *The Logic of Sense*, goes away after latter work: 'On the other hand, it seems to me that I have totally abandoned the notion of simulacrum, which is all but worthless.'[78] Deleuze has not thereby abandoned differential ontology in his later works, but in fact held fast to its most decisive condition.

Deconstruction as differential ontology

The next task is to defend the characterisation of Derrida's project as an 'ontology'. Prima facie, this would appear to be an absurd task, given the number of times that Derrida himself explicitly rejects such terminology. As ontology will attempt to formulate a 'sense' of 'being', and as being has been historically determined as presence, and as everything that Derrida does calls into question the unmediated simplicity of presence, am I not grossly misrepresenting Derrida's thought by characterising it as an 'ontology'? Indeed, Derrida writes explicitly of 'the impossibility of formulating the movement of supplementarity within the classical logos, within the logic of identity, within ontology'.[79] So if Derrida *is* giving us an ontology, what sort of ontology is it?

It almost goes without saying that there are few philosophers in the history of philosophy who have been as widely ridiculed, dismissed, and disregarded as Derrida.[80] The John Searle debacle, which ultimately culminated in the publication of Derrida's *Limited Inc.*, is well known; and though Searle himself refused to formally take up the debate again, he nevertheless continued in his published work to dismissively mock Derrida, poorly translating his infamous line '*Il n'y a pas de hors texte*'[81] as 'There exists nothing outside of texts.'[82] Another of Derrida's persistently dismissive attackers is Brian Leiter, who accuses Derrida of attempting to appear profound by being deliberately obscure.[83] In an interview, Leiter remarks that 'philosophers generally think that people like Derrida . . . are pretty bad philosophers, and say a lot of silly and foolish things about truth, about meaning, about knowledge, and so on', claiming that for Derrida, 'texts have no meaning . . . they can mean almost anything the interpreter wants them to mean'.[84] As we have seen, this is a reductive and gross mischaracterisation of Derrida. Finally there is the famous attempt, on the part of numerous professional philosophers (among them Willard Quine and David Armstrong) to prevent Derrida's being awarded an honorary degree from Cambridge University in 1992, citing his 'semi-intelligible attacks upon the values of reason, truth, and scholarship'.[85]

Deriding Derrida as deliberately obscure, irreverent, insincere, disrespectful, or frivolous is, in some academic circles, a badge of honour, one that can be flashed without need of defence or justification.

Yet, Derrida himself repeatedly asserts the seriousness and importance of his work. His earliest works on Husserl reflect a careful and thorough engagement with the philosopher who, more than any other in our epoch, sought to radicalise the Cartesian and Kantian projects, purging them of their errors and inconsistencies in the unrelenting and unwavering search for apodictic certainty, in order to once again establish philosophy as *the* rigorous science *par excellence*. *Writing and Difference* and *Margins of Philosophy*, the published collections of his early essays, contain such careful engagements with every significant movement and thinker in French philosophy in his day – Husserl, Levinas, Hegel, Foucault, Bataille, Structuralism, Freud, Artaud, Nietzsche, and others – and always with the same exigency and the same questions: what does this thought demand, and what economic structures and logics command its operation? What are the conditions for thought? What is the foundation of meaning? These are not the questions of someone who does not take philosophy seriously. Moreover, Derrida played a key role in the Groupe de Recherches sur l'Enseignement Philosophique (Greph), the Collège International de Philosophie (Ciph), and the Etats Généraux de la Philosophie (Estates General of Philosophy). These groups were all focused on concentrating efforts to ensure the continued teaching of philosophy in French secondary schools when it came under attack by the proposed Haby Reform.[86] The writings of this period are collected in Derrida's two *Right to Philosophy* volumes.[87] These actions are not the actions and preoccupations of someone who does not take philosophy seriously.

Why then the insistent and persistent mockeries and derisions of his work? First, as the signers of the Cambridge letter assert, Derrida's writings, especially in the United States in the late 1970s and early 1980s, had more of an impact in departments of literary theory, film and media studies, and cultural studies than they did in straightforward philosophy departments. This, however, hardly seems an adequate reason to dismiss out of hand a philosopher as a non-philosopher, given that, since its inception, philosophy has always addressed and spoken through the cultural media of its day, whatever they may be. Some of the Pre-Socratic philosophers wrote in the form of poetry. Plato addressed Homer, and wrote dramatised dialogues; Aristotle is believed to have written dialogues, as did Georges Berkeley and David Hume (who also wrote a six-volume history of England); Augustine philosophised through confessions and prayers; Boethius dramatised a dialogue between himself and a personified *Philosophia*; Nietzsche was a musician, a poet, and philologist. Moreover, in Eastern thought, the boundaries between poetry, scripture, and philosophy have *never* been hard and fast. It is only in the twentieth century that certain strains in Western thought have asserted that philosophy should be isolated from the arts, the rest of the world, and from every other academic discipline. Thus, that Derrida was influential in fields beyond philosophy is, if anything, a testament to his being firmly ensconced within the philosophical tradition, but it is certainly not a mark against him.

A second reason for the relentless dismissals is the fact that Derrida does not employ a traditional argumentative style. His 'arguments' are more evocative and phenomenological than they are straightforwardly argumentative. Rather than a premise-premise-conclusion model of argument, he attempts to evoke an experience of the logic of the text itself, drawing out the ways in which language makes possible, but also undermines, the argument structure of the text, which thus means that his 'arguments' can and often do go on for the duration of the engagement in question. It also means that he is very careful and selective with his own commitments, which can at times make it difficult to determine who is speaking, whether Derrida, his interlocutor, or his *reading* of his interlocutor. Then again, the rigid 'rules' of philosophical argumentation that today govern most of the discipline are, like the demand for academic and disciplinary purity, relatively recent, and obtain only among certain strains of twentieth-century, specifically Western, philosophy. Plato used literary works to make his arguments, and often relied upon the testimony of priests and priestesses. Hume's *Dialogues Concerning Natural Religion* quite intentionally and quite masterfully uses the interstices of a dialogue (rather than any one character's perspective) to make a philosophical argument about the nature of human beliefs.[88]

Finally, and for our purposes, the most important reason for the dismissals is that Derrida himself is seldom upfront about what he is up to, often being more assertive about what he is *not* doing, rather than what he *is*. 'Différance is not only irreducible to any ontological or theological – ontotheological – reappropriation, but as the very opening of the space in which ontotheology – philosophy – produces its system and its history, it includes ontotheology, inscribing it and exceeding it without return.'[89] *Différance* is 'neither a word nor a concept',[90] 'Such a *différance* would at once, again, give us to think a writing without presence and without absence, without history, without cause, without *archia*, without *telos*, a writing that absolutely upsets all dialectics, all theology, all teleology, all ontology',[91] 'at and beyond onto-theology'.[92] This "rationality" – but perhaps that word should be abandoned for reasons that will appear at the end of this sentence – which governs a writing thus enlarged and radicalized, no longer issues from a logos. Further, it inaugurates the destruction, not the demolition, but the de-sedimentation, the de-construction, of all the significations that have their source in that of the logos. Particularly the signification of *truth*.'[93] In the discussion following Derrida's presentation of the '*Différance*' essay, in response to the accusation by Brice Parain that *différance* 'is the God of negative theology', Derrida elusively replies, 'It is and it is not . . . It is above all not.'[94] In his 'Letter to a Japanese Friend', Derrida writes, 'All sentences of the type "deconstruction is X" or "deconstruction is not X" a priori miss the point, which is to say that they are at least false.'[95] In that same letter, Derrida explicitly asserts that deconstruction is not an analysis, a critique, a method, an act, or an operation. Deconstruction 'is' not even, strictly speaking, deconstruction, as deconstruction '*deconstructs itself*',[96] as the 'word "deconstruction," like any other, acquires its value only from its inscription in a chain of possible substitutions, in what is so blithely called a "context" '.[97] As we have seen, Derrida repeatedly insists that his thought moves in the spacing between philosophy and non-philosophy. Thus, the inability to satisfactorily label him is a structural feature of his own project.

Yet, we must ask ourselves why this is so. Why is Derrida so apparently coy, so quick to insist that his project is *not x, y*, or *z*? Why does he always seem to take such great pains to avoid being pinned down? Contrary to what his critics might think, it is not for the sake of playful cleverness or stubbornness. It is because any of the determinations by which one would label Derrida's thought fall under the headings organised and disseminated by the very tradition that his project calls into question. Derrida defines the *transcendental signified* as that which 'would place a reassuring end to the reference from sign to sign', and defines the *metaphysics of presence* as 'the exigent, powerful, systematic, and irrepressible desire for such a signified.'[98] In a certain sense then, much of what is at stake in Derrida's project is the insistent demand of the West to attach a label to things, as though in so labelling them we have at last arrived at their truth or their essence.

At the heart of Derrida's investigations are the origin and possibility of meaning itself. Hence his questions are almost always at least related to questions of language. Yet we err (once again) if we call his project a 'philosophy *of* language', as this presupposes a basic understanding of the nature of language, and typically involves the assumption that 'language' is the human system of signs whereby 'reality' (also a problematic term) is represented and thereby made accessible. Derrida's question, rather, is, *what makes meaning possible?* With this in mind, he constantly challenges the traditional binaries that govern Western thinking, chief among them the 'reality/representation' binary, as 'in the sign *the difference does not take place* between reality and representation'.[99]

Are we then to assert, echoing Derrida himself, that he is *not* doing an ontology? The answer to this question, I think, is, *no*. First, let us revisit the way in which we have characterised philosophy, following from the readings of Plato and Husserl. We first characterised the nature of philosophy as the disruption of the *doxa* in pursuit of the fundamental. We then defined the 'fundamental' as *whatever, in whatever sense of the term 'whatever', grounds, or conditions, whatever is*. In this inclusive and expansive sense, then, we characterised the fundamental in the terms of 'being', and therefore, philosophy in pursuit of the fundamental, we characterised as 'ontology'. Given these caveats and expansive conceptualisations, Derrida incontestably fits the description well. The fundamental in sight for Derrida is that which makes possible science, history, philosophy, and indeed, the world itself. He writes:

> If Being, according to the Greek forgetting which would have been the very form of its advent, has never meant anything except beings, then perhaps difference is older than Being itself. There may be a difference still more unthought than the difference between Being and beings. We certainly can go further toward naming it in our language. Beyond Being and beings, this difference, ceaselessly differing from and deferring (itself), would trace (itself) (by itself) – this *différance* would be the first or last trace if one still could speak, here, of origin and end.[100]

Again, 'Essentially and lawfully, every concept is inscribed in a chain or in a system within which it refers to the other, to other concepts, by means of the systematic play of differences. Such a play, *différance*, is thus no longer simply a concept, but rather, the possibility of conceptuality, of a conceptual process and system in general.'[101] *Différance* is the 'non-full, non-simple, structured and differentiating origin of differences'.[102] Again,

> within the decisive concept of ontico-ontological difference, *all is not to be thought at one go*; entity and being, ontic and ontological, 'ontico-ontological,' are, in an original style, *derivative* with regard to difference; and with respect to what I shall later call *différance*, an economic concept designating the production of differing/deferring. The ontico-ontological difference and its ground . . . are not absolutely originary. *Différance* by itself would be more 'originary,' but one would no longer be able to call it 'origin' or 'ground,' these notions belonging essentially to the history of onto-theology, to the system functioning as the effacing of difference.[103]

Finally, in *Voice and Phenomenon*, after effectively arguing that 'no pure transcendental reduction is possible', Derrida claims that nevertheless, 'it is necessary to pass through the reduction in order to recapture the difference in closest proximity to itself: not to its identity, nor its purity, nor its origin. It has none of these. But in closest proximity to the movement of *différance*'.[104] Thus, it seems undeniable that Derrida is attempting to think the *originary* and the *fundamental*, even if it is an 'originary' that complicates the very notion of 'origin'. As Jeffrey Bell writes, 'to the extent that "philosophies" within the "critique of metaphysics" and "end of philosophy" traditions attempt to think the uncommon condition for the possibility of common, everyday practices and beliefs, then they are doing what metaphysicians and philosophers ought to be doing. They are, in short, doing philosophy.'[105] Thus, keeping in mind all the necessary Derridean caveats, we can say that Derrida is indeed operating at the level of the ontological as we have characterised it.

Nevertheless, does he not persistently speak almost exclusively, and especially in the early writings, of *signs*? We must admit this is the case. He is after all, speaking of a *grammatology*, a science of writing that would be more basic and more fundamental than *either* science *or* writing. However, it is only in light of a presupposed traditional commitment to an absolute breach between thought and being that one must maintain that a philosophy of *signs* cannot be an ontology, a breach that the very movement of deconstruction, in its relentless problematisation of traditional binaries, would have to reject. Derrida writes, citing C. S. Peirce, 'From the moment there is meaning there are nothing but signs. We *think only in signs*.'[106] He then points us almost immediately back in the direction of Nietzsche, noting that this 'amounts to ruining the notion of the sign at the very moment when, as in Nietzsche, its exigency is recognized in the absoluteness of its right'.[107]

We recall that Derrida's Nietzscheanism embraces the liberation of the signifier from any presupposition to truth or to being in the form of the 'presence' of a signified. In one of his most infamous passages, Nietzsche writes, 'Against positivism, which halts at phenomena – "There are only *facts*" – I would say: No, facts is precisely what there is not, only interpretations . . . In so far as the word "knowledge" has any meaning, the world is knowable; but it is *interpretable* otherwise, it has no meaning behind it, but countless meanings. – "Perspectivism."'[108] Like Derrida, Nietzsche is often subjected to the most outlandish and ridiculous criticisms. This citation is one that has elicited some of those criticisms. But let us first look at what he is *not* saying. He is *not* endorsing a robust relativism, or saying that the world has no meaning other than the one that a would-be subject injects into it. Perspectivism does not entail an egoistic relativism;[109] as evidence, consider that Leibniz's monadology is, in a certain sense, a perspectivism. Indeed, egoism – and the 'interpretation' that it would impose upon the world – would itself be an interpretation, relying upon assumptions about the 'ego': '"Everything is subjective," you say; but even this is interpretation. The "subject" is not something given, it is something added and invented and projected behind what there is. – Finally, is it necessary to posit an interpreter behind the interpretation?

Even this is invention, hypothesis."[110] Let us look to this passage of *The Will to Power* more closely, as it is illuminative to understanding Derrida's ontology of signs.

Positivists, Nietzsche claims, halt at the phenomena, which they understand as 'facts'. The word 'fact' derives from the Latin 'factum', which is the nominal use of the past participle of the verb 'facere', meaning to make, compose, or do. A 'fact' is a given, a *something done*. In his reading of positivism, Nietzsche equates the 'fact' with the 'phenomena', or appearances. But given Nietzsche's relentless and unwavering attacks on the notion of 'substance', it is clear that his use of 'phenomena' here cannot be measured, in the Kantian sense, against a noumenal *thing in itself*. Phenomena here are *appearances*, but not of any self-standing *substantium*. The 'phenomena' as Nietzsche here uses the word must mean the appearances, or the expressions, of nature itself. In denying the status of these expressions of nature as 'facts', Nietzsche is rejecting the metaphysical assumption that the expressions of nature are ever just 'givens'. They are themselves interpretations, but not of any particular 'interpreter', if we again read this in a substantialist way.

On the contrary, Nietzsche is here asserting that *the world itself has countless meanings*. This removes the importance of the *human* interpreter from the equation. As Foucault writes, 'In our day, and once again Nietzsche indicated the turning-point from a long way off, it is not so much the absence or the death of God that is affirmed as the end of man (that narrow, imperceptible displacement, that recession in the form of identity, which are the reasons why man's finitude has become his end) . . . man will disappear.'[111] If the world itself has countless meanings, then long before human beings were here to subjectively 'interpret' the world, the world was 'expressing' itself in various ways. There is no *Meaning*, but countless *meanings*. That is to say, nature manifests itself as, itself, meaningful. In this sense, being is expressed in signs, and being 'interprets' being, with or without self-conscious agents to carry out the activity. The lava interprets the signs emitted by the minerality of the volcano as it courses down its side, and the volcano, in turn, interprets the signs of the lava, each 'reacting' accordingly. The weed interprets the sign of the concrete laid upon it, and responds accordingly, 'trying' to break through it or grow around it. The plant interprets the sign of the light and grows toward it. The spider interprets the sign of the subtle impact when its prey is ensnared by its web and responds accordingly. Being, we might say, has expressed itself meaningfully, by way of signs and interpretations, for billions of years prior to our arrival.[112] Thus, that Derrida concerns himself with signs certainly does not preclude his thinking an ontology.

To make the final decisive turn, linking Derrida's thought of the *sign* to the thought of the fundamental, we must look to his notion of *play* in *Of Grammatology*. The passage bears a lengthy citation:

> From the moment that there is meaning there are nothing but signs. We *think only in signs*. Which amounts to ruining the notion of the sign at the very moment when, as in Nietzsche, its exigency is recognized in the absoluteness of its right. One could call *play* the absence of the transcendental signified as limitlessness of play, that is to say as the destruction of ontotheology and the metaphysics of presence . . . This *play*, thought as absence of the transcendental signified, is not a play *in the world*, as it has always been defined, for the purposes of *containing* it, by the philosophical tradition and as the theoreticians of play also consider it . . . To think play radically the ontological and transcendental problematic must first be seriously *exhausted*; the question of the meaning of being, the being of the entity and of the transcendental origin of the world – of the world-ness of the world – must be patiently and rigorously worked through, the critical movement of the Husserlian and Heideggerian questions must be effectively followed to the very end, and their effectiveness and legibility must be conserved. Even if it were crossed out, without it the concepts of play and writing to which I shall have recourse will remain caught within regional limits and an empiricist, positivist, or metaphysical discourse. The counter-move that the holders of such a discourse would oppose to the precritical tradition and to metaphysical speculation would be nothing but the worldly representation of their own operation. It is therefore *the game of the world* that must be first thought; before attempting to understand all the forms of play in the world.[113]

That *we think only in signs* 'ruins' the very notion of the sign, in the sense that the sign no longer serves, as it has traditionally, as a stand-in for some presupposed, non-signifying, stratum of sense or a transcendental signified. This is why Derrida claims that Peirce, in a certain sense, goes further than does Husserl toward the deconstruction of the transcendental signified, in that, for Peirce, '*The thing itself is a sign*',[114] whereas, for Husserl, *the thing itself* is pre-expressive, and signs *come after*. That *we think only in signs* is thus a demolition of the traditional understanding of what a sign *is* and how signs function. The sign traditionally understood, both temporally and spatially, points toward a *presence* that *is not here*, and *is not now*. Signs are thus understood as essentially secondary. They tell us that so and so *was* here, but *is no more*, or that someone *will be* here at such and such a time. They tell us that we *are not* yet at our destination, but *will be*. Linguistically, they point the listener toward the internal experiences of a speaker, which the listener, as listener, can never *quite* grasp in the way that the speaker does, because it is held that our own experiences, immanent as they are to our personal consciousnesses, are full and complete, whereas the signs that we use to convey them are necessarily deficient. They point toward ideal senses. That *we think only in signs*, and only by way of a limitless series of referentiality and interpretation, without ever reaching a terminus, is tantamount to putting a notion of *play* at the heart of thinking.

But we must not, by that token, remain trapped within a Cartesian framework of a self-enclosed, self-contained subjectivity which would be responsible for the thinking, as this would merely reinstate the transcendental signified, in the mode of the 'I' that serves as the absolute ground of its thought. The subject thinks only in signs, even when she is thinking about *herself*, and signs always point elsewhere. So even in her efforts at self-understanding, the signs whereby she thinks the self will be infected with an *exteriority*, such that any rigid line between the *inside* of the subject and the *outside* of the subject will be unsustainable. As Derrida writes in *Voice and Phenomenon*, 'there is no absolute interiority'.[115] The 'I' opens out onto the world, but for the very same reasons, it is not sufficient to conceive *play* as play *within the world*, as this would simply reinstate the transcendental signified in the mode of the 'world', as though the world itself transcends, encompasses, and hence contextualises, the play, providing the *true* basis on which *play* must be conceived. It is for this reason that one must push the Husserlian and Heideggerian problematics through to their ends, effacing the transcendental signified in all its modes – the ego, Dasein, the meaning of being, the world-ness of the world, and so on. At the end of this investigation, Being itself is unmasked as play. 'It is therefore *the game of the world* that must be first thought.'[116] At precisely this point, Derrida cites, once again, Eugen Fink, who, in his book *Nietzsche's Philosophy*, writes of Nietzsche:

> There is a non-metaphysical originality in his cosmological philosophy of 'play' . . . Nietzsche makes the human playing, the playing of the child and the artist into a key concept for the universe. It becomes a cosmic metaphor. This does not mean that the human ontological modality is uncritically applied to being in its entirety. Rather vice versa: the human essence can only be conceived and determined through play if man is conceived in its ecstatic openness toward the existing world and not simply as a thing among other things within the cosmos distinguished by the faculties of mind and reason. Only where the cosmic play comes into view, where the conceptual view breaks through the Apollonian illusion and sees through the constructs of finite appearance to perceive the creative, productive and destructive 'life' itself – where the ascent and decline of the finite, temporal forms is experienced as a dance and a round, as the dice game of divine chance, covered by the innocent and careless heavens, man can experience himself in his playful productivity as connected to the life of the All, as embedded in the great play of the birth and death of all things and as immersed in the tragedy and comedy of universal being. The cosmos plays.[117]

That *we think only in signs* does not situate Derrida's thought as a differential token of philosophy of language, in the Saussurean mould, because the *language* he describes is the very play of the world itself – of which the thing that we most typically refer to as *language* is but one part. As he writes in *Of Grammatology*, 'For some time now, as a matter of fact, here and there, . . . one says "language" for action, movement, thought, reflection, consciousness, unconsciousness, experience, affectivity, etc. Now we tend to say "writing" for all that and more: to designate not only the physical gestures of literal pictographic or ideographic inscription, but also the totality of what makes it possible.'[118] That this 'play' operates at the level of the ontological is made even clearer in the 'Structure, Sign and Play in the Discourse of the Human Sciences' essay, where Derrida writes of 'the Nietzschean *affirmation*, that is the joyous affirmation of the play of the world and of the innocence of becoming, the affirmation of a world of signs without fault, without truth, and without origin which is offered to an active interpretation. *This affirmation then determines the noncenter otherwise than as loss of the center.*'[119] This play of the world constitutes subjects and objects, Being and beings, signifiers and signifieds. In this sense, there are signs of all sorts – genetic, chemical, physical, biological, sexual, artistic, literary, sociological, psychological, philosophical, etc. – hence we can say, echoing and paraphrasing Nietzsche, there are no *facts*, only *signs*, and hence, only *interpretations*. Being expresses itself as meaningful and playful, in a space of thought where these two adjectives are no longer mutually exclusive.

Thus it seems clear that, despite its deconstructive impetus, Derrida's thought is indeed a differential ontology, in the ways that we have described it. Even though he speaks of signs, the signs of which he speaks are not limited to signs in the way that the tradition understands them, in so far as for Derrida, signs go all the way down. But the assertion – *signs go all the way down* – is itself an ontological claim, as is 'the thing itself is a sign'. Even if most of his works engage closely with texts in the philosophical tradition, Derrida is in no way merely doing 'textual commentary',[120] and he is most certainly *not* asserting that 'There exists nothing outside of texts.' Rather he is continuing to think through the inherited problems of the tradition, *so that* the *play of the world* can be illuminated, and new avenues for thinking may be opened, paths tending 'toward the unnameable'.[121]

Positive and negative differential ontologies

What, then, distinguishes the differential ontology of Derrida from that of Deleuze? To address this question, let us first summarise the results of our investigation thus far. Through our exploration of Hegel in Part II, we learned that, while Derrida understands his own conception of *dif-*

férance as almost indistinguishable from Hegel's conception of difference – claiming, in fact, that 'the concept of *différance* took its place within metaphysics . . . with Hegel'[122] – Deleuze rejects Hegel's conception of difference in its entirety. For Derrida, 'We will never be finished with the reading or rereading of Hegel',[123] and 'all anti-Hegelian thinkers'[124] are much closer to Hegel than they realise, while for Deleuze, Hegel is so treasonous an enemy of the philosophical tradition that he does not even warrant an extended engagement. This divergence, we saw, rested on the fact that for Deleuze, *negation* – Hegelian difference – does not satisfy the conditions of a concept of difference. It is less profound than difference, indeed dependent on difference, as things must first *differ* before they can *oppose* one another. It derives from a view of life rooted in *ressentiment*, in that it can only think the nature of the thing by first negating everything else, and then must constantly affirm all of the 'evils' that it has already negated. Finally, difference conceived as negation collapses into identity, as it does in Hegelian dialectics when the oppositional terms are 'raised up' into the unity of the *Aufhebung*. Difference, for Deleuze, must be conceived without negation or it is, we might say, insufficiently difference. On the contrary, Derrida's criticism of Hegel's conception of difference is that it is *insufficiently negative*, because the binary oppositions in Hegel's system are ultimately *aufgehoben* into a higher, dynamic and homeostatic unity, thereby cancelling the opposition. The problem, for Derrida, is *not* that difference is conceived by Hegel as a *negation*, but rather that the negation is ultimately overcome. Derridean *différance*, we said, amounts to a *negativity so negative* that even the term 'negative' – laced as it is with Hegelian dialectics – cannot characterise it.

Then, through our investigations of Nietzsche in Part III, we saw that both Deleuze and Derrida reject Heidegger's reading of Nietzsche, and both understand Nietzsche as the pivotal figure in the overcoming of the Hegelian conception of difference. Like their rejections of Hegel, however, their reasons and strategies for rejecting Heidegger, as well as their understandings of the Nietzschean contribution, differ significantly. Derrida strenuously rejects Heidegger's reading of Nietzsche as an ontological thinker, writing that 'in wishing to restore a *truth* and an originary or fundamental *ontology* in the thought of Nietzsche, one risks misunderstanding, perhaps at the expense of everything else, the axial intention of his concept of interpretation'.[125] Given his rejection of Heidegger's ontological reading of Nietzsche, Derrida also rejects the two further points in Heidegger's reading, including Heidegger's understanding of Nietzsche as 'reversing Platonism': 'read otherwise, the Nietzschean demolition remains dogmatic and, like all reversals, a captive of that metaphysical edifice which it professes to overthrow'.[126] Derrida understands Nietzsche's most significant achievement as the 'liberation of the signifier from its dependence or derivation with respect to the logos',[127] which correlates, as we saw, with Derrida's understanding of the 'trace' as 'the trace of the trace, the trace of the erasure of the trace',[128] a 'Cinder as the house of being'.[129]

Deleuze, on the contrary, *affirms* an ontological reading of Nietzsche, but rejects the notion that this ontology commits him to a substantialist, 'presentist' metaphysics, in the way that Heidegger reads him (and as Derrida asserts is true of all ontologies). Rejecting the principle that 'all reversals remain captive' to that which they endeavour to reverse, Deleuze thinks through the implications of the Nietzschean injunction to reverse Platonism – 'the task of modern philosophy'[130] – arguing that this reversal in fact liberates a Platonic concept typically suppressed in the traditional, dyadic readings of the Platonic tradition: the simulacrum. Against the model/copy (form/particular) structure, which measures the nature of the thing by its internal *resemblance* to the form, the reversal of Platonism 'means to make the simulacra rise and to affirm their rights among icons and copies'.[131] Unlike the Platonic 'copy', the simulacrum is conceived on the basis of its internal *difference*.

This internal difference is Deleuze's basic ontological principle, the thought of which, Deleuze argues, is made possible by Nietzsche's notion of 'eternal return'. The 'internal difference' we saw in Deleuze as the notion of the 'intensity', the implicated multiplicity that constitutes the differential element for Deleuze. These intensities are connected in groupings known as 'series', the relations of which are modified by, and themselves modify, the intensities which constitute them. Then, 'two or more series'[132] connect and communicate to form what Deleuze calls 'systems'. At each level of Deleuze's ontology, the constitutive relations communicatively alter the natures of the things in question. Within a series, relations between intensities alter the intensities, while the intensities themselves impact the natures of the relations. Within a system, the relations between series alter the natures of the series, and the interactions between different systems impact the natures of the systems in relation as well. Most relevant about this account is that it is relational – as opposed to *negational* – all the way down. Nietzsche's eternal return is understood as the 'dicethrow' in the 'ideal game' of the cosmos, wherein each move introduces and reconfigures its own rules, fully immanent to the game itself, thus affirming chance through each move. It is the disjunctive synthesis, whereby the tensile relation between heterogeneous systems is creative and affirmative, rather than pernicious. Finally, the eternal return is understood by Deleuze as the unthinkable heartbeat of time, the selective, expulsive pulsation of repetition that selects out the negative and the identical in favour of the different, constituting 'the only Same of that which becomes'.[133] Deleuze's differential ontology is therefore positive and relational. Being (becoming), for Deleuze, is not manifested as lack or negation, but as pure affirmation, expression, relation, and creativity.

Derrida's ontology, on the other hand, is negative. In the simplest of terms, for Derrida, *différance* is understood as a *negativity so negative* that the term 'negative' as it is traditionally understood cannot grasp it, and the trace – the constituted effect of *différance* – is only ever the trace of other traces, constituted by their status as placeholders of absences. Derrida attempts to offer an account for the *play of the world*, but he does so in such a way that the *thing* is conceived, precisely in terms of what it is *not*, rather than what it *is*. In a certain sense, inasmuch as *is-ness* is understood by Derrida only in the mode of presence, this is a structural and essential necessity of the project of deconstruction. Derrida says, 'difference cannot be thought without the trace',[134] that '*the pure trace is différance*',[135] and that 'the trace must be thought before the entity'.[136] The trace is that on the basis of which the entity may be thought at all, and yet the trace '*does not exist*'.[137] The trace is what is produced by the play of *différance*, it is the self-effacing mark of otherness in the interiority of the same, that which announces the same only inasmuch as it at the same time occludes that very same and marks the announcement of the other, which the same *is not*. The trace is akin to ashes and cinders, remaining '*from* what is not, in order to recall at the delicate, charred bottom of itself only nonbeing or nonpresence'.[138]

For these reasons, I shall here borrow a designation from Eugen Fink to characterise Derrida's project. In his work, *Nietzsche's Philosophy*, Fink writes:

> Nietzsche's thesis is this: in truth there are no things, there are no substances, there is no 'being'. There is only the wavering flood of life, only the stream of becoming and the incessant up and down of its waves. Nothing endures, stays and persists, and all is in flux. But our cognition forges its reality and changes the flow falsely into the being of enduring things which endure in the change and which persist during the change of their states. The 'thing' or the substance is a fiction. It is a structure created by the will to power which violates the reality. It arrests, forges and grasps becoming and subjects it to the concept.[139]

Though reason insists to us that we see 'things', there are, for Nietzsche, no *things* to be seen, only waves, flows, and becomings. Fink goes on to say that, 'What looks like a separate thing is only a wave in the stream of life and temporary quantum and conglomeration of power which only presents a phase in the dynamic of the cosmic interplay.'[140] Fink therefore refers to Nietzsche's thought as a 'negative ontology of the thing'.[141]

Likewise, Derrida's differential ontology may be thought of as a *negative* differential ontology.[142] It is an *ontology* in that it attempts to think, even more *fundamentally* and *originarily*, the fundamental and the originary. It is *differential* in that it formulates the fundamental on the basis of *différance*, rather than a basis of identity or, in Derridean terminology, 'presence'. It is a *negative* differential ontology for two related reasons: (1) The fundamental for Derrida – *différance* – is understood, as we have seen numerous times in numerous contexts, as a fundamental *negativity*; a negativity more negative, oppositional, and conflictual than the Hegelian negative, in that 'this conflictuality of *différance* . . . can never be totally resolved'.[143] That forces are in *relation* for Derrida entails that they *oppose* one another, and do so in imbalanced but interdependent binaries, constituting terms which 'must appear as the *différance* of the other'.[144] (2) The constituted for Derrida – the trace – is conceptualised according to this same *super-negativity*. The trace consists only of 'traces of traces',[145] 'the trace of the trace, the trace of the erasure of the trace',[146] a 'Cinder as the house of being',[147] a '*nothing*'[148] that '*does not exist*',[149] remaining '*from what is not, in order to recall at the delicate, charred bottom of itself only nonbeing or nonpresence*'.[150] The trace, constituted by the play of *différance*, is but a placeholder of other, absent traces, themselves understood only in the senses of what they are *not*.

These two points of Derrida's negative differential ontology may be contrasted with the analogous points in Deleuze's thought: (1) The fundamental for Deleuze – *difference in itself* – is *not* understood as fundamentally negative or oppositional, but as relational. This relationality is rooted in Deleuze's understanding of the differential element, the intensity or self-infolded difference or multiplicity. Negation is a secondary *effect*, made possible only because of a primary *differentiation*:

> Negation is difference, but difference seen from its underside, seen from below. Seen the right way up, from top to bottom, difference is affirmation. This proposition, however, means many things: that difference is an object of affirmation; that affirmation itself is multiple; that it is creation but also that it must be created, as affirming difference, as being difference in itself. It is not the negative which is the motor. Rather, there are positive differential elements which determine the genesis of both the affirmation and the difference affirmed. It is precisely the fact that there is a genesis of affirmation as such which escapes us every time we leave affirmation in the undetermined, or put determination in the negative. Negation results from affirmation: this means that negation arises in the wake of affirmation or beside it, *but only as the shadow of the more profound genetic element* . . .[151]

These 'positive differential elements' are what we read as Deleuze's intensities, 'determining' the genesis of affirmation in the fundamental expressivity of being itself. These elements are related to others through communicative relations, each mutually shaping the other, aligned in series which are further connected in systems. But it would be inaccurate to characterise Deleuze's understanding of relationality as 'negative', in the way that we have Derrida's. For his part, Derrida only rarely mentions the correlate of a differential element. For instance, in *Of Grammatology*, he refers to the *grammè* as 'An element without simplicity'.[152] However, this element is synonymous, for Derrida, with the 'trace'[153] which, as we have seen, is constituted in terms of its fundamental *absences*, the traces of other traces. (2) In terms of the 'constituted', for Deleuze, the likeliest of candidates would be, especially in *Difference and Repetition*, the 'Idea'. The idea 'is an *n*-dimensional, continuous, defined multiplicity',[154] while Deleuze understands the multiplicity not as 'a combination of the many and the one, but rather an organization belonging to the many as such, which has no need whatsoever of unity in order to form a system'.[155] The Deleuzian Idea is 'thus defined as a structure',[156] a virtuality, the actualisation of which functions as the determinative basis for any given 'thing' (construed in the broadest sense possible):[157] 'There are Ideas which correspond to mathematical relations and realities, others which correspond to physical laws and facts. There are others which, according to their order, correspond to organisms, psychic structures, languages and societies: these correspondences without resemblance are of a structural-genetic nature.'[158] Ideas – like the systems, series, and intensities of which they are constituted – are themselves changed by their interactions with each other, as well as by their actualisations, but it would be entirely inaccurate to say that the Deleuzian Idea is constituted only by the marks of other, absent Ideas.

Conclusion

We concluded Part III with the question, what is the nature of philosophy for Derrida and Deleuze? We have now answered that question. Derridean deconstruction is best understood as a negative differential ontology. It is an ontology in the sense that it attempts to think the fundamental, it is differential in that '*différance* is originary',[159] and it is negative in that both its constitutive, differential mechanism as well as the traces constituted thereby are understood in terms of a fundamental 'not'. It is for this reason that Derrida's thought always operates in a deconstructive mode, because the entity can only ever be thought on the basis of the trace, and the trace, constituted on the basis of *différance*, is only ever understood on the basis of what it is not: 'The movement of this schema will only be able, for the moment and for a long time, to work over from within, from a certain inside, the language of metaphysics.'[160] The moment there is *constitution*, for Derrida, there is always already *negation*.

Deleuze's philosophy, on the other hand, we conceptualised as a positive differential ontology. Like Derrida, Deleuze attempts to think the fundamental, referring to himself as a 'pure metaphysician'.[161] Like Derrida, he does so on a relational or differential basis, where identity is considered as secondary to a constitutive play of forces. But unlike Derrida, difference for Deleuze should not be thought most fundamentally as negation, but as positive relationality and affirmation. The intensity, Deleuze's differential element, relates to other intensities through productive relations, themselves shaped by the intensities, which are in turn altered by their relations. These groupings form series, which in turn associate in larger groupings known as 'systems', 'structures', and 'Ideas'. At no point is there stasis, as each element and unit is modified by its relationality, but at the same time, at the virtual, ontological level, there is only positivity, as negation for Deleuze is a secondary phenomenon, made possible only by way of differentiation. Deleuze's is a relational, differential ontology, conceived on a basis of positivity. Thus, philosophy, for Deleuze, 'is a constructivism',[162] consisting of the creations of concepts, which will reshape the world, which in turn will reshape and demand new concepts.

In Chapter 10, we shall conclude by looking at the implications of these results, thereby further defending the conclusions I have drawn in this chapter. There are certain challenges that my reading must address. First, my characterisation of deconstruction as a 'negative differential ontology' has not yet taken into account Derrida's unwavering commitment to affirmation, to double affirmation, to an archi-originary yes. Indeed, in his remarks on the event of Deleuze's death, he explicitly cites Deleuze as a kindred spirit in this regard. Thus, I must examine the role of affirmation in Derrida's thinking. In addition, I want to stave off the concern that my reading of Derrida entails a quietism or political ineffectuality to Derrida's thinking. I do this by looking at the role of the 'not' in Derrida's concept of 'undecidability'. Finally, I look at the criticisms that both Derrida and Deleuze level against Hegel, turning those criticisms this time against Deleuze and Derrida themselves, to see which, if any, of these criticisms hold up. In the end, it seems to me that the one criticism of Deleuze's that has real bite when it comes to deconstruction is the idea that a negative conception of difference is *less profound* than difference. This is not an entirely unhappy point, however, as the 'power of the negative' in Derrida's thinking is that it arguably does a better job of providing a space of vocalisation and expression at existing sites of oppression, precisely because it leaves intact, while fundamentally destabilising, the binarities on which those oppressions are based. For formulating positive concepts *beyond* the binarities, however, Deleuze seems more useful. We shall see this by briefly looking at the ways in which feminist scholars have taken up and/or distanced themselves from Derrida and Deleuze.

Notes

1. *OG*, 6.
2. *WM*, 192–3.
3. *OG*, 7.
4. *OG*, 49.
5. *OG*, 50. Regarding the *representamen*: 'I confine the word *representation* to the operation of a sign or its *relation* to the object *for* the interpreter of the representation. The concrete subject that represents I call a sign or a *representamen*.' Peirce, *Collected Papers of Charles Sanders Peirce, Volume 1*, paragraph 540.
6. Peirce, *Peirce on Signs*, 251.
7. *MP*, 329.
8. *WM*, 193.
9. *MP*, 17.
10. *OG*, 75.
11. *P*, 26.
12. *LI*, 116–17.
13. *LI*, 120.
14. *WD*, 80.
15. *WD*, 79. It is absolutely necessary to note, however, that Derrida never espouses a simple 'death' of philosophy, and in fact, explicitly rejects such a death: 'I try to keep myself at the *limit* of philosophical discourse. I say limit and not death, for I do not at all believe in what today is so easily called the death of philosophy (nor, moreover, in the simple death of whatever – the book, man, or god, especially since, as we all know, what is dead wields a very specific power)' (*P*, 6).
16. *OG*, 22.
17. *VP*, 53.
18. *LI*, 93.
19. *MP*, xxiii.
20. *MP*, 25.
21. *OG*, 314.
22. *MP*, 67.
23. *AL*, 73.
24. *AL*, 74
25. *WD*, 79.
26. Deleuze, 'Responses to a Series of Questions', 41–2.
27. *DI*, 15. Hyppolite defines philosophy as 'the expression of being in concepts or in discourse'. See *LE*, 10. For an important, well-written, and controversial counter-reading to the reading of Deleuze as an ontological thinker, see Zourabichvili, *A Philosophy of the Event, Together With the Vocabulary of Deleuze*.
28. *DR*, 147.
29. *DR*, xx.
30. *WP*, 5.
31. *WP*, 7.
32. *WP*, 9.
33. *WP*, 35.
34. *NP*, 106.

35. *DR*, 134.

36. *DR*, 136.

37. *DR*, 8.

38. *WP*, 9.

39. *TRM*, 365.

40. We use this term 'origin' in the full awareness that this origin is not, and cannot be, simple. Both Derrida and Deleuze are attentive to the historical interaction between 'Greek culture' and the surrounding cultures of antiquity, to the point that Derrida even complicates the very notion of a Platonic 'borrowing' (*D*, 85). 'What remains common to Heidegger and Hegel is having conceived of the relationship of Greece and philosophy as an origin and thus as the point of departure of a history internal to the West, such that *philosophy necessarily becomes indistinguishable from its own history*. However close he got to it, Heidegger betrays the movement of deterritorialization because he fixes it once and for all between being and beings, between the Greek territory and the Western earth that the Greeks would have called Being' (*WP*, 95). Indeed, at the heart of Deleuze's philosophy is the conviction that thought only occurs by way of an *encounter*, and this too lies at the heart of his understanding of the 'origins' of philosophy: 'What we deny is that there is any internal necessity to philosophy, whether in itself or in the Greeks (and the idea of a Greek miracle would only be another aspect of this pseudonecessity) . . . The birth of philosophy required an *encounter* between the Greek milieu and the plane of immanence of thought' (*WP*, 93). Derrida, as the thinker of 'originary contamination', could hardly espouse a dogmatic adherence to a robust Occidentalism, and indeed, much of his 'Plato's Pharmacy' essay is dedicated to complicating the notion of a simple Greek origin. See *D*, 84–94, esp. 85n15. Nevertheless, taking into consideration all of these important caveats, both Derrida and Deleuze would also agree that the strategies and methodologies that we associate with philosophy trace their lineage to the ancient Greek city-state, and in particular to Plato. Deleuze and Guattari will specifically associate the gestation of philosophy with the Greek political structure, arising, as it did, in the margins and on the fringes of ancient imperialism. See also Tampio, 'Not All Things Wise and Good are Philosophy', *Aeon*, https://aeon.co/ideas/not-all-things-wise-and-good-are-philosophy.

41. This 'origin' is no less complicated than the other. The so-called split between analytic and continental philosophy does not really emerge proper until the mid-twentieth century, and the figures traditionally associated with the early continental camp – Heidegger, Sartre, Levinas, and Jaspers – claim inspiration in multiple, diverse figures – Kant, Hegel, Dostoevsky, Kierkegaard, Schopenhauer, and Nietzsche, among others. It is also important to note that Husserl himself develops his own consciousness philosophy alongside that of Bergson, whom Husserl ultimately eclipses in France. See Cisney, 'Duration and Immanence: The Question of A Life in Deleuze'. Lee Braver traces the origins of the continental tradition to Kant in *A Thing of this World: A History of Continental Anti-Realism*. Nevertheless, our choice of Husserl as the 'origin' is based upon the fact that the split proper is forged in the fires of the Heidegger-Carnap-Marcuse controversy, and Heidegger's methodology is deeply and explicitly indebted to Husserl, not to mention the fact that Husserl provides the intellectual air in which French philosophy in the mid-1960s began to breathe.

42. *WD*, 81.

43. *WP*, 93.

44. Merleau-Ponty, 'The Philosopher and His Shadow', in *Signs*, 159–81.

45. Hegel, *Elements of the Philosophy of Right*, 'Preface'.

46. *DI*, 15.

47. *The Republic*, 480a.

48. Parmenides too, though he does not specifically use the term 'philosopher', distin-

guishes explicitly between 'the steadfast heart of persuasive truth' and the 'opinions of mortals' (βροτῶν δόξας). Parmenides, *Fragments*, 1.29–30.

49. *DR*, 129.
50. I use this term quite consciously aware of the complicated history that accompanies it in the twentieth century, specifically in the works of Heidegger, Levinas, and Derrida. In 1927, Heidegger's *Sein und Zeit* outlined a project of 'fundamental ontology', both terms of which Heidegger would later abandon (and Derrida would speak approvingly of this abandonment). See Heidegger, *Introduction to Metaphysics*, 43–4; and *OG*, 22. See also Levinas, 'Is Ontology Fundamental?', in *Basic Philosophical Writings*, 1–10.
51. Here I am thinking of Derrida. See, for instance, *OG*, 35–7, 65, 74; and *VP*, 5, 52, 59, 71, 79, 81
52. de Beistegui, *Truth and Genesis*, ix.
53. *IPP*, §27.
54. *IPP*, §24.
55. *IPP*, §32.
56. *CES*, §41. Most of my account of the *epoché* and the reduction are taken from *The Crisis* text, which differs from the account of the reduction(s) given in *Ideas I*, §§27–34. Husserl himself makes explicit his own criticisms of his earlier formulations (which he refers to as the 'Cartesian way' in *The Crisis*, §43). Briefly, by *not* distinguishing between the *epoché* and the reduction, Husserl claims, we encounter the ego, but one that is apparently devoid of any content, as opposed to recognising the sense-bestowing nature of the ego, which he claims is made possible only by the division between *epoché* and reduction, as explicated in *The Crisis*.
57. *CES*, §41.
58. Zahavi, *Husserl's Phenomenology*, 46.
59. Heidegger, *Kant and the Problem of Metaphysics*, §34, 132–6.
60. *PCT*, §§7–31.
61. *PCT*, §11.
62. *PCT*, §§11–14.
63. Incidentally, the failure to make this distinction is, according to Husserl, the error of Brentano. See *PCT*, §§1–6.
64. *NP*, 48.
65. Kierkegaard, *The Concept of Anxiety*, 85.
66. I do not here deal with, but am very sensitive to, Derrida's emphasis on the importance of the *presence of the present* for Husserl, as discussed extensively in *VP*, and in all of his Husserl writings.
67. Augustine, *Confessions*, XI.26.
68. See *DR*, 76.
69. *DR*, 76.
70. *CM*, §60.
71. It is in these senses, I think, and these senses only, that Zourabichvili makes his compelling case that 'If there is an orientation of the philosophy of Deleuze, this is it: *the extinction of the term "being" and therefore of ontology*.' Zourabichvili, *Deleuze: A Philosophy of the Event*, 37.
72. *DR*, 194.
73. *DR*, xx.
74. Gasché, *The Tain of the Mirror*, 7.
75. *MP*, 3.
76. DeLanda, *Intensive Science and Virtual Philosophy*, 202.
77. Smith, *Essays on Deleuze*, 122–3.
78. *TRM*, 366.
79. *OG*, 314.
80. This assessment does not include careful and thoughtful critiques of deconstruc-

tion, such as: Ellis, *Against Deconstruction*, and May, *Reconsidering Difference: Nancy, Derrida, Levinas, Deleuze*, 77–128.

81. Derrida, *De la grammatologie*, 227.
82. Searle, *Mind, Language, and Society*, 19. This is an extraordinarily, almost laughably, bad translation of this line.
83. Leiter, *Routledge Philosophy Guidebook to Nietzsche on Morality*, xiv.
84. Leiter, 'Brian Leiter on Nietzsche Myths', *Philosophy Bites* 108, at http://hwcdn. libsyn.com/p/d/1/6/d1677410823f120c/Brian_Leiter_on_Nietzsche_Myths. mp3?c_id=1779634&expiration=1500748097&hwt=744ffebdf3192b0a9f176f3e58 df0fd6.
85. Derrida, '*Honoris Causa*: This is Also Extremely Funny', in *Points*, 420–1.
86. 'A state proposal for drastic educational restructuring named after the then newly appointed Minister of Education, René Haby (who served in the "Gaullist" [right-wing] government of Giscard d'Estaing), the Haby Reform promised to reduce the number of classroom hours available for philosophy instruction in the *lycée*. Moreover, the imperatives of the "Giscard-Haby" plan very much threatened the future of the discipline in the university. The consternation that the severity of its edicts bred about the overarching or longer-ranging ramifications of this preemptive intervention on the part of the State into teaching-learning was one of the factors that eventually led to the "official mobilization" of the GREPH against the Haby Reform in January 1975.' Trifonas, *The Ethics of Writing: Derrida, Deconstruction, and Pedagogy*, 75.
87. Derrida, *Who's Afraid of Philosophy: Right to Philosophy 1*; Derrida, *Eyes of the University: Right to Philosophy 2*. In his eulogy for Deleuze, Derrida notes that Deleuze had said to him at one point, 'It pains me to see you put so much time into this institution [the Collège International de Philosophie], I would prefer that you write' (*WM*, 193).
88. See Foley, 'Unnatural Religion: Indoctrination and Philo's Reversal in Hume's *Dialogues Concerning Natural Religion*'.
89. *MP*, 6.
90. *MP*, 7.
91. *MP*, 67.
92. *OG*, 23.
93. *OG*, 10.
94. Derrida, 'The Original Discussion of "*Différance*"', in Wood and Bernasconi (eds), *Derrida and* Différance, 84.
95. *PIA*, 5.
96. *PIA*, 4.
97. *PIA*, 5.
98. *OG*, 49.
99. *VP*, 43.
100. *MP*, 67.
101. *MP*, 11.
102. *MP*, 11.
103. *OG*, 23.
104. *VP*, 71.
105. Bell, *Philosophy at the Edge of Chaos*, 15.
106. *OG*, 50.
107. *OG*, 50.
108. *WTP*, 267.
109. Derrida too, many would be surprised to know, explicitly rejects relativism. 'For a proper understanding of the gesture that we are sketching here, one must understand the expressions "epoch," "closure of an epoch," "historical genealogy" in a new way; and must first remove them from all relativism' (*OG*, 14).

110. *WTP*, 267.
111. Foucault, *The Order of Things*, 420.
112. See Williams, *A Process Philosophy of Signs*; Hoffmeyer, *Biosemiotics: An Examination into the Signs of Life and the Life of Signs*; Wheeler, *The Whole Creature: Complexity, Biosemiotics, and the Evolution of Culture*; Cohn, *How Forests Think: Toward an Anthropology Beyond the Human*; von Uexküll, *A Foray Into the Worlds of Animals and Humans*.
113. *OG*, 50.
114. *OG*, 49.
115. *VP*, 73.
116. *OG*, 50.
117. Fink, *Nietzsche's Philosophy*, 171–2. Derrida is not citing *this* text in particular, but Fink, *Spiel als Weltsymbol*, French translation by Hildenbrand and Lindenberg, *Le jeu comme symbole du monde*. This text is also cited by Deleuze, *DR*, 332n5, and *DI*, 305n18.
118. *OG*, 9.
119. *WD*, 292.
120. *DI*, 260.
121. *VP*, 66.
122. Derrida, 'The Original Discussion of "*Différance*"', in Wood and Bernasconi (eds), *Derrida and* Différance, 95.
123. *P*, 77.
124. *WD*, 99.
125. *OG*, 286–7.
126. *OG*, 19.
127. *OG*, 19.
128. *MP*, 66.
129. *C*, 23.
130. *DR*, 59.
131. *LS*, 262.
132. *DR*, 117.
133. *DR*, 41.
134. *OG*, 57.
135. *OG*, 62.
136. *OG*, 47.
137. *OG*, 62.
138. *C*, 21.
139. Fink, *Nietzsche's Philosophy*, 148.
140. Ibid., 150.
141. Ibid., 145–54.
142. In characterising Derrida's thought in this manner, it is important to note that this is a designation that, in 'Violence and Metaphysics', Derrida explicitly rejects: 'This is why, here, when the thought of Being goes beyond ontic determinations it is not a negative theology, nor even a negative ontology' (*WD*, 146). However, he does so for the same reasons for which he rejects the term 'ontology' elsewhere, that 'ontos' designates 'being', and 'being' designates 'presence'. When describing (and rejecting) negative theology, he writes, 'This negative theology is still a theology and, *in its literality at least*, it is concerned with liberating and acknowledging the ineffable transcendence of an infinite existent, "Being above Being and superessential negation"' (*WD*, 146). Negative theology, though negating the positive claims one might make about God, nevertheless maintains the hyperessential *being* of God. Applying this to his rejection of negative ontology, then, we can say that, as Derrida would understand the term, 'negative ontology' would entail a hyperessential 'presence' beyond all capacities of language or representation. A

super-representational, abiding presence. We have characterised the task of 'ontology' differently.

143. *P*, 44.
144. *MP*, 17.
145. *P*, 26.
146. *MP*, 66.
147. *C*, 23.
148. *OG*, 75.
149. *OG*, 62.
150. *C*, 21.
151. *DR*, 55.
152. *OG*, 9.
153. 'If the theory of cybernetics is by itself to oust all metaphysical concepts – including the concepts of soul, of life, of value, of choice, of memory – which until recently served to separate the machine from man, it must conserve the notion of writing, trace, grammè [written mark], or grapheme, until its own historic-metaphysical character is also exposed' (*OG*, 9).
154. *DR*, 182.
155. *DR*, 182.
156. *DR*, 183.
157. See Cisney, 'Becoming-Other: Foucault, Deleuze, and the Nature of Thought'.
158. *DR*, 184.
159. *WD*, 203.
160. *VP*, 44.
161. Deleuze, 'Responses to a Series of Questions', 42.
162. *WP*, 35.

Chapter 10

Conclusion(s)

In this concluding chapter, I would like to clarify the results of this study, in particular the characterisation of deconstruction as a 'negative differential ontology', hopefully clearing up what I do *not* mean by this formulation. First, given that Derrida equates deconstruction with affirmation – 'launching a new phase in the process of deconstructive (i.e. affirmative) interpretation'[1] – I shall look at the ways in which Derrida explicitly takes up the theme of 'double affirmation',[2] contrasting it with the notion of 'double affirmation' in Deleuze.[3] Then we will examine Derrida's notion of 'undecidability' as it relates to the notion of the 'not' and to Derrida's understanding of the 'decision'. In so doing, I will further defend the differentiation I have proposed between the two thinkers, looking at the importance of binarity in Derrida's work, and showing how this played out in the receptions of these two thinkers by looking briefly at the feminist engagements with the works of Derrida and Deleuze. While deconstruction was quickly taken up in positive ways by some feminist thinkers, many feminist scholars initially and for a long time rejected the hypothesis of any positive applications of Deleuze's thought within a feminist context. The 'power of the negative' in the deconstructive mode is that it gives space for vocalisation at existing sites of oppression.

The joyously repeated affirmation

The first and most glaring obstacle to the reading I have here proposed is Derrida's repeated insistence on the theme of 'affirmation'. Indeed, in his remarks upon the event of Deleuze's death, when Derrida expresses his 'experience of a closeness or of a nearly total affinity'[4] with Deleuze, one of those affinities is found 'in the joyously repeated affirmation ("yes, yes")',[5] and this insistence upon affirmation can be found scattered throughout Derrida's earliest published writings.[6] In addition, Derrida frequently endeavours to *distinguish* deconstruction from its purely negative connotations. For instance, in his 'Letter to a Japanese Friend', as Derrida describes his reasoning for the selection of the term 'deconstruction', he says: 'But in French the term "destruction" too obviously implied an annihilation or a negative reduction much closer perhaps to Nietzschean "demolition" than to the Heideggerian interpretation or to the type of reading I was proposing. So I ruled that out.'[7] In the same letter, Derrida also writes that 'Structures were to be undone, decomposed, desedimented . . . But the undoing, decomposing, and desedimenting of structures, in a certain sense more historical than the "structuralist" movement it called into question, was not a negative operation. Rather than destroying, it was also necessary to understand how a "whole" was constituted and to reconstruct it to this end.'[8] The *thought of the trace,* as we have seen, 'escapes binarism and makes binarism possible',[9] so in deconstructing, deconstruction also simultaneously demonstrates the necessary logical and metaphysical impulses behind traditional *constructions.* Deconstruction, for Derrida, must be understood as fundamentally affirmative, and yet I have characterised it throughout this work as a 'negative differential ontology'; so let us look briefly at the Derridean theme of affirmation, taken up most explicitly in the 1987 piece on Michel de Certeau, titled, 'A Number of Yes',[10] where it is directly tied to the 'joyously repeated affirmation' of the 'yes, yes'.[11]

This essay addresses 'what Michel de Certeau writes about writing in the mystical text',[12] and in particular de Certeau's claim that 'God always says only Yes [or: I am].'[13] This 'infinite yes'[14] of 'originary affirmation',[15] on Derrida's reading, underlies, infects, haunts, and makes possible every other use of language, including the empirical, de facto employment of the word 'yes' itself that occurs in any given communicative affirmation. Derrida writes of this 'yes' that, 'implicated by all the other words whose source it figures, it also remains silent, the "silent accompanist" (a little like the "I think" in Kant that "accompanies" all our representations), and thus in a certain way foreign to language, heterogeneous to the set of terms [*vocables*] thus defined [*cernés*] and concerned [*concernés*] by its power'.[16] This originary affirmation is imperceptibly attached to every sign, securing its operation. The sign, in other words, is not 'neutral'. The very use of the sign asserts that the sign itself *says* what it *says*, even when it says 'no', 'a kind of archi-engagement, alliance, consent, or promise that merges with the acquiescence given to the utterance it always accompanies, albeit silently, and even if this utterance is radically negative'.[17] The sign, 'no', in other words, *asserts* (positively says 'yes' to) and thus *affirms* the 'no'. In this way, the originary affirmation to which Derrida here refers echoes the notion of the 'promise' that appears in 'Faith and Knowledge' and elsewhere: '*the promise, in the act of faith or in the appeal to faith that inhabits every act of language and every address to the other*'.[18] It is a 'yes' that precedes, accompanies, and conditions the expression of 'yes' in any communicative act: 'It is therefore a kind of inaudible term, inaudible even in the utterance of a determined *yes*, in one language or another, in a given sentence valid as an affirmation.'[19]

At the same time, any 'yes' is, as Derrida notes, a response, and any response entails the 'danger' of the other. Embedded within the originary 'yes' in Derrida's thinking is the notion of rupture, break, contamination, and threat, a distinction between a 'good' and a 'bad' repetition.[20] This passage bears a complete citation:

> Let us suppose a first *yes*, the archi-originary *yes* that engages, promises and acquiesces before all else. On the one hand, it is originarily, in its very structure, a response. It is *first second*, coming after a demand, a question, or another *yes*. On the other hand, as engagement or promise, it must *at least* and in advance be tied to a confirmation in another [*prochain*] *yes. Yes* to the other [*au prochain*], that is, to the other *yes* that is already there but nonetheless remains to come. The 'I' does not preexist this movement, nor does the subject; they are instituted in it. I ('I') can say *yes* ('yes-I') only by promising to keep the memory of the *yes* and to confirm it immediately. Promise of memory and memory of promise. This 'second' *yes* is a priori enveloped in the 'first.'[21]

The sign, as we have said, is not 'neutral'. There is an affirmation attached to every use of the sign, an *archi-originary* 'yes' or a *promise* that ensures the functioning of the sign. Yet, every 'yes', Derrida notes, is a *response*, every response indicates an 'other', and thus, this archi-originary *response* portends and entails a second 'yes', another *yes* that remains, in the archi-originary affirmation, yet 'to come'. This second *yes* – the promise to the other – must, as a condition of its execution, *forget* the archi-originary yes that infects every use of every sign. Otherwise, it would be merely a 'natural, psychological, or logical consequence'[22] of the archi-originary *yes*. The very notion of the promise, in other words, includes as a condition of its promissory status, the possibility of being *broken*. Nietzsche describes the promise as 'an active no-longer-wanting-to-get-rid-of, a willing on and on of something one has once willed, a true *memory of the will*',[23] and yet the very gravity of the promise that Nietzsche describes, the sanctity that we typically attach to the promise, rests upon the fact that *our word may be broken*, our *will* may weaken, our 'yes' may be violated. Thus the second *yes* 'must act *as if* the "first" had been forgotten, past enough to require a new, initial *yes*. This "forgetting" is not *psychological* or accidental, it is structural, the very condition of fidelity.'[24]

At root in the 'yes', therefore, is the 'danger' of oblivion: 'Thanks, if this can be said, to the threat of this oblivion, the memory of the promise, the promise itself can take its first step, namely, the second.'[25] There are other dangers as well – the danger that the repetition of the 'yes' will be merely mechanical (hence, lacking in the solemnity of the promise), that it will be broken (in infidelity), that the 'yes' is but 'simulacrum, fiction, fable'.[26] There is also the danger that the 'yes' opens us to the threat of harm from the other. Derrida notes in 'Faith and Knowledge' that '*The coming of the other can only emerge as a singular event when no anticipation* sees it coming, *when the other and death – and radical evil – can come as a surprise at any moment.*'[27] This danger at the heart of the second 'yes' is not unlike what, in 'Violence and Metaphysics', Derrida refers to as 'an original, transcendental violence, previous to every ethical choice, even supposed by ethical nonviolence'.[28] But to be clear, it is this aspect of threat that makes possible the welcoming of the other: 'For here the relationship of a *yes* to the Other, of a *yes* to the other and of one *yes* to the other *yes*, must be such that the contamination of the two *yeses* remains inevitable. And not only as a threat: but also as an opportunity.'[29] For this reason, Derrida speaks of the archi-originary *yes* as 'the opening *and* the cut'[30] of language – opening in so far as it ensures the functioning of language, *cutting* in so far as the danger always already inhabits the 'yes': 'Since the second *yes* inhabits the first, the repetition augments and divides, splits in advance the archi-originary *yes*.'[31] The 'double affirmation', for Derrida, is always already 'cut', 'threat', 'split', 'contaminated', 'divided', and 'pierced'.[32] The archi-originary 'yes' is always already a rupture or a break, a violence; in the language we have used throughout, the 'yes' is always already a 'not'.[33]

The 'double affirmation' has an entirely different sense in Deleuze's thought, rooted in the Nietzschean interpretation of '*The divine couple, Dionysus-Ariadne*'.[34] The Nietzschean celebration of the Dionysian is well known – 'Have I been understood? – *Dionysus versus the Crucified.*'[35] Less often commented on, however, is Nietzsche's frequent literary partnering of Dionysus with Ariadne: 'Nothing like this has ever been written, felt, or *suffered:* thus suffers a god, a Dionysus. The answer to such a dithyramb of solar solitude in the light would be Ariadne. – Who besides me knows what Ariadne is! – For all such riddles nobody so far had any solution; I doubt that anybody even saw riddles here.'[36] The dithyramb to which Nietzsche here refers is 'The Night Song' from *Thus Spoke Zarathustra* excerpted in *Ecce Homo*, which ends with the line, 'Night has come; now all the songs of lovers awaken. And my soul, too, is the song of a lover.'[37] Ariadne is the 'answer' to this 'immortal lament at being condemned by the overabundance of light and power, by his sun-nature, not to love'.[38] The daughter of King Minos of Crete, Ariadne helped Theseus in his quest to kill the Minotaur, on the condition that Theseus would afterward take Ariadne back to Athens with him and marry her. Ariadne provided Theseus with the instructions on locating the Minotaur, the strategy for escaping the labyrinth when finished, and the sword with which to carry out the task. Theseus agreed, defeated the Minotaur, and escaped from the labyrinth. On the way to Athens, 'they put in at the island of Naxos'[39] where, while Ariadne slept, Theseus abandoned her. There, Dionysus discovered her, fell in love with her, and married her. 'Who besides me knows what Ariadne is!', asks Nietzsche.

As Deleuze reads the Nietzschean understanding of the Ariadne myth, Ariadne and Dionysus represent a mutually beneficial complementarity, a marriage based upon admiration and reciprocal strengthening, as opposed to the co-dependent, sickly understanding of love and marriage that populates so much popular literature and film:

> Marriage: thus I name the will of two to create a one that is more than those who created it. Reverence for each other, as for those willing with such a will, is what I name marriage. Let this be the meaning and truth of your marriage. But that which the all-too-many, the superfluous, call marriage – alas, what shall I name that? Alas, this poverty of the soul in pair! Alas, this filth of the soul in pair! Alas, this wretched contentment in pair! Marriage they call this; and they say that their marriages are made in heaven. Well, I do not like it, this heaven of the superfluous.[40]

The sickly understanding of love and marriage is predicated upon two complementarily weak people finding each other and partnering up, each making up for the weaknesses of the other. It is a love based upon lack. As Nietzsche says, 'for the most part, two beasts find each other'.[41] There are religious and psychoanalytic interpretations of this 'love', but its pervasiveness in Western thought is undeniable. On the religious interpretation (the 'marriage made in heaven'), it is God who creates us as incomplete beings, beings who must then fulfil God's plan in our lives by finding that one person in the world who will 'complete' us in accordance with his design. (This language has also been used to buttress the religious opposition to same-sex marriage.) On the psychoanalytic interpretation, we marry the person who most reminds us of our other-sex parent, in the hopes that this person can 'heal' all of the wounds left by that parent. What both of these interpretations share in common is the perception of life as sickly, weak, and deficient, and in need of a partner to 'complete' one and to simply help one get by – the satisfaction of this *need* is called 'love'. It was *this* type of love that Ariadne had sought when she partnered with Theseus. Enamoured of the heroic 'manliness' of Theseus, the 'manliness' that slays monsters, Ariadne made herself small, reducing herself to the status of love-object for the hero, in cunning exchange for the promise of marriage to him. For his part, Theseus used Ariadne, without whom his defeat of the Minotaur would have been impossible, only to abandon her when it suited him. Paul Kirkland writes of Theseus, 'His return to Athens without her demonstrates his concealment of his dependence.'[42] As Deleuze notes, this particular image of the feminine in Ariadne is merely a sickly reflection of an already sickly image of the masculine: 'As long as woman loves man, as long as she is mother, sister, wife of man, even if he is the higher man, she is only the feminine image of man: the feminine power remains fettered in man . . . As terrible mothers, terrible sisters and wives, femininity represents the spirit of revenge and the *ressentiment* which animates man himself.'[43] Nietzsche writes elsewhere in *Thus Spoke Zarathustra*: 'There is little of man here; therefore their women strive to be mannish.'[44]

In *Thus Spoke Zarathustra*, Nietzsche writes: 'For this is the soul's secret: only when the hero has abandoned her, she is approached in a dream by the overhero.'[45] The soul in this passage is feminine – the *anima* – and the exit of the heroic is salutary for the *anima*. According to Kirkland, 'Dionysus is a worthy lover for Ariadne because unlike Theseus, he does not need. Nietzsche presents such love as the longing of one who is overfull.'[46] Such is a longing that derives from a saturation of one's being that desires to *give*, not to receive. In conversation with Claire Parnet, Deleuze says that one should strive to 'Become capable of loving without remembering, without phantasm and without interpretation, without taking stock',[47] to love based upon overflow rather than deficiency. Theseus' abandonment of Ariadne in fact makes possible her liberation from the sickly view of love. She 'senses the coming of a transmutation which is specific to her: the feminine power emancipated, become beneficent and affirmative, the Anima'.[48] In the writings of Carl Jung, *anima* (the Latin word for 'soul') is the feminine complement to the 'masculine consciousness', a power of the feminine that Western man suppresses in himself, as 'our Western mind, lacking all culture in this respect, has never yet devised a concept, nor even a name, for the *union of opposites through the middle path*',[49] which he characterises in the terms of the ancient Chinese notion of the Tao.

According to Deleuze, following the exit of Theseus, Ariadne signifies the discovery of the feminine power *within herself*. Hers is the power to *say* – Yes! Dionysus *is* the *yes* – the primary affirmation synonymous with being itself – but Ariadne is the power to *proclaim* the 'yes' and in so doing, to double the primary affirmation synonymous with Dionysian becoming. In *The Birth of Tragedy*, Nietzsche writes of the Dionysian, 'Now, with the gospel of universal harmony, each one feels himself not only united, reconciled, and fused with his neighbor, but as one with him, as if the veil of *māyā* had been torn aside and were now merely fluttering in tatters before the mysterious primordial unity.'[50] The Dionysian signifies the 'collapse of the *principium individuationis*', in which 'everything subjective vanishes into complete self-forgetfulness'.[51] In its purest sense, the '*Dionysian* world'[52] indicates the 'oneness' of the mysterious primordial unity, 'a monster of energy, without beginning, without end; . . . a sea of forces flowing and rushing together, eternally changing, eternally flooding back'.[53] Dionysus is the perpetually expressive power of being itself, according to Deleuze: 'Affirmation itself is being, being is solely affirmation in all its power . . . In itself and as primary affirmation, it is becoming.'[54] As the ceaseless, un-self-conscious ebbing and flowing of becoming, being is affirmation in a primary sense. But this affirmation must also become affirmation in a secondary sense, saying 'yes' to the flow of becoming – Dionysus longs for a lover. Ariadne, according to Deleuze, signifies this 'second affirmation' in Nietzsche's thought, 'the Anima that now corresponds to the Spirit that says yes'.[55] Becoming gives birth to beings capable of echoing this primary affirmation. As Laurence Lampert writes, 'to enhance humanity, Dionysos leads it into possession of the qualities of his beloved – he makes humanity truer to what *it* is and to *what is*'.[56] In the Dionysian mythos, according to Deleuze, Ariadne signifies this yes-saying: 'Nietzsche clearly distinguishes the two affirmations when he says "Eternal affirmation of being, eternally I am your affirmation." Dionysus is the affirmation of Being, but Ariadne is the affirmation of affirmation, the second affirmation or the becoming-active.'[57] Ariadne is the affirmation of chance that wilfully expels the negative, repeating that primary affirmation of becoming itself – she is, in other words, the eternal return personified, and it is for this reason that in *Thus Spoke Zarathustra*, the ring of eternal return is described no fewer than seven times as a wedding ring – 'the nuptial ring of rings'.[58]

It is therefore clear that while Derrida echoes the 'double affirmation' of Deleuze, he means it in an entirely different sense. The archi-originary 'yes' is an 'inaudible term' that inhabits and secures the functioning of every sign, according to Derrida. Any 'yes', however, is a response, and as such, the archi-originary yes portends a second yes – the promise to the other – which not only requires the forgetting of the archi-originary yes, but also opens one to the danger of radical evil. At the heart of the archi-originary yes, therefore, is the danger of oblivion, and the threat of harm from the other. The negativity of the 'cut' and of 'oblivion' therefore lies at the heart of Derrida's archi-originary yes.

On the contrary, the primary affirmation in Deleuze is synonymous with the expressive and affirmative power of becoming itself – the Dionysian in Nietzsche's thought. The Dionysian in its purest sense is the un-self-conscious ebbing and flowing of the 'mysterious primordial unity'. Such a sea of forces, however, lacks the capacity to speak. It cannot *say* 'yes' because it *is* 'yes'. The affirmation of being doubles upon itself, becoming a *hymn* to the cosmos, when becoming gives birth to beings who are capable of *saying* the 'yes' that *is* the nature of becoming itself – this is the wedding of Dionysus and Ariadne. 'Organisms awake to the sublime words of the third *Ennead*: all is contemplation!'[59] While, for Deleuze, the second affirmation is the proclaimed repetition of the expressive and affirmative power of becoming, for Derrida, the primary affirmation itself is already cut, split, and pierced.[60]

In the next section, we will address the notion of the decision in Derrida's thinking. In an effort to further clarify what I mean (and what I do *not* mean) by 'negative differential ontology, we shall look briefly at the 'combat zone'[61] of undecidability (itself a negative denomination), demonstrating that despite and because of the 'madness' associated with undecidability, a decision is not only *possible*, but demanded. The power of the negative in Derrida's thought is not an endorsement of indecision or inactivity.

Decision and undecidability

Tiqqun give voice to a commonly held misconception of deconstruction when they write, 'The only thought compatible with Empire – when it is not sanctioned as its official thought – is deconstruction . . . Deconstruction is a discursive practice guided by one unique goal: *to dissolve and disqualify all intensity, while never producing any itself*.'[62] Given my characterisation of Derrida's thought as a 'negative differential ontology', it may appear prima facie that I hold a similar view. For his part, Derrida struggles against this perception of his work throughout his life, asserting that 'what is currently called deconstruction would not at all correspond . . . to a quasi-nihilistic abdication before the ethico-political-juridical question of justice and before the opposition between just and unjust'.[63] In so far as deconstruction consists of Derrida's famously articulated 'double gesture' – 'We must first *overturn* the traditional concept of history, but at the same time mark the *interval*[64] – and in so far as the 'interval' consists of a *différancial* play of force, then contrary to Tiqqun's characterisation, deconstruction is focused almost in its entirety on the liberation and mobilisation of force. Moreover, it is difficult to think of many continental thinkers from the late twentieth century more focused on ethical and political concepts, such as responsibility and justice, than Jacques Derrida. But even then, Derrida typically formulates such concepts in negative terms, and given our taxonomic designation as 'negative differential ontology', we must for the sake of clarity look more closely at such concepts. One of the most important is the concept of 'undecidability', which plays a key role in Derrida's now-famous 'Force of Law' essay.

Though it assumes centre-stage in Derrida's project in the period that comes to be equated with his 'ethical turn',[65] the concept of 'undecidability' appears quite early in Derrida's work. In the 'Plato's Pharmacy' essay, Derrida analyses the *pharmakon* of writing as both 'poison' and 'cure', writing that 'Long before being divided up into occult violence and accurate knowledge, the element of the *pharmakon* is the combat zone between philosophy and its other. An element that is *in itself*, if one can still say so, *undecidable*.'[66] Elsewhere, in his analysis of the hymen in Mallarmé, Derrida writes: 'An undecidable proposition, as Gödel demonstrated in 1931, is a proposition which, given a system of axioms governing a multiplicity, is neither an analytical nor deductive consequence of those axioms, nor in contradiction with them, neither true nor false with respect to those axioms. *Tertium datur*, without synthesis.'[67] The *tertium datur* is the 'third given', or the 'third possibility', philosophically forbidden by the logical principle of the 'law of excluded middle', *tertium non datur*. The 'undecidable' functions in the essays in Derrida's *Dissemination* as the 'between', synonymous with *différance*:

> It is the 'between,' whether it names fusion or separation, that thus carries all the force of the operation. The hymen must be determined through the *entre* and not the other way around . . . The word 'between' has no full meaning of its own . . . What holds for 'hymen' also holds, *mutatis mutandis*, for all other signs which, like *pharmakon, supplément, différance*, and others, have a double, contradictory, undecidable value that always derives from their syntax.[68]

Like *différance*, which we have characterised as a play of opposing forces, pressing outwardly against each other in the creation of intervals, the undecidable is treated as 'neither one nor the other and both at once'.[69] While Western metaphysics labours to privilege one term *over* the other, the task of deconstruction is to push thought back into the fecund space in between the two, as Leonard Lawlor writes, into the 'experience of *undecidability*'.[70]

It is this emphasis on undecidability, however, that convinces some that deconstruction is politically and ethically useless. If thought only occurs in the 'between' space of undecidability, what possible significance can this thought have in a world rife with suffering, injustice, oppression, poverty, disease, and hunger – a world where life-or-death *decisions* must constantly be made? Does undecidability not simply amount to indecision? As Derrida says, 'There are no doubt many reasons why the majority of texts hastily identified as "deconstructionist" seem – I do say *seem* – not to foreground the theme of justice (as theme, precisely), nor even the theme of ethics or politics.'[71] It is precisely this mischaracterisation that Derrida begins to address in his 1989 essay, 'Force of Law: *The "Mystical Foundation of Authority"* '.

Contrary to the facile reading of undecidability – that it damns one to impasse or indecision – Derrida will argue that the 'madness' of *undecidability* is the very condition of decision. He writes, 'A decision that would not go through the test and ordeal of the undecidable would not be a free decision; it would only be the programmable application or the continuous unfolding of a calculable process.'[72] The word 'decision' is etymologically connected to the Latin infinitive, *caedere*, meaning 'to cut' (note its affinities with the surgical word, 'incision'). To 'decide' means 'to make a cut' in the fabric of things, to tear asunder the predictability of logically precise calculation, as when one 'cuts off' the oscillation of uncertainty. The decision is made in the face of what one cannot, can never, *know*, and hence it is made in a space of 'madness'. Repeating one of the epigraphs from 'Cogito and the History of Madness', Derrida writes, 'The instant of decision is a madness, says Kierkegaard. This is particularly true of the instant of the *just* decision that must rend time and defy dialectics.'[73] A decision, strictly speaking, *cuts*, and without this *caesura*, there is no 'decision'. If it is merely the unreflective execution of a law, the logical outcome or the sum total of all the various inputs, it is purely mechanical and hence it is not a 'decision' and it certainly does not qualify as 'just'. Undecidability is thus the *condition* of the decision.

Moreover, once the decision is made, it is always 'haunted' by the ghost of the undecidable, in two senses: (1) Whatever else one might say henceforth of the decision that has been made, it will *always* be the case that this decision *was made* in the face of undecidability. The decision, once made, can never be guaranteed to have been the *right* decision, there can be no absolute guarantor of its justice – otherwise, we find ourselves back in the conundrum that the decision was mere mechanical execution (and hence, not a decision) – 'the memory of the undecidability must keep a living trace that forever marks a decision as such'.[74] (2) From the other direction, the decision, once made, will have followed *some* rule, even if only the instantaneously invented rule that '*x* is what must be done'. A decision that would follow no rule at all would not be just; nor would it even be, strictly speaking, a 'decision'. It would be merely an arbitrary, anarchic, and accidental enactment of whatever un-self-conscious, unreflective precursors had engendered it. The decision must always *refer* to a rule, law, or principle, even if it must not do so unreflectively, and even if it must also suspend the rule in doing so. But given that the decision must always refer to a rule, there can never be an absolute guarantee that the decision was *not* mechanical execution. The status of the decision *as* decision is forever undecidable as well.

Finally, and most importantly for our purposes, despite and because of these paradoxes and aporias, the decision *must* be made. The madness of undecidability does not free one from the burden of the decision, as the demand for justice does not wait. The urgency is such that one cannot languish in indecision so as to embark upon the infinite task of gathering the relevant information to assist one in making the decision. There is no decision without undecidability, but there is also no justice without a decision: 'only a decision is just'.[75] It is only when there has been an interpretation and application of the law that we can answer 'yes' or 'no' to the question of 'justice'. Thus, to leave thought suspended in the space of undecidability is itself unjust: 'a just decision is always required *immediately*, right away, as quickly as possible'.[76]

It is this dually conflicted exigency that makes deconstruction possible and necessary. The decision must be made, and yet, once made, it will always be haunted by the spectre of the undecidable. It is precisely this undecidability that ensures that the decision will always be deconstructible. We are always able to go back and recalibrate, reconsider, and reconfigure. Pure justice is *impossible*, but for precisely this reason, we must ever strive for it. As Derrida writes, 'Deconstruction takes place in the interval that separates the undeconstructibility of justice from the deconstructibility of law. Deconstruction is possible as an experience of the impossible.'[77]

With this in mind, let us now draw conclusions on the relation between our characterisation of Derrida's thought as a 'negative differential ontology' and the theme of undecidability as it occupies his work from his early writings through his 'ethical turn'. To begin, we can note that undecidability bears the markings by which we characterised Derrida's thought as a negative differential ontology. The two aspects by which we did so were: (1) *Différance* is itself understood as a 'not', as opposition, conflictuality, even characterised by Derrida at times as 'contradiction' (understood in a non-dialectical, i.e., irresolvable, way). That it is so, for Derrida, entails that the forces subsisting in a conflictual imbalance do so each as the other to the other. They subsist in precisely interdependent relationships; (2) the constituted thing – the trace – is also understood as a 'not'; in our earlier analyses the trace was defined as the trace of other, absent traces, akin to spectres and ashes.

In his early dealings with the concept of undecidability, as we have seen, Derrida characterises it as synonymous with a double, contradictory value,[78] a 'combat zone',[79] expressing, in other words, the oppositional interdependency of forces characteristic of *différance* itself. It is therefore no wonder that 'undecidability' is used as an explicit description of the signs of *pharmakon*, *supplément*, and *différance*. This oppositional status remains when the notion of undecidability is later applied within the ethico-political-juridical domains, as the opposition and conflictuality are then understood as obtaining 'between just and unjust',[80] where 'each of the terms must appear as the *différance* of the other'.[81] Our first condition of the 'negative' aspect of Derrida's thought is thus met in the notion of undecidability.

The second – that the constituted thing is itself understood in negative terms – also holds. The constituted in this case is the *decision* – '*X* is just' – and the decision is always constituted and marked by the spectre or trace of undecidability. The decision is only a decision because of the undecidability – 'neither one nor the other and both at once'[82] – in the face of which and out of which it was made. But this fact ensures at the same time that the status of the decision – both as a *decision* and/or as *just* – is forever deconstructible. The 'demand for infinite justice',[83] coupled with the infinite deconstructibility of the decision, entails a 'responsibility without limits',[84] the endless commitment to the task of deconstruction which, for Derrida, is synonymous with justice itself: '*Deconstruction is justice.*'[85] One must always *decide*, but one's decision will always be constituted by *undecidability*, which demands the infinite *deconstruction* of one's decisions. As it pertains to undecidability, just as it did to *différance*, the constituted thing – the decision – is constituted by a 'not'. Thus, the concept of undecidability in Derrida's work coheres with my characterisation of his thought as a negative differential ontology.

Nevertheless, we must be equally clear that neither the negative characterisation of Derrida's philosophy generally, nor the concept of undecidability specifically, amounts to a quietism or ethical ineffectuality. As we have seen, undecidability is the condition, the *sine qua non*, of the decision. Moreover, undecidability does not divest one of the responsibility of deciding. On the contrary, the demand for justice impresses itself upon us with unmistakable and unavoidable urgency, and languishing in undecidability would be unjust. Justice does not wait, and the decision must be made: 'a just decision is always required *immediately*'.[86] Therefore the negative ontological aspects of deconstruction do not entail resignation or inaction.

In the next section, we shall revisit the implied criticisms of each other that, in Chapter 8, we extracted from the projects of Deleuze and Derrida, in order to assess the extent to which these criticisms hit and miss their mark. What we shall see is that, of the three criticisms that Deleuze poses against the conception of difference as negativity, the one that seems most damning is the first, that difference, conceived as negation, is *less than difference*. This will come out in the ways in which, despite all of his powerful critical work regarding the logocentric binaries of Western thought, Derrida's own philosophy maintains a constant affinity with binarity.

Derrida contra Deleuze: the last dance

At the end of Chapter 8, we posed some speculative criticisms between Deleuze and Derrida, on the basis of their conceptions of difference which we extracted from their criticisms of Hegel in Chapters 3 and 4, and their mobilisations of Nietzsche in Chapters 6 and 7. We should first remind ourselves, in summary fashion, of the stark differences between Deleuze and Derrida, to precisely pave the road for the targets of those criticisms. To do so, I shall briefly explore Deleuze's forceful proclamation that 'There is no possible compromise between Hegel and Nietzsche.'[87] However much Derrida may critique Hegel, it is undeniably the case that Derrida's own brand of Nietzscheanism dances very close to Hegel's thought – Derrida says so explicitly, as we have seen numerous times. Deleuze, after rejecting any possible compromise between Hegel and Nietzsche, goes on to characterise the three primary aspects of the dialectic, each of which, as we shall see, corresponds to a significant element of Derrida's thought:

> Three ideas define the dialectic: the idea of a power of the negative as a theoretical principle manifested in opposition and contradiction; the idea that suffering and sadness have value, the valorization of the 'sad passions', as a practical principle manifested in splitting and tearing apart; the idea of positivity as a theoretical and practical product of negation itself. It is no exaggeration to say that the whole of Nietzsche's philosophy . . . is the attack on these three ideas.[88]

We can take these in turn, and show the different stances Deleuze and Derrida occupy vis-à-vis each of them. Deleuze rejects the 'power of the negative as a theoretical principle, manifested in opposition and contradiction'. Derrida's thought, on the contrary, seeks a 'negativity so negative'[89] that the term 'negative' cannot even grasp it. Deleuze rejects the productive significance of opposition and contradiction, while Derrida explicitly celebrates it: 'this conflictuality of *différance* . . . can never be totally resolved'.[90] Indeed, Hegel's 'labour of the negative'[91] foreshadows Derrida's 'work of mourning'.[92] This ties in to the second of these 'three ideas' defining the dialectic: Deleuze rejects the valorisation of the sad passions, while Derrida understands *mourning* as central to the notion of *work*, and in particular, to the notion of *bringing forth* (as in bringing forth *the new*):

> Work: that which makes for a work, for an *oeuvre,* indeed that which works
> – and works to open: *opus* and *opening, oeuvre* and *overture:* the work or

labor of the *oeuvre* in so far as it engenders, produces, and brings to light, but also labor or travail as suffering, as the enduring of force, as the pain of one who gives. Of the one who gives birth, who brings to the light of day and gives something to be seen, who enables or empowers, who gives the force to know and to be able to see – and all these are powers of the image, the pain of what is given and of the one who takes the pains to help us see, read, and think . . . One cannot hold a discourse *on* the 'work of mourning' without taking part in it, without announcing or partaking in death, and first of all in one's own death . . . All work in general works *at mourning*. In and of itself. Even when it has the power to give birth, even and especially when it plans to bring something to light and let it be seen.[93]

Work is tied to the notion of *opening* which, as we saw with the archi-originary 'yes', is tied to the notion of the *cut*. The cut in this case evokes the sense of giving birth, which is at once a *bringing forth* and a *rending in two*. These concepts are all woven into the concept of *mourning*, for Derrida. As Rosi Braidotti writes, the 'Levinas-Derrida tradition of ethics . . . is centered on the relationship between the subject and Otherness in the mode of indebtedness, vulnerability, and mourning'.[94] Thus, on the second aspect of the dialectic that Deleuze identifies and rejects – the valorisation of the sad passions – he and Derrida stand undeniably far from one another. The final element in the cited passage from Deleuze is the 'idea of positivity as a theoretical and practical product of negation'. We saw this negative notion of positivity in Derrida's philosophy as well. The trace is always the trace of other, absent traces. The decision is always based upon undecidability. Even the notion of the archi-originary yes, the primary affirmation, is constituted by a 'split', a 'cut', a 'threat'. For each of these three characteristics by which Deleuze distinguishes Nietzsche's philosophy from that of Hegel, we can see stark differences between Deleuze and Derrida. With that let us turn to and evaluate the explicitly formulated criticisms from Chapter 8, abstracted, as they were, from the criticisms of the Hegelian notion of difference as found in Chapters 3 and 4. I shall work backwards through the three formulated Deleuzian criticisms of Hegel, assessing the extent to which each of these criticisms may or may not be applied to Derrida's thought, as it is in this direction, I think, that the criticisms gain in persuasive force. This strategy will also allow me to simultaneously address what I understand as the Derridean criticism of Deleuze.

The collapse into identity

We begin with Deleuze's final criticism of Hegelian difference, that difference, conceived as negation, collapses into identity. In Hegel's thought, as Deleuze understands it, difference is always already implicitly contradiction, such that the opposition of self and other must finally be pushed to the point of infinite distance. The 'I' is conceived as the 'not-not-I', as the 'negation of the other',[95] and this pure reflection, '*Pure* self-recognition in absolute otherness',[96] necessitates the overcoming of the contradiction which was the telos of the difference to begin with. Thus, at precisely the moment that the difference is attained, it is surpassed. For Deleuze, this collapse into identity is a characteristic of all negative conceptions of difference.

But however much this criticism may work against Hegel's philosophy, it does not adequately function as a criticism of Derrida's philosophy. As a matter of fact, Derrida's own criticisms of Hegel – rooted in the Heideggerian critique of ontotheology – function quite similarly to the criticisms of Deleuze, as we saw in Chapter 5. Derrida, no less than Deleuze, worries about the Hegelian conception of difference on account of what he sees as its collapsing into identity, 'the self-presence of an onto-theological or onto-teleological synthesis'.[97] Moreover, in Derrida's own thought, we do not see a Hegel-esque collapse into identity. At no point in anything we have read out of Derrida have we seen anything resembling a stasis, not even a Hegelian homeostasis. What we see, on the contrary, is the disruption and dislocation – we might even call it the inversion – of the Hegelian *Aufhebung*, grounded upon the understanding that forces in tension are never on an equal footing, a conviction Derrida shares with Deleuze. So, on this point, Deleuze appears to be wrong – Hegel's negative conception of difference may collapse into identity, but this is not a necessary feature of all negative conceptions of difference, as it does not seem to apply in the case of Derrida's *différance*.

Negation as a symptom of ressentiment

With that, we move on to the second of Deleuze's criticisms, an ethical criticism that is a bit more complicated than the first. The second criticism of Hegel (and by extension, of Derrida) is that negative conceptions of difference are indicative of a spirit of *ressentiment* against life. The difference between the Nietzschean master and slave is that, while the master first affirms herself as good, and only secondarily judges the other to be 'bad', and even then, bad only in the sense of 'not flourishing',[98] the slave cannot affirm herself without first *negating* the otherness of the other. Her moment of self-affirmation is nothing more than the double-negation of the other: 'for the affirmation of self it substitutes the negation of the other, and for the affirmation of affirmation it substitutes the famous negation of the negation'.[99] It is this fact, and nothing else, that makes her a slave in the sense that Nietzsche or Deleuze (or Spinoza, for that matter) would under-stand the term: 'A slave does not cease to be a slave by taking power, and it is even the way of the world, or the law of its surface, to be led by slaves.'[100]

Deleuze then extrapolates this structure from the ethical to the onto-logical level – a negative conception of difference accompanies a negative conception of positivity – and from here, he concludes that a negative difference entails that affirmation of *any* kind is not possible without a primary and fundamental moment of negation. This is indicative of a negative or nihilistic comportment of thought, rooted in *ressentiment*. We should point out that there are elements of this criticism that certainly ring true where Derrida's thought is concerned. The trace, as we saw – the constituted 'effect' of *différance* – is but a nexus of negation: 'It remains *from* what is not, in order to recall at the delicate, charred bottom of itself only nonbeing or nonpresence.'[101] The trace is only ever the trace of other, absent traces, and as such, its own 'identity' – its positivity – is akin to that of the spectre or even the ash: a 'Cinder as the house of being'.[102] We further saw that while for Derrida 'justice, however unpresentable it remains, does not wait',[103] and as such, a just decision is always neces-sary, it is nevertheless the case that the decision is always constituted by undecidability, and as such, the decision will always be deconstructible, entailing a 'responsibility without limits'.[104]

It is, moreover, worth noting that even Derrida's notion of archi-originary affirmation is marked by a fundamental 'cut', 'threat', and 'obliv-ion'. For Deleuze, the primary affirmation is redoubled in the hymnic affirmation of Ariadne: 'Affirmation turns back on itself, then returns once more, carried to its highest power.'[105] 'Affirmation', as he says, 'must divide in two'[106] in the sense of the distinction between the primary affir-mation that *is* synonymous with becoming itself – the Dionysian – and the secondary affirmation that is the song of Ariadne – the stamp of being upon the flow of becoming. But for Derrida, the primary affirmation is itself already torn asunder by the second affirmation that it portends.

Nevertheless, Derrida's negative conception of positivity does not seem to *entail* in any robust sense that affirmation can *only* occur by way of double negation. The situation is far more complicated where Derrida is concerned, because Derrida's own negative conception of *différance* is far more complicated than that of Hegel. As we have seen, Derrida is explicit in his embrace of affirmation, and he understands deconstruction as a fundamentally affirmative practice, taking great pains over the course of his life to clarify that deconstruction is not to be understood as a negative endeavour. He is, furthermore, absolutely uncompromising and unwaver-ing in his explicit affirmation of life itself in the face of death. Here it behoves us to remind ourselves of Derrida's final interview:

I maintained that survival is an originary concept that constitutes the very structure of what we call existence, *Dasein*, if you will. We are structurally survivors, marked by this structure of the trace and of the testament. But, having said that, I would not want to encourage an interpretation that situates surviving on the side of death and the past rather than life and the future. No, deconstruction is always on the side of the *yes*, on the side of the affirmation of life. Everything I say . . . about survival as a complication of the opposition life/death proceeds in me from an unconditional affirmation of life. This surviving is life beyond life, life more than life, and my discourse is not a discourse of death, but, on the contrary, the affirmation of a living being who prefers living and thus surviving to death, because survival is not simply that which remains but the most intense life possible. I am never more haunted by the necessity of dying than in my moments of happiness and joy. To feel joy and to weep over the death that awaits are for me the same thing. When I recall my life, I tend to think that I have had the good fortune to love even the unhappy moments of my life, and to bless them. Almost all of them, with just one exception. When I recall the happy moments, I bless them too, of course, at the same time as they propel me toward the thought of death, toward death, because all that has passed, come to an end . . .[107]

This notion of *survival* echoes a discovery that Derrida had made at least as early as *Voice and Phenomenon*. In the final pages, Derrida characterises the history of metaphysics, and in particular Hegel as its culmination, as '*the absolute wanting-to-hear-itself speak*'.[108] Hegel's goal is to bring to completion Aristotle's 'self-thinking thought' from the *Metaphysics*. In order to do so, as we have seen with the notion of the *Aufhebung*, Hegel conceptualises a progressively expanding positing of otherness, followed in turn by movements of reconciliation. Hegel thus posits fundamental moments of difference or mediation as the condition of the self-thinking thought of the absolute, but simultaneously cancels those differences. But in cancelling difference, Hegel thereby cancels mediation in every meaningful sense, and without mediation, there is no movement – no life. The absolute attainment of self-presence (traditionally synonymous with 'life') therefore amounts to the simultaneous cancellation of that life, making it '*at once absolutely alive and absolutely dead*'.[109] As Nietzsche notes in *The Antichrist*, 'true life' is synonymous with '*nothingness*'.[110] Against this notion of *absolute life*, Derrida posits a new conception of life, one that in the Heideggerian spirit is in constant relation to death and hence, a concept of life that is essentially and irrevocably finite:

Only a relationship to my-death can make the infinite différance of presence appear. By the same token, compared to the ideality of the positive infinite, this relation to my-death becomes an accident of finite empiricity. The appearing of infinite différance is itself finite. Différance, which is nothing outside of this relationship, thereupon becomes the finitude of life as the essential relation to itself as to its death. *The infinite différance is finite.*[111]

It is this conception of life, as *différance*, that Derrida later christens with the name of 'survival'.[112] As it is a life that has at its core a relation to death, this death, not unlike the 'cut' at the heart of Derrida's conception of archi-originary affirmation, entails a doubling of this notion of life, protending forth in a life that remains, like Derrida's second affirmation, ever *to come*. It is therefore a life lived as an openness to the unforeseeable future, and it is in this way that the notion of survival, for Derrida, amounts to 'the most intense life possible'. This reflection and explication appear to be definitive. However negative Derrida's understanding of *différance* may be, it does not, at least in Derrida's view, *entail* a nihilistic spirit or a *ressentiment* against life. It is a 'death' at the heart of life, and a 'not' or a 'cut' at the heart of the archi-originary *yes*, to be sure, but nevertheless, Derrida is unflinching in his assertion of the affirmation of life. Taking him at his word, let us then explore the distinction between him and Deleuze on this point.

Above, we distinguished the joyously repeated affirmation in Derrida from the double affirmation in Deleuze. We did so by noting that for Derrida, the primary, archi-originary 'yes' is an 'inaudible term' that secures the functioning of the sign, and in so far as it portends a second 'yes', it is already cut open by the oblivion required for the second yes, as well as the threat of radical evil in the openness to the other. For Deleuze, on the other hand, the primary affirmation is synonymous with the Dionysian, un-self-conscious ebbing and flowing of the 'mysterious primordial unity', given explicit voice in the second affirmation, which we characterised as the cosmic 'yes' in the hymn of Ariadne. This was prefigured by our analysis in Chapter 7, where we explored Deleuze's understanding of Nietzsche's concept of eternal return. The third sense of the eternal return, we characterised as 'the selective heartbeat of time', the centrifugal, expulsive pulsation of repetition itself, which abolishes both the self-identical and the negative, constituting the only remaining sense of the 'same', as the different. The mechanism by which it expels the negative is the repetition of the affirmation (Ariadne's song), which at the same time *affirms* the negative, turning it into a repetition of the negative itself, which thereby turns the negative against itself, transmuting it into affirmation. In this sense the eternal return is the transvaluation whereby reactive forces change their quality and become-active.

With Derrida's sense of affirmation, however, we have something different. In so far as Derrida's affirmation of life is synonymous with a death at the heart of life, and in so far as this entails the constant haunting of the necessity of death at the heart of every moment of joy, then we can say that while for Deleuze affirmation is primary and negation is a secondary epiphenomenon, for Derrida affirmation is primary *only because* it puts the negative at the heart of it. This structure is even more salient in the sense that, for Deleuze, the *affirmation of the negative*, which results from the repetition of the Dionysian, ultimately *abolishes* the negative, while for Derrida, on the other hand, the affirmation of the negative affirms the repetition of the negative *as negative*, in perpetuity. It affirms the negative, to be sure, but only in the seemingly interminable *yes-saying* to the negativity of the negative itself, 'because it can no longer permit itself to be converted into positivity'.[113] Life's 'unhappy moments' are not transfigured, they are blessed *as unhappy*. 'And that is why whoever thus works *at* the work of mourning learns the impossible – and that mourning is interminable. Inconsolable. Irreconcilable.'[114] With that, we are back to the 'Hegelianism without reserve', the 'negativity so negative' that it is unencapsulable by the term.

In spite of all of Derrida's protestations to the contrary, Deleuze would almost certainly understand Derrida's thought as imbued with the spirit of nihilism and of *ressentiment*. Even if, for Derrida, the archi-originary *yes* is 'a *yes* that affirms, prior to, before or beyond any possible question',[115] and hence prior to any de facto 'yes' or 'no', nevertheless, there is no primary affirmation in Derrida that is not always already rent asunder by oblivion and the threat of radical evil. Contrary to Spinoza's famous dictum that '*A free man thinks of death least of all things*',[116] there is no sense of the affirmation of life in Derrida that does not require as a constitutive constant a meditation upon death. There is no moment of happiness or joy in Derrida's thought that does not at the same time propel one toward the thought of death. There is no 'I' that is not, in its self-determination, already pointing toward its death: '*I am* means therefore originarily *I am mortal*.'[117] There is no *friendship* that does not already anticipate death: 'To have a friend . . . is to know in a more intense way, already injured, already insistent, and more and more unforgettable, that one of the two of you will inevitably see the other die.'[118] The affirmation of the negative in Derrida entails the interminable carrying of the negative within, the 'blessings' of sadness, the 'interminable work of mourning'. It is difficult *not* to see in this view the terms of Deleuze's characterisation of '*bearing, taking upon oneself*',[119] the 'affirmation of the ass'.[120]

In light of all of this, it is not surprising that Derrida's critique of Hegel's conception of difference is that Hegelian difference is *insufficiently negative*, or that Derrida distinguishes *différance* 'from Hegelian difference . . . precisely at the point at which Hegel, in the greater *Logic*, determines difference as contradiction only in order to resolve it, to interiorize it, to lift it up . . . into the self-presence of an onto-theological or onto-teleological synthesis'.[121] We must now address the extent to which this criticism may serve as a criticism of Deleuze on the part of Derrida. As we saw in the previous section, this characterisation could not be applied *in toto* as a criticism of Deleuze because, while in Hegel's thought the *resolution of the contradiction* amounts to what both Deleuze and Derrida understand as a collapse into identity, this cannot be said of Deleuze's thought. Deleuze's ontology consists of intensities, series, and systems, none of which is ever self-identical, static, or completely stable. There is no 'essence' to the concept of force *as such* that does not already include the notion of other forces, in communication with each other; and there are never perfectly counterbalanced forces, according to Deleuze, just as for Derrida. Deleuze's is a system that functions always, in Bell's words, 'at the "edge of chaos"'.[122]

Nevertheless, if Hegel's conception of difference is insufficiently negative for Derrida, this criticism would also have to apply, *a fortiori*, to Deleuze, who seeks not merely to *resolve* the negative into an ontotheological synthesis, but to abolish it from ontology almost entirely,[123] explicitly in the name of an 'anti-Hegelianism'.[124] For Deleuze, as we have seen, 'The negative is an epiphenomenon',[125] an oppositional surface effect possible only *on the basis* of difference. The philosophical conviction that difference must be conceived in terms of the negative is based upon the nihilistic perspective of the reactive type, the spirit of *ressentiment*, 'difference seen from its underside, seen from below'.[126] But at the ontological level, according to Deleuze, 'being is full positivity and pure affirmation',[127] and the traditional philosophical connection between difference and the negative is, according to Deleuze, an 'unholy bond'.[128]

There are, I think, three criticisms – one philosophical and two ethical – that Derrida would bring against Deleuze. We begin with the philosophical criticism – there can be no philosophy of difference that is not at the same time and commensurably a philosophy of identity. Derrida's early remarks on this point are decisive: when he critiques Levinas in the closing pages of 'Violence and Metaphysics' for seeking the '*dream* of a purely *heterological* thought at its source. A *pure* thought of *pure* difference' that goes by the name of empiricism, which has 'ever committed but one fault: the fault of presenting itself as a philosophy',[129] it would seem that this criticism would have to also apply to Deleuze. As we saw, Deleuze's notion of the intensity is his elemental difference or his differential element: 'This element is intensity, understood as pure difference in itself',[130] and the expression, 'pure difference' runs throughout the entirety of *Difference and Repetition*. Against this *pure difference*, Derrida writes, 'Pure difference is not absolutely different (from nondifference). Hegel's critique of the concept of pure difference is for us here, doubtless, the most uncircumventable theme. Hegel thought absolute difference, and showed that it can be pure only by being impure.'[131] The 'impurity' of pure difference, contaminated as it is with identity, is 'most uncircumventable'. He then goes on to affirmingly cite Hegel, who, in the *Science of Logic*, writes: 'Difference in itself is self-related difference; as such, it is the negativity of itself, the difference not of an other, but *of itself from itself*; it is not itself but its other. But that which is different from difference is identity. Difference is therefore itself and identity.'[132] Derrida is the thinker of originary contamination, and as such, *any* pure notion, even that of 'pure difference', will be suspect.

This criticism, however, seems to have teeth only if we operate with the assumption that identity must be understood in the sense of static and abiding presence. Deleuze clearly does not reject in its entirety the notion of identity. He does, however, reject the notion that 'what differentiates difference is identity',[133] or in the translation of Hegel, 'that which is different from difference is identity'.[134] Rather, Deleuze attempts to formulate a philosophy wherein the identical is always a secondary, surface effect of the play of difference: 'All identities are only simulated, produced as an optical "effect" by the more profound game of difference and repetition.'[135] Deleuze's ontology, as we have seen, consists of intensities and the relations between them – singularities, series, and systems. At no point in this ontology is there anything resembling stasis, but that does not *exclude*, but rather *reformulates*, the notion of identity. The question where Deleuze is concerned, therefore, is not whether one's philosophy can do without the concept of identity entirely, but rather the status of the concept of identity vis-à-vis the concept of difference. This brings us to the second and third criticisms – the ethical criticisms that I suspect Derrida would bring against Deleuze.

If Deleuze would characterise Derrida's thought as *nihilistic* or as exemplifying the spirit of *ressentiment*, we can say from the other direction that Derrida would almost certainly characterise Deleuze's thought, in failing to take adequate stock of the negative, as lacking a dimension of responsibility. It is important to note, the 'not' or the 'cut' at the heart of the 'yes', the 'death' at the heart of 'life', are for Derrida the ground of his notion of responsibility, occupying Derrida's thought from his earliest writings. The first ethical criticism that Derrida would bring against Deleuze has to do with a certain responsibility or fidelity to the tradition of philosophy itself. 'Violence and Metaphysics' opens with a series of problems and questions, focused on the 'dying nature' of philosophy:

> That philosophy died yesterday, since Hegel or Marx, Nietzsche, or Heidegger – and philosophy should still wander toward the meaning of

its death – or that it has always lived knowing itself to be dying . . . that beyond the death, or dying nature, of philosophy, perhaps even because of it, thought still has a future, or even, as is said today, is still entirely to come because of what philosophy has held in store; or, more strangely still, that the future itself has a future – all these are unanswerable questions . . . It may even be that these questions are not *philosophical*, are not *philosophy's* questions. Nevertheless, these should be the only questions today capable of founding the community, within the world, of those who are still called philosophers; and called such in remembrance, at the very least, of the fact that these questions must be examined unrelentingly.[136]

The *question* of the 'death of philosophy', and in particular of the way in which philosophy is essentially and perennially understood as *related* to death, and to its death in particular, are *the* questions that *ought* to ground today's community of philosophers, even if they cannot be addressed from within the philosophical tradition itself. From Plato's proclamations in the *Phaedo* through Heidegger's notion of *Sein-zum-Tode*, the question of death haunts the very practice of philosophical engagement, and in particular, in the wake of Hegel, Marx, Nietzsche, and Heidegger, it is the question of our epoch, according to Derrida. As he writes in *The Gift of Death*, 'The *Phaedo* explicitly names philosophy: it is the attentive antici-pation of death, the care brought to bear upon dying, the meditation on the best way to receive, give, or give oneself death, the experience of a *vigil* over the possibility of death, and over the possibility of death as impos-sibility.'[137] Philosophy only occurs through a meditation upon its death, Derrida says, a death at the heart of philosophy's life. This, of course, pushes thought into a space that is not, strictly speaking, philosophical, nevertheless we *owe* it to the philosophical tradition to be its 'responsible guardians'[138] in this way.

This epochal 'responsibility' is one that Deleuze simply rejects without a second thought: 'In any case, the death of metaphysics or the overcom-ing of philosophy has never been a problem for us: it is just tiresome, idle chatter',[139] and 'questions that address "the death of philosophy" or "going beyond philosophy" have never inspired me'.[140] Nevertheless, Deleuze maintains a constant relation between philosophy and non-philosophy that must not be overlooked: 'For me, the system must not only be in perpetual heterogeneity, it must also be a *heterogenesis*, which as far as I can tell, has never been tried',[141] and 'The nonphilosophical is perhaps closer to the heart of philosophy than philosophy itself.'[142] This, however, is not a meditation upon the *death* of philosophy, according to Deleuze, but rather, the *life* of philosophy in communication with life *outside* of philosophy, which is why in *What is Philosophy?* Deleuze and Guattari characterise it in the terms of 'geophilosophy'.[143]

But the second, more pernicious, charge that Derrida would likely bring against Deleuze in his avoidance of the negative would lie in his lack of an adequate sense of responsibility to *the other*. Thinking back to our reflection upon Derrida's engagement with the archi-originary 'yes', we recall that this primary affirmation portended a second affirmation as a response, but as a response *to an unforeseeable other*, a 'yes' in the mode of the promise. It was this 'yes' – its attendant oblivion and the threat of radical evil – that cut open the primary 'yes' of the archi-originary affirmation. But this cutting open is the very condition of possibility of the ethical realm, according to Derrida: 'an original, transcendental violence, previous to every ethical choice, even supposed by ethical nonviolence'.[144] This sensibility is one that Deleuze explicitly, point by point, rejects:

> Thus Zarathustra's Ass says yes, but for him to affirm is to bear, to assume or to shoulder a burden. He bears everything: the burdens with which he is laden (divine values), those which he assumes himself (human values), and the weight of his tired muscles when he no longer has anything to bear (the absence of values). This Ass and the dialectical ox leave a moral aftertaste. They have a terrifying taste for responsibility, as though one could affirm only by expiating, as though it were necessary to pass through the misfortunes of rift and division in order to be able to say yes.[145]

To be clear, there is a profound and undeniable ethical dimension running through the entirety of Deleuze's thought, but it is not oriented, as it is for Derrida (and Levinas), by the responsibility in the face of radical alterity. It is not one that emphasises values that have been traditionally associated with the Judeo-Christian tradition (such as 'hospitality' and 'forgiveness').[146] In fact, it is an ontology and an ethics that is explicitly focused on 'the innocence of becoming',[147] a philosophy commensurate with the fact that 'existence is not responsible or even blameworthy'.[148] In rejecting the negative or the cut at the heart of the primary affirmation, Derrida would argue, Deleuze is disallowed this ethical dimension of alterity. Indeed, in his remarks on Deleuze's death, it appears that Derrida stealthily acknowledges this as a criticism: 'Deleuze was the one among all of this "generation" who "was doing" philosophy the most gaily, the most innocently. I don't think he would have liked me using the word "thinker" earlier. He would have preferred "philosopher." In this regard, he once described himself as "the most innocent (the one who felt the least guilt about 'doing philosophy')."'[149] However polite, even warm, these comments may seem, they are most assuredly *not*, in Derrida's vernacular, compliments.

It seems to me that both of these ethical criticisms between Derrida and Deleuze have teeth, depending upon one's perspective. It does appear to be the case that there is a fundamental rift or cut at the heart of Derrida's thinking, one that situates mourning as central to Derrida's conception of joy and a 'not' at the core of the archi-originary affirmation, which thereby distinguishes his thinking from one that is purely affirmative. It also appears to me that, by focusing so heavily on pure affirmation and on pure immanence, Deleuze lacks, and even explicitly rejects, an emphasis on any robust sense of responsibility, and if ethics *requires* a robust notion of responsibility (a view that Deleuze would reject), this is problematic for Deleuze. Though I myself side with Deleuze on this question, it seems to me that it is a question of preference. It seems to me to come down to a difference of interpretation of the following aspect of Nietzsche's thought:

> Have you ever said Yes to a single joy? O my friends, then you said Yes too to *all* woe. All things are entangled, ensnared, enamored; if ever you wanted one thing twice, if ever you said, 'You please me, happiness! Abide, moment!' then you wanted *all* back. All anew, all eternally, all entangled, ensnared, enamored – oh, then you *loved* the world. Eternal ones, love it eternally and evermore; and to woe too, you say: go, but return! *For all joy wants – eternity.*[150]

It is the difference between the Deleuzian *yes* that transfigures woe, and the Derridean *yes* that celebrates woe *as* woe; the repetition of *woe* that transmutes reactive forces into active, versus the repetition of *woe* that sustains the woeful. In his book on Deleuze, Alain Badiou writes:

> But, all in all, if the only way to think a political revolution, an amorous encounter, an invention of the sciences, or a creation of art as distinct infinities is by sacrificing immanence and the univocity of Being, then I would sacrifice them. If, in order to render eternal one of those rare fragments of truth that traverse here and there our bleak world it is necessary to restrict oneself to the Mallarméan doctrine of the trace then I would do so it is a question of taste.[151]

This appears to me to be the most fitting response to this particular difference between Derrida and Deleuze – it comes down to a question of taste.

Negation as less than difference

From a strictly philosophical perspective, the Deleuzian critique of Hegel that seems to me to have the *most* teeth against Derrida's thought is that difference conceived as negation is in fact *less than*, which is to say, *less profound than*, difference. Put otherwise, conceived as negation, difference retains vestiges of the traditional, static conception of identity, which entails at the same time that difference itself is understood as at least retaining aspects of the traditional conception of difference, as *difference-between* two 'things'. We have just seen that negative difference does not *necessarily* collapse into identity in the robust, dialectical Hegelian sense. But this charge of 'less than difference' is more subtle than that. Above, we saw Deleuze critique Hegel on the ground that it is only because things *first* differ that they can *then* oppose or negate one another. So to think of difference in negative terms is to maintain semblances of static identity as the basis of difference. Given everything we have hitherto said about Derrida's thinking, this should come as no surprise. There is a rift at the heart of the archi-originary 'yes', and a rift always entails, in some sense, a *two*-ness.

This brings us to the primary way in which it seems that Derrida is subject to this critique. We see an abiding affiliation with the structure of binarity running through the entirety of Derrida's thought. *Différance* is unthinkable without the 'trace', but the trace only ever marks other, absent traces – the 'one' always points to the 'other'. *Différance* is inconceivable without the thought of the 'not', and is inseparable from 'conflictuality' (requiring two, in some senses 'constituted', forces); its forces vie in imbalanced but interdependent dualities, which in *Dissemination* Derrida refers to as having 'a double, contradictory, undecidable value'.[152] He consistently celebrates the term 'contradiction' (which requires a *two*-ness), provided it is kept separate from its Hegelian (resolvable) senses. Most damningly, the creation of concepts, and the practice of philosophy itself, is for Derrida not comprehensible *except* as proceeding by way of the 'either/or', the 'all or nothing'. Derrida is explicit about this:

> Every concept that lays claim to any rigor whatsoever implies the alternative of 'all or nothing.' Even if in 'reality' or in 'experience' everyone believes he knows that there is never 'all or nothing,' a concept determines itself only according to 'all or nothing.' Even the concept of 'difference of degree,' the concept of relativity is, qua concept, determined according to the logic of all or nothing, of yes or no: differences of degree *or* nondifference of degree. It is impossible or illegitimate to form a *philosophical concept* outside this logic of all or nothing.[153]

Différance is the productive play of forces that constitutes the nature of thought, for Derrida, and as such, *différance* is always already *on the way* to being manifested in binary terms. It is for this reason that Derrida 'grumbles' at Deleuze's definition of philosophy as the creation of concepts,[154] and it is why philosophy can only be, for the foreseeable future, deconstruction: 'The movement of this schema will only be able, for the moment and for a long time, to work over from within, from a certain inside, the language of metaphysics.'[155] Indeed the thought of *différance* and the thought of the trace is, Derrida says, 'a *thought* because it escapes binarism and makes binarism possible on the basis of *nothing*',[156] but it would seem that if *différance* is understood 'essentially' as that which makes binarism possible, it does not completely escape binarism after all. In this way, it seems to me that Deleuze's criticism, that difference, conceived as negation, is somehow *less profound* than difference, is *less* than difference, is the most applicable criticism where Derrida's thinking is concerned. In the next and final section of the book, I will conclude by pointing toward potential avenues of investigation that might grow out of this work.

Conclusion

This work has likely raised as many questions as it has answered. That is not necessarily a bad thing. I offer this remark merely as a suggestion or announcement of what I take to be future paths of exploration between Derrida and Deleuze. In particular, it seems to me that the question of the meaning of affirmation in these two thinkers, as well as the meaning of *life*, and the distinction in terms of their ethical concerns, all of which are merely touched upon in this chapter, could and should be explored in much greater depth in future projects.

Moreover, I want it to be clear that in arguing that deconstruction maintains an affiliation with binarity, I in no way mean to suggest that it is somehow *deficient* in comparison with the philosophy of Deleuze. On the contrary, it seems to me that the 'power of the negative' in Derrida's thinking is that it tends in the direction of real, concrete spaces of empowerment, giving voice to the voiceless, in a way that is arguably more immediate than one finds in Deleuze. This is *because* of its lingering affinities with binarism. *Because* deconstruction problematises binary identities and in its ontological mode attempts to articulate the discursive mechanisms whereby they arise, *because* it attempts to destabilise these identities, provoking slippages of force between them, *without* dissolving them entirely into their purely ontological depths, deconstruction *gives place* to existing sites of oppression and marginalisation.

This is most immediately evident in the ways that certain feminist thinkers have engaged with the works of Derrida and Deleuze. It is certainly the case that the feminist reception of Derrida's work has been complicated, and that Derrida has faced a great deal of criticism from feminist thinkers. As Nancy Holland writes, 'Some would deny any positive relationship between Derrida and feminism, most would have reservations about asserting baldly that one exists.'[157] Furthermore, even among those feminist scholars who *have* positively adopted aspects of Derrida's thinking, the tendency persists to do so only in a qualified sense, or with specific caveats in place. Elizabeth Grosz, one of the more sympathetic thinkers when it comes to feminist appropriations of Derrida, writes: 'This is not, however, to suggest that Derrida's work should be accepted wholesale as feminist or as readily compatible with and amenable to feminism',[158] while Spivak writes that deconstruction is not 'feminism as such'.[159] Nevertheless, it is also the case that, with Derrida, there *have* been a number of prominent feminist thinkers – among them Drucilla Cornell, Gayatri Spivak, Hélène Cixous, Peggy Kamuf, Elizabeth Grosz, and Barbara Johnson – who engaged seriously with and were influenced by his work; while in the case of Deleuze, the feminist reception was, for a long time, lukewarm at best, and in many cases hostile.

It seems to me that this is *because* of Derrida's lingering entanglements with binarity, which destabilise the hierarchies of the 'phallogocentric space'[160] without obliterating the constituted sites entirely. The philosophical effort to think *past* those sites or *without* those sites would be for Derrida a feigned vision of neutrality that would, in all likelihood, merely serve to reinstate the traditional, oppressive hierarchy – a restoration of the domination by the primary term, now buttressed by the excluded other in the seemingly innocuous name of neutrality: 'the motif of neutrality, in its negative form, paves the way for the most classical and suspect attempts at reappropriation'.[161] Elsewhere, Derrida ties this concern explicitly to the question of sexual difference: 'the classical interpretation gives a masculine sexual marking to what is presented either as a neutral originariness or, at least, as prior and superior to all sexual markings'.[162] According to Elizabeth Grosz, 'Derrida's gift to feminism, which we may receive as a gift even though it was never given to feminists as such – a true gift, a gift given not as gift – is this concept of difference',[163] and Grosz explicitly understands *différance* as the 'originary tearing' and the 'active movement of tearing, cutting, breaking apart'.[164] This 'originary tearing', we have seen throughout our work, entails an essential *two*-ness to the operation of *différance*, such that the spaces, however destabilised they may be, are left intact. And the power of Derrida's negative ontology is that it provokes the slippages of force whereby 'woman' – and the space of 'the other' more generally, those who have been marginalised and excluded from the 'phallogocentric space' – is lit up, opened, and expanded, without cancelling that space of the other. We can see this more clearly when we contrast it with the feminist reception of Deleuze.

One of the earliest and most consistent criticisms of Deleuze on the part of feminist thinkers has been precisely that his ontology seeks to obliterate those sites, and in so doing, it would blow past millennia of patriarchal oppression, overlooking the immediate and concrete needs of *actual* women. This has been especially true of the concept, formulated in the writings with Félix Guattari, of 'becoming-woman'. In the context of *Capitalism and Schizophrenia*, this concept marks an initial stage of a journey from a life of 'molarity' centred on the 'I' and the things that pertain to the 'I' – the least adaptive and least intensive life one can live, the life most like death, for Deleuze – to a life of 'molecularity', a life lived in the liberation, enhancement, and mobilisation of those constitutive, intensive forces themselves. The stage of 'becoming-woman' is merely the first on the way 'toward becoming-imperceptible',[165] according to Deleuze and Guattari, with the ultimate endgame being 'the production of a thousand sexes, which are so many uncontrollable becomings'.[166] Deleuze and Guattari admit that 'It is, of course, indispensable for women to conduct a molar politics, with a view to winning back their own organism, their own history, their own subjectivity',[167] but nevertheless, this concept is unquestionably not *focused* specifically on such questions or concerns. Indeed, while Deleuze frequently cites in a laudatory manner the writings of Virginia Woolf, one of the most admirable aspects of Woolf's project, according to Deleuze, was that Woolf 'was appalled at the idea of writing "as a woman"'.[168] For many feminist thinkers, Deleuze's work simply had no practical value for the actual concerns of women. As Frida Beckman notes in her most recent book, 'To a feminist movement to which the struggle for the specificity of a female subject position was central, Deleuzian ideas that insist on moving beyond such molar politics became problematic.'[169]

This indeed was the heart of criticisms offered by Luce Irigaray. For Irigaray, Deleuze and Guattari's concept of 'becoming-woman' is merely a male romanticisation and exploitation of the hard-fought victories of the women's liberation movement, one that seeks to abolish the uniquely feminine pleasures and subjectivities that actual, historical women had only begun to assert:

> isn't a multiplicity that does not entail a rearticulation of the difference between the sexes bound to block or take away something of a woman's pleasure? In other words, is the feminine capable, at present, of attaining this desire, which is *neutral* precisely from the viewpoint of sexual difference? Except by miming masculine desire once again.[170]

In this vein, Alice Jardine notes (in 1984) that the American reception of Deleuze and Guattari's work is 'an active and politically pragmatic one, but one which often seems out of synchrony with immediately feminist concerns'.[171] To bring this point back into contrast with the reception of Derrida, let us look to Gayatri Spivak's classic article, 'Can the Subaltern Speak?' Speaking of Deleuze and Foucault, Spivak writes, 'These philosophers will not entertain the thought of constitutive contradiction – that is where they admittedly part company from the Left. In the name of desire, they reintroduce the undivided subject into the discourse of power.'[172] Later, in reference to Derrida, Spivak writes:

> As a postcolonial intellectual, I am not troubled that he does not *lead* me (as Europeans inevitably seem to do) to the specific path that such a critique makes necessary. It is more important to me that, as a European philosopher, he articulates the *European* Subject's tendency to constitute the Other as marginal to ethnocentrism and locates *that* as the problem with all logocentric and therefore also all grammatological endeavors.[173]

Then, in an explicit contrast between Foucault and Deleuze on one side, and Derrida on the other, Spivak writes that while 'Foucault's and Deleuze's immediate, substantive involvement with more "political" issues – the latter's invitation to "become woman" . . . can make their influence more dangerous', on the contrary, 'Derrida marks radical critique with the danger of appropriating the other by assimilation.'[174] Derrida highlights the danger of *appropriating* the site of the other through efforts to neutralise that site, while Deleuze and Foucault, more immediate and more radical though they may be, attempt just such a neutralisation.

What we see in these briefly formulated remarks on the feminist receptions of Derrida and Deleuze is that the second-wave feminists of the 1970s and 1980s recognised the distinction between Deleuze and Derrida for which I have argued throughout this book – that oppositionality lay at the heart of Derrida's notion of *différance*, while Deleuze endeavours to think a purely relational multiplicity. While figures like Irigaray and Spivak *rejected* the ontologico-political prescriptions of Deleuze on the ground that they too quickly obliterated the oppositional spacing whereby a uniquely feminine subjectivity might be explored, many feminists were at least more open to the offerings that Derridean *différance* afforded, to its 'constitutive contradiction', as Spivak notes. This recognition would seem to offer further support for the thesis I have advanced. It seems to me that the 'power of the negative' in Derrida's thought is that it provokes those slippages that give space to existing sites of oppression, without attempting to *appropriate* those spaces itself, and without attempting to overlook or forget them. At the same time, given that *différance* is always on the way toward binarity, then, to echo the programme of Protevi's *Political Physics*, it seems to me that in order to envision the world *beyond* binarity, the world of the 'unnameable'[175] of which Derrida speaks (without speaking), Deleuze's positive differential ontology is more useful. This world, we should carefully note, may be little more than a dream. But given this compelling landscape of feminist thought about the relative value of Derrida and Deleuze for feminism, it seems clear that there is a lot of interesting work waiting to be done at the intersections of Deleuze, Derrida, and questions concerning gender,[176] and by extrapolating to the site of the marginalised 'other' more generally – race, class, nationality, and sexuality as well.

In a world on fire, the challenges posed against the traditional images of thought by Deleuze and Derrida could not be more necessary. For these two thinkers, more than any other in the twentieth century, carried thought to places it had never been before, forever complicating the tradition's most cherished idols, destabilising identities, thinking every ground as essentially *ungrounded*, and every centre as perpetually *decentring*. The philosophies of Derrida and Deleuze are, to their cores, philosophies of the future, written in the hope of '*a new earth, a new people*'.[177] For even if this new earth *is* but a dream, it is nevertheless a dream worth dreaming. As Derrida writes, 'the future can only be anticipated in the form of an absolute danger'.[178] We dance, with fear, trembling, and exuberance, toward the space of that danger.

Notes

1. *SNS*, 37.
2. *FL*, 235.
3. *NP*, 186–9.
4. *WM*, 192.
5. *WM*, 193.
6. It appears numerous times throughout *Writing and Difference*, for instance, including in the 'Force and Signification' essay, first published in 1963. It also figures prominently in *Dissemination*, in particular in the 'Plato's Pharmacy' and 'Dissemination' essays.
7. *PIA*, 2.
8. *PIA*, 3.
9. *WD*, 230.
10. See *PIA*, 231–40.
11. *See PIA*, 240. Another very important piece for this theme is 'Ulysses Gramophone', in *AL*, 256–309.
12. *PIA*, 231.
13. *PIA*, 233. This quote is found in de Certeau, *The Mystic Fable, Volume I*, 175. The quote itself alludes to a passage in the writings of St Paul: 'For the Son of God, Jesus Christ, who was preached among you by us – by me and Silas and Timothy – was not "Yes" and "No," but in him it has always been "Yes"' (2 Corinthians 1:19).
14. *PIA*, 233. Originally in de Certeau, *The Mystic Fable, Volume I*, 174.
15. *PIA*, 232.
16. *PIA*, 235.
17. *PIA*, 238.
18. *FK*, 56.
19. *PIA*, 235–6.
20. *PIA*, 240.
21. *PIA*, 239–40.

22. *PIA*, 240.
23. *GM*, 35–6.
24. *PIA*, 240.
25. *PIA*, 240.
26. *PIA*, 240.
27. *FK*, 56.
28. *WD*, 125.
29. *AL*, 304.
30. *PIA*, 231.
31. *PIA*, 240.
32. *PIA*, 234.
33. For an alternative reading, see Noys, *The Persistence of the Negative*, 23–50. Noys writes: 'We have characterised Derrida as a "weak affirmationist", and the relative weakness of his affirmationism lies in his consistent attempt to develop an excessive form of negativity' (30). Noys is operating with completely different criteria in his evaluation than I am in mine: 'my solution is to push for a stronger conception of the practice of negativity against any subordination' (16). Taking Derrida at his word when he writes of the fundamental affirmation at the heart of the archi-originary yes, Noys characterises Derrida's thought as an 'affirmationism', but he further qualifies this affirmationism with the designation of 'weak' precisely because of the 'persistence of the negative' in Derrida's thought. For Noys, Derrida is insufficiently negative, *because* of his explicit insistence on affirmation.
34. *NP*, 187.
35. *EH*, 791.
36. *EH*, 764. See Crawford, *To Nietzsche: Dionysus, I Love You! Ariadne*.
37. *EH*, 764.
38. *EH*, 762.
39. Hamilton, *Mythology: Timeless Tales of Gods and Heroes*, 152.
40. *Z*, 182.
41. *Z*, 183.
42. Kirkland, *Nietzsche's Noble Aims*, 82.
43. *NP*, 187.
44. *Z*, 281.
45. *Z*, 231.
46. Kirkland, *Nietzsche's Noble Aims*, 82.
47. *Dialogues*, 47.
48. *NP*, 187.
49. Jung, *Two Essays on Analytical Psychology*, 205. Jung writes that 'His system is tuned in to woman from the start, just as it is prepared for a quite definite world where there is water, light, air, salt, carbohydrates, etc. The form of the world into which he is born is already inborn in him as a virtual image. Likewise parents, wife, children, birth, and death are inborn in him as virtual images, as psychic aptitudes' (190). Deleuze writes affirmingly of Jung in *Nietzsche and Philosophy* and *Difference and Repetition*.
50. *BT*, 37.
51. *BT*, 36.
52. *WTP*, 550.
53. *WTP*, 550.
54. *NP*, 186.
55. *CC*, 103.
56. Lampert, *Nietzsche's Task: An Interpretation of Beyond Good and Evil*, 293.
57. *CC*, 103. The quote from Nietzsche is from the poem, 'Fame and Eternity', in Nietzsche, *Dithyrambs of Dionysus*: 'ewiges Ja des Seins, ewig bin ich dein Ja'.
58. *Z*, 340–3.

59. *DR*, 75.
60. See also Bearn, 'Differentiating Derrida and Deleuze'. Employing a different strategy, Bearn argues a case similar to the one I have argued in this section, though his conclusion is more forceful than mine: 'The difference between Derrida and Deleuze is simple and deep: it is the difference between No and Yes . . . the difference between Derrida's No, which reeks of the thick smell of Schopenhauer . . . and Deleuze's Yes, blowing in, fresh and salty, off Nietzsche's new seas. . . . It is the difference between playing a Derridean game you can never win and a Deleuzian game you can never lose. It is the difference between No and Yes' (441).
61. *D*, 138.
62. Tiqqun, *Introduction to Civil War*, 145.
63. *FL*, 247.
64. *P*, 59.
65. See Baker, *Deconstruction and the Ethical Turn*; Critchley, *The Ethics of Deconstruction: Derrida and Levinas*; Anderson, *Derrida: Ethics Under Erasure*.
66. *D*, 138.
67. *D*, 219.
68. *D*, 220–1.
69. *D*, 259.
70. Lawlor, 'Translator's Introduction', *VP*, xxvii.
71. *FL*, 235. It is worth noting, of course, that Derrida goes on to show, as he does in numerous contexts, that themes pertaining to justice, hospitality, ethics, animality, right, power, responsibility, violence, and so on, appear throughout his works from beginning to end.
72. *FL*, 252.
73. *FL*, 255. See also Bennington, 'A Moment of Madness: Derrida's Kierkegaard'.
74. *FL*, 253.
75. *FL*, 253.
76. *FL*, 255.
77. *FL*, 243.
78. *D*, 220–1.
79. *D*, 138.
80. *FL*, 247.
81. *MP*, 17.
82. *D*, 259.
83. *FL*, 248.
84. *FL*, 247.
85. *FL*, 243.
86. *FL*, 255.
87. *NP*, 195.
88. *NP*, 195–6.
89. *WD*, 308n4.
90. *P*, 44. See also *D*, 220–1.
91. *PH*, 10.
92. *WM*.
93. *WM*, 142–3.
94. Braidotti, 'Affirmation Versus Vulnerability: On Contemporary Ethical Debates', 237.
95. *NP*, 196.
96. *PH*, 14.
97. *P*, 44.
98. Which is to say, not 'bad' in the sense of 'deserving of eternal hellfire'.
99. *NP*, 196.
100. *DR*, 54.

101. *C*, 21.
102. *C*, 23.
103. *FL*, 255.
104. *FL*, 247.
105. *NP*, 197.
106. *CC*, 103.
107. Derrida, *Learning to Live Finally. The Last Interview*, 51–2.
108. *VP*, 88.
109. *VP*, 88. See also Cisney, *Derrida's* Voice and Phenomenon, 189–91.
110. Nietzsche, *The Antichrist*, in *The Portable Nietzsche*, 573.
111. *VP*, 87.
112. See also Vitale, 'Living On: The Absolute Performative', in Senatore (ed.), *Performatives After Deconstruction*, 131–45.
113. *WD*, 259.
114. *WM*, 143.
115. *PIA*, 233.
116. Spinoza, *Ethics*, Part IV, p67.
117. *VP*, 46. It is significant to note that one of the three epigraphs to *Voice and Phenomenon* is a quotation from Edgar Allan Poe's story 'The Facts in the Case of M. Valdemar': 'Yes; – no; – *I have been sleeping* – and now – now – *I am dead.*'
118. *WM*, 107.
119. *NP*, 181.
120. *NP*, 180.
121. *P*, 44.
122. Bell, *Philosophy at the Edge of Chaos*, 4.
123. As we have already seen, the story is far more complicated than this. In reality, there is a powerful critical component to Deleuze's philosophy that is now beginning to get some scholarly attention. In addition to the aforementioned Kaufman book, see also Culp, *Dark Deleuze*; Toscano, 'In Praise of Negativism', in O'Sullivan and Zepke (eds), *Deleuze, Guattari, and the Production of the New*, 56–67.
124. *DR*, xix.
125. *DR*, 54.
126. *DR*, 55.
127. *DR*, 269.
128. *DR*, 269.
129. *WD*, 151.
130. *DR*, 144.
131. *WD*, 320n91.
132. *GL*, 417.
133. *WD*, 320n91.
134. *GL*, 417.
135. *DR*, xix.
136. *WD*, 79.
137. Derrida, *The Gift of Death, Second Edition & Literature in Secret*, 14.
138. Derrida, *Rogues: Two Essays on Reason*, 134.
139. *WP*, 9.
140. *TRM*, 365.
141. *TRM*, 365.
142. *WP*, 41.
143. *WP*, 85–113. See also Gasché, *Geophilosophy: On Gilles Deleuze and Félix Guattari's* What is Philosophy?
144. *WD*, 125.
145. *DR*, 53.
146. See, among other works, Derrida, *On Cosmopolitanism and Forgiveness*.

147. *NP*, 22.
148. *NP*, 24.
149. *WM*, 193–4.
150. *Z*, 435.
151. Badiou, *Deleuze: The Clamor of Being*, 90–1.
152. *D*, 220–1.
153. *LI*, 116–17.
154. *WM*, 193.
155. *VP*, 44.
156. *WD*, 230.
157. Holland, 'Introduction', in Holland (ed.), *Feminist Interpretations of Jacques Derrida*, 7.
158. Grosz, 'Ontology and Equivocation: Derrida's Politics of Sexual Difference', in Holland (ed.), *Feminist Interpretations of Jacques Derrida*, 94.
159. Spivak, 'Can the Subaltern Speak?', in Nelson and Grossberg (eds), *Marxism and the Interpretation of Culture*, 308.
160. *SNS*, 97.
161. *D*, 207n24.
162. Derrida and McDonald, 'Choreographies: Interview', in Holland (ed.), *Feminist Interpretations of Jacques Derrida*, 35.
163. Grosz, 'Derrida and Feminism: A Remembrance', 88–9.
164. Ibid., 91.
165. *ATP*, 279.
166. *ATP*, 278.
167. *ATP*, 276.
168. *ATP*, 276.
169. Beckman, *Gilles Deleuze*, 117.
170. Irigaray, *This Sex Which is Not One*, 140–1.
171. Jardine, 'Deleuze and His Br(others)', 48.
172. Spivak, 'Can the Subaltern Speak?', in Nelson and Grossberg (eds), *Marxism and the Interpretation of Culture*, 274.
173. Ibid., 293.
174. Ibid., 308.
175. *VP*, 66.
176. It is also worth noting that *both* Derrida and Deleuze employ some version of the notion of 'becoming-woman' (*devenir-femme*). See *SNS*, 86–9; *ATP*, 248–86.
177. *WP*, 99.
178. *OG*, 5.

Bibliography

Agamben, Giorgio. 'Absolute Immanence'. In ed. and trans. Daniel Heller-Roazen. *Potentialities.* Stanford: Stanford University Press, 1999.

Anderson, Nicole. *Derrida: Ethics Under Erasure.* London and New York: Bloomsbury Academic Publishing, 2012.

Ansell-Pearson, Keith. *Germinal Life: The Difference and Repetition of Deleuze.* New York: Routledge, 1999.

Anselm of Canterbury. *The Major Works.* Ed. Brian Davies and G. R. Evans. Oxford: Oxford University Press, 2008.

Aquinas, Thomas. *Aquinas's Shorter Summa: Saint Thomas's Own Concise Version of His Summa Theologica.* Trans. Cyril Vollert, S. J. Manchester: Sophia Institute Press, 1993.

Aristotle. *Complete Works of Aristotle: The Revised Oxford Translation, 2 Volumes.* Ed. Jonathan Barnes. Princeton: Princeton University Press, 1984.

Aschheim, Stephen. *The Nietzsche Legacy in Germany: 1890–1990.* Berkeley, Los Angeles, and London: University of California Press, 1992.

Augustine of Hippo. *Eighty-Three Different Questions.* Trans. David L. Mosher. Washington, DC: The Catholic University of America Press, 2002.

Augustine of Hippo. *The Confessions of Saint Augustine.* Trans. Gary Wills. New York: Penguin Books, 2006.

Badiou, Alain. *Deleuze: La clameur de l'Etre.* Paris: Hachette Littératures, 1997. Trans. Louise Burchill. *Deleuze: The Clamor of Being.* Minneapolis: University of Minnesota Press, 2000.

Baker, Peter. *Deconstruction and the Ethical Turn.* Gainesville: University Press of Florida, 1995.

Barnett, Stuart, ed. *Hegel After Derrida.* London and New York: Routledge, 1998.

Baugh, Bruce. *French Hegel: From Surrealism to Postmodernism.* London and New York: Routledge, 2003.

Bearn, Gordon C. F. 'Differentiating Derrida and Deleuze'. *Continental Philosophy Review,* Vol. 33 (2000): 441–65.

Beckman, Frida. *Gilles Deleuze.* London: Reaktion Books, 2017.

Behler, Ernst. *Confrontations: Derrida/Heidegger/Nietzsche.* Stanford: Stanford University Press, 1991.

Beistegui, Miguel de. *Truth and Genesis: Philosophy as Differential Ontology.* Bloomington and Indianapolis: Indiana University Press, 2004.

Bell, Jeffrey A. *Philosophy at the Edge of Chaos: Gilles Deleuze and the Philosophy of Difference.* Toronto: University of Toronto Press, 2006.

Bell, Jeffrey A. *The Problem of Difference: Phenomenology and Poststructuralism*. Toronto: University of Toronto Press, 1998.

Bennington, Geoffrey. 'A Moment of Madness: Derrida's Kierkegaard'. *Oxford Literary Review*, Vol. 33, No. 1 (2011): 103–27.

Bennington, Geoffrey. *Derridabase*. Chicago and London: University of Chicago Press, 1993.

Bogue, Ronald. *Deleuze and Guattari*. London and New York: Routledge, 1989.

Braidotti, Rosi. 'Affirmation Versus Vulnerability: On Contemporary Ethical Debates'. *Symposium: Canadian Journal of Continental Philosophy*, Vol. 10, No. 1 (Spring/Printemps 2006): 235–54.

Braver, Lee. *A Thing of this World: A History of Continental Anti-Realism*. Evanston: Northwestern University Press, 2007.

Breazeale, Daniel. *Philosophy and Truth: Selections from Nietzsche's Notebooks of the Early 1870s*. Amherst: Humanity Books, 1999.

Bryden, Mary, ed. *Deleuze and Religion*. London and New York: Routledge, 2001.

Buchanan, Ian and Colebrook, Claire, eds. *Deleuze and Feminist Theory*. Edinburgh: Edinburgh University Press, 2000.

Butler, Judith. *Subjects of Desire: Hegelian Reflections in Twentieth-Century France*. New York: Columbia University Press, 1999.

Certeau, Michel de. *La Fable Mystique, XVIe–XVIIe Siecle*. Paris: Les Éditions Gallimard, 1982. Trans. Michael B. Smith. *The Mystic Fable, Volume I: The Sixteenth and Seventeenth Centuries*. Chicago: University of Chicago Press, 1992.

Choat, Simon. *Marx Through Post-Structuralism: Lyotard, Derrida, Foucault, Deleuze*. London and New York: Bloomsbury, 2010.

Cisney, Vernon W. 'Becoming-Other: Foucault, Deleuze, and the Nature of Thought'. *Foucault Studies*, No. 17, Special Issue: Foucault and Deleuze (April 2014): 36–59.

Cisney, Vernon W. *Derrida's* Voice and Phenomenon: *An Edinburgh Philosophical Guide*. Edinburgh: Edinburgh University Press, 2014.

Cisney, Vernon W. 'Duration and Immanence: The Question of A Life in Deleuze'. *Studia Universitatis Babeş-Bolyai, Philosophia*, LIII, 1–2 (2008): 71–84.

Clark, Timothy. *Derrida, Heidegger, Blanchot: Sources of Derrida's Notion and Practice of Literature*. New York: Cambridge University Press, 2008.

Cohn, Eduardo. *How Forests Think: Toward an Anthropology Beyond the Human*. Berkeley: University of California Press, 2013.

Colebrook, Claire. *Deleuze and the Meaning of Life*. London and New York: Continuum International Publishing, 2010.

Conway, Anne. *The Principles of the Most Ancient and Modern Philosophy*. Ed. Allison P. Coudert and Taylor Corse. Cambridge: Cambridge University Press, 1996.

Copleston, Frederick. *A History of Philosophy, Volume III: Ockham to Suárez*. Westminster: The Newman Press, 1960.

Crawford, Claudia. *To Nietzsche: Dionysus, I Love You! Ariadne*. Albany: State University of New York Press, 1994.

Critchley, Simon. 'No Exit For Derrida: Jeremy Butman interviews Simon Critchley'. *Los Angeles Review of Books*, 9 October 2014.

Critchley, Simon. *The Ethics of Deconstruction: Derrida and Levinas*. Third Edition. Edinburgh: Edinburgh University Press, 2014.

Culp, Andrew. *Dark Deleuze*. Minneapolis: University of Minnesota Press, 2016.

Cusset, François. *French Theory: Foucault, Derrida, Deleuze & Cie et les mutations de la vie intellectuelle aux États-Unis*. Paris: Les Éditions La Découverte, 2003. Trans. Jeff Fort. *French Theory: How Foucault, Derrida, Deleuze, & Co. Transformed the Intellectual Life of the United States*. Minneapolis: University of Minnesota Press, 2008.

Davis, Colin. *Critical Excess: Overreading in Derrida, Deleuze, Levinas, Žižek, and Cavell*. Stanford: Stanford University Press, 2010.

DeLanda, Manuel. *Intensive Science and Virtual Philosophy*. New York: Continuum, 2002.

Deleuze, Gilles. *Anti-Oedipus Seminar* (14 January 1974), https://www.webdeleuze.com/textes/176.

Deleuze, Gilles. *Critique et Clinique*. Paris: Les Éditions de Minuit, 1993. Trans. Daniel W. Smith and Michael A. Greco. *Essays Critical and Clinical*. Minneapolis: University of Minnesota Press, 1997.

Deleuze, Gilles. *Deux Régimes de fous, textes et entretiens 1975–1995*. Ed. David Lapoujade. Paris: Les Éditions de Minuit, 2003. Trans. Ames Hodges and Mike Taormina. *Two Regimes of Madness*. New York: Semiotext(e), 2006.

Deleuze, Gilles. *Différence et repetition*. Paris: Presses Universitaires de France, 1968. Trans. Paul Patton. *Difference and Repetition*. New York: Columbia University Press, 1994.

Deleuze, Gilles. *Empiricism and Subjectivity: An Essay on Hume's Theory of Human Nature*. Trans. Constantin Boundas. New York: Columbia University Press, 1991.

Deleuze, Gilles. *Le Bergsonisme*. Paris: Presses Universitaires de France, 1966. Trans. Hugh Tomlinson and Barbara Habberjam. *Bergsonism*. New York: Zone Books, 1988.

Deleuze, Gilles. *L'Île déserte et autres texts, textes et entretiens 1953–1974*. Paris: Les Éditions de Minuit, 2002. Trans. Mike Taormina. *Desert Islands and Other Texts*. New York: Semiotext(e), 2003.

Deleuze, Gilles. *Logique du Sens*. Paris: Les Éditions de Minuit, 1969. Trans. Mark Lester with Charles Stivale. *The Logic of Sense*. New York: Columbia University Press, 1990.

Deleuze, Gilles. *Nietzsche et la philosophie*. Paris: Presses Universitaires de France, 1962. Trans. Hugh Tomlinson. *Nietzsche and Philosophy*. New York: Columbia University Press, 1983.

Deleuze, Gilles. *Pourparlers 1972–1990*. Paris: Les Éditions de Minuit, 1990. Trans. Martin Joughin. *Negotiations 1972–1990*. New York: Columbia University Press, 1995.

Deleuze, Gilles. 'Réponses à une série de questions', interview with Arnaud Villani. In Arnaud Villani. *La guêphe et l'orchidée: Essai sur Gilles Deleuze*. Paris: Belin, 1999: 129–31. Trans. 'Responses to a Series of Questions'. In ed. Robin Mackay. 'Unknown Deleuze', *Collapse III* (2007, reissued 2012): 39–44.

Deleuze, Gilles. *Spinoza et la problème de l'expression*. Paris: Les Éditions de Minuit, 1968. Trans. Martin Joughin. *Expressionism in Philosophy: Spinoza*. New York: Zone Books, 1992.

Deleuze, Gilles. *Spinoza: Philosophie pratique*. Paris: Les Éditions de Minuit, 1981. Trans. Robert Hurley. *Spinoza: Practical Philosophy*. San Francisco: City Lights, 1988.

Deleuze, Gilles and Guattari, Félix. *Capitalisme et schizophrénie tome 1: l'Anti-Œdipe*. Paris: Les Éditions de Minuit, 1972. Trans. Robert Hurley, Mark Seem, and Helen Lane. *Anti-Oedipus: Capitalism and Schizophrenia*. Minneapolis: University of Minnesota Press, 1983.

Deleuze, Gilles and Guattari, Félix. *Capitalisme et schizophrénie tome 2: Mille Plateaux*. Paris: Les Éditions de Minuit, 1980. Trans. Brian Massumi. *A Thousand Plateaus: Capitalism and Schizophrenia*. Minneapolis: University of Minnesota Press, 1987.

Deleuze, Gilles and Guattari, Félix. *Qu'est-ce que la philosophie?* Paris: Les Éditions de Minuit, 1991. Trans. Graham Burchell and Hugh Tomlinson. *What is Philosophy?* New York: Columbia University Press, 1994.

Deleuze, Gilles and Parnet, Claire. *Dialogues*. Paris: Flammarion, 1977. Trans. Hugh Tomlinson and Barbara Habberjam. *Dialogues II*. New York: Columbia University Press, 2007.

Derrida, Jacques. *Acts of Literature*. Ed. Derek Attridge. London and New York: Routledge, 1992.

Derrida, Jacques. *Aporias*. Trans. Thomas Dutoit. Ed. Werner Hamacher and David E. Wellbery. Stanford: Stanford University Press, 1993.

Derrida, Jacques. *Apprendre à vivre enfin: Entretien avec Jean Birnbaum*. Paris: Les Éditions Galilee/Le Monde, 2005. Trans. Pascale-Anne Brault and Michael Naas. *Learning to Live Finally: The Last Interview: An Interview with Jean Birnbaum*. Hoboken, NJ: Melville House Publishing, 2007.

Derrida, Jacques. *De la Grammatologie*. Paris: Les Éditions de Minuit, 1967. Trans. Gayatri Spivak. *Of Grammatology*. Baltimore: The Johns Hopkins University Press, 1974.

Derrida, Jacques. *Donner la mort*. Paris: Les Éditions Galilee, 1999. Trans. David Wills. *The Gift of Death, Second Edition & Literature in Secret*. Chicago: University of Chicago Press, 1995, 2008.

Derrida, Jacques. *Edmund Husserl's Origin of Geometry: An Introduction*. Trans. John P. Leavey, Jr. Lincoln: University of Nebraska Press, 1989.

Derrida, Jacques. *Eyes of the University: Right to Philosophy 2*. Trans. Jan Plug and others. Stanford: Stanford University Press, 2004.

Derrida, Jacques. *Feu la cendre*. Paris: Les Éditions des Femmes, 1987. Trans. Ned Lukacher. *Cinders*. Minneapolis: University of Minnesota Press, 2014.

Derrida, Jacques. 'Foi et savoir: Les deux sources de la «religion» aux limites de la simple raison'. In ed. Jacques Derrida and Gianni Vattimo. *La religion*. Paris: Les Éditions de Seuil, 1996. Trans. Samuel Weber. 'Faith and Knowledge: The Two Sources of "Religion" at the Limits of Reason Alone'. In ed. Gil Anidjar. *Acts of Religion*. New York: Routledge, 2010: 40–101.

Derrida, Jacques. *Force de loi*. Paris: Les Éditions Galilée, 1994. Trans. Mary Quintance, 'Force of Law: The "Mystical Foundation of Authority"'. In ed. Gil Anidjar. *Acts of Religion*. New York: Routledge, 2010: 228–98.

Derrida, Jacques. *Glas*. Paris: Les Éditions Galilée, 1974. Trans. John P. Leavey, Jr. and Richard Rand. *Glas*. Lincoln: University of Nebraska Press, 1986.

Derrida, Jacques. 'Interpreting Signatures (Nietzsche/Heidegger): Two Questions'. Trans. Diane Michelfelder and Richard E. Palmer. *Philosophy and Literature*, Vol. 10, No. 2 (October 1986): 246–62

Derrida, Jacques. *La Dissémination*. Paris: Les Éditions de Seuil, 1972. Trans. Barbara Johnson. *Dissemination*. Chicago: University of Chicago Press, 1981.

Derrida, Jacques. *La voix et le phenomena*. Paris: Presses Universitaires de France, 1967. Trans. Leonard Lawlor. *Voice and Phenomenon*. Evanston: Northwestern University Press, 2011.

Derrida, Jacques. *L'écriture et la différence*. Paris: Les Éditions de Seuil, 1967. Trans. Alan Bass. *Writing and Difference*. Chicago: University of Chicago Press, 1978.

Derrida, Jacques. *Limited Inc*. Paris: Les Éditions Galilée, 1990. Trans. Samuel Weber. Evanston: Northwestern University Press, 1988.

Derrida, Jacques. *Marges de la philosophie*. Paris: Les Éditions de Minuit, 1972. Trans. Alan Bass. *Margins of Philosophy*. Chicago: University of Chicago Press, 1982.

Derrida, Jacques. *Of Spirit: Heidegger and the Question*. Trans. Geoffrey Bennington and Rachel Bowlby. Chicago: University of Chicago Press, 1989.

Derrida, Jacques. *On Cosmopolitanism and Forgiveness*. Trans. Mark Dooley and Michael Hughes. London and New York: Routledge, 2001.

Derrida, Jacques. *Points de suspension: Entretiens*. Paris: Les Éditions Galilée, 1992. Trans. Peggy Kamuf and others. *Points . . . Interviews, 1974–1994*. Stanford: Stanford University Press, 1995.

Derrida, Jacques. *Positions*. Paris: Les Éditions de Minuit, 1972. Trans. Alan Bass. *Positions*. Chicago: University of Chicago Press, 1981.

Derrida, Jacques. 'Preface'. In Catherine Malabou. *L'Avenir de Hegel*. Paris: Librairie Philosophique J. Vrin, 1996. Trans. Lisabeth During. *The Future of Hegel: Plasticity, Temporality, and Dialectic*. London and New York: Routledge, 2005: vii–xlvii.

Derrida, Jacques. *Psyché: Inventions de l'autre, tome II*. Paris: Les Éditions Galilée, 2003. Ed. Peggy Kamuf and Elizabeth Rottenberg. *Psyche: Inventions of the Other, Volume II*. Stanford: Stanford University Press, 2008.

Derrida, Jacques. *Spurs: Nietzsche's Styles/Éperons: Les Styles de Nietzsche*. Trans. Barbara Harlow. Chicago: University of Chicago Press, 1978.

Derrida, Jacques. *The Problem of Genesis in Husserl's Philosophy*. Trans. Marian Hobson. Chicago: University of Chicago Press, 2003.

Derrida, Jacques. *The Work of Mourning*. Ed. and trans., and with introduction by Pascale-Anne Brault and Michael Naas. Chicago: University of Chicago Press, 2001.

Derrida, Jacques. *Voyous: Deux essais sur la raison*. Paris: Les Éditions Galilee, 2003. Trans. Pascale-Anne Brault and Michael Naas. *Rogues: Two Essays on Reason*. Stanford: Stanford University Press, 2005.

Derrida, Jacques. *Who's Afraid of Philosophy: Right to Philosophy 1*. Trans. Jan Plug. Stanford: Stanford University Press, 2002.

Derrida, Jacques and McDonald, Christie V. 'Choreographies: Interview'. In ed. Nancy Holland. *Feminist Interpretations of Jacques Derrida*. University Park: Pennsylvania State University Press, 1997: 23–41.

Descartes, René. *The Philosophical Writings of Descartes, Volume I*. Ed. and trans. John Cottingham, Robert Stoothoff, and Dugald Murdoch. Cambridge: Cambridge University Press, 1985.

Descartes, René. *The Philosophical Writings of Descartes, Volume II*. Ed. and trans. John Cottingham, Robert Stoothoff, and Dugald Murdoch. Cambridge: Cambridge University Press, 1984.

Descombes, Vincent. *Le Même et L'Autre*. Paris: Les Éditions de Minuit, 1979. Trans. Lorna Scott-Fox and J. M. Harding. *Modern French Philosophy*. Cambridge: Cambridge University Press, 1980.

Dicker, Georges. *Descartes: An Analytical and Historical Introduction*. Oxford: Oxford University Press, 1993.

Donkel, Douglas L. *The Understanding of Difference in Heidegger and Derrida*. New York and Berlin: Peter Lang Publishing, 1993.

Duns Scotus, John. *Philosophical Writings: A Selection*. Trans. Allan B. Wolter. Indianapolis: Hackett Publishing Company, 1987.

Ellis, John M. *Against Deconstruction*. Princeton: Princeton University Press, 1989.

Fink, Eugen. *Nietzsche's Philosophy*. Trans. Goetz Richter. New York: Continuum, 2003.

Fink, Eugen. *Spiel als Weltsymbol*. Stuttgart 1960. French translation by Hildenbrand and Lindenberg. *Le jeu comme symbole du monde*. Paris: Éditions de Minuit, 1960.

Foley, Rich. 'Unnatural Religion: Indoctrination and Philo's Reversal in Hume's *Dialogues Concerning Natural Religion*'. *Hume Studies*, Vol. 32, No. 1 (April 2006): 83–112.

Foucault, Michel. *Histoire de la folie à l'âge classique – Folie et déraison*. Paris: Plon, 1961. Ed. Jean Khalfa. Trans. Jonathan Murphy and Jean Khalfa. *History of Madness*. London and New York: Routledge, 2006.

Foucault, Michel. *Les mots et les choses*. Paris: Éditions Gallimard, 1966. Trans. Alan Sheridan. *The Order of Things: An Archaeology of the Human Sciences*. London and New York: Routledge, 1970.

Foucault, Michel. *L'ordre du discours*. Paris: Les Éditions Gallimard, 1971. Trans. Alan Sheridan. 'The Discourse on Language'. In *The Archaeology of Knowledge and The Discourse on Language*. New York: Pantheon Books, 1972.

Foucault, Michel. 'Theatrum Philosophicum'. In ed. James D. Faubion. Trans. Robert Hurley et. al. *The Essential Works of Foucault: 1954–1984, Volume 2: Aesthetics, Method, and Epistemology*. Series ed. Paul Rabinow. New York: The New Press, 1998.

Freud, Sigmund. 'A Note upon the "Mystic Writing-Pad"'. In ed. Philip Rieff. *General Psychological Theory: Papers on Metapsychology*. New York: Macmillan, 1963.

Freud, Sigmund. *Beyond the Pleasure Principle*. Ed. and trans. James Strachey. New York and London: Norton, 1961.

Freud, Sigmund. *The Interpretation of Dreams*. In ed. and trans. Dr A. A. Brill. *The Basic Writings of Sigmund Freud*. New York: Random House, 1938.

Gasché, Rodolphe. *Geophilosophy: On Gilles Deleuze and Félix Guattari's What is Philosophy?* Evanston: Northwestern University Press, 2014.

Gasché, Rodolphe. *The Tain of the Mirror: Derrida and the Philosophy of Reflection.* Cambridge and London: Harvard University Press, 1986.

Gendron, Sarah. *Repetition, Difference, and Knowledge in the Work of Samuel Beckett, Jacques Derrida, and Gilles Deleuze.* New York: Peter Lang Publishing, 2008.

Goddard, Jean-Christophe. *Violence et subjectivité. Derrida, Deleuze, Maldiney.* Paris: Vrin, 2008.

Gorman, Clare. *The Undecidable: Jacques Derrida and Paul Howard.* Newcastle Upon Tyne: Cambridge Scholars Publishing, 2015.

Grosz, Elizabeth. 'Derrida and Feminism: A Remembrance'. *differences: A Journal of Feminist Cultural Studies,* Vol. 16, No. 3 (2005): 88–94.

Grosz, Elizabeth. 'Ontology and Equivocation: Derrida's Politics of Sexual Difference'. In ed. Nancy Holland. *Feminist Interpretations of Jacques Derrida.* University Park: Pennsylvania State University Press, 1997: 73–101.

Halpern, Catherine, ed. *Foucault, Derrida, Deleuze: Pensées rebelles.* Paris: Les Éditions Sciences Humaines, 2013.

Hamilton, Edith. *Mythology: Timeless Tales of Gods and Heroes.* New York and Scarborough, Ontario: Signet, 1940.

Hegel, Georg W. F. *Elements of the Philosophy of Right.* Ed. Allen W. Wood. Trans. H. B. Nisbet. Cambridge: Cambridge University Press, 1991.

Hegel, Georg W. F. *Enzyklopädie der philosophischen Wissenschaften I: Werke in zwanzig Bänden, Bd. 8.* Ed. E. Moldenhauer and K. M. Michel. Frankfurt am Main: Suhrkamp Verlag, 1971. Trans. William Wallace. *Hegel's Logic: Being Part One of the Encyclopedia of the Philosophical Sciences (1830).* Oxford: Oxford University Press, 1975.

Hegel, Georg W. F. *Lectures on the Philosophy of World History, Introduction: Reason In History.* Trans. H. B. Nisbet. Cambridge: Cambridge University Press, 1975.

Hegel, Georg W. F. *Phänomenologie des Geistes: Werke in zwanzig Bänden, Bd. 3.* Ed. E. Moldenhauer and K. M. Michel. Frankfurt am Main: Suhrkamp Verlag, 1971. Trans. A. V. Miller. *Hegel's Phenomenology of Spirit.* New York: Oxford University Press, 1977.

Hegel, Georg W. F. *Wissenschaft der Logik: Werke in zwanzig Bänden, Bd. 5–6.* Ed. E. Moldenhauer and K. M. Michel. Frankfurt am Main: Suhrkamp Verlag, 1971. Trans. A. V. Miller. *Hegel's Science of Logic.* Amherst, NY: Humanity Books, 1969.

Heidegger, Martin. *Basic Questions of Philosophy: Selected 'Problems' of Logic.* Trans. Richard Rojcewicz and André Schuwer. Bloomington: Indiana University Press, 1994.

Heidegger, Martin. *Holzwege.* Frankfurt am Main: Vittorio Klostermann GmbH, 1950. Trans. J. Young and K. Haynes. *Off the Beaten Track.* Cambridge: Cambridge University Press, 2002.

Heidegger, Martin. *Identität und Differenz.* Pfullingen: Verlag Günther Neske, 1957. Trans. J. Stambaugh. *Identity and Difference.* Chicago: University of Chicago Press, 1969.

Heidegger, Martin. *Introduction to Metaphysics.* Trans. Gregory Fried and Richard Polt. New Haven and London: Yale University Press, 2000.

Heidegger, Martin. *Kant and the Problem of Metaphysics.* Trans. Richard Taft. Bloomington and Indianapolis: Indiana University Press, 1990.

Heidegger, Martin. *Nietzsche,* 2 Vols. Pfullingen: Verlag Günther Neske, 1961.

Heidegger, Martin. *Nietzsche, Volume I: The Will to Power as Art.* Ed. and trans. David Farrell Krell. San Francisco: Harper and Row, Publishers, Inc., 1979.

Heidegger, Martin. *Nietzsche, Volume II: The Eternal Recurrence of the Same.* Ed. and trans. David Farrell Krell. New York: Harper and Row, Publishers, Inc., 1984.

Heidegger, Martin. *Nietzsche, Volume III: The Will to Power as Knowledge and Metaphysics.* Ed. and trans. David Farrell Krell. New York: Harper and Row, Publishers, Inc., 1987.

Heidegger, Martin. *Nietzsche, Volume IV: Nihilism.* Ed. and trans. David Farrell Krell. San Francisco: Harper and Row, Publishers, Inc., 1982.

Heidegger, Martin. *Nietzsche, Volumes I and II: The Will to Power as Art; The Eternal*

Recurrence of the Same. Ed. and trans. David Farrell Krell. New York: HarperCollins Publishers, 1991.

Heidegger, Martin. *Nietzsche, Volumes III and IV: The Will to Power as Knowledge and as Metaphysics; Nihilism*. Ed. and trans. David Farrell Krell. New York: HarperCollins Publishers, 1991.

Heidegger, Martin. *On the Way to Language*. Trans. Peter D. Hertz. San Francisco: Harper and Row, 1971.

Heidegger, Martin. 'Only a God Can Save Us: *Der Spiegel's* Interview (September 23, 1966)'. Trans. Maria P. Alter and John D. Caputo. In ed. Manfred Stassen. *Philosophical and Political Writings*. New York and London: Continuum, 2003.

Heidegger, Martin. 'Overcoming Metaphysics'. *The End of Philosophy*. Trans. Joan Stambaugh. Chicago: University of Chicago Press, 1973.

Heidegger, Martin. *Poetry, Language, Thought*. Trans. Albert Hofstadter. New York: Harper Perennial Classics, 2001.

Heidegger, Martin. *Sein und Zeit*. Tübingen: Max Niemeyer Verlag, 1927. Trans. John Macquarrie and Edward Robinson. *Being and Time*. New York: Harper and Row, 1962.

Heidegger, Martin. 'The Question Concerning Technology'. *The Question Concerning Technology and Other Essays*. Trans. William Lovitt. New York: Harper and Row, Publishers, Inc., 1977.

Heidegger, Martin. *Was heißt Denken?* Tübingen: Max Niemeyer, 1954. Trans. J. Glenn Gray. *What is Called Thinking?* New York: Harper and Row, Publishers, Inc., 1968.

Heidegger, Martin. *Wegmarken*. Frankfurt am Main: Vittorio Klostermann GmbH, 1967. William McNeill, ed. *Pathmarks*. Cambridge: Cambridge University Press, 1998.

Heraclitus. *Fragments: A Text and Translation With a Commentary By T.M. Robinson*. Toronto: University of Toronto Press, 1987.

Hodge, Joanna. *Derrida on Time*. London and New York: Routledge, 2007.

Hoffmeyer, Jesper. *Biosemiotics: An Examination into the Signs of Life and the Life of Signs*. Scranton: University of Scranton Press, 2009.

Holland, Nancy, ed. *Feminist Interpretations of Jacques Derrida*. University Park: Pennsylvania State University Press, 1997.

Houle, Karen and Vernon, Jim, eds. *Hegel and Deleuze: Together Again for the First Time*. Evanston: Northwestern University Press, 2013.

Hughes, Joe. *Deleuze and the Genesis of Representation*. London and New York: Continuum, 2008.

Hughes, Joe. *Deleuze's* Difference and Repetition: *A Reader's Guide*. London and New York: Continuum, 2009.

Hume, David. *An Enquiry Concerning Human Understanding, with A Letter from a Gentleman to His Friend in Edinburgh and Hume's Abstract of A Treatise of Human Nature*, Second Edition. Ed. Eric Steinberg. Indianapolis: Hackett, 1993.

Hume, David. *A Treatise of Human Nature, Second Edition With Text Revised and Notes by P. H. Nidditch*. Oxford: Oxford University Press, 1978.

Husserl, Edmund. *Cartesianische Meditationen und Pariser Vorträge. Husserliana Band I*. The Hague: Martinus Nijhoff, 1960. Trans. Dorion Cairns. *Cartesian Meditations: An Introduction to Phenomenology*. Dordrecht, Boston and London: Kluwer Academic Publishers, 1999.

Husserl, Edmund. *Die Krisis der europäischen Wissenschaften und die transzendentale Phänomenologie. Husserliana Band VI*. The Hague: Martinus Nijhoff, 1962. Trans. David Carr. *The Crisis of European Sciences and Transcendental Phenomenology: An Introduction to Phenomenological Philosophy*. Evanston: Northwestern University Press, 1970.

Husserl, Edmund. *Ideen zu einer reinen Phänomenologie und Phänomenologischen Philosophie. Erstes Buch. Husserliana Band III*. Den Haag: Martinus Nijhoff, 1950.

Trans. Fred Kersten. *Ideas Pertaining to a Pure Phenomenology and to a Phenomenological Philosophy, First Book.* Dordrecht: Kluwer Academic Publishers, 1983.

Husserl, Edmund. *Logische Untersuchungen, Erster Theil: Prolegomena Zur Reinen Logik.* Leipzig: Verlag Von Veit & Comp., 1900. Trans. J. N. Findlay. *Logical Investigations, Volume I: Prolegomena to Pure Logic.* London and New York: Routledge, 1970.

Husserl, Edmund. *Zur Phänomenologie des inneren Zeitbewusstseins (1893–1917). Husserliana Band X.* The Hague: Martinus Nijhoff, 1992. Trans. John Barnett Brough. *On the Phenomenology of the Consciousness of Internal Time (1893–1917).* Dordrecht: Kluwer Academic Publishers, 1992.

Hyppolite, Jean. *Genèse et Structure de la Phénoménologie de l'esprit de Hegel.* Paris: Editions Montaigne, 1946. Trans. S. Cherniak and J. Heckman. *Genesis and Structure of Hegel's Phenomenology of Spirit.* Evanston: Northwestern University Press, 1974.

Hyppolite, Jean. *Logique et existence.* Paris: Presses Universitaires de France, 1953. Trans. Leonard Lawlor and Amit Sen. *Logic and Existence.* Albany: State University of New York Press, 1997.

Irigaray, Luce. *Ce Sexe qui n'en est pas un.* Paris: Les Éditions de Minuit, 1977. Trans. Catherine Porter with Carolyn Burke. *This Sex Which is Not One.* Ithaca: Cornell University Press, 1985.

Irigaray, Luce. *Marine Lover of Friedrich Nietzsche.* Trans. Gillian Gill. New York: Columbia University Press, 1991.

Jardine, Alice. 'Deleuze and His Br(others)'. *SubStance*, Vol. 13, No. 3/4, Issue 44–5: Gilles Deleuze (1984): 46–60.

Jung, Carl Gustav. *Two Essays on Analytical Psychology, Second Edition.* Trans. R. F. C. Hull. London: Routledge, 1966.

Kant, Immanuel. *The Metaphysical Foundations of Natural Science.* In ed. and trans. Ernest Belfort Bax. *Kant's Prolegomena and Metaphysical Foundations of Natural Science.* London: George Bell and Sons, 1891.

Kates, Joshua. *Essential History: Jacques Derrida and the Development of Deconstruction.* Evanston: Northwestern University Press, 2005.

Kaufman, Eleanor. *Deleuze, The Dark Precursor: Dialectic, Structure, Being.* Baltimore: The Johns Hopkins University Press, 2012.

Kaufmann, Walter. *Nietzsche: Philosopher, Psychologist, Antichrist.* Princeton: Princeton University Press, 1974.

Kierkegaard, Søren. *Fear and Trembling.* Ed. and trans. Howard V. Hong and Edna H. Hong. *Kierkegaard's Writings, Volume VI.* Princeton: Princeton University Press, 1983.

Kierkegaard, Søren. *The Concept of Anxiety.* Ed. and trans. Reidar Thomte in collaboration with Albert B. Anderson. *Kierkegaard's Writings, Vol. VIII.* Princeton: Princeton University Press, 1980.

Kierkegaard, Søren. *Works of Love.* Ed. and trans. Howard V. Hong and Edna H. Hong. *Kierkegaard's Writings, Volume XVI.* Princeton: Princeton University Press, 1995.

Kirkland, Paul E. *Nietzsche's Noble Aims: Affirming Life, Contesting Modernity.* Lanham, MD: Lexington Books, 2009.

Kraut, Richard. 'Introduction to the Study of Plato'. In ed. Richard Kraut. *The Cambridge Companion to Plato.* Cambridge: Cambridge University Press, 1992.

Lampert, Laurence. *Nietzsche's Task: An Interpretation of Beyond Good and Evil.* New Haven: Yale University Press, 2001.

Lapoujade, David. *Aberrant Movements: The Philosophy of Gilles Deleuze.* Trans. Joshua David Jordan. Los Angeles: Semiotext(e), 2017.

Laruelle, François. *Philosophies of Difference: A Critical Introduction to Non-Philosophy.* Trans. Rocco Gangle. New York: Continuum International Publishers, 2011.

Lawlor, Leonard. *Early Twentieth-Century Continental Philosophy.* Bloomington: University of Indiana Press, 2011.

Lawlor, Leonard. 'The Beginnings of Thought: The Fundamental Experience in Derrida and Deleuze'. In ed. Paul Patton and John Protevi. *Between Deleuze and Derrida*. London and New York: Continuum, 2003: 67–83.

Lawlor, Leonard. *Thinking Through French Philosophy: The Being of the Question*. Bloomington: University of Indiana Press, 2003.

Lawlor, Leonard. 'Translator's Introduction'. *Voice and Phenomenon*. Evanston: Northwestern University Press, 2011: xi–xxviii.

Leibniz, G. W. *Philosophical Essays*. Ed. and trans. Roger Ariew and Daniel Garber. Indianapolis and Cambridge: Hackett Publishing Company, 1989.

Leibniz, G. W. *Philosophical Papers and Letters*. Ed. and trans. Leroy E. Loemker. Dordrecht: Kluwer Academic Publishers, 1989.

Leiter, Brian. 'Brian Leiter on Nietzsche Myths'. *Philosophy Bites* 108, http://hwcdn.libsyn. com/p/d/1/6/d1677410823f120c/Brian_Leiter_on_Nietzsche_Myths.mp3?c_id=177 9634&expiration=1500748097&hwt=744ffebdf3192b0a9f176f3e58df0fd6.

Leiter, Brian. *Routledge Philosophy Guidebook to Nietzsche on Morality*. New York: Routledge, 2002.

Levinas, Emmanuel. *Basic Philosophical Writings*. Ed. Adriaan Peperzak, Simon Critchley, and Robert Bernasconi. Bloomington and Indianapolis: Indiana University Press, 1996.

Levinas, Emmanuel. 'Is Ontology Fundamental?' Trans. Peter Atterton, revised by Simon Critchley and Adriaan Peperzak. In ed. Adriaan Peperzak, Simon Critchley, and Robert Bernasconi. *Basic Philosophical Writings*. Bloomington and Indianapolis: Indiana University Press, 1996.

Levinas, Emmanuel. *Le temps et l'autre*. Montpellier, France: Fata Morgana, 1979. Trans. Richard A. Cohen. *Time and the Other*. Pittsburgh: Duquesne University Press, 1987.

Levinas, Emmanuel. *Totalité et infini: essai sur l'extériorité*. The Hague: Martinus Nijhoff Publishers, 1961. Trans. Alphonso Lingis. *Totality and Infinity: An Essay on Exteriority*. Pittsburgh: Duquesne University Press, 1969.

Locke, John. *An Essay Concerning Human Understanding*. Oxford: Oxford University Press, 1975.

Long, A. A. and Sedley, D. N., eds and trans. *The Hellenistic Philosophers, Volume I: Translations of the Principal Sources, with Philosophical Commentary*. Cambridge: Cambridge University Press, 1987.

Lovejoy, Arthur. *The Great Chain of Being: A Study of the History of an Idea*. Cambridge: Harvard University Press, 1976.

Malabou, Catherine. *L'Avenir de Hegel*. Paris: Libraire Philosophique J. Vrin, 1996. Trans. Lisabeth During. *The Future of Hegel: Plasticity, Temporality, and Dialectic*. London and New York: Routledge, 2005.

Malabou, Catherine. 'Who's Afraid of Hegelian Wolves?' Trans. David Wills. In ed. Paul Patton. *Deleuze: A Critical Reader*. Cambridge: Blackwell, 1996: 114–38.

Marrati, Paola. *Genesis and Trace: Derrida Reading Husserl and Heidegger*. Trans. Simon Sparks. Stanford: Stanford University Press, 2004.

May, Todd. *Gilles Deleuze: An Introduction*. Cambridge: Cambridge University Press, 2005.

May, Todd. *Reconsidering Difference: Nancy, Derrida, Levinas, and Deleuze*. University Park: The Pennsylvania State University Press, 1997.

Mayr, Ernst. *What Evolution Is*. New York: Basic Books, 2001.

Merleau-Ponty, Maurice. *Signs*. Trans. Richard C. McCleary. Evanston: Northwestern University Press, 1964.

Müller-Lauter, Wolfgang. *Heidegger und Nietzsche: Nietzsche-Interpretationen III*. Berlin: Walter de Gruyter, 2000.

Nealon, Jeffrey. 'Beyond Hermeneutics: Deleuze, Derrida and Contemporary Theory'. In ed. Paul Patton and John Protevi. *Between Deleuze and Derrida*. London and New York: Continuum, 2003: 158–68.

Nelson, Cary and Grossberg, Lawrence, eds. *Marxism and the Interpretation of Culture.* Urbana and Chicago: University of Illinois Press, 1988.

Nietzsche, Friedrich. *Also sprach Zarathustra: Ein Buch für Alle und Keinen.* Chemnitz: Verlag von Ernst Schmeitzner, 1883. Trans. Walter Kaufmann. *Thus Spoke Zarathustra: A Book for All and None.* In ed. Walter Kaufmann. *The Portable Nietzsche.* New York: Penguin Books, 1954.

Nietzsche, Friedrich. *Der Wille zur Macht. Versuch einer Umwerthung aller Werthe (Studien und Fragmente).* Leipzig: Druck und Verlag von C. G. Naumann, 1901. Trans. Walter Kaufmann. *The Will to Power.* New York: Vintage, 1967.

Nietzsche, Friedrich. *Die fröhliche Wissenschaft, Neue Ausgabe mit einem Anhange: Lieder des Prinzen Vogelfrei.* Leipzig: Verlag von E. W. Fritzsch, 1887. Trans. Walter Kaufmann. *The Gay Science, With a Prelude in Rhymes and an Appendix of Songs.* New York: Vintage, 1974.

Nietzsche, Friedrich. *Die Geburt der Tragödie aus dem Geiste der Musik.* Leipzig: Verlag von E. W. Fritsch, 1872. Trans. Walter Kaufmann. *The Birth of Tragedy out of the Spirit of Music.* In ed. Walter Kaufmann. *Basic Writings of Nietzsche.* New York: The Modern Library, 1967.

Nietzsche, Friedrich. *Dithyrambs of Dionysus (German and English Edition).* Trans. R. J. Hollingdale. Manchester: Carcanet Press, 2004.

Nietzsche, Friedrich. *Ecce Homo, Wie man wird, was man ist.* Leipzig: Insel-Verlag, 1908. Trans. Walter Kaufmann. *Ecce Homo: How One Becomes What One Is.* In ed. Walter Kaufmann. *Basic Writings of Nietzsche.* New York: The Modern Library, 1967.

Nietzsche, Friedrich. *Götzen-Dämmerung oder Wie man mit dem Hammer philosophirt.* Leipzig: Verlag von C. G. Naumann, 1889. Trans. Walter Kaufmann. *Twilight of the Idols or, How One Philosophizes With a Hammer.* In ed. Walter Kaufmann. *The Portable Nietzsche.* New York: Penguin Books, 1954.

Nietzsche, Friedrich. *Jenseits von Gut und Böse: Vorspiel einer Philosophie der Zukunft.* Leipzig: Druck und Verlag von C. G. Naumann, 1886. Trans. Walter Kaufmann. *Beyond Good and Evil: Prelude to a Philosophy of the Future.* In ed. Walter Kaufmann. *Basic Writings of Nietzsche.* New York: The Modern Library, 1967.

Nietzsche, Friedrich. *Nachgelassene Fragmente.* Volume 13 of ed. Giorgio Colli and Mazzino Montinari. *Kritische Studienausgabe Herausgegeben.* Berlin and New York: Deutscher Taschenbuch Verlag de Gruyter, 1967.

Nietzsche, Friedrich. 'On Truth and Lies in a Nonmoral Sense'. In ed. and trans. Daniel Breazeale. *Philosophy and Truth: Selections from Nietzsche's Notebooks of the Early 1870's.* Amherst: Humanity Books, 1999.

Nietzsche, Friedrich. *Selected Letters of Friedrich Nietzsche.* Ed. and trans. Christopher Middleton. Indianapolis and Cambridge: Hackett Publishing Company, Inc., 1969.

Nietzsche, Friedrich. *The Antichrist.* In ed. Walter Kaufmann. *The Portable Nietzsche.* New York: Penguin Books, 1954.

Nietzsche, Friedrich. *Zur Genealogie der Moral: Eine Streitschrift.* Leipzig: Verlag von C. G. Naumann, 1887. Trans. M. Clark and A. J. Swensen. *On the Genealogy of Morality.* Indianapolis: Hackett Publishing, 1998.

Noys, Benjamin. *The Persistence of the Negative: A Critique of Contemporary Continental Theory.* Edinburgh: Edinburgh University Press, 2010.

Oliver, Kelly. *Womanizing Nietzsche: Philosophy's Relation to the 'Feminine'.* New York and London: Routledge, 1995.

Oliver, Kelly and Pearsall, Marilyn, eds. *Feminist Interpretations of Friedrich Nietzsche (Re-Reading the Canon).* State College: Penn State University Press, 1998.

Ormiston, Gayle L. 'Traces of Derrida: Nietzsche's Image of Woman'. *Philosophy Today,* Vol. 28 (Summer 1984): 178–88.

O'Sullivan, Simon and Zebke, Stephen, eds. *Deleuze, Guattari, and the Production of the New.* London and New York: Continuum, 2008.

Parmenides. *Fragments: A Text and Translation With an Introduction By David Gallop*. Toronto: University of Toronto Press, 1984.

Patton, Paul, ed. *Deleuze: A Critical Reader*. Cambridge: Blackwell, 1996.

Patton, Paul and Protevi, John, eds. *Between Deleuze and Derrida*. London and New York: Continuum, 2003.

Peirce, Charles Sanders. *Collected Papers of Charles Sanders Peirce, Volume 1, Principles of Philosophy*. Ed. Charles Hatshorne and Paul Weiss. Cambridge, MA: Harvard University Press, 1931.

Peirce, Charles Sanders. *Peirce on Signs: Writings on Semiotics by Charles Sanders Peirce*. Ed. James Hooper. Chapel Hill: University of North Carolina Press, 1991.

Plato. *Complete Works*. Ed. John M. Cooper. Associate ed. D. S. Hutchinson. Indianapolis: Hackett Publishing Company, 1997.

Plotnitsky, Arkady. *In the Shadow of Hegel: Complementarity, History, and the Unconscious* Gainesville: University Press of Florida, 1993.

Plotnitsky, Arkady. 'Points and Counterpoints: Between Hegel and Derrida'. *Revue internationale de philosophie* 52 (1998): 451–76.

Porphyry. *Introduction*. Trans. Jonathan Barnes. Oxford: Oxford University Press, 2003.

Protevi, John. *Political Physics: Deleuze, Derrida, and the Body Politic*. London and New York: The Athlone Press, 2001.

Protevi, John. *Time and Exteriority: Aristotle, Heidegger, Derrida*. Lewisburg: Bucknell University Press, 1994.

Rapaport, Herman. *Heidegger and Derrida: Reflections on Time and Language*. Lincoln: University of Nebraska Press, 1991.

Roudinesco, Elizabeth. *Philosophes dans la tourmente*. Paris: Fayard, 2005. Trans. William McQuaig. *Philosophy in Turbulent Times: Canguilhem, Sartre, Foucault, Althusser, Deleuze, Derrida*. New York: Columbia University Press, 2008.

Sallis, John. *Delimitations: Phenomenology and the End of Metaphysics*. Bloomington: Indiana University Press, 1995.

Sallis, John. *Echoes: After Heidegger*. Bloomington: Indiana University Press, 1990.

Sato, Yoshiyuki. *Pouvoir et Resistance: Foucault, Deleuze, Derrida, Althusser*. Paris: L'Harmattan, 2007.

Sauvagnargues, Anne. 'Hegel and Deleuze: Difference or Contradiction?' Trans. Marc Champagne, with Niels Feuerhahn and Jim Vernon. In ed. Karen Houle and Jim Vernon. *Hegel and Deleuze: Together Again for the First Time*. Evanston: Northwestern University Press, 2013.

Schacht, Richard. *Nietzsche*. London: Routledge and Kegan Paul, 1983.

Schrift, Alan D. *Nietzsche and the Question of Interpretation: Between Hermeneutics and Deconstruction*. New York and London: Routledge, 1990.

Schrift, Alan D. *Nietzsche's French Legacy: A Genealogy of Poststructuralism*. New York: Routledge, 1995.

Schrift, Alan D. *Twentieth-Century French Philosophy: Key Themes and Thinkers*. Malden, MA: Blackwell Publishing, 2006.

Schwab, Gabriele, ed. *Derrida, Deleuze, Psychoanalysis*. New York: Columbia University Press, 2007.

Searle, John. *Mind, Language, and Society: Philosophy in the Real World*. New York: Basic Books, 1998.

Senatore, Mauro, ed. *Performatives After Deconstruction*. London and New York: Bloomsbury Publishing, 2013.

Sergeant, Phillippe. *Deleuze, Derrida: Du danger de penser*. Paris: Les Éditions de la Différence, 2009.

Sextus Empiricus. *Outlines of Skepticism*. Ed. Julia Annas and Jonathan Barnes. Cambridge: Cambridge University Press, 2000.

Smith, Daniel W. 'Deleuze and Derrida, Immanence and Transcendence: Two Directions in Recent French Thought'. In ed. Paul Patton and John Protevi. *Between Deleuze and Derrida*. London and New York: Continuum, 2003: 46–66.

Smith, Daniel W. *Essays on Deleuze*. Edinburgh: Edinburgh University Press, 2012.

Smith, Daniel W. and Protevi, John. 'Gilles Deleuze'. *The Stanford Encyclopedia of Philosophy* (Winter 2015 Edition). Ed. Edward N. Zalta, https://plato.stanford.edu/archives/win2015/entries/deleuze.

Somers-Hall, Henry. *Hegel, Deleuze, and the Critique of Representation: Dialectics of Negation and Difference*. Albany: State University of New York Press, 2012.

Spinoza, Benedict. *Complete Works*. Ed. Michael L. Morgan. Trans. Samuel Shirley. Indianapolis: Hackett Publishing Company, 2002.

Spivak, Gayatri Chakravorty. 'Can the Subaltern Speak?' In ed. Cary Nelson and Lawrence Grossberg. *Marxism and the Interpretation of Culture*. Urbana and Chicago: University of Illinois Press, 1988: 271–313.

Spivak, Gayatri Chakravorty. 'Translator's Preface'. In Jacques Derrida. *De la grammatologie*. Paris: Les Éditions de Minuit, 1967. Trans. Gayatri Spivak. *Of Grammatology*. Baltimore: The Johns Hopkins University Press, 1974: ix–lxxxvii.

Stark, Hannah. *Feminist Theory After Deleuze*. London and New York: Bloomsbury, 2017.

Steigmann-Gall, Richard. *The Holy Reich: Nazi Conceptions of Christianity, 1919–1945*. Cambridge: Cambridge University Press, 2003.

Stellardi, Giuseppe. *Heidegger and Derrida on Philosophy and Metaphor: Imperfect Thought*. Amherst, NY: Prometheus Books, 2000.

Tampio, Nicholas. 'Not All Things Wise and Good are Philosophy'. *Aeon*, https://aeon.co/ideas/not-all-things-wise-and-good-are-philosophy.

Tiqqun. *Introduction à la guerre civile*. Paris: Éditions La Fabrique, 2009. Trans. Alexander R. Galloway and Jason E. Smith. *Introduction to Civil War*. Los Angeles: Semiotext(e), 2010.

Tolstoy, Leo. *The Kingdom of God is Within You*. Radford, VA: Wilder Publications, 2008.

Toscano, Alberto. 'In Praise of Negativism'. In ed. Simon O'Sullivan and Stephen Zepke. *Deleuze, Guattari, and the Production of the New*. London and New York: Continuum, 2008: 56–67.

Trifonas, Peter Pericles. *The Ethics of Writing: Derrida, Deconstruction, and Pedagogy*. Lanham, MD: Rowman and Littlefield, 2000.

von Uexküll, Jakob. *A Foray Into the Worlds of Animals and Humans: With a Theory of Meaning*. Trans. Joseph D. O'Neill. Minneapolis: University of Minnesota Press, 2010.

Vattimo, Gianni. *The Adventure of Difference: Philosophy After Nietzsche and Heidegger*. Trans. Cyprian Blamires with Thomas Harrison. Baltimore: The Johns Hopkins University Press, 1993.

Vitale, Francesco. 'Living On: The Absolute Performative'. In ed. Mauro Senatore. *Performatives After Deconstruction*. London and New York: Bloomsbury Publishing, 2013: 131–45.

Wheeler, Wendy. *The Whole Creature: Complexity, Biosemiotics, and the Evolution of Culture*. London: Lawrence and Wishart, 2006.

Widder, Nathan. *Genealogies of Difference*. Urbana: University of Illinois Press, 2002.

Williams, James. *A Process Philosophy of Signs*. Edinburgh: Edinburgh University Press, 2016.

Wood, David, ed. *Of Derrida, Heidegger, and Spirit*. Evanston: Northwestern University Press, 1993.

Wood, David and Bernasconi, Robert, eds. *Derrida and* Différance. Evanston: Northwestern University Press, 1988.

Zahavi, Dan. *Husserl's Phenomenology*. Stanford: Stanford University Press, 2003.

Zourabichvili, François. *A Philosophy of the Event, Together With The Vocabulary of*

Deleuze. Ed. Gregg Lambert and Daniel W. Smith. Trans. Kieran Aarons. Edinburgh: Edinburgh University Press, 2012.

Zuckert, Catherine H. *Plato's Philosophers: The Coherence of the Dialogues*. Chicago: University of Chicago Press, 2009.

Index